Keegan, Ava, Jenna, Coby, Sa_____
Alysse, Sierra, Tama_____
Puffy, Xena, Quenti_____

Pocket T Names . . . With the durability of an
American fashion classic, these names are flexible,
suited to all shapes and sizes, casual or dressy.
Try on Aaron, Adam, Andrew, Anthony or
Becca, Belle, Bridget

Trendy Suspenders . . . Names that ride the crest
of popularity and, like Mork's rainbow suspenders,
just might end up in the back of your closet. So
watch out for Garth, Logan, Parker or
Felicia, Lindsay, Nevada

Positive Image Names . . . Ben and Connor
sound honest and handsome; Katherine and Maria
project confidence and beauty

And for Cuddly Bear Names. check out Cody, Cory,
Jamie or *Little House on the Prairie*-types
Hannah, Emily, Sarah

With lists of top choices,
helpful commentary, and thousands of names!

JOAL RYAN is a writer for *E! Online,* and has written for *Swing*
magazine, the *Los Angeles Times,* and other publications. Her parents created her name by combining parts of their first names,
John and Alice. Joal was born in California in 1967, and lives in
New York City.

Puffy, Xena, Quentin, Uma

And 10,000 Other Names for Your New Millennium Baby

JOAL RYAN

A PLUME BOOK

PLUME
Published by the Penguin Group
Penguin Putnam Inc., 375 Hudson Street, New York, New York 10014, U.S.A.
Penguin Books Ltd, 27 Wrights Lane, London W8 5TZ, England
Penguin Books Australia Ltd, Ringwood, Victoria, Australia
Penguin Books Canada Ltd, 10 Alcorn Avenue, Toronto, Ontario, Canada M4V 3B2
Penguin Books (N.Z.) Ltd, 182–190 Wairau Road, Auckland 10, New Zealand

Penguin Books Ltd, Registered Offices:
Harmondsworth, Middlesex, England

First published by Plume, a member of Penguin Putnam Inc.

First Printing, June 1999
10 9 8 7 6 5 4

 REGISTERED TRADEMARK—MARCA REGISTRADA

LIBRARY OF CONGRESS CATALOGING-IN-PUBLICATION DATA

Ryan, Joal.
    Puffy, Xena, Quentin, Uma, and 10,000 other names for your New
Millennium baby / Joal Ryan.
        p.   cm.
    Includes bibliographical references.
    ISBN 0-452-28091-5
    1. Names, Personal—Dictionaries.   I. Title.   II. Title: Puffy,
Xena, Quentin, Uma.
CS2377.R93   1999
929.4'003—dc21   98-50403
                                                         CIP

Printed in the United States of America
Set in Times New Roman
Designed by Julian Hamer

BOOKS ARE AVAILABLE AT QUANTITY DISCOUNTS WHEN USED TO PROMOTE PRODUCTS OR SERVICES.
FOR INFORMATION PLEASE WRITE TO PREMIUM MARKETING DIVISION, PENGUIN PUTNAM INC.,
375 HUDSON STREET, NEW YORK, NEW YORK 10014.

Contents

Acknowledgments

Thanks to: Dennis Bent, Bellevue University professor Cleveland Evans, Ryan O Ryan, Steve Ryfle, and the dozens of parents who shared their real-life baby name experiences with me over the Internet.

Special thanks to: my agent, Peter Rubie; my editor, Jennifer Moore; my research assistant, Raechel Fittante; and my parents, John and Alice Ryan, without whom I would have remained nameless.

Introduction:
So, the Kid Needs a Name

S o, it's come to this, has it? You, with the living room full of cheap Swedish furniture and the decade-old college loan debt. You, with the fly-by-the-seat-of-your-jeans home-based business and the expansive video-game collection. You, friend, have just had your ticket to Grown-up Land punched: You're expecting a baby. *You?*

Yeah, you. Now quit resting on your reproductive laurels because there's something the whole world wants to know: What are you gonna name the kid?

The Importance of Being Jennifer

"My parents named me **Jennifer** *because they thought it was so beautiful—but so did ten million other parents their age."*

"My name is spelled **Lesli** *because my hippie folks wanted something a little unusual."*

"I want my kids to feel they have unique names without feeling they are too 'weird,' like naming a kid **Mountain Moonglow** *or something."*

These are the voices of our peers—the nearly fifty million Americans who came of age in the 1970s and early 1980s—raised on *Sesame Street,* disco, double-digit inflation, and [insert appropriate, clichéd *Reality Bites*–like memory here]. We're the people—ages twenty-one to thirty-five, in 1998—that advertisers label "Generation X." The ones media pundits analyze as "slackers." In these pages, we're simply parents.

As parents, we have a wholly unique perspective on this baby name business. We grew up the children of Depression-era kids, hippie-dippie Jerry Garcia disciples, reformed tie-dyers, and budding yuppies. We got dumped on with a mishmash of names: from **Frank** to **Freedom** to **Frederick.** Exposed to everything from the sublime to the silly, we were treated to a first-class education in the importance and potential pitfalls of first names. Too-common names (like, say, **Jennifer**), we realized, help us blend in—sometimes too well. Faddish names (paging **Rainbow**) make us stand apart, and yet link us to an era or movement that we didn't ask to be a part of. Shaped by extremes, it is our destiny, our desire, to seek the middle ground—to make our children feel unique, not unusual. That is our mandate.

Choosy Moms Choose Jif (but Not as a Name)

You can name a kid anything—from **Bob** to **Butt-head.** Really, they can't stop you. (Although, perhaps someone should.) Any random combination of letters you string together will suffice. That's how you make a name. But what makes a *good* name?

Here are the top criteria for Generation X–era parents:

Pocket T names: The white pocket T-shirt is an American fashion classic. Durable, flexible, flattering to almost all shapes and sizes, and casual or dressy (depending on your flair for accessories).

What we're looking for in baby names isn't too different. We want the pocket Ts. We want the names that will sound as solid to the ears in 2028 as in 1998. Pocket Ts aren't going out of style in our lifetimes, and probably neither are the likes of **Michael, Matthew, Sarah,** and **Emily.**

The downside (and there always is one) is that some pocket Ts, like **Michael,** are so widely popular today that your child runs the risk of being one of a dozen **Michael Somebodies** in his first-grade class. While this might encourage your child to carve out his own niche—his way of distinguishing himself from a world of Michaels—it also might leave him feeling like a mere name clone.

The upside here (and, fortunately, there's always one of those too) is that almost any pocket T is better than a pair of trendy suspenders. You know trendy suspenders—maybe they're the rainbow-striped getups you saw Robin Williams wear on *Mork & Mindy* and *just had to have.* Or maybe they're the slick ones you saw Michael Douglas don in *Wall*

Street and *just had to have*. Once your unbridled enthusiasm for such things was bridled, did you ever want to wear them again, must less admit you ever thought they were remotely happening? Didn't think so.

Beware, then, of the trendy suspenders of the baby name world. They may seem like the cutest things going right now—**Brianna, Kayla, Cody, Dakota,** and the like—but do you envision the new millennium embracing names that sound as if they were cribbed from daytime TV, circa the mid-1990s?

In fashion, you can always stash a pair of trendy suspenders in the back of your closet once the trend runs its course. In baby names, you—and your child—are stuck with your purchase for life (barring a name change, of course).

Same old stuff, with a twist: Maybe you really like the name **John.** Can't get more pocket T than that. Still, every time you think of naming your son **John,** you hesitate. You had your heart set on something special for your baby. What you want is a twist on an old standby. What you want is wiggle room.

Instead of John, maybe you opt for its Scottish variation, **Ian.** Instead of **Allison,** it's **Alysse.** Instead of **Christopher,** it's **Kristoff.** Instead of **Mary,** it's **Maura.**

With a little research, a little creativity, we can play both sides of the street—and get our exotica grounded in the ordinary.

Unique, Unique, Unique: For some, perhaps even the majority of Gen Xers, pocket Ts and wiggle room are not enough. These parents want "unique" names—and they want them at all costs. No movie is unwatched, no cereal box unread, no magazine article unmarked. Everything and everyone is potential fodder for that elusive, singular, unique name. When the usual leads dry up, the undeterred Gen Xer gets out the pad, the pencil, and starts tinkering. **Jane** becomes **Jaeyne; Michael** becomes **Mychkell,** or some such concoction. (Wake-up call: It's still going to sound like **Jane** and **Michael.** All you're doing is creating a lifetime of headaches for public servants who work at the DMV.)

Still, maybe only a generation that was saddled in multiples with the Wonder Bread likes of **Kimberly, Robert,** and (yes) **Jennifer** can understand a desire to give our children unique names. If this means we lose the ability, or sense, to spell, then so be it. Finding the unique name, at all costs, is the ambition, and the blind spot, of Generation X parents.

Gen Xers are in a, well, "unique" position to pursue this obsession—feeling less bound, less obligated than ever to follow family tradition. Extended families, less pressure from prospective grandparents, and a general do-your-own-thing ethos has all but obliterated a sense of "doing your duty," nursery-style. If you love **Hunter,** you name your son **Hunter** regardless of whether the eldest son on your family's side has *always* been named **John.**

It wouldn't be the first, or last, time a Gen Xer decided to wing it.

Here are some traditional baby name criteria used by all parents, Generations A to X:

Sound check: We want the baby's first name to jibe with her last name. **Danielle,** for instance, is a perfectly good name. But does it work if your family's last name is Shell? Or Manuel?

Or what about the syllable thing? Let's say the family surname is a short, succinct, one beat—like Wong. Maybe you want to give the kid's overall name a little more play. Tag him with **Jonathan,** as opposed to **Tom.** And if you've got a lengthy sonata of a surname—like Vanderheyden, maybe less is more. **Kris** instead of **Mercedes**.

And by the way, if Mom and Dad have different last names, have you figured out which—or what—last name the baby is going to get? Just something else to add to your to-do list.

Family tradition: Yes, even Gen Xers want to honor loved ones. No need to sweat: Baby **Elmer** can be made to understand that your Uncle Elmer was the dearest person in the world to you, and that you wanted to pass on his spirit to your child—even if that meant labeling him with an out-of-the-mainstream name.

The image: We want baby names to project positive things. **Ben** and **Connor** sound honest and handsome; **Katherine** and **Maria,** confident and beautiful.

In their day, **Clyde, Homer, Matilda,** and **Zsa Zsa** must have spoken of equally good things. But this, unfortunately, is not their day. Clyde may well be Welsh for "warm," but you're likely to be the only person to know that.

The Baby Name Climate

What's the weather like out there with **Gary**s and **Doug**s right now? Pretty chilly. Want some heat? Try **Josh**. Below are the top ten baby names (for girls and boys), according to a survey of the nation's fifteen most populated states, using the most recent data available—1996 in most cases. Keep in mind, these stats reflect, in part, the baby boomers' last gasp at parenthood prior to their biological clocks striking midnight.

Most Popular Boy Names

1. Michael
2. Matthew
3. Christopher
4. Jacob
5. Nicholas
6. Joshua
7. Tyler
8. Daniel
9. Austin
10. Joseph

Honorable mentions: Andrew, Brandon, Cody, David, Jonathan, Joseph, Ryan, Zachary

Most Popular Girl Names

1. Emily
2. Ashley
3. Jessica
4. Samantha
5. Sarah
6. Taylor
7. Hannah
8. Rachel
9. Amanda
   Nicole
10. Madison

Honorable mentions: Alexis, Brittany, Caitlyn, Elizabeth, Haley, Megan, Stephanie

How to Use This Book

Now, not to sound medieval or anything, but for the sake of quick referencing, this book is divided into two parts: names for boys; names for girls.

From there, it's the old alphabet at work—names from A to Z. For those of you who just want the facts, the basic stuff's there: name, meaning, country of origin. Listings include a sampling of variations and common nicknames. Popular variations, the **Sean/Shaun** contingent, for instance, rate separate entries. Depending on your spelling whims, there arguably are dozens of variations for any given name. Here, you'll find a couple—sometimes a dozen—to give you an idea of how a name looks with, say, an extra *e* or *l* tagged on the end. But let's make this clear: I'm not going to crunch *all* the letters or suggest you do an end run from **David** to some bogus **Dayevidd** thing. There is a limit to the extent I'm willing to "misspell" names.

If you've got a couple extra minutes to peruse this thing, there are some handy extras to enjoy.

Plus/minus: So, you're considering **Abraham.** What's the upside? What's the downside? Selected entries tell you just that, with handy-dandy plus/minus indicators. Example: **Abraham**'s doable because it's sort of **Joshua**-esque—a plus. The minus? You trying being a little **Abe** when President's Day rolls around. Yes, it's that simple.

Each plus is meant as a sincere statement of a name's upsides; each minus is meant as commentary on the potential problems presented by the choice. (Is there a high teasability factor? Is the name very, very, *very* popular?)

Whatever: Other names are tagged with "Whatever"—assorted commentary, random thoughts, related trivia. This is where you'll learn that ex–New Kids on the Block singer Donnie Wahlberg has a son named **Xavier,** or that **Andre** is the sixth most popular boy name in Colorado.

The gloss: Plus/minus and Whatever entries rely on a certain amount of shorthand to make their pithy points. Nothing too complex. Self-explanatory in most cases. But to ensure the most pleasurable—and least confusing—reading experience possible, you may want to peruse the list of definitions below. You will not be quizzed later.

A comer: A name that may be on its way to becoming the Next Big Thing. Examples: **Parker** (boy); **Ava, Cali** (girls).

Cuddly bear: A big, plush, huggable toy parading as a baby name (usually, but not always, a boy name). Examples: **Coby, Cody, Cory, Spencer** (boys).

Dynasty *names:* A name full of drama and opulence—the sort of thing you'd hear on an episode of the glitzy 1980s prime-time soap (usually, but not always, a girl name). Examples: **Alexis, Chase, Krystle** (girls); **Hawk** (boy).

Flannel shirt: A comfortable, no-fuss effort that sounds "real" and wears like a well-worn flannel shirt. (Boy names only.) Examples: **Ben, Gil, Hank.**

Irish lass: A girl name that sounds, well, Irish—one of our most endearing baby name trends. Examples: **Bridget, Tamony.**

Lil' cowpoke: A snuggly-wuggly name (usually for boys) with a Western flavor that sounds fit for the littlest rangers. Examples: **Cody, Dakota, Kit** (boys); **Cassidy, Sierra** (girl).

Little House on the Prairie *names:* A selection that captures the essence of one of our new hot trends—an old-fashioned girl name that sounds as if it could pass as the moniker of a classmate (or school marm) of Laura Ingalls. Example: **Amanda, Hester, Jessica.**

Little princess: An exquisite tiara-ready, girlie-girl name that bleeds pink. Examples: **Alexandra, Savannah, Tamara.**

A Madonna: A name indelibly identified with a superstar personality. Not recommended for use by a mere mortal. Examples: **Cher, Goldie, Madonna.**

Map name: A name inspired from an actual city, region, state, or nation. Examples: **Brooklyn, Winona** (girls); **Dallas** (boy).

Museum piece: A girl name that's beautiful to look at but fragile to the touch—and not exactly made for today. Example: **Penelope.**

Nerdy cool: A boy name that, against all odds and random associations with busted eyeglasses, sounds nifty in a retro sort of way—and at the very least, projects decency. Examples: **Albert, Herman, Jarvis.**

Peanut-butter-and-jelly sandwich: A name not unlike the type that the typical Gen Xer got tagged with in the 1960s and 1970s—nice, safe, generic, easily digestible. A peanut-butter-and-jelly sandwich is not bad

(Who doesn't like a PB&J?), just (arguably) bland. Sometimes even pocket Ts can double as the sack-lunch fodder. Examples: **Jill, Karen, Linda** (girls); **Alan, Jeff, Keith** (boys).

Pick to click: A name that you won't find in a top ten list, a name that you ordinarily skip over—a name that if you just stop to consider for a second you may find is a cool alternative to the prevailing wisdom. Examples: **Daria, Palmer, Tandy** (girls); **Carter, Gordon, Harper** (boys).

Power name: Not royal enough to be a little princess, not delicate enough to be a pretty girl (see below), the power name is a girl name that makes an impression. Or else. Examples: **Ariana, Bronwen, Shelby.**

Pretty girl: A girl name that, while not as grand as a little princess, is every bit as pink and dainty—and trendy. Examples: **Ashley, Brittany, Samantha.**

Sensitive, cute boy: A tad more on the adult side than the cuddly bear, the sensitive, cute boy conjures images of kind eyes, a nice smile, and an unspoken ability to "understand." Examples: **Ethan, Kevin, Kyle.**

Spelunkers: Prospective parents who troll underwater caves to find the *perfect* name.

A Thurston Howell III: An ultrapreppie, wimpy boy name that will look lousy on a playground but not too bad in a boarding school.

Vowel action/vowel-friendly: A key component of today's girl and boy names: It's got to end in a cutesy-wutesy vowel sound. An *ah* or *ee* in the last syllable can make or break a name and mean the difference between a museum piece and a pretty girl.

Crib notes: Babies . . . cribs . . . ah, the cleverness abounds. Crib notes top every chapter. There you'll find veritable factoids galore: **Celebrity As** (or Bs or Cs, etc.); top Pocket Ts and Trendy suspenders; and something called **"Think long, think hard,"** a roundup of names that should be avoided at most reasonable costs.

Chapters are offset with mini-features on everything from how to select a baby name from an old yearbook to how to make up your very own baby name creation.

All this and opinion too. Everyone's got an opinion on what's a "good" name, what's a "bad" name and why. This book is no different. I'm not shy in espousing likes and dislikes, but (not to deflate the aura of authority I've so carefully constructed to this point) that's all they are—*personal* likes and dislikes leavened with some conventional wisdom. In the end, there are no rights and wrongs. Just varying degrees of therapy bills.

So, just what *is* a Generation X name anyway? For someone who has immersed herself in the subject matter lo these many months, an answer, surprisingly, doesn't come easy. I stutter, stammer, and finally blurt out something like, "Um . . . **Brianna**?" My voice trails in a question mark because even as the words leave my mouth, I think: What am I doing? There's no such thing as a Generation X *name*. We are not all **Brianna** worshipers. We do not all bow at the temple of **Kurt**. . . . Geez, I don't even *believe* in Generation X.

A crisis of conscience ensues: Should I take the money of "the Man" and perpetuate the Gen X myth? Then, a cooler, clearer-thinking, less-persecuted head prevails. This is not a book about Generation X baby names. It's a book for, and about, Generation X–era parents. It's about names we connect with, and why. And that's OK. That's a valid thing.

The bottom line is, for all generations the name game is tricky (How were our parents supposed to *know* seemingly every third girl on their block was either a **Jennifer** or a **Kristen**?), fraught with peril (witness well-meaning parents who named their boys **Adolf,** pre–World War II), and ultimately thankless (When was the last time you hugged one of your parental units for *not* knighting you **Starshine**?). Well, we better get used to it. Raising kids isn't a lot different from naming them. Just more diaper-intensive.

Best of luck.

A

CRIB NOTES

Famous As: **Abraham** Lincoln (U.S. President); **Ace** Frehley (rocker, Kiss); **Adam** Horovitz (rapper, the Beastie Boys); **Aidan** Quinn (actor, *Legends of the Fall*); **Alan** Alda (TV's *M*A*S*H* guy); **Alec** Baldwin (actor); **Alfred** E. Neuman (*Mad* magazine mascot); **Anson** Williams (TV's Potsie, *Happy Days*); **Anthony** Michael Hall (the geek, *The Breakfast Club*); **Antonio** Banderas (actor); **Aristotle** Onassis (tycoon); **Arthur** Miller (playwright, *Death of a Salesman*); **Axl** Rose (rocker, Guns n' Roses)

Pocket Ts: Aaron, Adam, Andrew, Anthony

Trendy suspenders: Alexander, Austin

Think long, think hard: **Ace** (Only slightly better than naming the kid **Stud.**); **Adolf** (Uh, no.); **Adonis** (Please. You can't afford the therapy bills.); **Alfred/Alf** (Ruined by the aforementioned comic-book guy, and a 1980s sitcom E.T., respectively.); **Algernon** (Once and forever, the rodent from the 1968 movie *Charly*.); **Alvin** (Blame it on the Chipmunks.); **Amadeus** (Great movie, lousy baby name.); **Ambrose** (For nineteenth-century misanthropes only.); **America** (Wanna get patriotic? Try voting.); **Amiel** (Like throwing fresh meat to the schoolyard bullies.); **Amos** (Two words: And **Andy.**); **Angus** (Too livestock-y); **Apollo** (*See* **Adonis.**); **Arvid** (*Head of the Class* nerd name.); **Ashley** (A name that's gone to the girls, in no small part due to *Gone With the Wind* Nancy-boy **Ashley** Wilkes.)

Aaron (Hebrew: high mountain). Also, **Aaren, Aron, Aren.** *Plus:* Strong, earnest, biblical, timeless. A name that's a worthy peer of

Jacob and **Joshua.** It's got a tidy level of popularity—not too big, not too out. A nearly faultless pocket T. *Minus: Nearly* faultless. Reminds you of the fractious Los Angeles season of MTV's *Real World* and the budding accountant guy named **Aaron.**

Ab (Latin: away). Also, **Abb.** Familiar, **Abbott, Abner.** *Whatever:* This one's probably best left to the gym rats—"Work those abs!"

Abbott (English: monastery member; variation of **Abraham,** "father of many"). Also, **Abbot, Abot, Abott.** Familiar, **Ab.**

Abe (Hebrew: variation of **Abraham, Abram, Abrams, Avraham, Avram, Avrams**). *Plus:* **Abe** is more than a nickname—it's **Abraham** unplugged, a selection that cuts to the soul of Gen X. Comfortable, dependable, unpretentious—a veritable flannel shirt. *Minus:* It'll be murder for your poor kid come President's Day.

Abel (Hebrew: breath, vanity). Also, **Abil, Able, Abyl.**

Abdul (Arabic: servant).

Abdullah (Arabic: servant to God). Also, **Abdula, Abdulah, Abdulla.**

Abdullahi (Arabic: variation of **Abdullah,** "servant to God"). Also, **Abudulahi, Abdulahy, Abudullahy.**

Abiel (Hebrew: God is my father). Also, **Abeel.**

Abner (Hebrew: father of light). Familiar, **Ab.** *Plus:* If **Jacob** can make the long climb back, why not **Abner**? *Minus:* One word: Lil'.

Abraham (Hebrew: father of many). Also, **Abrahem, Abrahym, Abreham, Abrehem, Abrehym, Abryham, Abryhem.** Familiar, **Abe.**

Abram (Hebrew: father of many; variation of **Abramson,** "son of **Abram**"). Also, **Abrem, Abrym.** Familiar, **Abe.**

Abrams (Hebrew: variation of **Abram,** "father of many"). Also, **Abrems, Abryms.** Familiar, **Abe.**

Abramson (Hebrew: son of **Abram**). Also, **Abramsen, Abremsen, Abremson, Abrymsen, Abrymson.** Familiar, **Abram.**

Adair (Scottish: of the oak tree). Also, **Adare.**

Adam (Hebrew: the maker; variation of **Adamson,** "son of **Adam**"). Also, **Adem, Adym.** *Whatever:* This one has impeccable credentials. Cute on a boy, manly on a man. A classic, not Jurassic pocket T. And don't forget, it's got a *Bewitched* connection—an association that's done wonders for **Samantha. Adam** was **Samantha** Stevens's good little warlock of a son.

Adams (Hebrew: variation of **Adam,** "the maker"). Also, **Adems, Adyms.**

Adamson (Hebrew: son of **Adam**). Also, **Adamsen, Ademsen, Ademson, Adymsen, Adymson**. Familiar, **Adam**.

Adder (English: viper). Also, **Ader**.

Addis (Hebrew: variation of **Adam, Addison**). Also, **Addiss, Addys, Addyss, Adis, Adiss, Adys, Adyss**.

Addison (Hebrew: variation of **Adam**, "the maker"). Also, **Adisen, Adison, Addysen, Addyson, Adysen, Adyson**. Familiar, **Addis**. *Plus:* Thurston Howell III preppie. *Minus:* Namesake of a kidney disorder.

Adell (German: noble; variation of **Adelson**, "son of Adel"). Also, **Adel**.

Adelson (German: son of **Adel,** noble). Also, **Adelsen**. Familiar, **Adel**.

Adlai (Hebrew: my ornament). Also, **Adlae, Adlay**. *Plus:* **Adlai** Stevenson III is one of our most fondly remembered statesmen. *Minus:* He might have been one of our most fondly remembered presidents, except he ran for the White House twice—and lost.

Adler (German: eagle).

Adrian (Greek: manly, brave). Also, **Adryan, Adrien, Adryen**. *Plus:* "Manly?" "Brave?" Who says this is a girl name? Heck, **Adrian** Zmed played hotheaded cop Vince Romano on TV's *T. J. Hooker* (1982–87). *Minus:* Zmed was a fluke. It's a girl name.

Ahmad (Arabic: most praiseworthy). Also, **Ahmaad**.

Ahmed (Arabic: praiseworthy).

Ahmir (Hebrew: variation of **Amir**, "mighty"). Also, **Ahmeer, Ahmyr**.

Aidan (Irish: fire). Also, **Aiden, Aidyn**. *Plus:* Lyrical, handsome, uncommon—in a good way. *Minus:* A wimpy **Adrian** sound-alike.

Al (English/Italian/Scottish/Spanish: variation of **Alan, Albert, Alberto, Alejandro, Alesandro, Alfonse, Alfonso, Alfonze, Alfonzo, Alonso, Alonzo, Alphonse, Alphonso**).

Alan (Scottish: handsome). Also, **Alen, Allan, Allen, Allyn, Alyn**. Familiar, **Al**. *Whatever:* A name in transition. "Slick and cool" in the 1960s and 1970s has morphed into "bland and unexciting" today. **Alan** doesn't sound wrong—it just kind of sounds there. A peanut-butter-and-jelly sandwich.

Albert (English: bright, noble). Familiar, **Al, Bert**. *Plus:* At first glance it's no hipper than **Alan,** maybe even nerdier. And yet . . . it's so old school, so not hip, it's sort of nerdy cool. *Minus:* One word: Fat.

Alberto (Italian: variation of **Albert**, "bright, noble"). Also, **Albirto**. Familiar, **Al**.

Alden (English: wise guardian). Also, **Aldin, Aldyn.**

Alder (English: small birch tree).

Alec (English: variation of **Alex,** "protector, defender"). Also, **Aleck, Alek, Alic, Alick, Alik, Alyc, Alyck, Alyk.**

Alejandro (Spanish: variation of **Alexander,** "protector, defender"). Also, **Alijandro, Alyjandro.** Familiar, **Al.**

Alesandro (Italian: variation of **Alexander,** "protector, defender"). Also, **Alisandro, Alysandro.** Familiar, **Al.**

Alex (English/French: variation of **Alexander, Alexandre**). Also, **Alix, Alyx.**

Alexander (Greek: protector, defender). Also, **Alixander, Alyxander.** Familiar, **Alex.** *Plus:* Here's a power name for the America that drives four-wheel-drive utility vehicles, not cars. **Alexander** is blowing past the kingly likes of **Richard** and **James** in popularity lists. *Minus:* **Alexander** is a touch on the opulent side; **Alex** a touch on the **Max** side—that side being precious and pretentious. (Witness Judd Nelson's caddish **Alex** in *St. Elmo's Fire.* It's a name that in a decade could look as affected as Pat Riley's slicked-back hair. A potential pair of trendy suspenders.

Alexandre (French: variation of **Alexander,** "protector, defender"). Also, **Alexandrae, Alexandray, Alixandrae, Alixandray, Alixandre, Alyxandrae, Alyxandray, Alyxandre.** Familiar, **Alex.**

Alexi (Greek: variation of **Alexander,** "protector, defender"). Also, **Alexey, Alexy, Alixi, Alixey, Alixy, Alyxi.**

Alfonse (Spanish: eager). Also, **Alfons.** Familiar, **Al.**

Alfonso (Spanish: variation of Alfonse, "eager"). Familiar, **Al.**

Alfonze (Italian: eager). Also, **Alfonz.** Familiar, **Al.**

Alfonzo (Italian: variation of Alfonze, "eager"). Familiar, **Al.**

Allister (English: variation of **Alexander,** "protector, defender"). Also, **Alister, Allyster, Alyster.**

Alonso (Spanish: eager). Familiar, **Al, Lon, Lonnie.**

Alonzo (Italian: eager). Familiar, **Al, Lon, Lonnie.**

Alphonse (German: eager). Also, **Alphons.** Familiar, **Al.**

Alphonso (Italian: variation of Alphonse, "eager").

Alston (English: nobleman's town). Also, **Alsten.**

Alt (German: aged). Also, **Alte.**

Amir (Hebrew: mighty). Also, **Ameer, Amyr.**

Amram (Hebrew: father of **Aaron** and **Moses**). Also, **Amrem, Amrym.**

Ander (German: another).

Andes (Greek: variation of **Andrew,** "brave").

Andre (French: variation of **Andrew,** "brave"). Also, **Andrae, Andray.** Familiar, **Drew, Dre.**

Andres (Spanish: variation of **Andrew,** "brave"). *Whatever:* Here's an example of the power of celebrity: While the rest of the country is ga-ga for **Andrew,** this is the sixth most popular name in Colorado. Why? Baseball slugger **Andres** Galarraga, formerly of the hometown Col-orado Rockies. But watch out—Galarraga departed Denver. There goes the stock.

Andrew (Greek: brave). Also, **Andru, Andruw.** Familiar, **Andy, Drew.** *Plus:* A popular pocket T that wears long, wears true. **Andrew** is a snuggly cuddly bear that'll grow with your son. *Minus:* It's too popu-lar. No challenge for spelunkers.

Andy (Greek: variation of **Andrew,** "brave"). Also, **Andey.** *Plus:* Makes you think of footsie pajamas. *Minus:* Makes you think of that *Matlock* guy.

Anfernee (American: variation of **Anthony,** "priceless"). Also, **An-ferney, Anferny.**

Angel (English: angel). Also, **Angil, Angyl.** *Whatever:* Celestial an-gels, for lack of a better term, are hot.

Angelo (Spanish: angel, messenger). Also, **Angilo, Angylo.**

Anson (English: son of Anne, gracious). Also, **Ansen.**

Anthony (Latin: priceless). Also, **Anthoney.** Familiar, **Tony.** *Plus:* **Alexander,** minus the fanfare. Steady, dependable, versatile. A pocket T. *Minus:* Fodder for "**Tony** the Tiger" taunts.

Antoine (French: variation of **Anthony,** "priceless").

Anton (Slavic: variation of **Anthony,** "priceless"). Also, **Antonn.**

Antony (Italian: variation of **Anthony,** "priceless"). Also, **Antoney.** Fa-miliar, **Tony.**

Antwan (American: variation of **Anthony,** "priceless"). Also, **Antwon.**

Arch (English: variation of **Archibald,** "bold, genuine"). Also, **Arche.** *Whatever:* The "**Archie**" comics association aside, **Arch** is kinda nifty.

Archibald (German: bold, genuine). Also, **Archybald.** Familiar, **Arch, Archie.** *Whatever:* With smoking jacket and elbow patches, **Archibald** is the perfect complement for a future Oxford English pro-fessor.

Archie (English: variation of **Archibald,** "bold, genuine"). Also, **Archey, Archy.**

Arden (Latin: ardent). Also, **Ardin, Ardyn.**

Ares (Greek: god of war).

Areus (Greek: warlike). Also, **Arius, Aryeus.**

Ari (Hebrew: lion; Hebrew/Greek: variation of **Ariel, Aristotle**). Also, **Arey, Ary.** *Whatever:* A pick to click. Uncommonly classic.

Aric (Scandinavian: variation of **Eric,** "mighty lord, hero"). Also, **Arick, Arik, Aryc, Aryck.**

Ariel (Hebrew: lion of god). Also, **Aryel.** Familiar, **Ari.** *Whatever:* A name that was usurped by Disney's Little Mermaid herself. Might want to stick with **Ari.**

Aristotle (Greek: optimistic). Also, **Arystotle.** Familiar, **Ari.** *Whatever:* A bit too-too—unless you're a Richie Rich shipping magnate. It's included here as another way to get to **Ari** if you think that selection will look a little bare on the birth certificate.

Arlen (Irish: vow). Also, **Arlin, Arlyn.**

Arlis (Hebrew: oath). Also, **Arlys, Arliss, Arlyss.**

Arlo (Spanish: berry tree). *Whatever:* A sly way of paying tribute to the 1960s without getting too hippie-dippie. **Arlo** is the namesake of "Alice's Restaurant" folk singer **Arlo** Guthrie.

Armand (German: army leader; Latin: noble). Also, **Armond, Armonde.**

Armando (Spanish: variation of **Armand,** "noble"). Also, **Armondo.**

Armen (Armenian: Armenian). Also, **Armin, Armyn.**

Armin (Hebrew: high fort). Also, **Armyn.**

Aronin (Hebrew: variation of **Aaron,** "high mountain"). Also, **Aronyn.**

Arsenio (Greek: masculine, virile). Also, **Arsenyo, Arsinio, Arsinyo.** *Plus:* Comic **Arsenio** Hall is proof that boys can survive *not* being named **Michael;** maybe even thrive. *Minus:* If you want to give the kid a challenge, make him buy his own bicycle—don't go around saddling him with a Madonna.

Art (Latin: a creative work; English: variation of **Artemus, Arthur, Artur, Arturo**). *Whatever:* The question you must ask: Is **Art** best served in a museum or a baby nursery?

Artemus (Greek: of the hunt). Also, **Artimus, Artymus.** Familiar, **Art, Artie.**

Arthur (Celtic: bear). Also, **Arther.** Familiar, **Art, Artie.** *Whatever:* A perfectly fine name going through some downtime. It's still usable, just not happening or hip.

Artie (English: variation of **Artemus, Arthur**). Also, **Artey, Arty.**

Artur (Russian: variation of **Arthur**, "bear"). Also, **Arter.** Familiar, **Art.**

Arturo (Spanish: variation of **Arthur**, "bear"). Also, **Arturro.** Familiar, **Art.**

Arum (Greek: plant).

Asa (Hebrew: doctor, healer). Also, **Assa.**

Ash (English: ash; variation of **Ashby, Ashcroft, Asher, Ashford, Ashland, Ashton**). Also, **Ashe.**

Ashby (English: ash trees). Also, **Ashbey.** Familiar, **Ash.** *Plus:* The new **Ashley.** *Minus:* You're too late. This Southern gentleman favorite is going to the girls too.

Ashcroft (English: crossing at the ash trees). Also, **Ashcrofte.** Familiar, **Ash.**

Asher (Hebrew: happy). Familiar, **Ash.**

Ashford (English: river crossing at the ash trees). Also, **Ashforde.** Familiar, **Ash.**

Ashland (English: land of the ash trees). Also, **Ashlande.** Familiar, **Ash.**

Ashton (English: town by the ash trees). Also, **Ashten.** Familiar, **Ash.** *Whatever:* Slightly higher on the manly man sound scale than **Ashley.**

Atom (Greek: not to cut).

Aton (Egyptian: god of sun).

Aubrey (Scottish: wealthy). Also, **Aubry.**

August (Latin: awe-inspiring).

Augustus (Latin: "venerable").

Austin (Latin: variation of **Augustus**, "venerable"). Also, **Austen, Austyn.** *Plus:* A lil' cowpoke of a higher order. A rangy entry that can be used to pay tribute to the romance of the West, or the romance of Jane Austen's England. *Minus:* If Hollywood keeps committing the Jane Austen catalog to film, every blinkin' kid in kindergarten is going to be **Austin.** It's a name that's storming the popularity lists, replacing the sensitive, cute boy likes of **Brian.** Given that, chances are that one day your little **Austin** will demand to know how many times you went to see *Sense and Sensibility.* Potential trendy suspenders.

Avens (English: clove). Also, **Avins, Avyns.**

Averell (English: wild boar). Also, **Averel, Averil, Averill, Averyl, Averyll.**

Avery (English: ruler). Also, **Averey.** *Whatever:* The name of the son of TV's Murphy Brown.

Avraham (Hebrew: variation of **Abraham,** "father of many"). Also, **Avrahem, Avrahym, Avreham, Avrehem, Avrehym, Avryham, Avryhem.** Familiar, **Abe.**

Avram (Hebrew: variation of **Abraham, Avramson**). Also, **Avrem, Avrym.** Familiar, **Abe.**

Avrams (Hebrew: variation of **Abraham,** "father of many"). Also, **Avrems, Avryms.** Familiar, **Abe.**

Avramson (Hebrew: variation of **Abraham,** "father of many"). Also, **Avramsen, Avremsen, Avremson, Avrymsen, Avrymson.** Familiar, **Avram.**

Avril (English: wild boar). Also, **Avrill, Avryl, Avryll.**

Axel (German: shoulder; variation of **Axelrod,** "shoulder, wheel"). Also, **Axl, Axle, Axyl.**

Axelrod (German: shoulder, wheel). Also, **Axlerod, Axlrod, Axylrod.** Familiar, **Axel.**

B

CRIB NOTES

Famous Bs: **Bailey** Salinger (cute boy, TV's *Party of Five*); **Balthazar** Getty (actor, *Lord of the Flies*); **Barry** Bonds (baseball player); **Beck** Hansen (singer/songwriter); **Benson** Dubois (lieutenant governor, TV's *Benson*); **Bill** Clinton (U.S. president); **Bing** Crosby ("White Christmas" guy); **Bono** (rocker, U2); **Boris** Becker (tennis player); **Brad** Pitt (actor); **Brady** Anderson (baseball player); **Brandon** Walsh (sideburns poster boy, TV's *Beverly Hills, 90210*); **Brendan** Fraser (actor); **Bruce** Lee (actor/kung-fu icon)

Pocket Ts: Ben, Benjamin

Trendy suspenders: Brandon

Think long, think hard: **Barnaby** (The last notable **Barnaby** was geriatric TV private detective **Barnaby** Jones. That ought to speak volumes to its hip factor.); **Barney** (A certain purple dinosaur has driven the final stake in this one.); **Bartholomew/Bart** (One's a museum piece. The other's been co-opted by outlaws from Black **Bart** to **Bart** Simpson); **Beavis** (No . . . That goes double for **Butt-head**.); **Benedict** (Remember the angst Peter Brady endured merely *portraying* **Benedict** Arnold in a school play? Imagine the angst if he *was* a **Benedict**.); **Benji** (So 1970s it might as well be a mood ring.); **Blane** ("That's a major appliance. That's not a name!" —Duckie, *Pretty in Pink*.); **Brick** (How very Tennessee Williams. In fact, *too* very.); **Bud** (Let the kid's locker room buddies dub him **Bud**. No use going out of your way to christen him in honor of a beer and/or the kid from *Married . . . with Children*.); **Butch** (So manly man as to sound positively goofy.)

Bacchus (Greek/Latin: god of wine and revelry). Also, **Bachus, Bacus.**

Bach (German: after composer Johann Sebastian **Bach**).

Bade (English: to urge, encourage). Also, **Baide, Bayde.**

Bailey (English: overseer of estate). Also, **Baily, Baley, Baly, Bayley.** *Whatever:* A comer. Look for this one to pick up steam as a boy name, thanks to nice-'n'-cute good guy **Bailey** Salinger from TV's *Party of Five.*

Bairn (Scottish: child). Also, **Bairne.**

Baize (Latin: brown cloth). Also, **Bayze, Baze.**

Baldric (Latin: belt). Also, **Baldryc, Baldrick, Baldryck, Baldrik, Baldryk.**

Baldwin (English: bold, friend). Also, **Baldwyn.**

Bale (German: ball or bundle). Also, **Baile, Bayle.**

Baltazar (Greek: variation of **Balthazar,** one of the Three Wise Men). Also, **Baltasar, Baltesar, Baltysar, Baltezar, Baltyzar.** Familiar, **Balto.**

Balthazar (Greek: one of the Three Wise Men). Also, **Balthasar, Balthesar, Balthysar, Balthezar, Balthyzar.** Familiar, **Balto.** *Whatever:* Gen X–era actor **Balthazar** Getty proves that some old bones, i.e., **Balthazar,** are worth digging up.

Balto (Greek: variation of **Baltazar, Balthazar**).

Balzac (French: after novelist Honoré de **Balzac**). Also, **Balzack, Balzak.**

Bane (English: fair). Also, **Baine, Bayne.**

Banner (English: flag).

Bantam (English: small, aggressive). Also, **Bantem, Bantym.**

Banyan (Sanskrit: fig tree). Also, **Banyen, Banyn.**

Bard (Celtic: poet). Also, **Barde.**

Barker (English: sideshow announcer).

Barley (English: cereal grain). Also, **Barly.**

Barnard (German: variation of **Bernard,** "brave bear").

Barnes (English: of the barns). Also, **Barns.**

Barnhard (German: variation of **Bernard,** "brave bear").

Baron (Hebrew: son of **Aaron;** English: nobleman). Also, **Baren, Barron.** *Whatever:* A boy version of a little princess.

Barrett (German: a bear, a ruler). Also, **Barret, Barrit, Barritt, Barryt, Barrytt.**

Barrow (English: hill). Also, **Barow.**

Barry (Irish: spear). Also, **Barrey.** *Plus:* A virile, manly man moniker. *Minus:* Currently used by used-car salesmen the nation over.

Basil (Greek: herb). Also, **Basyl.**

Batiste (French: fine cloth).

Baxter (English: baker). *Plus:* Buttoned-down, professional. *Minus:* Stuffy.

Bay (Latin: laurel wreath).

Baye (African: straightforward).

Baylor (English: horse trainer). Also, **Bayler.**

Beach (English: a beach, a sandy shore). Also, **Beache.**

Beau (Latin: suitor; French: handsome; variation of **Beaumont,** "handsome mountain"). *Plus:* A leading-edge lil' cowpoke that's demonstrated enviable staying power. It's not hot but not too silly sounding either. *Minus:* The **Cody** of the 1970s.

Beaumont (French: handsome mountain). Also, **Beaumonte.** Familiar, **Beau.**

Beck (German: brook). Also, **Bec, Bek.** *Whatever:* A pick to click. While everybody else goes to the Emerald Isle to find surnames that work as first names, why don't you throw 'em for a loop? Visit Germany. "Loser" singer **Beck** proves this one a nifty, cool entry.

Beech (English: tree, wood). Also, **Beech.**

Bell (English: a bell). Also, **Bel.**

Belshazar (Hebrew: last king of Babylon). Also, **Belshasar, Belshesar, Belshysar, Belshezar, Belshyzar.**

Ben (Hebrew/Latin/English: variation of **Benjamin, Bennett, Benson, Benton**). Also, **Benn.** *Plus:* A no-brainer pocket T getting a big-time boost from Oscar-winner **Ben** Affleck. *Minus:* Every time you hear **Ben,** you think *Ben,* the 1972 movie about rats.

Benjamin (Hebrew: son of right hand). Also, **Benjamyn.** Familiar, **Ben, Bennie.** *Plus:* Decent, honest, intelligent, soft-spoken. This pocket T has been selling its virtues since before **Benjamin** Franklin, and after *The Graduate*'s befuddled **Benjamin** Braddock. Like the level-headed name it is, its popularity has never approached unmanageable levels. It's familiar and friendly, not common and trendy.

Bennett (Latin: blessed). Also, **Bennet, Bennit, Bennitt, Bennyt, Bennytt.** Familiar, **Ben, Bennie.**

Bennie (Hebrew/Latin/English: variation of **Benjamin, Bennett, Benson**). Also, **Benney, Benny.**

Benson (English: son of **Ben**). Also, **Bensen, Benssen, Bensson.** Familiar, **Ben, Bennie.**

Benton (English: town of **Ben**). Also, **Benten.** Familiar, **Ben.**

Berber (African: tribe of North Africa).

Berke (French: fortress; English: variation of **Berkeley,** "birch wood").

Berkeley (English: birch wood). Also, **Berkely, Berkley, Berkly.** Familiar, **Berke.** *Plus:* To West and East Coasters, **Berkeley** is a map name that sounds less precious than, say, **Dakota.** *Minus:* To the rest of the country, it's a map name that sounds more precious than, say, **Dakota.**

Berm (Dutch: roadside shoulder). Also, **Berme.**

Bern (German: bear). Also, **Berne.** *Whatever:* An easy target for fire-related jokes but not out of the question. In fact, it's a pick to click in this book. Why? Just sounds kinda cool.

Bernard (German: brave bear). Familiar, **Bernie.**

Bernhard (German: variation of **Bernard,** "brave bear"). Familiar, **Bernie.**

Bernie (German: variation of **Bernard, Bernhard**). Also, **Berney, Berny.**

Berry (English: a fruit). Also, **Berey, Berrey, Bery.**

Bert (English: bright, variation of **Albert, Bertland, Bertram**). Also, **Berte.** *Plus: Sesame Street*'s **Bert** is a dear soul who taught Gen Xers to spell. *Minus:* **Bert** is a Muppet. And the name just doesn't sound right without the accompanying **Ernie.**

Bertland (English: variation of **Burtland,** "bright land"). Also, **Bertlande.** Familiar, **Bert.**

Bertram (German: strength). Also, **Bertrem, Bertrym.** Familiar, **Bert.**

Bill (English: variation of **William,** "will, helmet").

Billy (English: variation of **William,** "will, helmet"). Also, **Billey.** *Plus: Ally McBeal*'s **Billy** is cute. *Minus: Melrose Place*'s **Billy** is stupid.

Billy Joe (American: combination of **Billy** and **Joe**). Also, **Billyjoe.**

Bing (German: a hollow). Also, **Byng.** *Plus:* Different, in a harmless way. *Minus:* Harmless?! A name that rhymes with *ding, ping, zing,* and a dozen other things?!

Blade (English: leaf). Also, **Blaide, Blayde.**

Blair (Scottish: clear plain). Also, **Blaire, Blare**. *Plus:* A preppie classic . . . *Minus:* . . . stolen by them darn girls.

Blake (English: fair-haired). Also, **Blaike, Blayke**. *Whatever:* A *Dynasty* name.

Blakely (English: fair meadow). Also, **Blaikeley, Blakeley, Blaykeley, Blaikly, Blaykely**.

Bo (American: variation of **Beau**, "handsome, suitor").

Bob (English: variation of **Robert**, "bright, flame").

Bobbin (French: spool of thread). Also, **Bobin, Bobbyn, Bobyn**.

Bobby (English: variation of **Robert**, "bright, flame"). Also, **Bobbey**.

Bobby Joe (American: combination of **Bobby** and **Joe**). Also, **Bobbyjoe**.

Bomont (American: variation of **Beaumont**, "handsome mountain"). Also, **Bomonte**. Familiar, **Bo**.

Bon (Italian/French: good). Also, **Bonn**.

Bond (English: cord, rope).

Bono (Italian: good). *Whatever:* Just so you know, **Bono** is *not* **Bono**'s "real" name. The former Paul Hewson cribbed it from a speaker system—the Bono Vox.

Boone (French: good, jovial). *Whatever:* A doable lil' cowpoke that should look as good on your future adult as it does on your toddler.

Booth (English: hut). Also, **Boothe**.

Boris (Slavic: warrior). Also, **Boriss, Borys, Boryss**.

Boston (English: town near the shrubs). Also, **Bosten**. *Whatever:* A map name before map names were trendy. Actor Kurt Russell welcomed son **Boston** into the world in 1980.

Bowie (Irish: fair-headed). Also, **Bowey, Bowy**.

Boyd (Scottish: fair-complected). Also, **Boyde**.

Brad (English: variation of **Bradford, Bradley**). *Whatever:* **Brad** was a B.M.O.C. when Gen Xers roamed school halls. He was the jock with the good teeth and good skin—think **Brad** Pitt today. It's lucky for **Brad** that Pitt's around, otherwise this swingin' ladies' man would be looking about as hip as a neckful of gold chains.

Braden (English/German: broad). Also, **Bradin, Bradyn, Brayden, Braydin**.

Bradford (English: wide ford, water crossing). Also, **Bradforde**. Familiar, **Brad**.

Bradley (English: wide meadow). Also, **Bradly**. Familiar, **Brad**.

Brady (Irish: spirited). Also, **Bradey.** *Plus:* The new **Brad.** *Minus:* The inevitable *Brady Bunch* jokes.

Bram (Irish: raven). Also, **Bramm.** *Plus:* Dignified and unusual, **Bram** sounds enough like **Brad** to avoid being *too* unusual. *Minus:* Creepy factor? **Bram** Stoker wrote *Dracula.*

Brandon (English: bright hill). Also, **Branden.** *Plus:* Well, not every kid in kindergarten is named after this popular cuddly bear entry. *Minus:* No, it's every *other* kid. Put the blame for this entry's hot-ticket status on Jason Priestley's sanctimonious, but cute, **Brandon** Walsh character of TV's *Beverly Hills, 90210.* Rate this trendy suspenders.

Brant (English: steep, wild goose). Also, **Brante.** *Whatever:* Another **Brad** sound-alike that can be used to soft-pedal the swingin' one's overt studlyness.

Braxton (English: badger, town). Also, **Braxten.**

Brendan (Irish: aflame). Also, **Brenden, Brendyn.** *Whatever:* **Brendan** isn't the red-hot cuddly bear that **Brandon** is. Down the road, this may mean it won't sound as cloyingly **Cody**-ish.

Brennan (Irish: raven). Also, **Brenan, Brenen, Brennen, Brennyn, Brenyn.**

Brent (English: steep hill; variation of **Brentland, Brenton, Brentwood**). Also, **Brente.**

Brentland (English: land near the steep hill). Also, **Brentlande.** Familiar, **Brent.**

Brenton (English: town near the steep hill). Also, **Brenten.** Familiar, **Brent.**

Brentwood (English: forest near the steep hill). Also, **Brentwoode.** Familiar, **Brent.**

Brett (French: from Britain). Also, **Bret.**

Brian (Celtic: strong). Also, **Briann, Brien, Bryan, Bryen.** *Whatever:* The sort of edible but bland peanut-butter-and-jelly sandwich that got stuffed in a *Six Million Dollar Man* lunchbox, circa 1975. Back then, **Brian** was as hip as **Brandon** or **Brendan.** But now those two monster Bs have sapped **Brian**'s power to pass itself off as the state-of-the-art cuddly bear. The party is still far from over for **Brian.** It's just getting a little quieter.

Brice (Irish: variation of **Bryce,** "ambition").

Brigham (English: bridge, village). Also, **Brigam, Brigem, Brighem.**

Brighton (English: bridge, town). Also, **Brighten.**

Brock (English: stream, marshland).

Broderick   (English: broad, ridge). Also, **Broderic, Broderik, Broderyc, Broderych, Broderyk.**

Brody (Scottish: steep rock overhang). Also, **Brodey, Brodie.** *Whatever:* A pick to click. Handsome, strong, contemporary.

Brogan (Gaelic: work shoe). Also, **Brogen, Brogyn.**

Bronson (English: brown). Also, **Bronsen.** *Whatever:* Actor **Bronson** Pinchot played Mypos native Balki Bartokomous on TV's *Perfect Strangers* (1986–93).

Brooks (English: small river). Also, **Brookes.**

Bruce (English: the brush). *Plus:* A name for heroes—from Batman alter ego **Bruce** Wayne to real-life martial arts legend **Bruce** Lee. *Minus:* A name for the guy who brought us *Hudson Hawk.*

Bruno (German: brown).

Bryant (Scottish: strong). Also, **Briant, Brient, Bryent.**

Bryce (Irish: ambition). *Plus:* The hipper alternative to **Bruce.** *Minus:* Could use a little of **Bruce**'s spare testosterone.

Bryson (English: son of **Brian,** "strong"). Also, **Brysen.**

Bryton (English: variation of **Brighton,** "bridge, town"). Also, **Bryten.**

Buck (English: male deer).

Buddy (English: friend). Also, **Buddey.**

Burkeley   (English: variation of **Berkeley,** "birch wood"). Also, **Burkely, Burkley, Burkly.**

Burl (French: knot in a tree trunk). Also, **Burle.**

Burr (Scottish: a burr; Scandinavian: prickly seed).

Burt (English: bright; variation of **Burtland, Burton**). Also, **Burte.**

Burtland (English: bright land). Also, **Burtlande.** Familiar, **Burt.**

Burton (English: fortress). Also, **Burten.** Familiar, **Burt.**

Byron (English: cottage). Also, **Byren.** *Plus:* Literary, romantic. *Minus:* Bookish, wimpy.

C

CRIB NOTES

Famous Cs: **Calvert** DeForest (Larry "Bud" Melman); **Calvin** Klein (designer); **Cameron** Crowe (filmmaker, *Jerry Maguire*); **Campbell** Scott (actor, *Dying Young*); **Cary** Grant (actor/charmer); **Chad** Everett (actor, TV's *Medical Center*); **Charlie** Parker (jazz great); **Charlton** Heston (actor/Moses); **Chet** Baker (jazz great); **Chipper** Jones (baseball player); **Christian** Slater (actor); **Clarence** Thomas (U.S. Supreme Court justice); **Clint** Eastwood (actor); **Clive** Barker (horror author); **Cobi** Jones (soccer player); **Cody** Gifford (talk-show hostess's son); **Conan** O'Brien (talk-show host); **Crispin** Glover (actor, *Back to the Future*)

Pocket Ts: **Cameron, Chrisitan, Christopher**

Trendy suspenders: **Coby, Cody, Cory**—the cuddly bear triplets.

Think long, think hard: **Casper** (The friendly ghost.); **Cecil** (With or without Beany, an unsalvageable nerd name.); **Chauncey** (In this enlightened age, one would like to believe that the notion of sissies has been discarded. One would be wrong.); **Cheech** (**Cheech** and **Chong** are best enjoyed as a comedy duo, not as a source of baby name inspiration.); **Chester** (Perfectly fine name that rhymes with a perfectly heinous act. Don't think this will be lost on the budding poets in your son's class.); **Claude** (With all due respect to the late actor **Claude** Akins [*Movin' On*], **Claude** sounds like "clod."); **Clem** (Sad, but true mental image: The lost member of *The Beverly Hillbillies*.); **Cletus** (*See* **Clem.**)

Cab (French: carriage). Also, **Cabb.** *Whatever:* **Cab** Calloway was the heppest of hepcats.

Cable (English: rope maker). Also, **Cabel.**

Cabot (French: small head). Also, **Cabbott.** *Plus:* A Thurston Howell III name that's Ivy League ready. *Minus:* Set your watch by it. There *will* be "cabbage" taunts.

Cade (Scottish: little warrior). Also, **Caide, Cayde.**

Caden (English: variation of **Cade,** "little warrior"). Also, **Cadin, Cadyn.**

Caesar (Latin: virile).

Cain (Hebrew: spear). Also, **Cane, Cayne.**

Cairn (Scottish: stone monument). Also, **Cairne.**

Cal (English/Latin: variation of **Calvert, Calvin**).

Caleb (Hebrew: faithful). Also, **Calib, Calyb.** *Plus:* The **Cody** Less Traveled, **Caleb** is a handsome entry that lacks the attendant trendiness or over-the-top cuteness of its cuddly bear cousin. *Minus:* Spelunkers know that **Caleb** isn't exactly the find of the century.

Calvert (English: cattle herder). Familiar, **Cal.** *Whatever:* Even lower on the hip scale than **Calvin.** Included here as another way to get to **Cal,** a nifty nickname.

Calvin (Latin: bald). Also, **Calvyn.** Familiar, **Cal.** *Plus:* Exudes shades of "**Calvin** and Hobbes." *Minus:* Exudes shades of Urkel.

Cam (Dutch: a comb, a wheel; variation of **Camden, Cameron**). Also, **Camm.**

Cambridge (English: wheel, bridge; English town). Also, **Cambrydge.**

Camden (English: crooked valley). Also, **Camdin, Camdyn.** Familiar, **Cam.**

Cameron (Gaelic/Scottish: crooked nose). Also, **Cameren, Cameryn, Camiren, Camiron, Camiryn, Camren, Camron, Camryn, Camyren, Camyron.** Familiar, **Cam.** *Plus:* A durable pocket T that sounds strong and steady. *Minus:* Reminds you of **Cameron,** the neurotic sidekick in *Ferris Bueller's Day Off.* It also doesn't help that it's starting to boom popularity-wise.

Campbell (Gaelic/Scottish: crooked mouth). Also, **Cambell, Campbel.** *Plus:* The less trendy alternative to **Cameron.** *Minus:* The soup thing.

Cannon (Latin: artillery, cane). Also, **Canen, Cannen, Canon.**

Carl (English: man; variation of **Carlson, Carlton**). *Whatever:* Outmoded but not impossible.

Carlin (Irish: little champion). Also, **Carlyn.**

Carlo (Italian: variation of **Charles,** "man, valiant, strong").

Carlos (Spanish: variation of **Charles,** "man, valiant, strong").

Carlson (English: son of **Carl**). Also, **Carlsen.** Familiar, **Carl.**

Carlton (English: man's town). Also, **Carlten.** Familiar, **Carl.**

Carmine (Latin: song). Also, **Carmyne.** *Whatever:* Eddie Mekka played **Carmine** "the Big Ragu" Ragusa on TV's *Laverne and Shirley* (1976–83).

Carol (English: variation of **Charles,** "man, valiant, strong"). Also, **Carroll, Carrol, Carroll.** *Whatever:* Nice but pretty much the exclusive property of the girls.

Carr (English: marsh). Also, **Carre.**

Carson (English: son of **Carr**). Also, **Carsen, Carssen, Carsson.**

Carter (English: cart driver). *Plus:* A pick to click. **Carter** is like a classic Western burger: substantial with a tangy kick. *Minus:* Dredges up bad memories of the Jimmy **Carter** administration.

Cary (Irish: dark-complected). Also, **Carey, Carrey, Carry.** *Plus:* Thanks to **Cary** Grant, a name that always sounds fit for a tuxedo . . . *Minus:* . . . or an evening gown. **Cary** has pretty much gone the way of the opposite sex.

Casey (Irish: vigilant). Also, **Casy.**

Cass (English: maker of copper pots). Also, **Cas.**

Cedric (Celtic: war chieftan). Also, **Cedrick, Cedrik, Cedryc, Cedryck, Cedryk.**

Cesar (Spanish: variation of **Caesar,** "virile").

Cesario (Spanish: variation of **Cesaro,** "virile"). Also, **Cesaryo.**

Cesaro (Spanish: variation of **Caesar,** "virile"). Also, **Cesarro.**

Chad (English: variation of **Chadwick,** "from Chadwick"). Also, **Chadd.** *Whatever:* Peaked in the 1960s when it was New Frontier swingin' cool along with the likes of **Roger** and **Steve. Chad** is still doable, just not exciting.

Chadwick (English: from Chadwick). Also, **Chadwic, Chadwik, Chadwyc, Chadwyck, Chadwyk.** Familiar, **Chad.**

Chaise (French: carriage). Also, **Chayse.**

Chance (English: luck; English/Latin: variation of **Chancellor, Channing**). *Plus:* Better than **Chauncey.** *Minus:* Still a low notch on the manly man scale.

Chancellor (Latin: government official). Also, **Chanceller, Chanciller, Chancillor, Chancyller, Chancyllor.** Familiar, **Chance.**

Chandler (French: candlemaker). Also, **Chandlor.** *Whatever:* Like **Rachel, Chandler** is another name getting a boost thanks to TV's *Friends.*

Channing (English: wise). Also, **Channyng.** Familiar, **Chance.**

Chanson (French: song). Also, **Chansen.**

Chapel (English: church).

Charles (English: man, valiant, strong). Familiar, **Charlie, Chas, Chip, Chipper, Chuck.** *Whatever:* Clearly, **Charles** is a name that's here to stay. But it falls short of pocket T status because, like **Richard** and **William,** it's feeling too formal for these cuddly bear times. The viability of **Charles** could well rest with a certain British prince. If the royal one can put his image on "defrost," this name may just have a shot at likeability in the new century.

Charleston (English: town of **Charles**). Also, **Charlesten.**

Charlie (English: variation of **Charles,** "man, valiant, strong"). Also, **Charley, Charly.**

Chas (English: variation of **Charles,** "man, valient, strong"). Also, **Chaz.**

Chase (French: hunter). Also, **Chaise, Chayse.** *Whatever:* One to watch—it's cracking the top fifty in states such as Washington.

Chaucer (English: for poet Geoffrey **Chaucer**)

Che (Spanish: God will add). *Whatever:* **Che** Guevara helped Fidel Castro come to power in Cuba in the 1950s. This is the revolutionary, hip baby name for parents with axes to grind.

Chet (English: variation of **Chester,** "fort"). Also, **Chett.** *Plus:* Just sounds cool coming out of the mouth. It's succinct, efficient, clipped. *Minus:* Rent *Barton Fink.* Fast forward to the Steve Buscemi scene. Study.

Chico (Spanish: boy). Also, **Cheeco, Chyco.**

Chip (English: small piece of wood; variation of **Charles,** "man, valiant, strong"). Also, **Chipp, Chyp, Chypp.**

Chipper (English: good spirits; variation of **Charles,** "man, valiant, strong").

Chris (Greek: variation of **Christian, Christianio, Christobal, Christofer, Christoph, Christophe, Christopher, Christopherson**). Also, **Cris.**

Christian (Greek: follower of Christ). Also, **Cristian.** Familiar, **Chris.** *Plus:* It's almost an understatement to tag this one a pocket T. Impeccable credentials position it as a timeless standard. *Minus:* Strange but true: Did you ever meet a **Christian** at school who *wasn't* incorrigible?

Christianio (Spanish: variation of **Christian,** "follower of Christ"). Also, **Christianyo, Cristianio, Cristianyo.** Familiar, **Chris.**

Christobal (Spanish: variation of **Christopher,** "Christ-bearer"). Also, **Cristobal.** Familiar, **Chris.**

Christofer (American: variation of **Christopher,** "Christ-bearer"). Also, **Cristofer.** Familiar, **Chris.**

Christoph (German: variation of **Christopher,** "Christ-bearer"). Also, **Cristoph.** Familiar, **Chris.**

Christophe (French: variation of **Christopher,** "Christ-bearer"). Also, **Cristophe.** Familiar, **Chris.**

Christopher (Greek: Christ-bearer). Also, **Christofer, Cristofer, Cristopher.** Familiar, **Chris, Kit.** *Whatever:* A monster on the popularity lists, **Christopher** won't please spelunkers, but others will be comforted by the sound of this perennial. When sensitive, cute boys like **Kyle** have been sent packing, **Christopher** will still be here. A heavyweight pocket T.

Christopherson (English: son of **Christopher**). Also, **Christophersen, Cristophersen, Cristopherson.** Familiar, **Chris.**

Chuck (English: variation of **Charles,** "man, valiant, strong").

Clarence (English: clear, bright). Also, **Clarince, Clarynce.** *Whatever:* In the old-fogy dumper until **Clarence** Thomas came along. It's debatable as to whether the judge helped its cause, but at least the name sounds more relevant.

Clark (English: clergy). Also, **Clarke.** *Plus:* The *Lois and Clark* TV series in particular, and the Superman legend in general, freshen up this bookish entry. *Minus:* The **Clark** Kent jokes will get real tired, real fast.

Clay (English: moist earth; variation of **Clayborne, Clayton**). Also, **Claye.**

Clayborne (English: stream near the clay). Also, **Clayborn, Claybourn, Claybourne.** Familiar, **Clay.**

Clayton (English: town near the clay). Also, **Clayten.** Familiar, **Clay.**

Clement (Latin: merciful).

Clete (English: fastener). Also, **Cleet, Cleete.**

Cleve (English: cling). Also, **Cleeve.**

Clevis (English: variation of **Cleve**, "cling"). Also, **Cleviss, Clevys, Clevyss.**

Cliff (English: a cliff; variation of **Clifford, Clifton, Heathcliff, Northcliff**). Also, **Clif, Cliffe.** *Plus:* Cliff is straightforward and unpretentious. *Minus:* It's the namesake of *Cheers* postal worker **Cliff** Clavin.

Clifford (English: cliff by the stream). Also, **Clifforde.** Familiar, **Cliff.**

Clift (English: variation of **Clifton**, "home on a hill"). Also, **Clifte.**

Clifton (English: home on a hill). Also, **Cliften.** Familiar, **Cliff, Clift.**

Clint (English: hill; variation of **Clinton**, "town on a hill"). Also, **Clinte.** *Whatever:* Call this one the new **Glen**—a moniker that projects ruggedness. A pick to click.

Clinton (English: town on a hill). Also, **Clinten.** Familiar, **Clint.** *Whatever:* Remember when parents used to name their babies after the president? Well, no, not really. Fortunately, **Clinton** has **Clint** going for it.

Clive (English: cliff). Also, **Clyve.** *Whatever:* Distinctive and dignified. Another pick to click.

Coby (Hebrew: variation of **Jacob**, "following after"). Also, **Cobey, Cobi, Cobie.** *Plus:* Very today. A leading member of the cuddly bear club. *Minus:* A name needs to be more than adorable to wear well over a lifetime. Remember: Even the most comforting teddy bears fall apart after repeated washings. This one's got trendy suspenders potential.

Cody (English: cushion; helper, assistant). Also, **Codey, Codi.** *Plus:* Cody is, perhaps, *the* leading member of both the cuddly bear and lil' cowpoke contingents. *Minus:* This is what Kathie Lee Gifford and the era of the daytime talk show have wrought: thousands of kids named after the kids of their parents' favorite TV hosts. (*See* **Parker.**) Kathie Lee's incessant **Cody** chatter has swelled **Cody**'s popularity—and oversaturation is exactly what this cuddly bear doesn't need. The gut feeling here is that an inevitable, impending backlash will make **Cody** the **Benji** of 2020. Total trendy suspenders.

Colby (English: dark). Also, **Colbey.** *Whatever:* A little too *Dynasty* for its own good. (Indeed, *The Colbys* was the name of a short-lived *Dynasty* spin-off). If you really want to use it, wait a few years and let the 1980s nostalgia boom kick in big time.

Cole (English: variation of **Nicholas, Colson**). *Whatever:* Good-bye, **Troy.** Good-bye, **Steve.** What the golden-boy quarterbacks of the new century will be named.

Coleman (English: miner).

Colin (French: variation of **Nicholas,** "victor of the people; Scottish: dove). Also, **Collin, Collyn, Colyn.**

Colins (Irish: variation of **Colin,** "young"). Also, **Collins, Collyns, Colyns.**

Collier (English: coal miner). Also, **Collyer, Colier, Colyer.**

Colm (Irish: dove). Also, **Colme.**

Colorado (Latin: color, strong).

Colson (English: son of **Cole**). Also, **Colesen, Coleson, Colsen.** Familiar, **Cole.**

Colt (English: young male horse; variation of **Colton,** "homestead of **Colton**"). Also, **Colte.**

Colton (English: homestead of **Colton**). Also, **Coleton, Coleten, Colten.** Familiar, **Colt.** *Whatever:* A grown-up sounding alternative to **Coby** or **Cody.**

Colum (Irish: dove).

Conall (Irish: high, mighty). Also, **Conal.**

Conan (Irish: high). Also, **Conen, Conyn.** *Whatever:* Watch *Late Night* talker **Conan** O'Brien take this one back from "the Barbarian" and make it safe for baby names again.

Concord (Latin: together, heart). Also, **Concorde.**

Conlan (Irish: mighty). Also, **Conlen, Conlyn.** Familiar, **Connie.** *Whatever:* A pick to click. An alternative to the more popular likes of **Cameron.**

Connery (Scottish: variation of **Connor,** "desired"). Also, **Connory.**

Connie (Irish/German: variation of **Conlan, Conrad**). Also, **Conney, Conny.** *Plus:* **Connie** Mack is a Hall of Fame baseball manager. *Minus:* **Connie** Mack died about a hundred years ago. His name's been taken over by the girls.

Connor (Irish: desired). Also, **Conner.** *Whatever:* A comer. The new **Spencer.**

Connors (Irish: variation of **Connor,** "desired"). Also, **Conners.**

Conrad (German: bold counselor). Familiar, **Connie.** *Whatever:* Beware the curse of *Diff'rent Strokes.* **Conrad** Bain played TV father to that troubled sitcom brood.

Coolidge   (English: for U.S. President Calvin **Coolidge**). Also, **Coo-lydge.**

Cooper   (English: bucket maker).

Corbell   (Latin: piece of stone or wood). Also, **Corbel.**

Corbett   (English: raven black). Also, **Corbet, Corbit, Corbitt, Corbyt, Corbytt.**

Corbin   (English/French/Irish: raven black). Also, **Corbyn.**

Cordell   (French: rope maker). Also, **Cordel.**

Cormac   (Irish: raven's son). Also, **Cormack, Cormak.**

Corwin   (English: near the castle). Also, **Corwyn.**

Cory   (Irish: hollow). Also, **Corey.** *Whatever:* Another **Coby** and **Cody.** Another pair of trendy suspenders.

Courtnay   (French/Irish: variation of **Courtney.**) Also, **Courtenay, Courtnae, Courtenae.**

Courtney   (French: count; Irish: drinking cup). Also, **Courteney, Courteny, Courtny.** *Whatever:* Classy, handsome, but pretty much gone to the girls.

Cowan   (Irish: hillside; Scottish: blacksmith). Also, **Cowen, Cowyn.**

Craig   (Scottish: rock). Also, **Creg.** *Plus:* No surprises with **Craig.** It's a pleasant peanut-butter-and-jelly sandwich. No funny aftertaste. *Minus:* Running on fumes, following headier times in the 1960s and 1970s.

Crispin   (Latin: curled). Also, **Crispyn.**

Curt   (Latin: short, brief; French: variation of **Curtis,** "courteous"). *Whatever:* Does **Curt** have the stuff to be the new **Nick**? Or is **Nick** the new **Curt**? Confused? That's what they make **Michael** for—it's the great compromise name.

Curtis   (French: courteous). Also, **Curtiss, Curtys, Curtyss.** Familiar, **Curt.**

Cy   (Persian: variation of **Cyrus,** "throne"). Also, **Cye.**

Cyrus   (Persian: throne). Also, **Cyruss.** Familiar, **Cy.**

D

CRIB NOTES

Famous Ds: **Dan** Marino (football player); **Dana** Carvey (comedian); **Darius** Rucker (rocker, Hootie and the Blowfish); **Davy** Jones (tambourine specialist, the Monkees); **Dean** Cain (TV's Superman, *Lois and Clark*); **DeForest** Kelley (TV's "Bones," *Star Trek*); **Deion** Sanders (football player); **Dennis** Rodman (basketball player); **Denzel** Washington (actor); **Dermot** Mulroney (actor, *My Best Friend's Wedding*); **Desi** Arnaz ("Luuuuuucy!" guy); **Desmond** Howard (football player); **Donny** Osmond (erstwhile teen idol); **Drew** Carey (comedian); **Dustin** Hoffman (actor); **Dwight** Eisenhower (U.S. president); **Dylan** Thomas (poet)

Pocket Ts: Daniel, David, Derrick

Trendy suspenders: Dakota, Dillon, Dylan

Think long, think hard: **Dagwood** (From "Blondie" to "Beatle Bailey," the funny pages are not the most inspired baby name resources.); **Dar** (Not so much a name as a sound that slips out of your throat.); **Dax** (For use only in Pine Valley—or some other fictional soap-opera town.); **DeForest** (With all due respect to Trekkers, this one's DeTooOld.); **Delbert** (A "Dilbert" sound-alike. Remember, beware the Sunday comics.); **Dexter** (Strictly pen-holder, busted-glasses material.); **Dick** (As far as you're concerned, there is no such thing as a "familiar" form of **Richard**.); **Dudley** (A Do-Wrong name.); **Duke** (Yes, but the German shepherd might get jealous.); **Dunston** (A little too close to "dunce" for comfort.)

Daejon (American: variation of **John,** "God is gracious"). Also, **Daejohn, Dayjohn, Dayjon.**

Daemarcus (American: variation of **Marcus,** "warlike"). Also, **Daemarckus, Daemarkus, Daymarcus, Daymarckus, Daymarkus.**

Daemarius (American: variation of **Marius,** "warlike"). Also, **Daemaryus, Daymarius.**

Daemon (Greek: guiding spirit). Also, **Daemen.**

Daequon (American: variation of **Juan,** "God is gracious"). Also, **Daequan, Dayquan.**

Daeshon (American: variation of **Sean,** "God is gracious"). Also, **Daesean, Daeshaun, Daeshawn, Daysean, Dayshaun, Dayshon, Dayshawn.**

Daewon (American: variation of **Juan,** "God is gracious"). Also, **Daewan, Daywan, Daywon.**

Dajon (American: variation of **John,** "God is gracious"). Also, **Dajohn, Dejon, Dejohn.**

Dakota (A language of the Sioux, meaning "friend"). Also, **Dakotah.** *Plus:* What all lil' cowpokes (who aren't named **Cody**) are wearing this season. *Minus:* Trendy suspenders city. Here's why: (1) It came from Hollywood—popularized by celeb couples, like Don Johnson and Melanie Griffith; (2) Sooner, rather than later, it's going to occur to us that there are better things we could name our future middle-aged accountant sons.

Dale (English: bushy valley). Also, **Daile, Dayle.** *Whatever:* Looking plain in a **Dakota** world. Depending on your tolerance for the lil' cowpokes, that's not necessarily a bad thing.

Daley (Irish: gathering). Also, **Daly.**

Dallas (Scottish: place on the plain). Also, **Dalas.** *Whatever:* The big southern city version of **Dakota.**

Dalt (English: variation of **Dalton,** "town on the plain"). Also, **Dalte.**

Dalton (English: town on the plain). Also, **Dalten.** Familiar, **Dalt.** *Whatever:* All the cowpoke-ness of **Dakota,** half the cuteness. A comer.

Damarcus (American: variation of **Marcus,** "warlike"). Also, **Damarckus, Damarkus, Demarcus, Demarckus, Demarkus.**

Damarius (American: variation of **Marius,** "warlike"). Also, **Damaryus, Demarius, Demaryus.**

Damian (Greek: to tame). Also, **Damien, Damyan, Damyen.** *Plus:* A veteran sensitive, cute boy. In its relative old age **Damian** has developed into a trusty performer. *Minus:* **Damien** was the name of the little devil kid in *The Omen.*

Damon (Sanskirt: to rule; Greek: friendship). Also, **Damen.**

Dan (English: variation of **Daniel,** "the Lord is just"). Also, **Dann.** *Whatever:* Doesn't have the salt-of-the-earth cachet of **Hank** or **Jake.** It just sounds plain—a plainness that makes you (almost) admire the spunk of **Cody.**

Dana (Celtic: darling). *Plus:* A pioneering alternative to the All Boys Must Be Named **Michael** school of thought. *Minus:* Sounded more cutting edge in the 1940s and 1950s—before it was stolen by the girls.

Dane (English: forest). Also, **Daine, Dayne.** *Plus:* Offbeat, strong. *Minus:* Like **Duke,** a name that's virtually been taken over by canines.

Daniel (Hebrew: the Lord is just; English: variation of **Danielson,** "son of **Daniel**"). Also, **Danyel.** Familiar, **Dan, Dano, Danny.** *Plus:* An apple-pie-and-hot-dog name that won't keep you up nights—"Did we do the right thing?" **Daniel** is a solid, still-popular pocket T. (The number one pick in California.) *Minus:* Apple pie? Hot dog? Ha, say spelunkers, try a peanut-butter-and-jelly sandwich. **Daniel** is far, far, from an adventurous choice—assuming you're looking for adventure. (And if you *are* looking for adventure, you might want to consider rock climbing.)

Daniels (English: variation of **Daniel,** "the Lord is just"). Also, **Danyels.**

Danielson (English: son of **Daniel**). Also, **Danielsen, Danyelsen, Danyelson.** Familiar, **Daniel.**

Danny (English: variation of **Daniel,** "the Lord is just")

Dano (English: variation of **Daniel,** "the Lord is just"). Also, **Danno.** *Whatever:* Two words: Book 'em.

Dante (Italian: to endure). Also, **Dantae, Dantay, Dantaye.** *Whatever:* Popularized by the fourteenth-century Italian poet. Brought into the New World by the twentieth-century filmmaker Kevin Smith. (**Dante** is the lead character in Smith's comedy *Clerks.*)

Daquon (American: variation of **Juan,** "God is gracious"). Also, **Daquan, Dequan, Dequon.**

Darby (English: freeman; Scandinavian: deer settlement). Also, **Darbey.** *Whatever:* If your boy's going to be safely hidden away in prep school, **Darby** should be OK. If not, take out extra insurance. You have a **Percy** on your hands.

Darian (Greek: daring). Also, **Darrian, Darien, Darrien, Darryan, Daryan, Daryen.** *Plus:* Contemporary, artsy. The new **Darren.** *Minus:* A new girl name.

Darius (Persian: to preserve). Also, **Darrius, Darryus, Daryus.** *Whatever:* Contemporary, artsy—*and* a touch more on the manly man side than **Darian.** A pick to click.

Darnell (English: hidden nook). Also, **Darnel, Darnil, Darnill, Darnyl, Darnyll.**

Darrell (English: brave, bold). Also, **Darel, Darell, Darrel, Darryl, Darryll, Daryl, Daryll.** *Plus:* A standard-issue boy name that's fancier than **Michael,** not as trendy as **Tyler.** *Minus:* Done great harm by *Newhart,* the sitcom with the noncommunicative, hayseed brothers **Darryl** and **Darryl.**

Darren (Irish: great). Also, **Daren, Darin, Darrin, Darryn, Daryn.** *Whatever:* Gen Xers know from **Darren.** We went to school with enough of them. But as a baby name today, **Darren** is in limbo—neither classic enough to qualify for **David** status nor contemporary enough to be a **Dylan.** It's an entry that's in desperate need of a new champion. *Bewitched*'s **Darin** Stevens has done all he can.

Dashon (American: variation of **Sean,** "God is gracious"). Also, **Dasean, Dashaun, Dashawn, Desean, Deshaun, Deshshawn, Deshon.**

Dave (English: variation of **David, Davis**).

David (Hebrew: beloved; English: variation of **Davidson,** "son of David"). Also, **Davyd.** Familiar, **Dave, Davy.** *Whatever:* You don't need a baby name book to sell you on **David,** but just so you get your money's worth, here goes: **David** is a popular boy name! No, really. Slumping slightly since its top-ranking heyday in the 1960s, there's still life left in this popular perennial. An easy call—a pocket T.

Davidson (English: son of **David**). Also, **Davidsen, Davydsen, Davydson.** Familiar, **David.**

Davis (English: variation of **David, Davison**). Also, **Daviss, Davys, Davyss.** Familiar, **Dave, Davy.**

Davison (English: son of **Davis**). Also, **Davisen, Davysen, Davyson.** Familiar, **Dave, Davis, Davy.**

Davy (English: variation of **David, Davis**). Also, **Davey, Davie.**

Dawayne (American: variation of **Dwayne,** "poem, song"). Also, **Dawaine, Dawane, Dewaine, Dewane, Dewayne.**

Dawes (English: days).

Dawon (American: variation of **John,** "God is gracious"). Also, **Dawan, Dewan, Dewon.**

Deacon (English: priest). Also, **Deacen, Deecen, Deecen.**

Dean (English: valley). Also, **Deane, Deen, Deene.** *Whatever:* Gen Xers know **Dean** too. Not as well as **Darren,** but we shared English class with him once or twice. In his day, **Dean** was the smooth-operating bud of **Steve.** Now, slick guys like **Dean** and **Steve** have been replaced by the cuddly bears.

Deandre (American: variation of **Andre,** "brave"). Also, **Deandrae, Deandray.**

Decker (German: roofer).

Dee (Irish: good luck; English: dark water). *Whatever:* **Dee** Snyder of the 1980s heavy-metal outfit Twisted Sister didn't seem to mind this girl-controlled moniker. Of course, Snyder was a hard read. He was always covered in makeup.

Deion (Greek: from Dionysus, "god of wine"). Also, **Deon, Deione.** *Whatever:* The flashy likes of **Deion** Sanders make this name a happening event. Cool and current.

Dell (English: valley). Also, **Del.** *Plus:* As stripped and real as **Hank** or **Gil.** *Minus:* As hip as **Mel** or **Phil.**

Delaney (Irish: challenger). Also, **Delany.**

Denholm (Scottish: town). Also, **Denholme.** Familiar, **Denny.**

Dennis (English/Irish: fighter, warrior). Also, **Denis, Dennys, Denys.** Familiar, **Denny.** *Whatever:* Your call. **Dennis** is either (a) the quintessential bad-boy name; or (b) a virtually trend-proof longtimer.

Denny (English/Irish/Scottish: variation of **Denholm, Dennis, Denton**). Also, **Denney.**

Denton (English: home in the valley). Also, **Denton.** Familiar, **Denny.**

Denver (English: green valley). *Whatever:* The Ds are chock-full of map names. As far as **Denver** goes, it's not as popular as **Dakota** and not as glamorous as **Dallas.** An in-between bowl of porridge.

Denzell (English: a British town). Also, **Denzel, Denzil, Denzill, Denzyl, Denzyll.** *Whatever:* Another contemporary-sounding alternative to **Darren** and **Darrell.**

Derek (English: variation of **Derrick,** "ruler"). Also, **Derik, Deryk.**

Dermot (Celtic: father of the oaks). Also, **Dermott.** *Plus:* A mostly undiscovered country as far as Irish names go. It's still a rarity in our world of **Kevin**s, **Ryan**s, and **Patrick**s. *Minus:* Doesn't exactly roll off your tongue. **Dermot** is a name that's intellectually handsome but not spoken-word handsome.

Derrick (German: ruler). Also, **Derick, Derik, Derrik, Derryck, Derryk, Deryck, Deryk.** *Whatever:* An old-school sensitive, cute boy that's holding its own against the youngens. With that sort of staying power, you get to be a pocket T.

Desi (Latin: yearning). *Plus:* A michievous alternative to **Dennis**? Boy names aren't often allowed to be winsome, but carefree **Desi** lets you push that border. *Minus:* You'd have to be a pretty big (obsessive?) *I Love Lucy* fan to actually try this.

Desmond (Celtic: worldly). Also, **Desmon, Desmonde.**

Devlin (Irish: black pool). Also, **Devlyn.**

Devon (Celtic: poet). Also, **Deven.** *Whatever:* Solid choice. **Devon** is contemporary and cute—but not precious.

DeWitt (Dutch: fair-complected). Also, **Dewit, Dewitt, Dewyt, Dewytt.** *Plus:* Here's one for parents who love **Dwight** but fear it's too ordinary. *Minus:* In general, you probably want to stay away from heavy *duh* sounds.

Dezmond (American: variation of **Desmond,** "worldly"). Also, **Dezmon, Dezmonde.**

Dillon (Welsh: variation of **Dylan,** "ocean"). Also, **Dilen, Dillen, Dilon.** *Whatever:* With **Dylan,** a pair of trendy suspenders.

Dino (Italian: variation of **Dean,** "valley"). *Plus:* Good way to initiate your boy into the lounge scene that you love. *Minus:* Good way to name your boy after the doggie dinosaur in *The Flintstones.*

Dion (Greek: from **Dionysus,** god of wine). Also, **Dionn, Dyon, Dyonn.**

Dirk (Danish: ruler of the people). Also, **Dirke.** *Whatever:* Familiarity is about the only thing **Dirk** has left to sell. This is a former golden boy who's losing his good looks. Parents are finally awakening to the fact that it rhymes with "jerk."

Dobber (English: variation of **Dobbs,** "bright flame"). Also, **Dober.**

Dobbs (English: bright flame; variation of **Dobson,** "son of **Dobbs**"). Also, **Dobs.**

Dobry (English: rounded summit). Also, **Dobrey.**

Dobson (English: son of **Dobbs**). Also, **Dobbsen, Dobbson, Dobbssen, Dobbsson, Dobsen, Dobssen, Dobsson.** Familiar, **Dobbs.**

Dodds (English: fame, spear; variation of **Dodson,** "son of **Dodds**"). Also, **Dods.**

Dodson (English: son of **Dodds**). Also, **Dodsen, Dodssen, Dodsson.** Familiar, **Dodds.**

Dolan (Irish: dark-complected). Also, **Dolen, Dolyn.**

Dom (Latin/Spanish: variation of **Dominic, Domingo**). *Whatever:* Cool nickname.

Domingo (Spanish: variation of **Dominic,** "of the Lord"). Also, **Domyngo.** Familiar, **Dom.**

Dominic (Latin: of the Lord). Familiar, **Dom.** *Whatever:* Classic, uncommon. In a just world, **Dominic** is welcomed into a neighborhood of **Austin**s.

Don (Irish/Scottish: variation of **Donal, Donald**). Also, **Donn.**

Donal (Irish: variation of **Donald,** "mighty chieftan"). Also, **Donel, Donyl.** Familiar, **Don, Donny.** *Whatever:* Another underutilized gem.

Donald (Scottish: mighty chieftan). Familiar, **Don, Donny.** *Plus:* **Donald** is a passable and harmless peanut-butter-and-jelly sandwich—even if it does sound more fit for one of your dad's office buddies than your newborn. *Minus:* Duck.

Donat (Italian: given). Also, **Donatt.**

Donner (German: god of thunder). *Whatever:* Too reindeer-esque?

Donny (English: variation of **Donal, Donald**). Also, **Donney, Donnie.**

Donovan (Irish: brown, poet). Also, **Donevan.** *Whatever:* Is this the much-needed **Dylan** Less Traveled? Or a name that evokes hippie-dippie images of "Mellow Yellow" guy **Donovan**? Here's betting the former. This one's a comer.

Donte (Italian: variation of **Dante,** "to endure"). Also, **Dontae, Dontay, Dontaye.**

Doran (Irish: alien; Greek: gift). Also, **Doren, Doryn.**

Dorat (French: a gilder). Also, **Doratt.**

Dorn (English: stronghold). Also, **Dorne.**

Dorsey (French: stronghold). Also, **Dorsy.**

Dory (French: golden). Also, **Dorey.**

Doug (English: variation of **Douglas,** "dark or black stream"). *Plus:* A B.M.O.C. name. *Minus:* In the long-ago sitcom worlds of *The Brady Bunch* and *The Facts of Life.*

Douglas (Irish: dark or black stream). Also, **Douglass.** Familiar, **Doug.** *Whatever:* A bit stuffy but doable.

Doyle (Irish: swarthy, stranger).

Dragan (English: to draw). Also, **Dragen, Dragyn.**

Drake (English: dragon). Also, **Draike, Drayke.**

Dram (Greek: handful, measure of weight). Also, **Dramm.**

Draper (English: cloth dealer). Also, **Draiper, Drayper.**

Dray (English: cart). Also, **Draye.**

Dre (American: variation of **Andre,** "brave"). Also, **Drae.**

Drew (English: wise; variation of **Andrew,** "brave"). Also, **Druw.**

Dru (American: variation of **Drew,** "wise"). Also, **Drue.**

Duane (Celtic: variation of **Dwayne,** "poem, song").

Duncan (Scottish: castle). *Whatever:* The closer you live to a Dunkin' Donuts, the rougher your little **Duncan**'s formative years will be.

Dunne (Irish: dark-complected). Also, **Dun, Dunn.**

Duran (Latin: variation of **Durant,** "enduring"). Also, **Duren, Duryn.**

Durant (Latin: enduring). Also, **Durante.**

Dustin (English: dusty homestead, a battler). Also, **Dustyn.** Familiar, **Dusty.** *Plus:* This sensitive, cute boy has been too popular too long to be a fly-by-night. *Minus:* For as long as it's been around, it sounds almost *too* today. It's so . . . *so* precious.

Dusty (English: dusty; variation of **Dustin,** "battler"). Also, **Dustey.**

Dwayne (Celtic: poem, song). Also, **Dwaine, Dwane.** *Whatever:* Important, must-be-asked question: Can you ever think of **Dwayne** without thinking "**Dah-wayne, Dah-wayne, Dah-wayne,**" à la TV's *What's Happening!!* (1976–79)?

Dwight (English: light-complected). Also, **Dwite.**

Dylan (Welsh: ocean). Also, **Dylen, Dyllan, Dyllen, Dyllon, Dylon.** *Plus:* To crib from a pizza commercial, **Dylan** is hot, fresh, now. *Minus:* This is a name that seemed a whole lot fresher before *Beverly Hills, 90210* made it the "officially" cool name it is today. Anything that owes its popularity to *90210* must be tagged a potential pair of trendy suspenders.

Dyson (Greek: variation of **Dionysus,** god of wine). Also, **Dysen.**

E

CRIB NOTES

Famous Es: **Earvin** "Magic" Johnson (basketball legend); **Edsel** Ford (auto-industry heir); **Elijah** Wood (actor); **Elton** John (pop star); **Elvis** Presley (the King); **Emilio** Estevez (Brat Pack alum); **Ernest** Hemingway (author); **Ethan** Hawke (actor, *Reality Bites*); **Evan** Dando (rocker, the Lemonheads); **Evander** Holyfield (boxer); **Ewan** McGregor (actor, *Trainspotting*)

Pocket Ts: **Edward, Elijah, Eric, Erik, Ethan**

Trendy suspenders: None

Think long, think hard: **Ebenezer** (The Scrooge thing.); **Edsel** (By its second model year, the Ford **Edsel** wasn't a half-bad automobile. You and Mr. Ford remember this. Everybody else thinks **Edsel** is synonymous with "loser."); **Egbert** (America is a land of opportunity. Unless you're named **Egbert**. In which case it's your own personal tour of hell.); **Elmer** (Fudd. Say no more.); **Elmo** (This is the way it works: you *tickle* **Elmo**. You *name* your son a *human* name. **Elmo**'s been taken over by the Muppets. Move on.); **Elwood** (Blues Brothers association notwithstanding, this one's another **Egbert**.); **Engelbert** (Singer **Engelbert** Humperdinck needed open-neck shirts and sideburns to prove he was cool in spite of his dorkhead name. What questionable fashion crutches will your little **Engelbert** resort to?); **Enos** (Too *Dukes of Hazzard*.); **Evel** (Maybe, if **Evel** Knievel had cleared that Snake River Canyon jump. Maybe then an appreciative nation would have named her sons in honor of the daredevil motorcycle rider. Nice dream. Now wake up.)

Eamon (Irish: fortunate warrior). Also, **Eamen.**

Earvin (English/German: sea, friend). Also, **Earvyn.** Familiar, **Erv.**

East (English: a direction, from the East; variation of **Eastman, Easton**). Also, **Easte.**

Eastman (English: man of the East). Familiar, **East.**

Easton (English: eastern town). Also, **Easten.** Familiar, **East.**

Eaton (English: town near the river). Also, **Eaten.**

Eaves (English: edges).

Eb (Hebrew: variation of **Ebenezer**, "stone of help"). Also, **Ebb.** *Plus:* It's accepted that **Ebenezer** is unusable (the Scrooge thing). But what about its nickname? If you think about it, **Eb** makes for an uncommonly cool entry. It's a stripped-down, salt-of-the-earth name ready for the Gen X universe. *Minus:* Have you ever actually known an **Eb**—not counting a guest character who turned up on *Petticoat Junction*?

Ed (English/French/Spanish: variation of **Edgar, Edgard, Edgardo, Edison, Edmond, Edmund, Eduardo, Edward, Edwin**). Also, **Edd.** *Whatever:* One word: Mister.

Eddie (English/French/Spanish: variation of **Edgar, Edison, Edgardo, Edmond, Edmund, Eduardo, Edward, Edwin**). Also, **Eddey, Eddy.** *Whatever:* One word: Munster.

Edgar (English: happy warrior, spear). Also, **Edger.** Familiar, **Ed, Eddie.** *Whatever:* Old-fashioned by today's ears but not without its charms. Think of **Edgar** as another **Oscar**—a workhorse of a name that doesn't get a lot of respect but gets the job done when given the chance.

Edgard (French: variation of **Edgar**, "happy warrior, spear"). Also, **Edgarde.** Familiar, **Ed, Eddie.**

Edgardo (Spanish: variation of **Edgar**, "happy warrior, spear"). Familiar, **Ed, Eddie.**

Edison (English: son of **Ed**). Also, **Edisen, Edysen, Edyson.** Familiar, **Ed, Eddie.** *Whatever:* On the nerdy side, yes, but a clever way to get to **Ed.**

Edmond (English: wealthy protector). Also, **Edmonde.** Familiar, **Ed, Eddie.**

Edmund (English: wealthy protector). Also, **Edmunde.** Familiar, **Ed, Eddie.** *Plus:* Traditional, strong. *Minus:* A three-piece suit in a dress-casual-Friday world.

Eduardo (Spanish: variation of **Edward,** "wealthy guardian"). Familiar, **Ed, Eddie.**

Edward (English: wealthy guardian). Also, **Edwarde.** Familiar, **Ed, Eddie, Ned, Ted, Teddy.** *Plus:* The bomb as far as **Ed**s go. Britain's royal family may not know a lot about manual labor or functional relationships, but they have a knack for baby names. **Edward** has been serving them well for centuries. It's done OK by the commoners too. It's vintage, polished, and pliable enough not to sound stuffy like **Edmund** in this age of hip-hop. A pocket T. *Minus:* Just because you're venerable doesn't mean you're an elder who gets respect. Not a hot name right now.

Edwin (English: happy friend). Also, **Edwyn.** Familiar, **Ed, Eddie.** *Whatever:* **Edward**'s on fire compared to **Edwin.**

Efrem (Spanish: variation of **Ephraim,** "fruitful"). Also, **Efrim, Efrym.**

El (English: variation of **Eldon, Eldridge, Elston, Elvin, Elwin**). *Whatever:* The exotic **Ed.**

Elan (French: with spirit). Also, **Elen, Elyn.**

Eldon (English: respected). Also, **Elden.** Familiar, **El.** *Whatever:* The modern **Edwin.**

Eldridge (English: plank of wood). Also, **Eldredge, Eldrydge.** Familiar, **El.** *Whatever:* A name that's no longer a political statement. **Eldridge** has lost its polemical edge since the 1960s and the days of Black Panther leader **Eldridge** Cleaver.

Eli (Hebrew: height; variation of **Elias, Elijah, Elisha**). Also, **Ely.** *Plus:* The **Max** Less Traveled. Like that modern favorite, it's time-worn, distinctive, and evocative of a seventy-five-year-old cigar-chomping uncle. The point is, if **Max** can become the rage of Montessori, then so can **Eli.** Unless . . . *Minus:* . . . you think it sounds really dorky.

Elias (Hebrew: Jehovah is God). Also, **Elyas.** Familiar, **Eli.** *Whatever:* There's something intangibly lovable about E names. Even the ones that aren't remotely happening—**Elias,** for instance—are still workable.

Elieser (Hebrew: variation of **Elias,** "Jehovah is God"). Also, **Elyeser.**

Elijah (Hebrew: Jehovah is God). Also, **Elija, Elyja, Elyjah.** Familiar, **Eli.** *Whatever:* A name with deep roots—roots that are still sucking up water. In fact, for all its biblical connection, **Elijah** is a virtual cuddly bear—cute, snuggly, and vowel-friendly. All this, plus it's nowhere near as cloying or oversold as its fellow plush toys. A pocket T.

Elisha (Hebrew: Lord is savior). Also, **Elishah, Elysha, Elyshah.** Familiar, **Eli.** *Whatever:* Offers wiggle room on the more popular **Elijah.**

Ellery (English: elder tree). Also, **Elery, Elerey, Ellerey.**

Elliott (English: Lord is my God). Also, **Eliot, Eliott, Elliot.** *Whatever:* A name that's reputation was sullied by one too many nerdy **Elliott** characters in the movies. Most recent, it's rep was improved (somewhat) by the non-nerdy but annoying **Elliott** character on *thirtysomething*. Bottom line: a wash.

Ellis (English: Lord is my God). Also, **Ellys.** *Plus:* A pick to click. The hip **Elliott.** *Minus:* An **Alice** sound-alike. Such factoids do not escape schoolyard foes.

Ellory (English: variation of **Ellery,** "elder tree"). Also, **Elory, Elorey, Ellorey.**

Elston (English: of a homestead). Also, **Elsten.** Familiar, **El.**

Elton (English: of a town). Also, **Elten.** *Whatever:* Keep in mind, **Elton** John was not *born* **Elton** John. Reginald Dwight picked his name from a blues record.

Elvin (English: friend.) Also, **Elvyn.** Familiar, **El.**

Elvis (Scandinavian: wise). Also, **Elvys.** *Plus:* Yes, it can be done. Pro football quarterback **Elvis** Grbac is among those who look no worse for taking on the King. *Minus:* This is a name with megabaggage. The legend of the Swivel-Hipped One looms larger than ever. Will your child ever be able to visit Las Vegas in peace?

Elwin (English: friend). Also, **Elwyn.** Familiar, **El.**

Emerson (English: industrious). Also, **Emersen.**

Emery (German: ruler). Also, **Emery.**

Emilio (Spanish: eager). Also, **Emylio.** *Plus:* You want your son to stand proudly apart from the world of **Michael**s and **Matthew**s. *Minus:* You want to name your kid after **Emilio** Estevez? . . . Rent *St. Elmo's Fire.* That should be sufficient tribute.

Emmanuel (Hebrew: God is with us). Also, **Emanuel, Emannuel, Emmannuel.** Familiar, **Manny.** *Whatever:* An apt name for a child of the new millennium?

Emmett (English: industrious). Also, **Emmet, Emmit, Emmitt, Emmyt, Emmytt.**

Emory (German: variation of **Emery,** "ruler"). Also, **Emorey.**

Ennis (English/Irish: the one). Also, **Ennys.** *Whatever:* Entertainer Bill Cosby and wife Camille gave each of their five children an E name— the E signifying "excellence." Here's predicting that **Ennis**—the Cosby son felled in an infamous murder—helps popularize this particular ode to excellence.

Enrico (Spanish: variation of **Henry,** "head of house"). Also, **Enreeco, Enryco.**

Enrique (Spanish: variation of **Henry,** "head of house"). Also, **Enryque.**

Ephraim (Hebrew: fruitful). Also, **Ephraime, Ephrame, Ephrayme.**

Eric (German: variation of **Erik,** "mighty lord, hero"). Also, **Erich, Eriq, Eryc, Erych.** With **Erik,** a pocket T.

Erie (English: one of the Great Lakes).

Erik (Scandinavian: mighty lord, hero; variation of **Erikson,** "son of **Erik**"). Also, **Erick, Eryck, Eryk.** *Plus:* How do you go wrong with **Erik?** You don't. It's like naming a dog **Woof**—it's a gimme. **Erik** worked for Gen X schoolyard peers of the 1970s; works today. A pocket T. *Minus:* A peanut-butter-and-jelly sandwich. Unchallenging, overdone.

Erikson (Scandinavian: son of **Erik**). Also, **Ericksen, Eriksen, Erycksen, Eryksen, Erykson.** Familiar, **Erik.**

Ernest (German/English: vigor, earnest). Familiar, **Ernie.** *Plus:* An old-school selection that's curiously underused in our back-to-basics craze. **Ernest** is every bit the peer of **Samuel** or **Charles.** It just needs a modern-day champion. *Minus:* It *has* a modern-day champion—that **Ernest** buffoon of *Ernest Saves Christmas* infamy. If you listen hard enough, you can almost hear Hemingway cursing the doofus for pillaging his name.

Ernesto (Spanish: variation of **Ernest,** "vigor, earnest"). Familiar, **Ernie.**

Ernie (German/English/Spanish: variation of **Ernest, Ernesto**). Also, **Erney, Erny.**

Erroll (Latin: wanderer; English: nobleman). Also, **Erol, Eroll, Errol.** *Plus:* Projects old-school chivalry. *Minus:* Yeah, if there's anything that goes over big in the locker room, it's old school chivalry.

Erv (English/German/Scottish: variation of **Earvin, Ervin, Erving**).

Ervin (Scottish: handsome). Also, **Ervyn.** Familiar, **Erv.** *Whatever:* Here's an example of the fickle nature of baby names: **Ervin** is simply **Erving** minus the *G,* and yet that one subtraction halves its nerd factor.

Erving (Scottish: green river; Irish: handsome). Familiar, **Erv.** *Whatever:* See **Ervin.**

Erwin (English/German: variation of **Earvin,** "sea, friend"). Also, **Erwyn.**

Esteban (Spanish: variation of **Stephen,** "crown"). Also, **Estiban, Estyban.**

Estevan (Spanish: variation of **Stephen,** "crown"). Also, **Estivan, Estyvan.**

Ethan (Hebrew: firm). Also, **Ethen, Ethyn.** *Whatever:* A pocket T. If the **Ethan** Hawke association makes you worry that this entry is *too* contemporary, just think of Edith Wharton's famed nineteenth-century novel, *Ethan Frome.* It's a name that works on many levels but chiefly as a fine sensitive, cute boy alternative to the more common **Ryan.**

Eugene (Greek: nobleman). Familiar, **Gene.** *Whatever:* Hip-challenged like **Elliott.** Reminds you of one of those checkered sports jackets modeled by **Gene** Rayburn on *The Match Game.*

Eustace (Greek: stable). Familiar, **Stace, Stacey.**

Evan (Welsh: variation of **John,** "God is gracious"). Also, **Even, Evyn.** *Whatever:* Another **Ethan.**

Evander (Greek: good, brave)

Evans (Welsh: variation of **John,** "God is gracious"). Also, **Evens, Evyns.**

Everest (English: from the mountain **Everest**).

Everett (English: boar, strong). *Whatever:* A stiff-upper-lip British entry that can hang in the hip-hop age. It's no more precious or dainty than **Ethan** or **Evan.**

Ewing (English: warrior). Also, **Ewying.**

Ezekiel (Hebrew: who sees God). Also, **Ezekyel, Ezikiel, Ezikyel, Ezykiel.** Familiar, **Zeke.** *Whatever:* A pick to click. Bible favorite **Ezekiel** is so out there, it's in. Its familiar form, **Zeke,** has real **Hank** appeal too.

Ezira (Hebrew: variation of **Ezra,** "helper"). Also, **Ezirah, Ezyra, Ezyrah.**

Ezra (Hebrew: helper). Also, **Ezrah.** *Whatever:* Alternative rock band Better Than **Ezra** used their fifteen minutes of musical fame to give this flatlining rock-of-ages name a mild shot of juice.

Ezri (Hebrew: variation of **Ezra,** "helper"). Also, **Ezrey, Ezry.**

F

CRIB NOTES

Famous Fs: **Fabio** (butter-substitute spokesmodel); **Felipe** Rose ("the Indian," the Village People); **Ferris** Bueller (title character, *Ferris Bueller's Day Off*); **Flip** Wilson (comedian); **Fox** Mulder (UFO-haunted FBI man, *The X-Files*); **Frank** Sinatra (legend); **Franklin** D. Roosevelt (U.S. president); **Frasier** Crane (TV shrink, *Frasier*); **Fred** Savage (actor)

Pocket Ts: Frank, Fred

Trendy suspenders: Fletcher, Frasier, Frazier

Think long, think hard: **Fabian** (For teen idols only.); **Fabio** (For strapping supermodels only.); **Fang** (Don't even joke about it.); **Farley** (The perfect name . . . for a shaggy dog.); **Farquar** (Beautiful to say— if you say it correctly. If you don't, it sounds like a certain two-syllable expletive.); **Faustus** (From legend and Christopher Marlowe's play—the one about the guy who sells his soul to the devil.); **Fergie** (For princesses only.); **Filbert** (Nutty *and* nerdy.); **Fonzie** (Question: Do you really want the world to know how much Nick at Nite you watch?)

Fairfax (English: golden).
Fairman (English: fair man). *Plus:* Decent. Honest. The literal **Hank** or **Henry**. *Minus:* Too literal. It sounds like it was cribbed from a Nathaniel Hawthorne novel.
Falcon (English: bird of prey).
Falconer (English: falcon trainer).
Falkner (English: variation of **Falconer,** "falcon trainer").

Falstaff (English: after the William Shakespeare play). Also, **Falstaf.**

Fane (English: with joy). Also, **Faine, Fayne.**

Faro (French: pharoah). Also, **Farro.**

Farr (English: traveler). Also, **Farre.**

Farrell (Irish: courageous). Also, **Farrel, Farryl, Farryll.**

Farren (English: traveler). Also, **Farrin, Farryn.**

Farrier (English: blacksmith).

Faulkner (English: variation of **Falconer,** "falcon trainer"). *Plus:* A real Southern gentleman, à la William **Faulkner.** *Minus:* Much like **Farquar,** you're going to have pronunciation problems with this one.

Fawke (English: people). *Plus:* Got a James Bond-ian swingin' cool to it. *Minus:* Indelicate but true: The bane of F names—**Falkner, Faulkner, Farquar, Fawke**—is the "F word."

Federico (Italian: variation of **Frederic,** "peaceful ruler"). Also, **Federyco.**

Felipe (Spanish: variation of **Phillip,** "lover of horses"). Also, **Felippe, Felype, Felyppe.**

Felix (Latin: happy). Also, **Felyx.** *Plus:* Repeated viewing of *The Odd Couple* reruns can make this prissy fussbudget seem retro cool. *Minus:* Two words: The cat.

Felton (English: field, town). Also, **Felten.**

Fen (English: swamp). Also, **Fenn.**

Fenton (English: marsh). Also, **Fenten.**

Ferdie (German/Spanish: variation of **Ferdinand, Ferdinando**). Also, **Ferdey, Ferdy.**

Ferdinand (German: brave adventurer). Also, **Ferdynand.** Familiar, **Ferdie.**

Ferdinando (Spanish: variation of **Ferdinand,** "brave adventurer"). Also, **Ferdynando.** Familiar, **Ferdie, Nando.**

Fergus (Irish: strong; variation of **Ferguson,** "son of **Fergus**"). Also, **Ferguss.**

Ferguson (Irish: son of **Fergus,** "strong"). Also, **Fergusen, Fergussen, Fergusson.** Familiar, **Fergus.** *Whatever:* A few years ago this name would have been right down there with **Filbert.** But the Nickelodeon sitcom *Clarissa Explains It All,* featuring a living, breathing (if smugly nerdy) **Ferguson** brought it a small degree of modern relevancy. *Clarissa* was on cable, so mind you, we said, "small degree."

Fernando (Spanish: variation of **Ferdinand,** "brave adventurer"). Familiar, **Nando.**

Ferris (Irish: rock). Also, **Ferriss, Ferrys, Ferryss, Feryss.** *Whatever:* Namesake of essential Gen X 1980s teen comedy *Ferris Bueller's Day Off.*

Fidel (Latin: faithful). *Plus:* Rebel cool. *Minus:* Moldy communist.

Field (English: a field, variation of **Fielding,** "field worker").

Fielding (English: field-worker). Familiar, **Field.** *Whatever:* What is it about F names for boys? Either they rhyme with raunchy four-letter words or sound stuffed and mounted. As problem Fs go, this one's doable. If the boy can survive his formative years, the name should sound rather dashing on a young man.

Filipe (Spanish: variation of **Phillip,** "lover of horses"). Also, **Filippe, Filyppe, Filype.**

Filipo (Spanish: variation of **Phillip,** "lover of horses"). Also, **Filippo, Filypo, Filyppo.**

Findlay (Irish: variation of **Findley,** "fair hero"). Also, **Findlae.**

Findley (Irish: variation of **Finley,** "fair hero").

Finley (Irish: fair hero). *Whatever:* See **Fielding.**

Finn (Irish: fair). Also, **Fin, Fyn, Fynn.** *Plus:* A pick to click. Here's an offbeat name for the New Millennium. It's puckish and left-of-center; short and simple. The character Douglas Coupland forgot to include in *Generation X. Minus:* The fish-association thing.

Finnegan (Irish: fair). Also, **Finegan, Finigan, Finnigan, Finnygan, Finygan.**

Fisher (English: a fisherman).

Fitch (English: small animal, like a weasel). Also, **Fitche.**

Fitz (Irish: son of; variation of **Fitzgerald, Fitzhugh, Fitzpatrick, Fitzroy**).

Fitzgerald (Irish: son of **Gerald,** "warrior chief"). Familiar, **Fitz.** *Whatever:* Like **Mac,** the **Fitz**-something names are nifty ways to dress up **Gerald, Hugh, Patrick,** and **Roy.** (They also can help you dodge the Junior issue.)

Fitzhugh (Irish: son of **Hugh,** "bright spirit"). Familiar, **Fitz.**

Fitzpatrick (Irish: son of **Patrick,** "nobleman"). Also, **Fitzpatric, Fitzpatrik, Fitzpatryc, Fitzpatryck, Fitzpatryk.** Familiar, **Fitz.**

Fitzroy (Irish: son of **Roy,** "red"). Also, **Fitz.**

Flanders (French: for the region in France and Belgium).

Flemming (English: from the valley). Also, **Fleming, Flemmyng.**

Fletch (English: variation of **Fletcher,** "arrow maker"). Also, **Fletche.**

Fletcher (English: arrow maker). Familiar, **Fletch.** *Plus:* Is there anything more adorable than the thought of a little **Fletcher** in footsie pajamas? And here's the good news: it'll wear OK once he progresses to shoes and socks too. *Minus:* Trendy suspenders potential. **Fletcher** smacks of latter-day yuppie.

Flick (English: a sudden, light striking motion). *Plus:* The name of a character in Gen X-era holiday movie *A Christmas Story.* **Flick** was the kid who stuck his tongue on the frozen schoolyard pole. *Minus:* The kid who played **Flick** grew up to star in a porn film. Make of that association what you will.

Flint (English: rock). Also, **Flinte.** *Plus:* A rugged **Clint** sound-alike. *Minus:* Why stop at **Flint**? Why not **Matches** or **Spark**?

Flip (English: herky-jerky motion; variation of **Philip,** "lover of horses"). Also, **Flipp.** *Whatever:* A name that could be another **Finn** except for the **Flip** Wilson problem. If you have fond memories of Mr. Wilson's 1970s variety show, it's cool. If you don't, it just sounds dated—like so many **Buddy**s and **Shecky**s.

Floyd (Welsh: gray). *Plus:* A nerdy cool candidate. Of course, it would help if somebody of this century popularized the thing, save for . . . *Minus:* The one they call "The Barber."

Flynn (Irish: son of a red-haired man). Also, **Flinn.**

Fob (German: pocket; English: pocket watch chain). Also, **Fobb.**

Ford (English: shallow stream). Also, **Forde.**

Forest (English: woods). Also, **Forrest, Forryst, Foryst.** *Whatever:* A perfectly good Southern gentleman moniker likely ruined for a generation by Tom Hanks's turn as **Forrest** Gump.

Forester (English: keeper of the forest). Also, **Forister, Forrester, Forrister, Forryster, Foryster.**

Forth (English: forward). Also, **Forthe.**

Foster (English: develop, nourish).

Fowke (English: variation of **Fawke,** "people").

Fox (English: a fox). Also, **Foxx.** *Whatever:* A comer, thanks to *The X-Files* and Agent Mulder. **Fox** achieves that rare double-double: It sounds book-smart *and* street-smart.

Francesco (Italian: variation of **Francis,** "free").

Francis (Latin: Frenchman; Welsh/French: free). Familiar, **Frank,**

Frankie. *Whatever:* Put **Francis** (or one of its variations) on the birth certificate, then go straight to **Frank,** a low-maintenance classic.

Francisco (Spanish: variation of **Francis,** "free"). Familiar, **Franco.**

Franco (Spanish: variation of **Francisco,** "free").

François (French: variation of **Francis,** "free").

Frank (English: variation of **Francis, Franklin**). This pocket T is decent and durable—plus it's got the Sinatra thing going for it. You could accuse **Frank** of being a peanut-butter-and-jelly sandwich, but would you dare risk offending the legacy of the Chairman of the Board?

Frankie (English: variation of **Francis, Franklin**). Also, **Frankey, Franky.**

Franklin (English: free landowner). Also, **Franklyn.** Familiar, **Frank.**

Frasier (Scottish: strawberry flowers; French: curly hair). Also, **Fraser.** Familiar, **Fraze.** *Plus:* Popularized by NBC sitcom of the same name. *Minus:* Popularized by NBC sitcom of the same name. Potential trendy suspenders.

Fraze (Scottish/French: variation of **Frasier, Frazier**). Also, **Fraize, Frayze.**

Frazier (Scottish/French: variation of **Frasier,** "strawberry flowers, curly hair"). Also, **Frazer.** Familiar, **Fraze.** *Whatever:* With **Frasier,** trendy suspenders material.

Fred (German: variation of **Frederic, Frederico**). *Plus:* A pocket T that perfectly mirrors the ethos of alternative rock. It's unplugged—bare, honest, real. *Minus:* It's *Flintstones*-esque.

Freddy (German: variation of **Frederic, Frederico**). Also, **Freddey, Freddie.**

Frederic (German: peaceful ruler). Also, **Frederich, Frederick, Frederik, Fredric, Fredrich, Fredrick, Fredrik.** Familiar, **Fred, Freddy, Fritz.**

Frederico (Spanish: variation of **Frederic,** "peaceful ruler"). Also, **Frederyco.** Familiar, **Fred, Freddie, Freddy.**

Freeborn (English: born free). Also, **Freeborne, Freebourn, Freebourne.**

Freeman (English: freeman). *Whatever:* In the same boat as **Fairman.** Good but terribly literal.

Fremont (English: free, mountain). Also, **Fremonte.**

Freso (Italian: fresh).

Friar (Latin: brother). Also, **Frier, Fryar, Fryer.**

Frick (English: brave, bold).

Friederic (German: variation of **Frederic,** "peaceful ruler"). Also, **Friederich, Friederick, Friederik, Friedric, Friedrich, Friedrick, Friedrik.** Familiar, **Fred, Freddy, Fritz.**

Frisco (Spanish: variation of **Francis,** "free").

Fritz (German: variation of **Frederic, Friederic**).

Frost (English: frozen dew). Also, **Froste.**

Fulbright (German: bright). Also, **Fullbright.**

Fuller (English: a cloth cleaner). *Whatever:* The **Fletcher** Less Traveled. **Fuller** is nowhere near as cute or trendy popular as its counterpart.

Fulton (English: field, town). Also, **Fulten.**

G

CRIB NOTES

FAMOUS GS: **Gabe** Kaplan (TV's Mr. Kotter, *Welcome Back, Kotter*); **Garry** Shandling (comedian); **Garth** Brooks (country singer); **Gavin** MacLeod (TV's Captain Stubing, *The Love Boat*); **George** Clooney (actor); **Gerald** Ford (U.S. president); **Geraldo** Rivera (talk-show host); **Grant** Goodeve (TV's David Bradford, *Eight Is Enough*)

Pocket Ts: Gabe, Gabriel, George

Trendy suspenders: Garth

Think long, think hard: Galahad (Frou-frou.); **Geraldo** (Even for a boy, **Oprah** would be a smarter choice.); **Gerardo** (One word: Rico. One other word: Suave.); **Gilligan** (Once a castaway, always a castaway.); **Gomer** (If we use baby names to project hopes on our offspring, what are we dreaming for a **Gomer**? A life as a ridiculed hayseed of a sitcom character?); **Grafton** (Thurston Howell III's spiritual cousin.); **Grover** (Coming up next: *Muppets Tonight*.)

Gabe (English: variation of **Gabriel,** "God is mighty"). *Whatever:* No longer the domain of eighty-year-old Old World immigrants, **Gabe** sounds salt-of-the-earth cool today. Cut from the same flannel shirt as **Ben** and **Hank**. A pocket T.

Gabie (English: variation of **Gabriel,** "God is mighty"). Also, **Gabey, Gaby.**

Gable (German: farmer, fork in the road). Also, **Gabel.** *Whatever:* True, it's more commonly a last name, but as a first name **Gable** gets you wiggle room on **Gabe** or **Gabriel.**

Gabor   (Hungarian: variation of **Gabriel,** "God is mighty"). *Plus:* Strong and dramatic. *Minus:* **Zsa-Zsa.**

Gabriel   (Hebrew: God is mighty). Also, **Gabryel.** Familiar, **Gabe, Gabie.** *Whatever:* **Gabriel** is on the money—solid, enduring, and acceptably musical for a boy. A pocket T.

Gabriele   (Italian: variation of **Gabriel,** "God is mighty"). Also, **Gabryele.**

Gage   (English: challenge). Also, **Gaige, Gayge.** *Plus:* Reminiscent of noble, hardworking paramedic John **Gage** of TV's *Emergency!* (1972–77). *Minus:* Reminiscent of a strapping stable-boy character on a soap opera.

Gaines   (English: profits). Also, **Ganes, Gaynes.** *Plus:* Preppy, gentlemanly. A doable Thurston Howell III. *Minus:* Dog food-esque.

Galen   (Greek: speaker). Also, **Galin, Galyn.** *Whatever:* A rarity: a delicate boy name that, to today's ears, sounds handsome not wussy.

Galfrid   (Latin: variation of **Geoffrey,** "God's peace"). Also, **Galfryd.**

Gamaliel   (Hebrew: the Lord is reward). Also, **Gamaleel, Gamalyel.**

Gamel   (Scandinavian: old).

Gannon   (Irish: fair-haired). Also, **Gannen.**

Gardener   (English: a gardener). Also, **Gardiner, Gardyner.**

Gardner   (English: from a garden).

Garmon   (Welsh: a German). Also, **Garmen.**

Garner   (English: protector, warrior).

Garnet   (English: little protector). Also, **Garnett.** *Whatever:* Look for this one's stock to rise with potential NBA superstar Kevin **Garnett.**

Garon   (Hebrew: the threshing floor, device used in food preparation). Also, **Garen.**

Garreth   (Welsh: gentle). Also, **Gareth, Garryth, Garyth.**

Garrett   (English: spear). Also, **Garret, Garryt, Garrytt, Garytt.** *Whatever:* A **Brandon** Less Traveled. Like that killer B, **Garrett** is tailor-made for boys who get shuttled to soccer practice in Range Rovers. But unlike that killer B, **Garrett** isn't overly precious or popular.

Garrison   (Greek: stationed troops). Also, **Garisen, Garison, Garrisen.**

Garth   (Scottish: hill). Also, **Garthe.** *Plus:* **Garth** Brooks is this name's big booster. He makes it seem both traditional and the stuff of a maverick. *Minus:* In twenty years' time, if **Garth** Brooks is still

Garth Brooks, the name will be fine. But when you're dealing with names popularized by celebrities, there's always the danger that you could be betting on the wrong horse. Go ask your friend **Ringo**. Potential trendy suspenders.

Gary (Irish: hunting dog). Also, **Garey, Garrey, Garry.** *Whatever:* This name, ubiquitous among Gen X-era classmates, is so *un*-today today. Its stock has fallen fast. **Gary** feels like something left over from the swingin' single scene. . . . On the upside, it's an accepted, generic boy name, so if you really love it, go for it. A peanut-butter-and-jelly sandwich is far from fatal.

Gaston (French: of a French village). Also, **Gasten.**

Gates (English: enclosed meadow). Also, **Gaites, Gaytes.** *Whatever:* A swell name—really. But consider: If we can assume Microsoft is going to be running the world by 2020, do you want your kid to feel owned by Bill **Gates** too?

Gavin (French/Scottish: battler, hawkish). Also, **Gaven, Gavyn.** *Whatever:* Fancy, not too fancy. Different, not too different. All in all, this is an entry that's very doable.

Gavriel (Hebrew: variation of **Gabriel,** "God is mighty"). Also, **Gavryel.**

Gavril (Russian: variation of **Gabriel,** "God is mighty"). Also, **Gavrill, Gavryl, Gavryll.**

Gawain (Welsh: hawk). Also, **Gawane, Gawayne.**

Gawin (German: district of land). Also, **Gawyn.**

Gaylord (English: happy). Also, **Gaylorde.** *Whatever:* One day the word and/or suffix *gay* will lose its power to evoke giggles among eleven-year-olds. But we're not there yet. Use at your kid's own risk.

Geary (Irish: hunting dog). Also, **Gearey.** *Whatever:* Really hung up on **Gary** but just can't envision one making waves in the twenty-first century? Sometimes a single vowel can make all the difference. **Geary** works for today.

Geer (German: virtue). Also, **Geere.**

Gene (Greek: variation of **Eugene,** "nobleman").

Geoff (English: variation of **Geoffrey,** "God's peace"). Also, **Geof.**

Geoffrey (English: God's peace). Also, **Geffrey, Geffry, Geoffry, Geofrey, Geofry.** Familiar, **Geoff.** *Whatever:* The Toys "Я" Us giraffe favors the G-man spelling. No matter. **Geoff** and identical cousin **Jeff** are the equivalent of mayo on white bread—names that go down easy, blend in well with walls, and don't challenge the senses. For the purposes of this book, a peanut-butter-and-jelly sandwich.

Georg (Scandinavian: variation of **George,** "farmer").

George (Greek: farmer). *Plus:* **George** walks among monosyllabic favorites **Jack, Nick,** and **Hank.** It's a humble, Father-of-Our-Country pocket T that endures thanks to modern-day namesakes, including actor **George** Clooney and *George* magazine. *Minus:* The *George of the Jungle* factor.

Georgio (Italian: variation of **George,** "farmer"). Also, **Georgyo.**

Gerald (German/French: warrior chief). Also, **Gerrald.** Familiar, **Gerry.** *Plus:* An old reliable. *Minus:* A boring pick.

Gerard (German: spear, hand). Also, **Gerrard.** Familiar, **Gerry.**

Gerbold (German: spear, bold). Also, **Gerbolde.**

German (English: a German).

Gerold (German/French: variation of **Gerald,** "warrior, chief"). Also, **Gerrold.** Familiar, **Gerry.** *Whatever:* The more contemporary **Gerald**—in sound and look.

Gerry (Greek/French: variation of **Gerald, Gerard, Gerold**). Also, **Gerrey.**

Gersh (Hebrew: variation of **Gershom,** "stranger"). Also, **Gershe, Gursh, Gurshe.**

Gershom (Hebrew: stranger). Also, **Gershem, Gurshem, Gurshom.** Familiar, **Gersh.**

Giancarlo (Italian: combination of **John** and **Charles**).

Gianni (Italian: variation of **John,** "God is gracious").

Gib (French: variation of **Gibbon, Gibbons, Gibson**). Also, **Gibb.** *Whatever:* If **Gib** wasn't quite so anonymous, it'd be a pocket T. As it is, it's a winner. A pick to click.

Gibbon (French: small ape). Also, **Gibben.** Familiar, **Gib.**

Gibbons (French: variation of **Gibbon,** "small ape"). Also, **Gibbens.**

Gibson (Scottish: son of **Gilbert,** "pledge"). Also, **Gibsen.** Familiar, **Gib.**

Gideon (Hebrew: mighty warrior). Also, **Gidion, Gidyeon.**

Gif (English: variation of **Giffin, Gifford**). Also, **Giff.**

Giffin (English: variation of **Geoffrey,** "God's peace"). Also, **Giffyn.** Familiar, **Gif.**

Gifford (German: give, bold, fierce). Also, **Giford.** Familiar, **Gif.**

Gil (Hebrew: my joy; Scottish/Spanish: variation of **Gilbert, Gilberto,**

Gilchrist). Also, **Gill.** *Plus:* A comer. **Gil** possesses a lot of **Ben**-ness. Its warm sound makes it a great good-guy name for today. *Minus:* The fish thing.

Gilbert (Scottish: pledge). Familiar, **Gil.** *Whatever:* A name that bears an unfortunate resemblance to **Herbert.** To be used only if you think **Gil** will look too naked on the Social Security card.

Gilberto (Spanish: variation of **Gilbert,** "pledge"). Familiar, **Gil.** *Whatever:* An exotic, appealing alternative to **Gilbert.**

Gilchrist (Gaelic: servant of Christ). Also, **Gilchryst, Gilcrist, Gilcryst.** Familiar, **Gil.**

Giles (Greek: shield). Also, **Gyles.**

Gilles (French: variation of **Giles,** "shield"). Also, **Gillis, Gillys.**

Gilman (Scottish: man servant). Also, **Gillman.**

Gilo (Latin: kid).

Gino (Italian: variation of **Gene,** "nobleman").

Glen (Irish/Scottish/Welsh: valley). Also, **Glenn.** *Whatever:* Another **Gary.** Another peanut-butter-and-jelly sandwich.

Glennon (Irish: small coat). Also, **Glenen, Glennen, Glenon.**

Glynn (Scottish; variation of **Glen,** "valley"). Also, **Glyn, Glin, Glinn.**

Goddard (German: god, hard). Also, **Godard, Godderd, Goderd.**

Godfrey (English: man of peace). Also, **Godfry.**

Godfried (German: variation of **Godfrey,** "man of peace"). Also, **Godfreed.**

Godric (English: powerful god). Also, **Godrick, Godrik, Godryc, Godryck, Godryk.**

Godridge (English: variation of **Godric,** "powerful god").

Godwin (English: god, friend). Also, **Godwyn.**

Goldin (English: variation of **Goldwin,** "gold, friend"). Also, **Golden, Goldyn.**

Goldwin (English: gold, friend). Also, **Goldwyn.**

Goodman (English: good man). Also, **Goodeman.**

Goodrich (English: variation of **Godric,** "powerful god"). Also, **Goodriche.**

Goodwin (English: friend of God). Also, **Goodewin, Goodewyn, Goodwyn.**

Gordie (Scottish: variation of **Gordon,** "big hill"). Also, **Gordey, Gordy.**

Gordo (Scottish: variation of **Gordon,** "big hill").

Gordon (Scottish: big hill). Also, **Gorden.** Familiar, **Gordie, Gordo.** *Whatever:* A pick to click. It's not a conventionally hip name, but if you think Dexter **Gordon** (the late jazz great), you may see how this moniker *can* swing.

Gotthard (German: variation of **Goddard,** "god, hard"). Also, **Gothard, Gotherd, Gottherd.**

Grady (Irish: noble, famous). Also, **Gradey.** *Plus:* A Southern-tinged **Brady.** *Minus:* **Grady** was the unfunny old man on TV's *Sanford and Son.*

Graem (English: variation of **Graham,** "gray house"). Also, **Graeme.**

Graham (English/Scottish: gray house). Also, **Gragham.** *Plus:* All the upper-crust dignity of **Giles,** less of the stuffiness. *Minus:* Cracker.

Grail (Latin: cup; biblical: cup used at the Last Supper). Also, **Grale, Grayle.**

Gram (Greek: writing, small weight). Also, **Gramm.** *Whatever:* Graham, for die-hard enthusiasts of the metric system.

Granger (English/Scottish: farmer). Also, **Grainger, Graynger.**

Grant (Scottish: swarthy; English: big man). Also, **Grante.**

Gray (English: gray-haired; variation of **Grayson,** "overseer, son of **Gray**"). Also, **Graye.** *Whatever:* A distinctive name of moderation— not hot, not cold, just **Gray.**

Grayson (English: overseer, son of **Gray**). Also, **Graysen.** Familiar, **Gray.**

Greeley (English: gray meadow). Also, **Greely.**

Greer (Scottish: watchful). Also, **Greere, Grier.**

Greg (Greek/English: variation of **Gregory, Gregson**). Also, **Gregg.** *Whatever:* Hot in the 1960s and 1970s—the age of **Greg** Brady. Today, it's staid peanut-butter-and-jelly sandwich fare. How very **Gary** and **Glen.**

Gregor (Scottish: variation of **Gregory,** "vigilant"). Also, **Greger.**

Gregory (Greek: vigilant). Also, **Greggory.** Familiar, **Greg.** *Plus:* Nice. *Minus:* Boring.

Gregson (English: son of **Greg**). Also, **Greggsen, Greggson, Gregsen.** Familiar, **Greg.** *Whatever:* The contemporary **Gregory.**

Grey (English: variation of **Gray, Greyson**).

Greyson (English: overseer, son of **Gray**). Also, **Greysen.** Familiar, **Grey.**

Griff (English: variation of **Griffin,** "mythical monster—part eagle, part lion"). Also, **Grif.**

Griffin   (English: mythical monster—part eagle, part lion). Also, **Grifin, Griffyn, Grifyn.** Familiar, **Griff.** *Whatever:* Anything that evokes images of birds of prey is kinda nifty.

Griffith   (Welsh: fearsome). Also, **Grifith, Griffyth, Grifyth.**

Grigg   (English: variation of Greg, "vigilant"). Also, **Grig.** *Whatever:* The contemporary **Greg.**

Grimbald   (English: gold, savage). Also, **Grimbold.**

Guillermo   (Spanish: variation of **William**, "will, helmet"). Also, **Guilermo.**

Gullet   (Latin: throat). Also, **Gullett.**

Gunnar   (Norwegian: war). Also, **Gunar.** *Whatever:* One of the identical twin guys of 1990s teen-idol pop band Nelson was named **Gunnar.** Make of that association what you will.

Gunner   (English: a soldier).

Gunthar   (Scandinavian: warlike). Also, **Gunther.** *Plus:* A big, strapping manly man name. *Minus:* Too much testosterone for its own good?

Gus   (Latin: majestic). Also, **Guss.** *Plus:* A flannel shirt. *Minus:* The name of a 1970s Disney movie about a football-playing mule.

Guthrie   (Scottish: windy). Also, **Guthrey, Guthry.**

Guy   (French: guide, man). *Whatever:* The next best thing to outfitting your boy with a permanent beret.

H

CRIB NOTES

Famous Hs: **Hank** Aaron (home run king); **Harlan** Ellison (sci-fi author); **Harrison** Ford (alter ego of Indiana Jones and Han Solo); Prince **Harry** (British royalty); **Heath** Shuler (football player); **Henry** Rollins (rocker/poet); **Hermann** Hesse (author); **Herschel** Walker (football player); **Holden** Caulfield (antihero, *The Catcher in the Rye*); **Hugh** Grant (actor); **Humphrey** Bogart (icon)

Pocket Ts: **Hal, Hank, Henry**

Trendy suspenders: **Harley, Hunter**

Think long, think hard: **Hamlet** (Not to be.); **Hammer** (Can't touch this.); **Herb** (Remember Burger King's failed "Herb" campaign? This name is always a tough sell. Same goes for **Herbert.**); **Hercules** (Not even **Herc** could lift a name with this much blinkin' baggage.); **Homer** (Yeah, Yeah, *you* know Homer as an epic storyteller. Problem is, the rest of the world thinks he's a jaundiced cartoon character with a beer gut.); **Horton** (Hears a Who.); **Horace** (**Herb** city.); **Hubert** (Ditto.); **Humbert** (Best left to the pages of Nabokov's *Lolita*.); **Humphrey** (**Humphrey** Bogart was a fluke. This name is too close to **"Humpty,"** as in "Humpty Dumpty," to be considered schoolyard safe.)

Haddock (English: cod). Also, **Haddoc, Haddok, Hadoc, Hadock, Hadok.**

Haden (Irish: variation of **Hayden,** "hill"). Also, **Hadin, Hadyn.**

Hadley (English: land owner). Also, **Hadly.**

Hal (English: sound body; variation of **Harold,** "host, army"). *Plus:*

The ethos of alternative rock: Basic, simple, decent, real. **Hal** is the **Ben** less traveled and a pocket T. *Minus:* The last notable person to champion the name wasn't a person at all, but the computer from *2001*.

Haldane (Scandinavian: half Danish). Also, **Haldaine, Haldayne.**

Halden (Scandinavian: half Danish). Also, **Haldin, Haldyn.**

Hale (English: sound health; Welsh: hiding place). Also, **Haile, Hayle.**

Hall (English: manor).

Halley (English: manor near the meadow). Also, **Hally.**

Halstead (English: manor on the homestead). Also, **Halsted.**

Hamill (English: home). Also, **Hamil, Hamyl, Hamyll.**

Hamilton (English: bare hill).

Hamish (Scottish: he who removes). Also, **Hammish, Hammysh, Hamysh.** Familiar, **Hamm, Hammie.** *Plus:* The **Hammish/Hamm/ Hammie** combo offers strong-sounding boy names. *Minus:* It offers names that sound like Easter dinner.

Hamm (English: home; variation of **Hammett, Hamish, Hammond**).

Hammett (English: village). Also, **Hammet, Hammit, Hammitt, Hammyt, Hammytt.** Familiar, **Hamm, Hammie.**

Hammie (Scottish/English: variation of **Hammett, Hamish, Hammond**). Also, **Hammey, Hammy.** *Whatever:* The comic strip *Baby Blues,* featuring infant **Hammie,** is trying to take this one back from the supermarket butcher. Usually, the comics are a bad place to hunt for baby names. (*Beetle Bailey,* anyone?) But *Baby Blues* might be on to something. *Might.*

Hammond (English: village). Also, **Hamond.** Familiar, **Hamm, Hammie.**

Hamon (Greek: faithful). Also, **Hamen.**

Hank (German: variation of **Henry,** "head of house"). *Whatever:* So dependable it's almost better than a pocket T—it's a comfy, well-worn flannel shirt. A name for this supposedly back-to-basics era, **Hank** is strong enough to work as a stand-alone, à la **Jack.**

Hans (Scandinavian: variation of **John,** "God is gracious").

Hanson (Scandinavian: son of **Hans**). Also, **Hansen, Hanssen, Hansson.** *Whatever:* "MmmBop, MmmBop, MmmBop." Get used to it. Running through your head. Constantly. Forever.

Hap (Scandinavian: luck). Also, **Happ.**

Harcourt (French: fortified house). Also, **Harcourte.**

Hardy (English: lasting). Also, **Hardey.**

Harlan (English: messenger). Also, **Harlen, Harlyn.**

Harland (English: army's land). Also, **Harlande.**

Harley (English: deer hunter). Also, **Harly.** *Plus:* Conjures images of a rough-and-ready free spirit of the West. Very contemporary. *Minus:* Will future sociologists look back and wonder if parents of the late twentieth century were under the mind control of biker gangs? Trendy suspenders fodder.

Harlow (English: army on a hill). Also, **Harlowe.**

Harmon (Greek: harmony). Also, **Harmen.**

Harold (English: host, army). Also, **Harrold.** Familiar, **Hal, Harry.** *Plus:* A classic. *Minus:* A nerd classic.

Harper (English: harp player). *Whatever:* A pick to click. Works for a Southern gentleman or a swingin' 1960s private detective.

Harris (English: variation of **Henry,** "head of house"). Also, **Haris, Hariss, Harriss, Harrys, Harryss, Harys, Haryss.** Familiar, **Harry.** *Whatever:* A hipper way than **Harold** to get to **Harry.**

Harrison (English: variation of **Henry,** "head of house"). Also, **Harisen, Harison, Harrisen, Harrissen, Harrisson, Harrysen, Harryson, Har-ryssen, Harrysson, Harysen, Haryson, Haryssen, Harysson.** Familiar, **Harry.** *Whatever:* Actor **Harrison** Ford has single-handedly knocked the stuffing, *er,* stuffiness out of this preppie classic.

Harry (English: variation of **Harold, Harris, Harrison, Henry**). *Whatever:* A comer. Look for the name to come into its own as a peer of **Jack, Hank, Ben,** et al., as Britain's young Prince **Harry** comes into his own.

Hart (English: red deer). Also, **Harte.**

Hartley (English: deer meadow). Also, **Hartly.**

Hartman (German: strong man). Also, **Harteman.**

Harve (French/Celtic: variation of **Harvey**). Also, **Harv.**

Harvey (French: bitter; Celtic: forward-thinking). Familiar, **Harve.** *Whatever:* Could be nerdy cool—someday. Right now, **Harvey** is in desperate need of a savior, à la **Harrison** Ford. You can try to forage this wilderness yourself—it's certainly not the biggest pair of busted eyeglasses out there. (*See* **Herb.**)

Haskell (Yiddish: God is powerful). Also, **Haskel, Haskil, Haskill, Haskyl, Haskyll.** *Plus:* Strong sound. *Minus: Leave It to Beaver*–esque.

Hatch (English: a grating; variation of **Hatcher,** "forest gate"). Also, **Hatche.**

Hatcher (English: forest gate). Familiar, **Hatch.**

Hawk (English: bird of prey). Also, **Hawke.** *Plus:* A unique way to pay homage to the West without jumping on the **Harley** bandwagon. *Minus:* A melodramatic *Dynasty* name.

Hayden (English: hedged valley). Also, **Haydin.**

Hayes (English: hedges, fences). Also, **Hays.**

Heath (English: heather; variation of **Heathcliff,** "cliff where the heather grows"). Also, **Heathe, Heethe.** *Whatever:* This name provides us with even more proof that so-called sissy names really don't exist. **Heath** Shuler didn't need to be called **Joe** or **Dan** to cut it as an NFL quarterback.

Heathcliff (English: cliff where the heather grows). Also, **Heathcliffe, Heathclif.** Familiar, **Cliff, Heath.** *Plus:* The romantic hero of *Wuthering Heights.* *Minus:* It's doubtful your boy's peers will appreciate the romance. The safe money says start with **Heathcliff** then ditch the first syllable for the more colloquial **Cliff,** à la TV's *The Cosby Show.*

Hector (Greek: steadfast). Also, **Hecter.**

Heinrick (German: variation of **Henry,** "head of house"). Also, **Heinric, Heinrik, Heinryc, Heinryck, Heinryk.**

Hendrick (Dutch: variation of **Henry,** "head of house"). Also, **Hendric, Hendrik, Hendryc, Hendryck, Hendryk.**

Henri (French: variation of **Henry,** "head of house").

Henry (German: head of house). Familiar, **Hank.** *Whatever:* The bomb, where names projecting dependability and honesty are concerned. **Henry** is **Henry** Fonda. It's **Henry** David Thoreau. It's a pocket T.

Herman (German: army of men). Also, **Hermann.** *Plus:* Among the Hs' unusually large nerd class, including **Herbert, Horace,** and **Hubert, Herman** is an upper-echelon name. Square but strong. *Minus:* One word: Munster.

Herrick (English: army commander). Also, **Herric, Herrik, Herryc, Herryck, Herryk.**

Herring (English: small fish).

Hersh (Yiddish: variation of **Hershel,** "deer"). Also, **Hersch, Hershe.**

Hershel (Yiddish: deer). Also, **Herschel, Herschell, Herschyl, Herschyll, Hershell, Hershyl, Hershyll.** Familiar, **Hersh, Shel.**

Hiatt (English: variation of **Hyatt**, "high gate"). Also, **Hiat.**

Highland (English: the highland). Also, **Highlande.**

Hill (English: a hill).

Hillel (Hebrew: praised). Also, **Hilel.** *Whatever:* Different (for the United States, anyway—it's popular in Israel) but doable.

Hilton (English: town on a hill). Also, **Hilten.**

Hoagie (English: sandwich). Also, **Hoagey, Hoagy, Hogey, Hogie.** *Plus:* Cute. *Minus:* Deli-esque.

Hob (English: elf, goblin). Also, **Hobb.**

Hobbs (English: variation of **Hob**, "elf, goblin"). Also, **Hobbes.** *Whatever:* One word: Calvin.

Hod (Scandinavian: a shovel). Also, **Hodd.**

Hogan (Irish: young). Also, **Hogen.**

Holden (English: deep valley; Teutonic: gracious). Also, **Holdin, Holdyn.** *Whatever:* **Holden** could be a pocket T except it owes its durability to a society that uses it as shorthand for "searching, alienated youth," thanks to *Catcher in the Rye.*

Holland (English: from the Netherlands, lowlands).

Hollis (English: holly tree). Also, **Holliss, Hollys, Holyss.**

Holm (English: holly tree). Also, **Holme.**

Holmes (English: variation of **Holm**, "holly tree"). Also, **Holms.** *Whatever:* You don't need to be Sherlock to know that this name, while classy, comes with a fair amount of baggage.

Holt (English: woods). Also, **Holte.**

Horner (English: trumpet player).

Hostler (English: stable caretaker).

Houston (Scottish: Hugh's town). Also, **Housten, Husten, Huston.** *Whatever:* The map name alternative to **Dallas.**

Howard (English: swordsman). Familiar, **Howie.** *Plus:* A baby name as oatmeal. Like that morning dish, **Howard** is a hardy, stick-to-the-ribs name that just *sounds* good for you. *Minus:* It won't win a popularity contest in the new millennium. This is a pair of brown shoes in a Nike world.

Howe (English: royalty).

Howell (Welsh: lordly). Also, **Howel.** *Whatever:* The ultimate Thurston Howell III but thankfully more preppie than stuffy.

Howie (English: variation of **Howard**, "swordsman"). Also, **Howey, Howy.**

Hoyle (English: from the book of rules by Edmond **Hoyle**).

Hoyt (Irish: merry). Also, **Hoyte.**

Hub (English: the center). Also, **Hubb.**

Hud (English: variation of **Hudson,** "son of **Hugh**"). Also, **Hudd.**

Hudson (English: son of **Hugh**). Also, **Hudsen.** Familiar, **Hud.**

Hugh (English: bright spirit). *Whatever:* A steadfast Anglo classic juiced up by actor **Hugh** Grant.

Hugo (Latin: variation of **Hugh,** "bright spirit").

Hume (English: holly tree).

Humes (English: variation of **Hume,** "holly tree").

Hunt (English: to hunt; variation of **Hunter, Huntley, Huntsville**). Also, **Hunte.**

Hunter (English: hunter). Familiar, **Hunt.** *Plus:* As lil' cowpokes go, **Hunter** is pretty low on the precious scale. *Minus:* So Range Rover ready. So trendy suspenders. So-so.

Huntley (English: hunter by the meadow). Also, **Huntly.** Familiar, **Hunt.**

Huntsville (English: village of the hunters). Familiar, **Hunt.**

Hutch (Latin: chest; English: variation of **Hugh,** "bright spirit"). *Whatever:* A pick to click. Don't let the *Starsky and Hutch* association scare you. In fact, that 1970s cop show just makes this moniker all the more cool. **Hutch** is a manly man lil' cowpoke name with style.

Hutton (English: village; German: cottage). Also, **Hutten.**

Hyatt (English: high gate). Also, **Hyat.**

Hyland (English: variation of **Highland,** "the highland"). Also, **Hylande.**

I

CRIB NOTES

Famous Is: **Ichabod** Crane (fictional scaredy-cat); **Ingmar** Bergman (filmmaker); **Ingo** Rademacher (soap actor, *General Hospital*); **Ira** Gershwin (composer); **Isaac** Hayes (composer, *Shaft*); **Isiah** Thomas (ex-basketball player); **Ivan** Rodriguez (baseball player)

Pocket Ts: Ian, Isaac, Isaiah

Trendy suspenders: Nothing trendy about Is. Even the popular entries (**Isaac, Isaiah**) work against the grain.

Think long, think hard: **Iago** (Brush up on your Shakespeare and pick another play. The villain from *Othello* ain't gonna fly.); **Ice** (Ice. Ice. Baby.); **Ichabod** (Unflattering mental picture, courtesy of Washington Irving: gangly, large Adam's apple, frightened easily by headless horsemen.); **Iggy** (A good name for a puppy—or any other creature that doesn't have to defend itself against spitball-armed peers.); **Igor** (Owned by Dr. Frankenstein's assistant.); **Ishmael** ("Call me **Ishmael**?" Clearly, the guy was a masochist.); **Izzy** (The Olympic mascot of the 1996 Summer Olympic Games tried to infuse relevancy into this long-in-the-tooth moniker and he, *er,* it, disappeared before the flame was out. A name beyond revival.)

Ian (Scottish: variation of **John,** "God is gracious"). Also, **Iain.** *Whatever:* **Ian** is every bit as dependable as its ubiquitous cousin—and every bit the pocket T.

Ib (Arabic: variation of Ibrahim, "father of many"). Also, **Ibb.**

Ibis (Egyptian: large bird). Also, **Ibiss, Ibys, Ibyss.**

Ibrahim (Arabic: variation of **Abraham,** "father of many"). Also, **Ibraheem, Ibreheem, Ibrehim, Ibryheem.** Familiar, **Ib.**

Ibsen (Scandinavian: for playwright Henrik **Ibsen**). Also, **Ibsin, Ibsyn.**

Ides (Latin: Fifteenth day of the month).

Ignacio (Spanish: variation of **Ignatius,** "ardent, spirited"). Also, **Ignacyo.**

Ignatio (Spanish: variation of **Ignatius,** "ardent, spirited"). Also, **Ignatyo.**

Ignatius (Latin: ardent, spirited).

Ignazio (Italian: variation of **Ignatius,** "ardent, spirited"). Also, **Ignazyo.**

Ike (English: variation of **Isaac,** "laughter"). *Whatever:* If you like **Hank,** you just might like **Ike** too. Both sound sturdy and earnest.

Ikey (English: variation of **Isaac,** "laughter").

Ilan (Hebrew: youth.) Also, **Ilann.**

Ilbert (German: iron, poet). Also, **Ilburt.**

Ilia (Russian: variation of **Ilias,** "Lord is my God"). Also, **Illia, Illya, Ilya.**

Iliad (Greek: for the epic Greek poem about the Trojan War). Also, **Illiad, Illyad.**

Ilias (Greek: Lord is my God). Also **Iliass, Ilyas, Ilyass.** Familiar, **Ilia.**

Imbert (German: variation of **Ilbert,** "iron, poet").

Immanuel (Hebrew: God is with us). Also, **Imanuel, Imannuel, Immannuel.** Familiar, **Manny.**

Imran (Arabic: host).

Ince (Hungarian: variation of **Incencio, Incenzio**).

Incencio (Spanish: innocent). Also, **Incencyo.** Familiar, **Ince.**

Incenzio (Italian: innocent). Also, **Incenzyo.** Familiar, **Ince.**

Ing (Scandinavian: god of peace; variation of **Ingamar, Ingavar, Ingmar**).

Ingall (English: angel). Also, **Ingal, Ingel, Ingell.**

Ingalls (English: variation of **Ingall,** "angel"). Also, **Ingals, Ingels, Ingells.**

Ingamar (Scandinavian: famous son). Also, **Ingemar.** Familiar, **Ing.**

Ingar (Scandinavian: son's army).

Ingavar (Scandinavian: **Ing**'s defender). Also, **Ingevar, Ingyvar.** Familiar, **Ing.**

Inge (Scandinavian: variation of **Ingmar,** "famous son").

Ingham (English: **Ing**'s home). Also, **Ingam, Ingamm, Inghamm.**

Ingle (English: variation of **Ingall,** "angel").

Ingles (English: variation of **Ingalls,** "angel").

Ingman (Norwegian: variation of **Inman,** "protector"). Also, **Ing-mann.**

Ingmar (Scandinavian: famous son). Familiar, **Ing.** *Plus:* Your tribute to Swedish art house films. *Minus:* The bane of your school-age boy's existence.

Ingo (Scandinavian: variation of **Ingmar,** "famous son"). *Whatever:* Can daytime heartthrob **Ingo** Rademacher turn this Euro staple into a monster American favorite? Probably not, but don't be surprised to see an **Ingo** or two taking up residence in the nursery next to your **Michael.**

Ingram (German: wings of angels; English: engrave). Also, **Ingramm.** *Whatever:* A win-win. **Ingram** is prep school ready but not too stuffy.

Ingvar (Scandinavian: **Ing**'s defender).

Inigo (Greek: variation of **Ignatius,** "ardent, spirited"). Also, **Inygo.**

Inman (Norwegian: protector). Also, **Inmann.**

Innis (Scottish: island). Also, **Inis, Iniss, Inniss, Innys, Innyss, Inys, Inyss.** *Whatever:* A pick to click. Like any good I, it's on the outer edge of the mainstream. But this one's got the goods. Classy, clean, not flashy.

Innocenzio (Italian: variation of **Incenzio,** "innocent"). Also, **Inno-cenzyo, Inocenzio, Inocenzyo.**

Iolo (Welsh: variation of **Julius,** "youthful, downy").

Ion (Irish: variation of **John,** "God is gracious").

Ionel (Greek: violet jewel). Also, **Ionell.** *Plus:* A spelunker's dream. This is a name that's different *and* doable. *Minus:* It'll sound like you wanted **Lionel** but got stuck with **Ionel** when the l fell off at the hospital.

Iorgos (Greek: variation of **George,** "farmer").

Ira (Arabic: swift, the watcher). *Plus:* A **Max** Less Traveled. A nerdy cool name for your baby to grow into . . . *Minus:* . . . when he's about forty-five.

Iram (English: shining bright). Also, **Iramm.**

Ireland (English: the country, one of the British Isles).

Irv (Scottish/English/German/Irish: variation of **Irvin, Irving**).

Irvie (Scottish/English/German/Irish: variation of **Irvin, Irving**). Also, **Irvey, Irvy.**

Irvin (Scottish: handsome; English/German: sea, friend). Also, **Irvyn.**

Familiar, **Irv, Irvie.** *Whatever:* Amazing what one little letter does. All **Irvin** is, is **Irving** minus the *g.* And yet that one subtraction adds a lot. Makes it sound infinitely hipper. (Even looks hipper than **Ervin.**)

Irving (Irish: handsome; Scottish: green river). Also, **Irvyng.** Familiar, **Irv, Irvie.** *Plus:* A "real" name—no pretensions, no frills. *Minus:* A "real" nerd name.

Irwin (Scottish/English/German: variation of **Erwin, Irvin**). Also, **Irwyn.**

Isa (Hebrew: variation of **Isaiah,** "God is helper"). Also, **Isah.**

Isaac (Hebrew: laughter). Also, **Isaak, Isac, Isak.** Also, **Ike, Ikey.** *Plus:* A model pocket T—classic, not Jurassic. **Isaac** is the biblical peer of **Jacob** and **Joshua.** *Minus:* When Gen Xers roamed gym class, **Isaac** would have been considered **Percy** material. As a result, you may have trouble reconciling **Isaac** as a cool boy name. But it's worth the effort.

Isaiah (Hebrew: God is helper). Also, **Isaia, Isaya, Isayah.** *Whatever:* The cuddly bear version of **Isaac.** The name's sensitive streak makes this equally biblical effort all the more contemporary. A pocket T.

Isaias (Hebrew: variation of **Isaiah,** "God is helper"). Also, **Isayas.**

Isan (German: iron).

Isha (Hindi: lord).

Isidore (Greek: gift). Also, **Isydore.**

Ismael (Arabic: variation of **Ishmael,** "God will hear"). Also, **Ismail, Ismale, Ismayle.** *Whatever:* The doable **Ishmael.**

Israel (Hebrew: wrestling with God). Also, **Isreal, Isreel.**

Issa (Swahili: God is our salvation).

Itzak (Hebrew: variation of **Isaac,** "laughter"). Also, **Itzac, Itzaac, Itzaak.**

Ivan (Russian: variation of **John,** "God is gracious"). Also, **Iven, Ivyn.** *Plus:* The Cold War's dead. Feel free to pinch this hardy standby from the Russians. *Minus:* "**Ivan** the Terrible" digs are inevitable.

Ivander (Hebrew: divine).

Ivar (Norwegian: archer).

Ivens (Welsh: young warrior, archer). Also, **Ivins, Ivyns.**

Ives (French: evergreen).

Ivo (German: evergreen tree).

Ivon (German: variation of **Ivo,** "evergreen tree").

Ivor (Irish/Scandinavian: archer).

Ivy (English: the climbing vine). Also, **Ivey.**

Iye (Native American: smoke).

Izaac   (Hebrew: variation of **Isaac,** "laughter"). Also, **Izaak, Izac, Izak.**

Izaiah   (Hebrew: variation of **Isaiah,** "God is helper"). Also, **Izaia, Izaya, Izayah.**

Izaias (Hebrew: variation of **Isaiah,** "God is helper"). Also, **Izayas.**

Izrael   (Hebrew: variation of **Israel,** "wrestling with God"). Also, **Izreal, Izreel.**

J

CRIB NOTES

Famous Js: **Jack** Nicholson (actor); **Jakob** Dylan (rocker, the Wallflowers); **James** T. Kirk (starship captain, TV's *Star Trek*); **Jared** Leto (actor, TV's *My So-Called Life*); **Jerry** Lewis (actor/director/French-certified genius); **Joaquin** Phoenix (actor/River's kid brother); **Joe** Montana (ex–football player); **John** Kennedy Jr. (sexiest magazine editor alive); **Judge** Reinhold (B.M.O.C. Brad, *Fast Times at Ridgemont High*); **Julian** Lennon (singer/scion)

Pocket Ts: Jack, Jacob, James, John, Jonathan, Joseph, Joshua

Trendy suspenders: Jesse, Jordan, Justin

Think long, think hard: No kidding—there's virtually not a boy J name that *won't* work. Even the usual suspects (presumably outmoded models such as **Jarvis** and **Jedidiah**) can't be discounted. Js are like type-O blood—they'll match anything. About the only stern warnings to offer here concern **Junior** (it's tough being born, the least you can do is reward the kid with his own name), **Jethro** (forever tainted by *The Beverly Hillbillies,* not to mention **Jethro** Tull), and **Judas** (uh, no). Other than that, happy hunting.

Jabez (Hebrew: height). Also, **Jabezz.**
Jabot (French: shirt ruffle).
Jack (English: man; variation of **Jackson,** "son of **Jack**"; common nickname for **John**). Also, **Jac, Jak.** *Plus:* As rakish as **Nick,** as decent as **Hank** or **Ben**—above all, a pocket T. *Minus:* Can you really just name a boy **Jack**? Yup. But if that feels too constricting, try **Jack-**

son, John, Jonathan—names that **Jack** is assumed to be merely an offshoot of.

Jackal (Sanskrit: wild dog). Also, **Jackel, Jackell, Jackyl, Jackyll.** *Plus:* Hey, **Dakota** probably sounds like a silly name at first, too. *Minus:* **Dakota** *still* sounds like a silly name, ditto for **Jackal.**

Jackie (English: variation of **Jack, Jackson**). Also, **Jackey, Jacky.**

Jackson (English: son of **Jack**). Also, **Jacsen, Jacson, Jacssen, Jacsson, Jacksen, Jackssen, Jacksson, Jaksen, Jakson, Jakssen, Jaksson.** Familiar, **Jack, Jackie.** *Whatever:* A fine Southern gentleman's name that can also serve as a suitable, less trendy alternative to **Jack.**

Jacksonville (English: **Jackson**'s village). Also, **Jacsonville, Jaksonville.**

Jacob (Hebrew: following after); variation of **Jacobson**, "son of **Jacob**"). Also, **Jakob.** Familiar, **Jake, Jakey.** *Plus:* Impeccable credentials. A cuddly bear with a grown-up bite, **Jacob** has traveled well from the rock of ages to the age of alternative rock. A slam-dunk pocket T. *Minus:* Everybody—*everybody*—loves **Jacob**. It's challenging, even besting, the all-powerful **Michael** in Kansas, Minnesota, and Washington.

Jacobs (Hebrew: variation of **Jacob**, "following after"). Also, **Jakobs.** Familiar, **Jakey.**

Jacobson (Hebrew: son of **Jacob**). Also, **Jacobsen, Jakobsen, Jakobson.** Familiar, **Jacob, Jake, Jakey.**

Jacobus (Latin: variation of **Jacob**, "following after"). Also, **Jakobus.**

Jacoby (Hebrew: variation of **Jacob**, "following after"). Also, **Jacobey, Jakobey, Jakoby.**

Jacquard (French: fabric design). Also, **Jackard, Jackarde, Jacquarde, Jaqard, Jaqarde, Jaquard, Jaquarde.**

Jacques (French: man). Also, **Jaques.**

Jaequon (American: variation of **John**, "God is gracious"). Also, **Jaequan, Jayquon, Jayquan.**

Jaewon (American: variation of **John**, "God is gracious"). Also, **Jaewan, Jaywan, Jaywon.**

Jago (Spanish: variation of **Jacob**, "following after").

Jahmal (Arabic: variation of **Jamal**, "handsome"). Also, **Jahmaal, Jahmall.**

Jahmil (Arabic: variation of **Jamil**, "handsome"). Also, **Jahmeel, Jahmyl.**

Jake (English: variation of **Jacob, Jacobson**). Also, **Jayke**. *Plus:* **Jack** with muscles. *Minus:* Hollywood cliché for the strong, silent, slightly dumb type—personified by *Melrose Place*'s **Jake** Hanson.

Jakey (English: variation of **Jacob, Jacobs, Jacobson**). Also, **Jaky**.

Jalen (American: calm). Also, **Jalin, Jalyn**.

Jamal (Arabic: handsome). Also, **Jamaal, Jamall**.

James (English: variation of **Jacob**, "following after"). Also, **Jaimes, Jaymes**. Familiar, **Jamie, Jamesy, Jim, Jimmy**. *Plus:* Rock of ages, rock solid, rock steady—and a pocket T to boot. What else could you ask for? *Minus:* A little imagination. We've been naming boys **James** forever (rough estimate). **James,** the **Michael** of the first half of this century, is slowly on its way down the charts.

Jamie (English: variation of **James**, "following after"). Also, **Jaimey, Jaymey, Jaimy, Jaymy**. *Whatever:* An early cuddly bear. **Jamie** is a touch on the 1970s side but doable.

Jamil (Arabic: handsome). Also, **Jameel, Jamyl**.

Jan (Scandinavian/Slavic: variation of **John**, "God is gracious").

Jansen (Scandinavian: son of **Jan**). Also, **Janson, Janssen, Jansson**.

Jantzen (Scandinavian: son of **Jan**). Also, **Jantzon**.

Janus (Latin: from the Roman god; keeper of the door). Also, **Januss**. *Plus:* Offbeat and strong—undeniably so. It's the thinking man's **Jake**. *Minus:* Sounds like **Janis**. As in **Janis**, the *girl*.

Jacquon (American: variation of **John**, "God is gracious"). Also, **Jaquan, Jequan, Jequon**.

Jared (Hebrew: descending). Also, **Jarod, Jarred, Jarrod**. *Whatever:* Contemporary, popular. A cuddly bear but with teeth.

Jarrett (English: brave, spear). Also, **Jaritt, Jarret, Jarrit, Jarritt, Jarryt, Jarrytt**.

Jarvis (English: spear, driver). Also, **Jarvys**. *Plus:* So out, it's nerdy cool. *Minus:* So out, it's out.

Jason (English: healer). Also, **Jaisen, Jaison, Jaysen, Jayson**. *Plus:* Like any good peanut-butter-and-jelly sandwich, this entry goes down easy. *Minus:* Gen Xers went to school with lots of clean-cut, improbably clear-skinned **Jason**s. It was a perfect 1970s name—so safely suburban, so safely un-1960s, so, well, safe. While it's still common, it's slipping against the likes of **Jordan** and **Justin**. Those *Friday the 13th* movies probably didn't help.

Jasper (English: wise man).

Javier (Spanish: home). Also, **Javyer.** Familiar, **Javy.**

Javy (Spanish: variation of **Javier,** "home"). Also, **Javey, Javie.**

Jawon (American: variation of **Juan,** "God is gracious"). Also, **Jawan, Jewan, Jewon.**

Jax (English: variation of **Jack,** "man"). Also, **Jaxx.**

Jay (English: songbird). Also, **Jaye.** *Whatever:* Perfectly doable. But like **Jason,** it's enjoying (if that's the word) the downside of hip.

Jed (Hebrew: variation of **Jedidiah,** "beloved of God"). Also, **Jedd.** *Plus:* Projects unpretentiousness. *Minus:* Projects *The Beverly Hillbillies.*

Jedidiah (Hebrew: beloved of God). Also, **Jedidia.** Familiar, **Jed.** *Whatever:* The **Elijah** Less Traveled.

Jeff (English: variation of **Jeffrey,** "God's peace"). Also, **Jef.** *Plus:* No fuss, no muss. *Minus:* The sort of name Gen Xers got saddled with in the 1960s because it sounded like, well a boy's boy name. . . . Today's take on **Jeff:** yawn.

Jeffrey (English: God's peace). Also, **Jeffry, Jefrey, Jefry.** Familiar, **Jeff.** *Whatever:* A peanut-butter-and-jelly sandwich.

Jem (English: variation of **Jim,** "following after"). Also, **Jemm.** *Plus:* The today **Jim.** *Minus:* The girlie **Jim.**

Jenkins (English: variation of **John,** "God is gracious"). Also, **Jenkyns.**

Jennett (French: variation of **John,** "God is gracious"). Also, **Jennet, Jennit, Jennitt, Jennyt, Jennytt.**

Jennings (French: variation of **John,** "God is gracious"). Also, **Jennyngs.**

Jenson (Dutch: variation of **Jansen,** "son of **John**"). Also, **Jensen, Jenssen, Jensson.**

Jerard (German: variation of **Gerald,** "warrior chief"). Also, **Jerrard.**

Jeremiah (Hebrew: God is high). Also, **Jeremia, Jerimia, Jerimiah, Jerymia, Jerymiah.** Familiar, **Jerry.** *Plus:* A comer. Old-fashioned and biblical—adorably so. Think of it as a more profound **Jeremy.** *Minus:* Think of it as really, really old-sounding.

Jeremias (Hebrew: variation of **Jeremiah,** "God is high"). Also, **Jerimias, Jerymias.**

Jeremy (English: variation of **Jeremiah,** "God is high"). Also, **Jeremey, Jeremie, Jerimey, Jerimy.** Familiar, **Jerry.** *Whatever:* A reliable, newly popular choice, **Jeremy** would be a pocket T if not for the suspicion that it's being boosted by the cuddly bear fad. Here's the theory:

Parents find themselves attracted by the cute-as-a-button *y* sound, figure it's as good as **Cody** and go for it. Fine and dandy. The problem is, when the gig's up for the cuddly bears will the undeserving **Jeremy** be dragged down with the rest of the cubs?

Jericho (Arabic: city of the moon). Also, **Jerico, Jericko, Jeriko, Jerycho, Jerycko, Jeryco, Jeryko.**

Jerold (German/French: variation of **Gerald,** "warrior chief"). Also, **Jerrold.** Familiar, **Jerry.**

Jerome (Greek: sacred name). Familiar, **Jerry.**

Jerram (English: variation of **Jerome,** "sacred name"). Also, **Jeram, Jerem, Jerrem, Jerrym, Jerym.** Familiar, **Jerry.**

Jerry (English/Hebrew/German/Greek: variation of **Jerard, Jeremiah, Jeremy, Jerold, Jerome, Jerram**). Also, **Jerrey.**

Jersey (English: reddish brown dairy cow). Also, **Jersy.**

Jess (Hebrew: variation of **Jesse, Jessie**). Also, **Jes.**

Jesse (Hebrew: God exists). Familiar, **Jess.** *Whatever:* An amazing transformation. When Gen Xers went to school **Jesse** was still regarded as an outlaw, à la Bobby Brady's false idol, **Jesse** James. But somewhere between Don Johnson giving one of his sons this name and today, **Jesse** has become unconventionally cool. Like **Dakota** (the moniker of Johnson's *other* son), it's a name of the West and wide open spaces. Is it a name for the twenty-first century? Too soon to tell, therefore it gets trendy suspenders status.

Jessie (Hebrew: variation of **Jesse,** "God exists"). Also, **Jessey, Jessy.** Familiar, **Jess.**

Jessop (English: variation of **Joseph,** "increaser, God will add"). Also, **Jesop, Jesopp, Jessopp, Jesup, Jesupp, Jessup, Jessupp.**

Jesús (Spanish: variation of *Jesus,* "Lord is salvation"). *Whatever:* That's "Hay-sus."

Jet (English: an airplane; a lush black). Also, **Jett.** *Whatever:* **Jett** is the name of aviation-enthusiast John Travolta's son.

Jetty (English: a pier). Also, **Jettey.**

Jevon (Welsh: variation of **John,** "God is gracious").

Jim (English: variation of **James,** "following after"). Also, **Jimm.** *Whatever:* A hardy name. Sticks to the roof of your mouth. Like PB&J on Wonder bread.

Jimmy (English: variation of **James,** "following after"). Also, **Jimmey, Jimmie.**

Jivon (Persian: young man).

Joab (Hebrew: God is father).

Joaquim (Hebrew: variation of **Joaquin,** "God judges"). Also, **Joaqueem, Joaqym.**

Joaquin (Hebrew: God judges). Also, **Joaqueen, Joaqyn.** *Whatever:* Actor Leaf (*Russkies*) Phoenix liked this one so much, he dropped his name like a leaf and went **Joaquin** (his given name). (Ended up with better film parts too.)

Job (English: persecuted; variation of **Jobson,** "son of **Job**"). Also, **Jobe.** *Plus:* A biblical **Hank.** *Minus:* Philistines will insist the name is pronounced "jawb," as in the place where they punch the clock.

Jobson (English: son of **Job**). Also, **Jobesen, Jobeson.** Familiar, **Job.**

Jock (Scottish: variation of **Jack,** "man"). Also, **Joc, Jok.** *Plus:* A **Jack** Less Traveled. Every bit the Gen X name of today—unfussy, direct, real. *Minus:* Can you hear the name without the theme song from *Dallas* running through your head? Or images of sweaty locker rooms flashing before your eyes?

Jody (Hebrew: praise). Also, **Jodey, Jodie.** *Whatever:* The perfect name for a child actor of the 1970s. You know the type: Wire-framed glasses, chubby cheeks, bangs. (*See* Cousin Oliver on *The Brady Bunch*.) And actually, the name *was* used by kid thespians (i.e., **Jodie** Foster). But, alas, **Jody** has found the passage of time a threat to its career, not unlike many a former child star. Outmatched on the cuddly bear front by **Cody** and **Coby, Jody** is a name in decline.

Joe (Hebrew: variation of **Josef, Joseph, Josephe**).

Joel (Hebrew: Jehovah is God). *Whatever:* **Joel** is a sensitive, cute boy of the Gen X formative era. It's not entirely dated today, it's just not entirely with it either.

Joey (Hebrew: variation of **Josef, Joseph, Josephe**).

Johann (German: variation of **John,** "God is gracious"). Also, **Johan.**

John (Hebrew: "God is gracious"; English: variation of **Johnson,** "son of **John**"). Familiar, **Jack, Johnnie.** *Plus:* No therapy bills, guaranteed. **John** is **John** is **John**—a name that's so common, so engrained, it's generic. This may not seem like high praise, but it's what makes it an ultimate pocket T. You can't imagine a scenario, a universe, where **John** goes out of style. *Minus:* How does your little **John** distinguish himself in a world of **John**s? (Uh-oh, maybe you better budget for therapy sessions after all.)

Johnnic (English: variation of **John, Jonathan**). Also, **Johnncy, Johnny.**

John Paul (English: combination of **John** and **Paul**; after Pope **John Paul**). Also, **Johnpaul.**

Johns (English: variation of **John**, "God is gracious").

Johnson (English: son of **John**). Also, **Johnsen.** Familiar, **John.**

Jon (Hebrew: variation of **John**, "God is gracious"). Also, **Jonn.**

Jonah (Hebrew: dove). Also, **Jona.** *Plus:* There's a lot of good stuff going on in the Js. **Jonah** is yet another strong Gen X choice—it's got deep roots, it's got a good sound. *Minus:* A whale of a choice.

Jonas (Welsh: variation of **John**, "God is gracious"). Also, **Jonahs.** *Whatever:* **Jonas** Grumby was the given name of the Skipper on TV's *Gilligan's Island* (1964–67). What do we take from that? **Jonas** works in any locale! Really, it's every bit a doable as the popular, old-school Js—**James, John, Joseph,** etc. More important, it's *not* one of the popular Js. It's different. A comer.

Jonathan (Hebrew: God gave). Also, **Johnathan, Johnathen, Johnathon, Johnethan, Johnethen, Johnethon, Jonathen, Jonethan, Jonethen, Jonethon.** Familiar, **Johnnie.** *Whatever:* This one's cutting into the audience of the more pedestrian-sounding **John.** ("Honey, can't we get something with a couple extra syllables? To go better with the Volvo.") Motives aside, **Jonathan** is worthy of the attention. A steady performer with just a touch of a cuddly bear in him, this one's a pocket T.

Jones (Welsh: variation of **John**, "God is gracious"). *Plus:* like **John** and **Jonathan,** but not. *Minus:* Too close for comfort to a certain slang phrase?

Joplin (English: city in Missouri). Also, **Joplyn.** *Whatever:* As a map name or a tribute to jazz great Scott **Joplin,** this makes for a classy, non-cutesy boy name.

Jordan (Hebrew: down-flowing river; English: variation of **Jordison,** "son of **Jordan**"). Also, **Jorden, Jordyn.** Familiar, **Jordy, Jory.** *Plus:* Modern, stylish, adaptable too. **Jordan** looks equally good on an athlete or an aesthete. *Minus:* Precious, studied. What the heir to Daddy's Land Rover is called these days. Trendy suspenders . . . Also, watch out—the girls are looking to claim this one for their own.

Jordane (Hebrew: variation of **Jordan**, "down-flowing river"). Also, **Jordaine, Jordayne.** Familiar, **Jordy, Jory.**

Jordison   (English: son of **Jordan**). Also, **Jordisen, Jordysen, Jordyson.** Familiar, **Jordy, Jory.**

Jordy   (Hebrew: variation of **Jordan, Jordane, Jordison**). Also, **Jordie, Jordey.**

Jory   (Hebrew: variation of **Jordan, Jordane, Jordison**). Also, **Jorey.**

Jose   (Spanish: variation of **Joseph,** "increaser, God will add"). *Whatever:* The second most popular boy name in California and Texas.

Josef   (German: variation of **Joseph,** "increaser, God will add"). Also, **Joseff.** Familiar, **Joe, Joey.**

Joseph   (Hebrew: increaser, God will add). Familiar, **Joe, Joey.** *Whatever:* Here's another entry that makes a baby name book superfluous. Heck, the phone book will suffice in this case. Go ahead, crack one open and take a look. **Joseph** is in there—probably on every page. **Joseph** is popular, perennial, and a pocket T.

Josephe   (French: variation of **Joseph,** "increaser, God will add"). Familiar, **Joe, Joey.**

Josh   (Hebrew: variation of **Joshua,** "God saves"). *Whatever:* A cuddly bear that manages to sound cute, not cloying.

Josha   (Sanskrit: satisfying). *Whatever:* A sound-alike alternative to **Joshua.**

Joshua   (Hebrew: God saves). Also, **Joshuah.** Familiar, **Josh.** *Plus:* The biblical **Cody, Joshua** is a cuddly bear with a track record that dates back to the apostles. A pocket T. *Minus:* A problem we should all have—**Joshua** is very (too?) popular.

Josiah   (Hebrew: God supports). Also, **Josia, Josya, Josyah.**

Jotham   (Hebrew: God is perfect). Also, **Jothem, Jothym.**

Jove   (Latin: alternate name of Jupiter, god of light).

Juan   (Spanish: variation of **John,** "God is gracious").

Juan Carlos   (Spanish: combination of **Juan** and **Carlos**). Also, **Juancarlos.**

Judah   (Hebrew: variation of **Jude,** "praise"). Also, **Juda.**

Judd   (English: confession; variation of **Judson,** "son of **Judd**"). Also, **Jud.** *Plus:* A prototypical Gen X name. No fuss, no muss, no B.S. It's just **Judd.** *Minus:* The **Judd** Nelson thing.

Jude   (Hebrew: praise; English: confession). *Whatever:* A pick to click. This one exudes a James Bond cool. And, as an added bonus, by the time your little **Jude** is of school age the Beatles' "Hey, **Jude**" will be almost forty years old, thereby mitigating the possible teasing factor.

Judge (English: arbiter).
Judson (English: son of **Judd**). Also, **Juddsen, Juddson, Judsen, Judssen.** Familiar, **Judd.**
Jule (English: variation of **Julius,** "youthful, downy").
Jules (French: variation of **Julius,** "youthful, downy").
Julian (English: variation of **Julius,** "youthful, downy"). Also, **Julien, Julyan, Julyen.**
Julio (Spanish: variation of **Julius,** "youthful, downy"). Also, **Julyo.**
Julius (Latin: youthful, downy). Also, **Julyus.**
Justin (English/Latin: honorable, fair). Also, **Justen, Justyn.** *Whatever:* **Jordan'**s doppelänger. It sounds like it. It's popular like it. And it's baby boomer–fied like it. The punch line: It's trendy suspenders material like it too.
Justinian (Latin: variation of **Justin,** "honorable, fair"). Also, **Justinyan.**
Justus (English: judge).
Jute (Sanskrit: matted hair).
Juwan (American: variation of **John,** "God is gracious"). Also, **Juwon.**

K

CRIB NOTES

Famous Ks: **Kadeem** Hardison (actor, TV's *A Different World*); **Kareem** Abdul-Jabbar (ex–basketball player); **Keenen** Ivory Wayans (*In Living Color* ringmaster); **Keyshawn** Johnson (football player); **Keith** Haring (pop artist); **Keanu** Reeves (actor/wannabe rocker); **Ken** Griffey Jr. (baseball player); **Kevin** Costner (actor); **Keifer** Sutherland (actor, *Flatliners*); **Kirby** Puckett (ex–baseball player); **Kirk** Cameron (erstwhile teen idol); **Kobe** Bryant (basketball player); **Kurt** Cobain (late rock icon)

Pocket Ts: The no-brainer pick here would be **Kevin,** but it's not. Read below. In the meantime, no pick here.

Trendy suspenders: Kobe, Kyle

Think long, think hard: **Kato** (Think we've had enough of the "trial of the century"—and all its players great and small—to last a couple of centuries.); **K.C.** (Four words: and the Sunshine Band.); **Keanu** (A total Madonna. Consider this one taken.); **Kermit** (Two words: the frog.); **Khan** (Naming a kid **Khan** in this age of relative peace is overkill—akin to driving an armored Humvee to the mall.); **Kid** (Cute but about as inventive as Tarzan naming his boy **Boy.**); **King** (Usurped by the dog kingdom.); **Kramer** (Strictly a *Seinfeld* thing.)

The "phony" Cs: A special note before we begin. Below, you won't find the likes of **Kaleb, Kalvin, Kameron, Kassidy, Klark, Klay, Kliff, Klyde, Kody, Konrad, Korman, Kornelius,** or **Kory.** Names that are commonly Cs—with no popular K variations to be had—are found in

the C section (no birthing-procedure pun intended). Clearly, you are free
to spell your baby's name any way you want. Make **Bob** into **Obob,** if
you wish. ("The *o*'s silent . . . like 'opossum!' ") Just a reminder: You
don't get style points for fudging with spelling. **Kody** is still **Cody.**

Kade (Irish/Scottish: wetlands, boggy). Also, **Kaid, Kayde.**

Kadeem (Arabic: servant). Also, **Kadym.**

Kadin (Arabic: friend). Also, **Kadeen, Kadyn.**

Kadir (Arabic: green, spring). Also, **Kadeer.**

Kahil (Turkish: young). Also, **Kaheel, Kahyl.**

Kailan (Irish: big warrior). Also, **Kailen, Kailyn.**

Kainan (Irish: tribute). Also, **Kainen, Kainyn.**

Kale (Irish: man). Also, **Kaile, Kayle.** *Whatever:* An uncommon alternative to the ubiquitous **Kevin.**

Kamm (German: mountain crest). Also, **Kam.**

Kane (German: warrior, soldier; Irish: tribute). Also, **Kaine, Kayne.**

Kannon (Polynesian: free). Also, **Kanen, Kannen, Kanon.**

Kareem (Arabic: generous, noble). Also, **Karim, Karym.** *Whatever:*
Kareem Abdul-Jabbar sued Miami Dolphins running back **Karim**
Abdul-Jabbar for infringing on the rights to *his* name. May want to
keep a lawyer on retainer if you plan to use this one.

Karl (German: man; variation of **Karlson,** "son of **Karl**"). *Whatever:*
Doesn't really look any cooler in K than it does in C, does it?

Karlson (German: son of **Karl**). Also, **Karlsen, Karlssen, Karlsson.**
Familiar, **Karl.**

Karr (Irish: spear). Also, **Karre.**

Kasey (Irish: vigilant). Also, **Kasy.**

Kavan (Irish: variation of **Kevin,** "handsome"). Also, **Kaven, Kavyn.**

Kavanaugh (Irish: variation of **Kevin,** "handsome").

Keagan (Irish: fiery). Also, **Keagen, Keagyn, Keegan, Keegen, Kee-
gyn.** *Whatever:* A pick to click. Strong-looking, manly sounding. Let's
see the girls steal this one.

Keane (Irish: quick, sharp). Also, **Kean, Keen, Keene.** *Whatever:* Seeing as how the word *keen* (as in "Golly, that's keen!") has been ex-
punged from our everyday dialogue, this one's probably safe for
general use again.

Kearney (Irish: victorious warrior). Also, **Kearny.**

Keating (Irish: urbane). Also, **Keeting.**

Keaton (English: of the hawk). Also, **Keaten, Keeten, Keeton.**

Keel (Scandinavian: the wooden runner along the bottom of a ship). Also, **Keal, Keale, Keele.**

Keelan (Irish: big warrior). Also, **Kealan, Kealen, Keelen.**

Keenan (Irish: ancient). Also, **Keenen, Kenan, Kenen.** *Whatever:* A comer. Very contemporary—witness Nickelodeon's teen comedy hit *Kenan and Kel.*

Keil (German: variation of **Keel,** "the wooden runner along the bottom of a ship"). Also, **Kiel.**

Keilly (Irish: graceful). Also, **Keiley, Keilley, Keily.** *Plus:* The **Kevin** for spelunkers. *Minus:* Could be confused with a girl name.

Keir (Irish: dark-complected). Also, **Keer, Kier.**

Keith (Scottish: woods; Irish: the wind). Also, **Keithe, Keyth, Keythe.** *Plus:* A familiar peanut-butter-and-jelly sandwich. *Minus:* A name of our youth—like **Gary** and **Greg**—that's in decline. **Keith** is sounding less and less like a name of the new millennium.

Kel (Irish: mighty warrior; variation of **Kellen, Kelly, Kelsey, Kelvin, Kelwin**). Also, **Kell.**

Kellen (Irish: big warrior). Also, **Kellin, Kellyn.** Familiar, **Kel.**

Keller (Irish: little, companion).

Kelly (Irish: warrior). Also, **Kelley.** Familiar, **Kel.** *Whatever:* A minor 1970s schoolyard favorite that's just becoming plain old minor as the years progress. Used to be a sensitive, cute boy. Now it looks better on a girl.

Kelsey (English: highland marsh). Also, **Kelsy.** Familiar, **Kel.** *Plus:* Dignified, handsome. *Minus:* Inevitable reaction from big-mouth friends and family: "Isn't that a girl name?"

Kelt (English: a Celtic). Also, **Kelte.**

Kelvin (English/Irish: warrior friend). Also, **Kelvyn.** Familiar, **Kel.** *Plus:* The coolest way to get to **Kel**—and a pretty cool moniker in its own right. *Minus:* If you're not planning to use the nickname, understand that **Kelvin** is but a hop, skip, and jump away from nerdy soundalike **Calvin.**

Kelwin (English/Irish: variation of **Kelvin,** "warrior friend"). Also, **Kelwyn.** Familiar, **Kel.**

Kemp (English: fighter).

Ken (English: variation of **Kenard, Kendall, Kendrick, Kennelly, Kenneth, Kenrick, Kenward, Kenwood**). Also, **Kenn.** *Whatever:*

Sounding slick and swingin' 1960s, à la **Kirk,** these days. And we haven't even gotten into the whole Barbie doll thing.

Kenard (English: brave, guard). Also, **Kennard.** Familiar, **Ken, Kenny.**

Kendall (English: the valley of Kent). Also, **Kendal, Kendel, Kendell, Kendyl, Kendyll.** Familiar, **Ken, Kenny.** *Whatever:* Don't look now, but the girls are stealing this hipper alternative to **Kenneth** too.

Kendrick (English: kingly). Also, **Kendric, Kendrik, Kendryc, Kendryck, Kendryk.** Familiar, **Ken, Kenny.**

Kenelm (English: brave, helmet). Also, **Kenhelm.**

Kennedy (Scottish: armored helmet). *Whatever:* Gen Xers don't name their sons after presidents, even ones featured in Oliver Stone movies.

Kennelly (Irish: scholar). Also, **Kenely, Kenelly, Kennely.** Familiar, **Ken, Kenny.**

Kenneth (Irish: leader). Also, **Keneth, Kenith, Kennith, Kennyth, Kenyth.** Familiar, **Ken, Kenny.** *Whatever:* Serviceable. This is a peanut-butter-and-jelly sandwich you won't lose sleep over. Nobody's gone into therapy because he was named **Kenneth.** And if somebody has, trust this: The guy had other problems.

Kenny (English: variation of **Kenard, Kendall, Kendrick, Kennelly, Kenneth, Kenrick, Kenward, Kenwood**). Also, **Kenney.** *Whatever:* Cult 'toon *South Park* is just about ruining this nickname with its incessant, "Omigod, they killed **Kenny!**" riffs.

Kenrick (English: royal, rule). Also, **Kenric, Kenrik, Kenryc, Kenryck, Kenryk.** Familiar, **Ken, Kenny.**

Kent (English: open country; variation of **Kenton,** "town of **Kent**"; Celtic: chief). Also, **Kente.** *Whatever:* Had its bright, shining moment in the early 1970s when quasi–teen idol Kent McCord co-starred as cop Jim Reed on TV's *Adam-12*. It was a name that seemed poised to become our new **Kirk.** Of course, then it was decided that we didn't really need the old **Kirk,** much less a new one.

Kenton (English: town of **Kent**). Also, **Kenten.** Familiar, **Kent.** *Whatever:* A Thurston Howell III that downsizes nicely to **Kent** for everyday use.

Kenward (English: king's guardian). Also, **Kenwarde.** Familiar, **Ken, Kenny.**

Kenwood (English: king's woods). Also, **Kenwoode.** Familiar, **Ken, Kenny.**

Kenyon (English: mountain; Irish: fair-complected). Also, **Kenyen.** *Whatever:* A **Keenan** Less Traveled.

Kern (Irish: heir). Also, **Kerne.**

Kernan (Irish: variation of **Kern,** "heir"). Also, **Kernen, Kernyn.**

Kerner (German: miller).

Kerns (Irish: variation of **Kern,** "heir"). Also, **Kernes.**

Kerr (English/Irish: marsh). *Plus:* A name that's defiantly obscure. It can never be out because it's never been here. *Minus:* Feels more like a growl *"Krrrrr"* than a name.

Kerry (English: captain; Irish: dark-complected). Also, **Kerrey.** *Plus:* Handsome. *Minus:* Girl-like.

Kershaw (English: boggy marsh).

Kerwin (Irish: dark-complected). Also, **Kerwyn.**

Keshawn (American: variation of **Sean,** "God is gracious"). Also, **Kesean, Keshaun, Keshon, Keysean, Keyshaun, Keyshawn, Keyshon.**

Kevin (Irish: handsome). Also, **Kevyn.** *Plus:* From Saint **Kevin** to Displaced **Kevin** in *Home Alone,* this supreme sensitive, cute boy has been through it all, his hair barely out of place. *Minus:* This is an entry that's threatening to become the new **Tom** or **Steve**—the preferred moniker of smooth-operating campus jocks. Its commonness is starting to tire our fair-haired boy.

Kiefer (English: a cooper). Also, **Keefer, Keifer.** *Plus:* Wins points for being acceptably rakish. *Minus:* Loses points for sounding like "keister."

Kieran (Irish: heir). Also, **Keiran, Keiren, Keiryn, Keiren, Keiryn.** *Whatever:* Child actor **Kieran** Culkin (*Father of the Bride*) is the sibling of *Home Alone* star Macaulay Culkin.

Kiernan (Irish: variation of **Kieran,** "heir"). Also, **Keirnan, Keirnen, Keirnyn, Kiernen, Kiernyn.**

Kileen (Irish: variation of **Killian,** "little warrior"). Also, **Killeen.**

Kiley (Irish: variation of **Keilly,** "graceful"). Also, **Kily.**

Killian (Irish: little warrior). Also, **Kilian, Kilien, Killien, Killyan, Kilyan.** *Whatever:* Here's another **Keagan,** and another pick to click—assuming the beer association doesn't bother you.

Kim (English/German: variation of **Kimball, Kimmell, Kimmer**). Also, **Kimm, Kym, Kymm.** *Plus:* A boy named **Kim**? It could happen. It's not like the girls use it anymore. *Minus:* Find Johnny Cash's "A Boy Named Sue." Take notes.

Kimball (English: hill). Also, **Kimbal, Kimbel, Kimbell, Kimble, Kimbyl, Kimbyll.** Familiar, **Kim.** *Whatever:* If you really, *really* like the sound of **Kim** for a boy, you would be strongly, *strongly* advised to start with **Kimball** (or **Kimmell**). This, in case the future heir decides *he* doesn't like the sound of **Kim** for a boy.

Kimmell (German: seed farmer). Also, **Kimmel, Kimmil, Kimmill, Kimmyl, Kimmyll.** Familiar, **Kim.**

Kimmer (English/German: variation of **Kimball, Kimmell**). Familiar, **Kim.**

Kin (English: family). Also, **Kinn.**

Kincaid (Scottish: battler). Also, **Kincade, Kincayde.**

Kinney (Irish: fiery). Also, **Kinny.** *Plus:* What today's names are about: being Irish, having vowel action, and sounding different. *Minus:* Does different have to include sounding like a shoe store?

Kipper (English: cured fish). *Plus:* Adorable . . . *Minus:* . . . for a guppy.

Kirby (English: church). Also, **Kirbey.** *Plus:* Nerdy cool. *Minus:* It's a nasal name—gets caught in your nose when you say it. Makes it sound more nerdy, less cool.

Kirk (Scottish: church; variation of **Kirkby, Kirkland, Kirkley, Kirkwell, Kirkwood**). Also, **Kirke, Kurk, Kurke.** *Whatever:* Used to be the stuff of devastatingly handsome hunks—witness actor **Kirk** Douglas or *Star Trek* Capt. James T. **Kirk.** Now it seems like a quaint throwback—the stuff of ex–teen idol **Kirk** Cameron.

Kirkby (English: by the church). Also, **Kirkbey, Kurkbey, Kurkby.** Familiar, **Kirk.**

Kirkland (English: church of the land). Also, **Kirklande, Kurkland, Kurklande.** Familiar, **Kirk.**

Kirkley (English: church by a meadow). Also, **Kirkly, Kurkley, Kurkly.** Familiar, **Kirk.**

Kirkwell (English: church by a spring). Also, **Kirkwelle, Kurkwell, Kurkwelle.** Familiar, **Kirk.**

Kirkwood (English: church in the woods). Also, **Kirkwoode, Kurkwood, Kurkwoode.** Familiar, **Kirk.**

Kit (English: a tub; variation of **Christopher,** "Christ-bearer"). Also, **Kitt.** *Plus:* An offbeat, kicky lil' cowpoke. *Minus:* Two words: And caboodle.

Kith (English: friends).

Knight (English: boy, chivalrous military man). Also, **Knighte.**

Knox (English: hills).

Knude (Scandinavian: kind, race). Also, **Knud.**

Knute (Scandinavian: variation of **Knude,** "kind, race"). Also, **Knut.** *Whatever:* For die-hard Notre Dame football fans only.

Kobe (Japanese: city of **Kobe**). Also, **Kobey, Kobi, Kobie, Koby.** *Plus:* Here's a cuddly bear sound-alike for **Coby** and **Cody**. Just as adorable, not as popular—less chance for backlash. *Minus:* This name has the goods to be as ubiquitous as Kathie Lee Gifford's lil' pardner, especially if budding NBA sensation **Kobe** Bryant takes off. Potential trendy suspenders.

Kogan (Polish: priest). Also, **Kogen, Kogyn.**

Kopeck (Russian: of the Russian ruble). Also, **Kopec, Kopek.**

Kordell (Latin: warm-hearted). Also, **Kordel.**

Koren (Hebrew: shining). Also, **Korin, Koryn.**

Kurt (French: variation of **Curtis,** "courteous"). Also, **Kurte.** *Whatever:* Do Gen Xers name their babies after **Kurt** Cobain, as boomers did with their chief rock icon, Bob **Dylan**? In a word, no. Here's why: (a) Our pop culture influences are more diverse; and (b) Cobain was a really depressed guy who killed himself—not exactly the stuff of inspiration.

Kyle (English: narrow river). Also, **Kile.** *Plus:* Is this the new **Kevin**? To be sure, this sensitive, cute boy is climbing the popularity charts— making its mentor look stale. *Minus:* Not enough of a track record as a top-drawer popular name. Will its good looks age well? Or will **Kyle** turn into the **Keith** of 2025? Trendy suspenders.

L

CRIB NOTES

Famous Ls: **Lance** Kerwin (1970s teen demi-idol, *James at 15*); **Langston** Hughes (poet); **Lee** Majors (bionic man, TV's *Six Million Dollar Man*); **Leif** Garrett (1970s teen mega-idol); **Lenny** Bruce (comedian); **Leonardo** DiCaprio (1990s teen mega-idol); **Liam** Neeson (actor); **Linus** Van Pelt (blanket-dependent, pumpkin-obsessed neurotic, "Peanuts"); **Lionel** Richie (singer); **Lukas** Haas (actor, *Witness*); **Luke** Skywalker (outerspace flyboy, *Star Wars*); **Lyle** Lovett (singer/songwriter); **Lyndon** B. Johnson (U.S. president)

Pocket Ts: **Lincoln, Lewis, Louis, Luke**

Trendy suspenders: **Logan**

Think long, think hard: **Lancelot** (Shining armor not included.); **Lazarus** (A certain figure of the Bible may rise again, but his name won't.); **Leander** (Better if you were christening, say, a pharmaceutical company, rather than a human being.); **Leroy** (Borderline. It's kind of retro cool. But it's mostly still stung by Jim Croce's "Bad, Bad **Leroy** Brown."); **Llewelyn** (The "L" version of **Percy**.); **Lucifer** (Uh, no.); **Lucky** (There is such a thing as being overly optimistic.); **Luka** (Hit songs about child abuse do not happy-go-lucky baby names make.)

Lachlan (Scottish: warlike). Also, **Lachlin, Lachlyn.**
Ladarius (American: variation of **Darius,** "to preserve"). Also, **Ladarrius, Ladarryus, Ladaryus, Ledarius, Ledarrius, Ledaryus.**
Ladd (English: attendant). Also, **Ladde.** *Whatever:* For people who *really* like **Kid** but can be persuaded that it ain't gonna fly.

Lake (English: body of water; variation of **Lakeland, Lakely, Lakewood**). Also, **Laike, Layke.**

Lakeland (English: land of lakes). Also, **Lakeland.** Familiar, **Lake.**

Lakely (English: lake by the meadow). Also, **Lakeley.** Familiar, **Lake.**

Lakewood (English: lake by the woods). Also, **Lakewoode.** Familiar, **Lake.**

Lamar (French: the sea). Also, **Lamarr, Lemar, Lemarr.** *Plus:* A baggage-free **Leroy** for our times . . . *Minus:* . . . assuming you don't count the wussy factor as baggage.

Lambard (German: variation of **Lambart,** "land, bright"). Also, **Lambarde.**

Lambart (German: land, bright). Also, **Lambert.**

Lamond (French: the world). Also, **Lamonde, Lemond, Lemonde.**

Lamont (Scottish: lawyer). Also, **Lamonte.** *Whatever:* Lamont Sanford was the "Son" of TV's *Sanford and Son* (1972–77), the level-headed complement to his irascible father.

Lance (Latin/French: small spear). *Plus:* The dress-casual-Friday version of **Lancelot.** *Minus:* Unless you have designs on your boy becoming a matinee idol, **Lance** is still probably a bit much.

Lander (English: washer of wool, landowner).

Landers (English: variation of **Lander,** "washer of wood, landowner").

Landis (English: plowed field). Also, **Landys.**

Landon (English: long hill). Also, **Landen.** *Whatever:* **Landon** was one of the stranded astronauts in the movie *Planet of the Apes.* (Full disclosure: **Landon** was the character's *last* name.)

Landreth (Scottish: court of law). Also, **Landrith, Landryth.**

Landry (French: powerful). Also, **Landrey.**

Lane (English: fertile land). Also, **Laine, Layne.** *Whatever:* A solid pick to click. It's the doable, more accessible version of **Lance.**

Lang (Scottish: tall man). Also, **Lange.**

Langdon (English: long hill). Also, **Langden, Langdin.** *Whatever:* A name that offers wiggle room on the trendier **Logan.**

Langley (English: long wood). Also, **Langly.** *Whatever:* A name that probably crosses the sissy line. If you love it, plan on enrolling the kid in boarding school where everybody's name is equally foppish.

Langston (English: long stone). Also, **Langsden, Langsdon, Langsten.**

Lansing (English: for the English town of **Lansing**). Also, **Lansyng.** *Whatever:* **Montana** schmontana. Let's here it for a map name from Michigan.

Larkin (English: variation of **Lawrence,** "crowned with laurel"). Also, **Larken, Larkyn.** *Whatever:* A generation ago **Larkin** would have been the schoolyard equivalent of fresh meat. Today, it can blend in with the likes of **Logan** and **Tristan.**

Larry (English: variation of **Laurence, Lawrence**). Also, **Larrey.** *Whatever:* Bowling leagues are about the only things keeping this one from slipping into obscurity and neglect.

Laughlin (Irish: servant of St. Secundus). Also, **Laughlyn, Loflin, Loflyn.**

Laughton (English: town on a hill). Also, **Laughten, Lawten, Lawton.**

Laurence (English: variation of **Lawrence,** "crowned with laurel"). Also, **Laurince, Laurynce.** Familiar, **Larry, Lorry.**

Laurens (Scandinavian: variation of **Laurence,** "crowned with laurel"). Also, **Laurins, Lauryns.**

Laurent (French: variation of **Lawrence,** "crowned with laurel"). Also, **Laurint, Laurynt.**

Lauris (Swedish: variation of **Lawrence,** "crowned with laurel"). Also, **Laurys.**

Lavon (Hebrew: white). Also, **Levon.**

Lawrence (English: crowned with laurel; Latin: bay tree). Also, **Lauwrence.** Familiar, **Larry, Lorry.** *Plus:* Standard, proven fare that evokes images of professionals: doctors, lawyers, even linebackers. *Minus:* Onetime NFL linebacker **Lawrence** Taylor aside, the name is sounding a little soft. A touch on the **Leonard** side.

Lawry (English: variation of **Lawrence,** "crowned with laurel"). Also, **Lauwrey, Lauwry, Lawrey.** *Plus:* The dressed-up **Larry.** *Minus:* The sound-alike for girl name **Lorie.**

Lawson (English: variation of **Lawrence,** "crowned with laurel"). Also, **Lawsen, Lawssen, Lawsson.**

Lawton (English: variation of **Laughton,** "town on a hill"). Also, **Lawten.**

Leaf (English: a leaf). Also, **Leef.** *Plus:* One of the acting Phoenix siblings (River, Rain, et al.) was named **Leaf.** *Minus: Was* named **Leaf.** The kid got over his hippie phase and went back to his given name **Joaquin.**

Lee (English: meadow). *Whatever:* Gen Xers went to school with a few **Lees**—even watched a couple on TV (chiefly, the bionic **Lee** Majors). But that was then, this is now. Today, naming a newborn baby **Lee** seems almost as alien as dubbing him **Gary**. **Lee** is another onetime cool guy name in a major funk. (Also, the **Lee** Harvey Oswald stigma, while diminished, is not erased.)

Leif (Scandinavian: beloved). Also, **Leife**. *Plus:* You're a firm believer that **Leif** Erikson, not Christopher Columbus, did the real legwork in discovering America and would like to honor his memory accordingly. *Minus:* You're chagrined to remember the hours you spent clipping **Leif** Garrett pictures out of *Tiger Beat* magazine.

Leigh (English: variation of **Lee**, "meadow"). *Plus:* Today's **Lee**. *Minus:* Yesterday, a boy name, today, a girl name, tomorrow, a girl name.

Leith (Scottish: overflowing). Also, **Leathe, Leeth.**

Leland (English: plowed land). Also, **Lelande.**

Lemuel (Hebrew: devoted to God). Also, **Lemuell.**

Len (German: variation of **Leonard**, "bold lion"). Also, **Lenn.**

Lennon (Irish: cape, cloak). Also, **Lenen, Lennen, Lenon.** *Plus:* In this post-*glasnost* era, **Lennon** is all about cool (as in "smart" Beatle John **Lennon**) and nothing about sounding like revolutionary V. I. **Lenin**. *Minus:* It *still* rhymes with "lemon."

Lennox (Scottish: elm trees). Also, **Lenex, Lennex, Lenox.** *Whatever:* An even-hipper-sounding **Lennon**. Plus, no lemon associations.

Lenny (German: variation of **Leonard**, "bold lion"). Also, **Lenney.**

Leo (Latin: lion; Italian: variation of **Leonardo**, "bold lion"). *Whatever:* A comer. The **Max** Less Traveled. Like **Max,** it evokes cigar-chomping, retirement home–bound uncles. And yet . . . there's something perversely cute about dubbing a baby **Leo** (or, before it became such a cliché, **Max.**) Championed by TV's *thirtysometing* in the early 1990s, it was the name of yuppies Michael and Hope Steadman's son.

Leon (Greek: brave; Spanish: variation of **Leo**, "lion"). *Whatever:* Could this be another **Leo** or **Max**? It is almost as absurd—and almost as perfect. Not for everybody's tastes, certainly. But at least you can be assured these are names that will grow with, and on, your child.

Leonard (German: bold lion). Also, **Lenard, Lenhard, Leonhard.** Familiar, **Len, Lenny.** *Plus:* You want a back-to-basics name but don't want your boy to march lockstep with the **Michael**s, **Daniel**s, and **Matthew**s? Here's **Leonard** to the rescue. Your boy can wear an old-as-dirt name and still be his own man. *Minus:* Your **Leonard** will be his own nerd.

Leonardo (Italian: variation of **Leonard**, "bold lion"). Familiar, **Leo**. *Whatever:* Look for this one to rise (fall?) in *Titanic* proportion to actor **Leonardo** DiCaprio's career.

Leopold (German: bold people). Also, **Leopolde**.

Les (Scottish/English: variation of **Lesley, Lester**). Also, **Less**. *Whatever:* A nickname that projects lowered expectations?

Lesley (Scottish: garden of holly, gray fort). Also, **Leslie, Lesly**. Familiar, **Les**. *Whatever:* Always an iffy prospect when a girl name doubles as a boy name. (Not as big an issue the other way around.) On the one hand, **Lesley** is the classic calling card of a gentleman. On the other hand, it's black-tie in a dress-casual universe—*and* it's a girl name.

Lester (Latin: army camp). Familiar, **Les**. *Whatever:* The most famous modern-day **Lester** belongs to the famed ventriloquist act Willie Tyler and **Lester**. **Lester** is the dummy.

Levi (Hebrew: devotion). Also, **Levy**. *Plus:* As sales of **Levi's** (the blue jeans) slip, **Levi** (the baby name) perks up. This newly hip comer is the biblical peer of **Aaron** and **Jacob**. *Minus:* Downward business trend or no, the blue jeans jokes *will* be there.

Lew (English/German: variation of **Lewis, Lewin**).

Lewelin (Latin: lionlike). Also, **Lewelinn, Lewelyn, Lewelynn**. *Plus:* The hip-looking version of **Llewellyn**. *Minus:* Still sounds like **Llewellyn**.

Lewin (English: beloved friend). Also, **Lewyn**. Familiar, **Lew**. *Whatever:* Attention, spelunkers: You have now arrived at the "unique" **Lewis/Louis**.

Lewis (German: to fight; English: variation of **Louis**, "glorious warrior"). Also, **Lewys**. Familiar, **Lew**. *Whatever:* With its virtual twin **Louis**, this name is a pocket T.

Lex (English: variation of **Alexander**, "protector, defender"). Also, **Lexx**. *Plus:* You love *Dynasty* names. *Minus:* You're partial to *Lois and Clark*—ain't no little **Lex** Luthor namesake coming into your house.

Lexie (English: variation of **Alexander**, "protector, defender"). Also, **Lexey, Lexy**.

Liam (Irish: variation of **William,** "will, helmet"). Also, **Liem, Lyam, Lyem.** *Whatever:* A comer. Utterly handsome, utterly *not* a peanut-butter-and-jelly sandwich. Popularized by actor **Liam** Neeson.

Linc (English: variation of **Lincoln,** "colony of lakes"). Also, **Lync.** *Whatever:* Can Gen X affection for 1970s retro bring this nifty *Mod Squad* favorite all the way into today? Some will certainly have fun trying.

Lincoln (English: colony of lakes). Also, **Lyncoln.** Familiar, **Linc.** *Whatever:* Anything associated with Abraham **Lincoln** has legs. Call this one a presidential pocket T.

Lindley (English: blue-flowered plant). Also, **Lindly, Lyndley, Lyndly.** *Whatever:* A total Thurston Howell III.

Lindsay (English: soft-spoken). Also, **Lindsae.**

Lindsey (English: variation of **Lindsay,** "soft-spoken"). Also, **Lindsy.** *Plus:* A preppie cuddly bear that will start looking good to Gen Xer parents in their midthirties—when the inevitable yuppiefication settles in, and the desire to raise a future litigator or law professor becomes more profound. *Minus:* A choice that will start looking good to all prospective parents of sons when it stops being a trendy girl name.

Linus (Greek: grief). Also, **Lynus.** *Plus:* Hey, why not? Who reads "Peanuts" anymore anyway? *Minus:* More people than you, or your child, would probably care to meet.

Lionel (French: variation of **Leo,** "lion"). Also, **Lionell.** *Whatever:* A pick to click. Sounds strong and, if not contemporary, then at least classically classy.

Lloyd (Welsh: gray). Also, **Loyd.** *Plus:* Nerdy cool. *Minus:* Nerdy, no cool.

Logan (Irish: love). Also, **Logen, Logyn.** *Whatever:* The hippest boy L name going. Great moniker for one of those future litigators and/or law professors if it didn't sound like it belonged to a bare-chested soap-opera studmuffin. In short, it's a tad dramatic. And because of its nouveau popularity, **Logan** is possible trendy suspenders material.

Lon (Irish: fierce; English: variation of **Alonso, Alonzo**). Also, **Lonn.** Familiar, **Lonnie.** *Plus:* Simple, honest, real. *Minus:* Actually, can we go back to **Logan** again? It's starting to look better.

London (English: fortress of the moon). Also, **Londen.** *Plus:* A very cool map name. **London** is a versatile pick that works on three levels: (1) You can use it to pay tribute to writer Jack **London;** (2) You can use it to make **Dakota**s feel provincial; and (3) You can use it because it just somehow sounds today. *Minus:* It somehow sounds like a girl name.

Lonnie   (Irish: variation of **Alonso, Alonzo, Lon**). Also, **Lonney, Lonny.**

Lorant   (Salvic: variation of **Lawrence,** "crowned with laurel"). Also, **Lorent, Lorynt.**

Loren   (Latin: lost; English: variation of **Lawrence,** "crowned with laurel"). Also, **Lorin, Loryn.** *Plus:* The today **Lawrence.** *Minus:* The girlie **Lauren** look-alike, sound-alike.

Lorenzo   (Italian: variation of **Lawrence,** "crowned with laurel"). Also, **Lorinzo, Lorynzo.**

Loris   (Scandinavian: clown). Also, **Loriss, Lorys, Loryss.**

Lorne   (Latin: bereft; English: variation of **Lawrence,** "crowned with laurel"). Also, **Lorn.**

Lorry   (English: variation of **Laurence, Lawrence**). Also, **Lorey, Lorrey, Lory.**

Lou   (French: variation of **Louis,** "glorious warrior"). *Whatever:* On paper *Lou* should be a candidate for Gen X boosterism. It's real, it's down to earth, yadda yadda yadda. In reality, it's a baby name with Ed (**Lou** Grant) Asner's face attached.

Louden   (English: low valley). Also, **Loudin, Loudyn.** *Whatever:* A doable Thurston Howell III. For the baby who will take his first steps in itty-bitty Topsiders.

Louie   (French: variation of **Louis,** "glorious warrior"). Also, **Louey.**

Louis   (French: glorious warrior). Also, **Louyis.** Familiar, **Lou, Louie.** *Whatever:* True, **Louis** won't win any popularity contests. But just because a pocket T isn't in, doesn't mean it's out—it's just sort of stuffed in the back of your closet. This is a name that's every bit as road-tested as **John** or **Robert.**

Lovell   (English: little wolf). Also, **Lovel, Lovil, Lovill, Lovyl, Lovyll.**

Lovett   (English: variation of **Lovell,** "little wolf"). Also, **Lovet, Lovit, Lovitt, Lovyt, Lovytt.**

Lowell   (English: beloved, young wolf). Also, **Llowel, Llowell, Lowel.** *Whatever:* A perfectly good preppie name that had a good twenty points knocked off its I.Q. thanks to TV's *Wings* and its dim-witted **Lowell** character. On the upside, that show's gone to the great beyond, so maybe nobody will remember. (Fat chance with all those cable reruns.) The safest bet may be to opt for **Lovell** and sidestep the issue entirely.

Lowery (English: variation of **Lawrence,** "crowned with laurel").

Lowry (English: variation of **Lawrence,** "crowned with laurel").

Luc (French: variation of **Lucius,** "daybreak"). Also, **Luk.**

Lucan (Irish: variation of **Lucius,** "daybreak"). Also, **Lucen, Lucyn.** *Plus:* Wiggle room on the trendier **Luke.** *Minus:* For students of 1970s TV, **Lucan** will forever be linked to *Lucan,* the show about the boy raised by wolves.

Lucas (Latin: variation of **Lucius,** "daybreak"). Also, **Luckas, Lukas.** Familiar, **Luke.** *Whatever:* An offbeat sensitive, cute boy that'll hold its own in homeroom against the **Justin**s and **Jordan**s.

Lucian (Latin: variation of **Lucius,** "daybreak"). Also, **Lucien.** Familiar, **Luke.**

Luciano (Italian: variation of **Lucius,** "daybreak").

Lucius (Latin: daybreak). Familiar, **Luke.**

Luigi (Italian: variation of **Louis,** "glorius warrior").

Luis (Spanish: variation of **Louis,** "glorious warrior").

Luke (Latin: variation of **Lucas, Lucian, Lucius**). *Plus:* More poular as a stand-alone than its root names, **Luke** is a contemporary peer of **Jack** and **Nick.** A long-lasting, ready-to-wear pocket T. *Minus:* None.

Luther (English: famous warrior). Also, **Luthor.** *Plus:* Sturdy, biblical. *Minus:* Another name with Superman villain issues.

Lyle (Scottish: little; English: island). Also, **Lile.** *Whatever:* All the sounds of **Kyle,** with little of the attendant preciousness or popularity.

Lyman (English: meadow, beside the waterfall). Also, **Liman.**

Lyndell (English: valley of lime trees). Also, **Lindel, Lindell, Lyndel.** Familiar, **Lynn.**

Lyndon (English: hill of lime trees). Also, **Linden, Lindon, Lynden.** Familiar, **Lynn.** *Whatever:* Another usable prosepct with presidential roots, à la **Lyndon** B. Johnson.

Lyndsay (English: variation of **Lindsay,** "soft-spoken"). Also, **Lyndsae.**

Lyndsey (English: variation of **Lindsay,** "soft-spoken"). Also, **Lyndsy.**

Lynel (French: variation of **Leo,** "lion"). Also, **Lynell.**

Lynn (Welsh: lake; English: variation of **Lyndell, Lyndon, Lynwood**). Also, **Lin, Linn, Lyn.** *Whatever:* Stay mindful of the girl-name dilemma and use with caution.

Lynwood (English: forest waterfall). Also, **Linwood, Linwoode, Lyn-woode.** Familiar, **Lynn.**

Lyon   (French: lion). *Whatever:* Pop-culture junkies will recall that **Lyon** Burke is the elusive dream man of Jacqueline Susann's *Valley of the Dolls.*

Lyonel (French: variation of **Lionel,** "lion"). Also, **Lyonell.**

M

CRIB NOTES

Famous Ms: **Macaulay** Culkin (former child star); **Malcolm** X (icon); **Mandy** Patinkin (actor, *The Princess Bride);* **Mark** Wahlberg (underwear model/actor); **Marlon** Brando (actor); **Marquis** Grissom (baseball player); **Martin** Scorsese (filmmaker); **Matthew** Mc-Conaughey (actor, *Contact*); **Mel** Gibson (actor); **Michael** Jordan (basketball god); **Mickey** Mantle (baseball god); **Montgomery** Clift (actor, *A Place in the Sun*)

Pocket Ts: **Mark, Martin, Matthew, Michael**

Trendy suspenders: **Max**

Think long, think hard: **Macbeth** (Shakespeare, schmakespeare. You're having a baby, not planning a night at the old Globe.); **Manfred** (Sounds like the first half of a drive-in double feature.); **Manley** (Real men don't go around telling people what real men they are.); **Marmaduke** (Yeah, **Marmaduke**'s cool—and his comic strip's funny too.); **Marv** (One word: Albert. Second and third words: Hair weave. Fourth word: Nooooo!); **Maurice** (**Nancy** would be a more macho choice.); **Maury** (Slice it, dice it, make a talk-show host out of it, **Maurice** doesn't get any better in nickname form.); **Maynard** (Bears an unsettling resemblance to "mayonnaise."); **Melvin** (No.); **Merlin** (If **Merlin** was so magical, how come he couldn't zap himself a better name?); **Merv** (Strictly a **Merv** Griffin thing.); **Millard** (No.); **Morley** (Sure, **Morley** Safer made it to *60 Minutes*. How many other **Morleys** walk the streets, crying, "Why me? . . . Why me?"); **Mortimer** (No.); **Munroe** (Namesake of the most unrelentingly annoying TV sitcom character *ever*—

Munroe Ficus of *Too Close for Comfort* infamy.); **Myron** (Pocket pencil holder not included.)

The "Macs": A note before we begin. The *Mac* prefix—Scottish for "son of"—presents an opportunity to make a Jr. without (exactly) doing the clone thing. Try attaching it as a prefix to **Adam, Andrew, Arthur, Cain, Daniel, Dermot, Henry, William.** Or better yet, *give the kid his own name.*

Mac (Scottish: son of; variation of **Macaulay, Macauliffe, Macdowell, Macgowan, Mackeane, Mackenna, Mackenzie, Mackinney, Maclean, Macleod**). Also, **Mack, Mak.** *Plus:* A rough-and-ready performer in the tradition of **Jack.** *Minus:* Two things: (1) Not enough name in the name. Where do you go from **Mac**?; (2) The Big **Mac** issue.

Macaulay (Scottish: son of the rock). Also, **Macalay.** Familiar, **Mac, Mackie.** *Whatever:* Its stock is tied to former *Home Alone* kid **Macaulay** Culkin.

Macauliffe (Scottish: son of ancestor's relic). Also, **Macaulif, Macauliff.** Familiar, **Mac, Mackie.**

Macdowell (Scottish: son of dark-complected foreigner). Also, **Macdowel.** Familiar, **Mac, Mackie.**

Macgowan (Scottish: son of the metalworker). Also, **Macgowen, Macgowyn.** Familiar, **Mac, Mackie.**

Mackeane (Scottish: son of the sharp man). Also, **Mackeene.** Familiar, **Mac, Mackie.**

Mackenna (Scottish: son of the fire god). Also, **Mackena.** Familiar, **Mac, Mackie.** *Whatever:* A perfect name for a TV cop.

Mackenzie (Scottish: son of fair, bright one). Also, **Mackenzey, Mackenzy.** Familiar, **Mac, Mackie.** *Whatever:* **Mackenzie** Astin played plucky orphan Andy Moffett on TV's *The Facts of Life.*

Mackeon (Scottish: son of wealthy man). Familiar, **Mac, Mackie.**

Mackie (Scottish: variation of **Mac, Macaulay, Macauliffe, Macdowell, Macgowan, Mackeane, Mackenna, Mackenzie, Mackeon, Mackinney, Maclean, Macleod**). Also, **Mackey.**

Mackinney (Scottish: son of fair hero). Also, **Mackinny.** Familiar, **Mac, Mackie.**

Maclean (Scottish: son of **John**). Also, **Macleen.** Familiar, **Mac,**

Mackie. *Whatever:* Namesake of McDonald's low-fat burger, the **McLean** Deluxe. Fortunately, McDonald's discovered consumers didn't really want low-fat burgers, so it discontinued the **McLean** Deluxe, leaving *M*A*S*H* costar **McLean** Stevenson as the name's more palatable standard-bearer. Unless you remember his after-*M*A*S*H* sitcom *Hello, Larry.*

Macleod (Irish: son of the people). Also, **Macloud.** Familiar, **Mac.** *Whatever:* Another perfect name for a TV cop. In fact, this *was* a name for a TV cop, Dennis Weaver's *McCloud* (1970-77).

Madden (Irish: little). Also, **Maddin, Maddyn, Maden, Madin, Madyn.**

Madison (English: variation of **Matthew,** "gift of God"). Also, **Madisen, Madysen, Madyson.** *Plus:* A map name (as in **Madison,** Wisconsin); a presidential name (as in commander in chief number four, James **Madison.**) *Minus:* Increasingly, a *girl* name.

Madoc (Celtic: fire). Also, **Maddoc, Maddock, Maddok, Madock, Madok.**

Mal (Latin: bad; variation of **Malcolm,** "servant"). *Whatever:* Just about the jazziest nickname going.

Malcolm (Celtic: servant). Also, **Malcom, Malcomb, Malcombe, Malcolme.** Familiar, **Mal.** *Whatever:* **Morgan** and **Madison** gone to the girls? **Malcolm** to the rescue. Strong and wide-shouldered—ain't no sister gonna steal this one's birthright. It may sound British to our ears, but, please, if we embraced the Spice Girls, we certainly can extend the same courtesy to **Malcolm.** A pick to click.

Malik (Hindi: king). Also, **Maleec, Maleek, Malic, Maleeque, Malique.**

Malone (Irish: devotee). *Plus:* You inexplicably love **Manley,** but acknowledge that it's a bit much. Still looking for something testosterone-charged, you stop at **Malone,** the namesake of Burt Reynold's 1987 shoot 'em-up flick, *Malone.* Now *that's* a boy name. *Minus:* Unless, of course, *that* becomes a girl name. Does **Malone** have the potential to become the new **Murphy**—another moniker that was swiped by the girls?

Mandy (Latin: beloved). Also, **Mandey.** *Whatever:* Swiped, stolen, taken by the girls—it's gone, totally. For die-hard **Mandy** Patinkin fans only.

Manning (English: son of a servant, little person). Also, **Mannyng.**

Manny (English: variation of **Emmanuel, Immanuel, Manuel**). Also, **Manney**.

Manse (English: minister's house).

Mansfield (English: parson's field). Also, **Mansfielde**.

Mantel (English: fireplace shelf). Also, **Mantell, Mantle**.

Manuel (Hebrew: variation of **Emmanuel**, "God is with us"). Familiar, **Manny**.

Marcel (French: variation of **Marcellus**, "warlike"). Also, **Marcell**.

Marcellus (Latin: variation of **Marcus**, "warlike"). Also, **Marcellous, Marcelous, Marcelus**.

March (French: military steps; English: the month). Also, **Marche**.

Marciano (Italian: variation of **Martin**, "warrior"). Also, **Marcyano**.

Marco (Italian: variation of **Marcus**, "warlike"). Also, **Marcko, Marko**. *Plus:* **Mark** with a twist. *Minus:* "**Marco** . . . Polo! **Marco** . . . Polo!" (The preceding taunt can be mitigated if you keep the kid at least one hundred yards away from *all* swimming pools at *all* times.)

Marcos (Spanish: variation of **Marcus**, "warlike"). Also, **Marcos, Markos**. Familiar, **Mark**.

Marcus (Latin: warlike). Also, **Marckus, Markus**. Familiar, **Mark**.

Mariner (English: sailor).

Mario (Italian: sailor).

Marius (Latin: warlike). Also, **Marrius**.

Mark (Latin: warrior; Spanish/Latin/English: variation of **Marcos, Marcus, Markham**). Also, **Marc, Marck**. *Plus:* A no-brainer pocket T. **Mark** may not excite, but it doesn't disappoint either. No future therapy bills (virtually) guaranteed. If you want to dress up the birth certificate, try starting with **Marcus** or **Marcos**, then downsizing. *Minus:* To adventuresome spelunkers, this is the sort of fish—or rather peanut-butter-and-jelly sandwich—you throw back. And maybe that's one reason **Mark** has been backsliding down the popularity charts since the 1960s.

Markham (English: border dweller). Also, **Marcham, Marchem, Marckham, Marckhem, Markham, Markhem**. Familiar, **Mark**. *Plus:* The fancy **Mark**. *Minus:* The prissy **Mark**. Again, try **Marcus** or **Marcos** first.

Marlon (French: falcon). *Whatever:* The power of one letter. *E* instead of *a* in the second position and you've got the less-than-magical **Merlin**. *A* instead of *e* and you've got the more adaptable **Marlon**. This borderline nerd name, though, was probably a lot hipper a couple, three, **Marlon** Brando waistlines ago.

Marlowe (English: hill by the lake). Also, **Marlow.** *Plus:* A tribute to existentialist tough guy Phillip **Marlowe.** *Minus:* A sound-alike for optimistic *That Girl,* **Marlo** Thomas.

Marque (French: a sign). Also, **Marcqe, Marcque, Marqe.**

Marques (Portuguese: noble). Also, **Marqes, Marqis, Marquis.**

Marquez (Spanish: noble). Also, **Marqez.**

Marquis (French: version of **Marcus,** "warlike"). Also, **Marqis, Marquys, Marqys.**

Marsden (English: border valley). Also, **Marsdin, Marsdyn.**

Marsh (English: a swamp). Also, **Marshe.**

Marshall (English: administrator, chief). Also, **Marshal, Marshel, Marshell.** *Plus:* A pick to click. This is an entry that projects strength, thanks to the likes of *Gunsmoke's* **Marshal** Matt Dillon. A worthy lil' cowpoke. *Minus:* Quit dreaming. It's but a couple of notches up on the nerd scale from **Maurice.**

Marston (English: town by the marsh). Also, **Marsten.**

Martin (Latin: warrior; French: swift). Also, **Martyn.** Familiar, **Marty.** *Plus:* A pocket T is made of such stuff: **Martin** is a classic worn by a sainted modern man, civil rights leader Reverend **Martin** Luther King Jr. *Minus:* The inevitable "**Martin,** the martian" taunts. (So much for lofty roots.)

Martino (Italian: variation of **Martin,** "warrior"). Also, **Martyno.** Familiar, **Marty.**

Marty (Latin/French/Italian: variation of **Martin, Martino**). Also, **Martie, Martey.**

Marvell (Latin: miracle, wonderful). Also, **Marvel, Marvil, Marvill, Marvyl, Marvyll.**

Mason (English: stonecutter). Also, **Masen.** *Whatever:* Wiggle room on the girl-swiped **Morgan**?

Mateo (Spanish: variation of **Matthew,** "gift of God"). Also, **Matteo.**

Mather (Greek: student; Hebrew: given).

Matheson (English: son of **Matthew**). Also, **Mathesen, Mathisen, Mathison, Mathysen, Mathyson.** Familiar, **Matt, Matty.**

Matheu (German: variation of **Matthew,** "gift of God"). Familiar, **Matt, Matty.**

Mathias (Swedish: variation of **Matthew,** "gift of God"). Familiar, **Matt, Matty.**

Matlock (English: oak trees). Also, **Matloc, Matlok.** *Plus:* Robust, sturdy. *Minus:* Andy Griffith-esque.

Mats (Scandinanvian: variation of **Matthew,** "gift of God").

Matt (English: variation of **Matheson, Matheu, Mathias, Matteus, Matthew, Matthews, Matthewson, Mattison**). Also, **Mat.**

Matteus (Scandinavian: variation of **Matthew,** "gift of God"). Also, **Mateus.** Familiar, **Matt, Matty.**

Matthew (Hebrew: gift of God; English: variation of **Matthewson,** "son of **Matthew**"). Also, **Mathew.** Familiar, **Matt, Matty.** *Whatever:* A monster pocket T. It's been on the rise since the 1970s when this soft-spoken entry meshed nicely with the decade's take-it-easy Eagles soundtrack. Today, **Matthew** is in a dogfight with **Michael** for boy name supremacy. In states like Kansas and Minnesota, it's even topping the big guy. So, the inevitable question: Is **Matthew** too popular? Today's preschools certainly do not want for little **Matthew**s and **Matt**s. Ordinarily, this would send parents scurrying to other, undiscovered countries. But **Matthew** isn't ordinary. It *really* is trend-proof. And don't expect it to cool anytime soon either. Not with two twentysomething movie stars (**Matthew** McConaughey and **Matt** Damon) flaunting its assets.

Matthews (English: variation of **Matthew,** "gift of God"). Also, **Mathews.** Familiar, **Matt, Matty.**

Matthewson (English: son of **Matthew**). Also, **Mathewsen, Mathewson, Matthewsen.** Familiar, **Matt, Matthew, Matty.**

Mattison (English: son of **Matthew**). Also, **Matisen, Matison, Mattisen, Mattysen, Mattyson, Matysen, Matyson.** Familiar, **Matt, Matty.**

Matty (English: variation of **Matheson, Matheu, Mathias, Matteus, Matthew, Matthews, Matthewson, Mattison**). Also, **Mattey, Maty.**

Max (English/Latin: variation of **Maxim, Maximilian, Maxwell**). Also, **Maxx.** *Plus:* What the coolest Hollywood babes are wearing today. *Minus:* Cigars are what the "coolest" Hollywood celebs are smoking today—and who won't bet that that fad fades fast? Total trendy suspenders.

Maxim (Latin: greatest). Also, **Maxum, Maxym.** Familiar, **Max.**

Maximilian (Latin: greatest). Also, **Maximillian, Maxymilian, Maxymillian.** Familiar, **Max.**

Maxwell (English: big spring). Also, **Maxwel.** Familiar, **Max.** *Plus:* The "unique" way to get to **Max.** *Minus:* If your ultimate goal is to "get to" **Max,** what's the point of trying to be "unique"?

Mead (English: meadow). Also, **Meade, Meed, Meede.**

Mel (Celtic/Latin: variation of **Melbourne, Melville**). Also, **Mell.** *Plus:* A comfortable flannel shirt. *Minus:* A character on *Alice.*

Melbourne (Latin: good fortune). Also, **Melborn, Melborne, Melbourn.** Familiar, **Mel.** *Whatever:* The doable way to get to **Mel** (over **Melvin**), if you are sufficiently inspired.

Melos (Greek: drama). Also, **Milos, Mylos.**

Melville (Celtic: chief of the people). Also, **Melvill.** Familiar, **Mel.** *Whatever:* For those who never got enough of sophomore American Lit.

Mercer (French: trader).

Merrick (English: work, rule). Also, **Merric, Merrik, Merryc, Merryck, Merryk.**

Merrill (English: famous). Also, **Merill, Merril.** *Plus:* Gentlemanly. *Minus:* Girlie.

Meyer (Hebrew: shining). Also, **Myer.**

Micha (Hebrew: variation of **Michael,** "who is like God?"). Also, **Mica, Micah, Michah.**

Michael (Hebrew: "who is like God?"). Also, **Michal, Mychael, Mychal.** Familiar, **Mick, Mickey, Mike, Mikey.** *Plus:* Remarkable. What else is there to say? Other than that **Michael** is ubiquitous, popular, common, classic, boring, proven, generic, meaningful. You love it. You hate it—you hate it like you hate McDonald's or some other all-encompassing corporation. You grouse about how America is being corrupted by sameness, and then you order a Big Mac—and enjoy it. **Michael** is standard-issue boy wear—the overall number one for nearly three decades now. You admire its credentials (**Michael**s become doctors, lawyers, movie stars, Chicago Bulls) even as you grow suspicious of its everywhereness. The bottom line: **Michael** is the sure thing. Gen Xers are comfortable with it—we were the first generation to come of age under its reign. It's our **John.** It sounds like what a baby boy should be named. *The* pocket T. *Minus:* One potential pop-culture sand trap: Is the erstwhile King of Pop **Michael** Jackson sufficiently famous and weird enough to put the brakes on the train? (He's probably not taken seriously enough for that, but you never know.)

And one last note to spelunkers: If you're naming the kid **Michael,** you're naming the kid **Michael**—*no matter how you spell it.*

Michel (French: variation of **Michael,** "who is like God?"). Also, **Mychel.**

Mick (Irish: variation of **Michael,** "who is like God?"). Also, **Mic, Mik.**

Mickey (Irish: variation of **Michael,** "who is like God?"). Also, **Micky.** *Plus:* Mantel. *Minus:* Mouse.

Miguel (Spanish: variation of **Michael,** "who is like God?"). Also, **Migel.**

Mikael (Scandinavian: variation of **Michael,** "who is like God?"). Also, **Mykael.**

Mike (English: variation of **Michael,** "who is like God?").

Mikhail (Russian: variation of **Michael,** "who is like God?"). Also, **Mikail.**

Miles (Greek: warrior). Also, **Myles.** *Whatever:* A pick to click. Nothing like a cool jazz man (in this case **Miles** Davis) to cast a name in his jazzy, cool image.

Mills (English: a mill). Also, **Mils.**

Milo (German: variation of **Miles,** "warrior"). Also, **Mylo.** *Whatever:* Best known (if at all) to Gen Xers as the revolutionary ape leader in the *Planet of the Apes* movies. But recently adopted by talk-show host Ricki Lake for her firstborn son.

Milt (English: variation of **Milton,** "mill town"). Also, **Milte.**

Miltie (English: variation of **Milton,** "mill town"). Also, **Miltey, Milty.** *Whatever:* Useful in evoking yahoo TV images of Uncle **Miltie,** who has always been more like Great-great-great-Uncle **Miltie** to Gen Xers.

Milton (English: mill town). Also, **Milten.** Familiar, **Milt, Miltie.** *Whatever:* Offbeat but useful in evoking refined, literary images of seventeenth-century poet John **Milton.**

Minnow (English: small fish). Also, **Minnowe, Minow, Minowe.** *Plus:* Different, unique. *Minus: Gilligan's Island*–esque.

Minter (Latin: banker).

Misha (Russian: variation of **Michael,** "who is like God?"). Also, **Meesha, Mysha.**

Mitch (English: variation of **Mitchell, Mitchum**). *Whatever:* **Mitch** has great Gen X credentials. In the tradition of **Hank** and **Jack,** it's stripped and sturdy, projecting a certain humble nobility. A flannel shirt and a pick to click.

Mitchell   (English: small loaf of bread). Also, **Mitchel.** Familiar, **Mitch.** *Whatever:* The classier way to get to **Mitch.**

Mitchum   (English: great homestead). Also, **Mitchem.** Familiar, **Mitch.**

Mohammed   (Arabic: great praise). Also, **Mohamed, Mohamid, Mohammid.**

Monte   (Latin: variation of **Montgomery,** "hunter"). Also, **Montey, Montie, Monty.** *Plus:* A comer. Once the stuff of cheesy game-show hosts (**Monty** Hall), it's now the stuff of R.E.M. songs (**Monty** makes the chorus of the band's track "**Monty** Got a Raw Deal"). *Minus:* It's also now the stuff of movies about male strippers (*The Full Monty*).

Montgomery   (Latin: hunter). Also, **Montgomry.** Familiar, *Monte.*

Moreland   (English: boggy land). Also, **Mooreland, Moorland, Moorlande, Morland, Morlande.**

Morgan   (Welsh: born of the sea, bright). Also, **Morgen, Morgyn.** *Whatever:* Once and, to a degree, *still* a preppie favorite, that's currently going the way of **Madison**—to the girls.

Morris   (Latin: dark; English: variation of **Morrison,** "son of **Morris**"). Also, **Morris, Morrys, Morryss.** Familiar, **Morry.** *Plus:* Not bad . . . *Minus:* . . . if you're having a spokescat.

Morrison   (English: son of **Morris**). Also, **Morrisen, Morrysen, Morryson.** *Whatever:* Sounds kind of kingly, as in the Doors' Lizard King, Jim **Morrison.** A possible.

Morrow   (English: by the marsh, the next day). Also, **Morrowe.**

Morry   (Latin: variation of **Morris,** "dark"). Also, **Morey, Morrey, Mory.** *Plus:* The slightly hipper-looking **Maury.** *Minus:* The just-as-dorky-sounding **Maury** (*See* Think long, think hard.)

Moses   (Hebrew: rescued from the water). Also, **Mosis, Mosys.** *Whatever:* Is the room getting crowded at **Noah**'s? **Moses** likes to think he's got a pretty good résumé too.

Moshe   (Russian: variation of **Moses,** rescued from the water).

Muhammad   (Arabic: for the founder of the Islamic religion; variation of **Mohammed** "great praise"). Also, **Muhamad, Muhamed, Muhammed.**

Mulder   (Dutch: a miller). *Whatever:* Can *The X-Files* get this surname cranking as a given name? Enough to make it a viable option—probably.

Muldoon (Irish: army commander). Also, **Muldoone, Muldune.**

Murdoch (Irish: sea man). Also, **Murdoc, Murdock, Murdok.**

Murph (Celtic: variation of **Murphy,** "sea warrior").

Murphy (Celtic: sea warrior). Also, **Murphey.** Familiar, **Murph.** *Whatever:* Blame **Murphy** *Brown*. This one's going to the girls too.

Mykal (American; variation of **Michael,** "who is like God?"). Also, **Mykel, Mykyl.**

N

CRIB NOTES

Famous Ns: **Nathaniel** Hawthorne (author, *The Scarlet Letter*); **Neil** Patrick Harris (TV's erstwhile *Doogie Howser, M.D.*); **Nelson** Mandela (South African president); **Newt** Gringrich (former U.S. speaker of the house); **Nicholas** Bradford (the littlest Bradford, TV's *Eight Is Enough*); **Noah** Wyle (actor, TV's *ER*); **Noam** Chomsky (writer); **Norm** Peterson (barfly, TV's *Cheers*)

Pocket Ts: **Nathan, Nathaniel, Neal, Neil, Nick, Noah**

Trendy suspenders: **Nevada**

Think long, think hard: **Napoleon** (A total Madonna.); **Nemo** (Buried—twenty thousand leagues under the sea.); **Nero** (All it takes is one fiddle-happy Roman emperor to ruin a good name.); **Nestor** (Express ride to Nerd City—no exits, no detours.); **Newman** (Was defamed almost weekly on *Seinfeld.*); **Nimrod** (Uh, no.); **Norbert** (Make that a double.); **North Dakota** ("It's **Dakota**-plus! Not just plain old **Dakota**—it's *North* **Dakota**." The preceding provided as a demonstration of how you can talk yourself into almost anything. Make sure you do your baby naming on a full stomach and with a clear head.)

Nadim (Arabic: friend). Also, **Nadeem, Nadym.**
Nadir (Arabic: pledge). Also, **Nadeer, Nadyr.**
Nahum (Hebrew: comforter). Also, **Nahumm.**
Nance (English: valley).
Nando (Spanish: variation of **Ferdinando,** "brave adventurer").
Naren (Hindi: superior). Also, **Narin, Naryn.**

Nash (English: ash tree). Also, **Nashe.** *Plus:* A lil' cowpoke name for our times. *Minus:* A Don Johnson cop show of the 1990s (*Nash Bridges).*

Nasim (Persian: fresh air). Also, **Naseem, Nasym.**

Nasir (Arabic: victor). Also, **Naseer, Nasyr.**

Nat (Hebrew/Spanish: variation of **Nataniel, Nathan, Nathaniel**).

Nataniel (Spanish: variation of **Nathaniel**). Also, **Natanyel.** Familiar, **Nat, Nate.**

Nate (Hebrew/Spanish: variation of **Nataniel, Nathan, Nathaniel**).

Nathan (Hebrew: gift of God). Also, **Nathen, Nathyn.** Familiar, **Nat, Nate.** *Plus:* Handsome and reliable, **Nathan** is a name that feels honest and right. A pocket T. *Minus:* **Nathan** is a name that reminds you of hot dogs.

Nathaniel (Hebrew: gift of God). Also, **Nathanyel.** Familiar, **Nat, Nate.** *Whatever:* A comer and a pocket T, this one's starting to chart in the top fifty in Pennsylvania. What's the secret to its success? Maybe it's being viewed as a similar-feeling, less-trendy alternative to the über N name, **Nicholas.**

Naughton (Irish: pure one). Also, **Naughten.**

Navarro (Spanish: the plains). Also, **Navaro.**

Neal (Irish: variation of **Neil,** "champion"). Also, **Neall.** With **Neil,** a pocket T.

Ned (English: variation of **Edward,** "wealthy guardian"). Also, **Nedd.**

Nehemiah (Hebrew: comforting Lord). Also, **Nehemia, Nehemya, Nehemyah.** *Plus:* Projects all the biblical strength and decency of a **Jacob** or **Joshua** at a fraction of the popularity. *Minus:* Baby naming isn't a time to bargain shop. You don't want your son to be the odd **Nehemiah** out in a playground of Joshes.

Nehemias (Hebrew: variation of **Nehemiah,** "comforting Lord"). Also, **Nehemyas.**

Neil (Irish: champion; variation of **Neilson,** "son of **Neil**"). Also, **Neill.** *Whatever:* A nifty number. It's rakish, it's dignified, it's long-wearing. A pocket T. Fit for outerspace, à la astronaut **Neil** Armstrong.

Neilson (Irish: son of **Neil**). Also, **Neilsen.** Familiar, **Neil.**

Nellis (Irish: variation of **Neil,** "champion"). Also, **Nellys.**

Nells (Scandinavian: variation of **Neil,** "champion"). Also, **Nels.**

Nelson (Scandinavian: son of **Neil**). Also, **Nelsen, Nelssen, Nelsson.** *Plus:* A good square—square, in this case, meaning sturdy. Almost nerdy cool. *Minus:* A reminder of early 1990s pop duo **Nelson.**

Nevada (Latin: snowy). *Plus:* Very today. It's a lil cowpoke, it's a map name. That's two—two!—hot name trends in one. *Minus:* Figure that at least one of these criteria is going to look pretty anachronistic in a decade. Tag this one trendy suspenders.

Neville (English: new town). Also, **Nevil, Nevill, Nevyl, Nevyll, Nevylle.**

Nevin (Irish: little bone). Also, **Nevyn.**

Newcombe (English: newcomer). Also, **Newcom, Newcomb, Newcome.**

Newel (Latin: supporting post). Also, **Newell.**

Newell (English: new hall). Also, **Newel.**

Newland (English: new land). Also, **Newlande.**

Newlin (English: variation of **Newland,** "new land"). Also, **Newlinn, Newlyn, Newlynn.**

Newsome (English: new house). Also, **Newsom.** *Whatever:* A manly man name that doesn't conk you over the head with its bulging biceps.

Newt (English: a small salamander; English/Scottish: variation of **Newton,** "new town"). *Whatever:* Not even during **Newt** Gingrich's brief Capitol Hill honeymoon did this name seem likely to catch the fancy of Americans. Its chances aren't likely to improve now that Gingrich is viewed as just another politician. That said, there *is* something intriguing and kicky about a **Newt.** Of course, maybe in more of a fish rather than a baby name way.

Newton (English/Scottish: new town). Also, **Newten.** Familiar, **Newt.** *Plus:* A worthy tribute to influential scientist and philosopher Sir Isaac **Newton.** *Minus:* One word: Fig.

Niall (Irish: variation of **Neil,** "champion"). Also, **Nial, Nyal, Nyall.**

Nicholas (Latin: victory of the people; English: variation of **Nicholson,** "son of **Nicholas**"). Also, **Nichlas, Nicklas, Nickolas.** Familiar, **Nick, Nicky.** *Whatever:* Is there anything more adorable than a chubby-cheeked, goo-gooing baby boy named **Nicholas?** The picture is warmer and fuzzier than a pair of footsie pajamas. And therein lies the monster appeal of **Nicholas.** It's a classy classic that transitions well from adorable little boy name to manly man moniker. The **Nicholas** revival began in the 1980s, the name being elevated from St. **Nick** familiarity to **Michael** celebrity. Safe money says the name is about to reach critical mass, i.e., the point at which prospective parents decide it's too-too—too trendy, too popular, too cuddly.

Nichols (English: variation of **Nicholas,** "victory of the people"). Also, **Nickols, Nicols, Nikols.** Familiar, **Nick, Nicky.**

Nicholson (English: son of **Nicholas**). Also, **Nicholsen, Nickolsen, Nickolson, Nicolsen, Nicolson.** Familiar, **Nick, Nicky.**

Nick (English: variation of **Nicholas, Nichols, Nicholson, Nicolas, Nikolaus**). Also, **Nic, Nik.** *Whatever:* **Nicholas** may rise, **Nicholas** may fall, but we're hooked on nickname **Nick.** A genuine pocket T. In the tradition of **Jack,** it's a name for a man's man—and a ladies' man.

Nicky (English: variation of **Nicholas, Nichols, Nicholson, Nicolas, Nikolaus**). Also, **Nickey, Nickie.**

Nico (Italian: variation of **Nicola, Nicolas**). Also, **Neeco, Nyco.**

Nicola (Italian: variation of **Nicholas,** "victory of the people"). Also, **Nycola.** Familiar, **Nico.**

Nicolas (Italian: variation of **Nicholas,** "victory of the people"). Also, **Nycolas.** Familiar, **Nick, Nicky, Nico.**

Nigel (Irish: champion). Also, **Nigil, Nygyl.**

Niklas (Scandinavian: variation of **Nicholas,** "victory of the people"). Also, **Niklos.**

Niko (Russian: variation of **Nikolai,** "victory of the people"). Also, **Neeko, Nyko.**

Nikolai (Russian: variation of **Nicholas,** "victory of the people"). Also, **Nickolai, Nickoli, Nicolai, Nicoli, Nikoli.** Familiar, **Niko.**

Nikolaus (German: variation of **Nicholas,** "victory of the people"). Also, **Nicholaus, Nickolaus, Nicolaus.** Familiar, **Nick, Nicky.**

Niles (English: variation of **Nicholas,** "victory of the people"). Also, **Nyles.**

Nils (Scandinavian: variation of **Nicholas, Nilson**). Also, **Nills.**

Nilson (Scandinavian: son of **Nils**). Also, **Nilsen, Nilssen, Nilsson.**

Noah (Hebrew: wandering, peace). Also, **Noa.** *Whatever:* A solid, if— be warned—increasingly popular choice. Reasons for the **Noah** boom are pretty evident. It's a Bible classic that values sturdy reliability over flashy opulence. Trendiness aside, **Noah** isn't going anywhere—it refuses to be washed away. A pocket T.

Noam (Hebrew: friendship). Also, **Noame.**

Noble (English: famous, noteworthy). Also, **Nobel.** *Whatever:* All the qualities of **Noah**—minus the starring role in the Bible—with none of the commonness.

Noe (French: variation of **Noah,** "wandering, peace").

Noel (Latin: born on Christmas Day). Also, **Noell.** *Plus:* A fine, under-exploited sensitive, cute boy name. *Minus:* Will your son grow to loathe Christmas carols?

Nol (Slavic: variation of **Noah,** "wandering, peace"). Also, **Noll.**

Nolan (Irish: noble, famous). Also, **Nolen, Nolyn.** *Whatever:* A pick to click. Crisp, clean, to the point.

Noonan (Irish: little, beloved one). Also, **Noonen, Noonyn.**

Noberto (Spanish: hero). Also, **Norbirto, Norbyrto.**

Norcott (English: northern cottage). Also, **Norcot.**

Norcross (English: northern crossing). Also, **Norcros.**

Norm (English: variation of **Norman,** "man of the North"). *Plus:* Salt of the earth. *Minus:* A *Cheers* barfly.

Norman (English: man of the North). Also, **Normen, Normyn.** Familiar, **Norm, Normy.** *Plus:* No trendy fly-by-night here. **Norman** has a long, long track record. *Minus:* As the namesake for *Psycho* psycho **Norman** Bates, this is a name that just can't catch any breaks. Author **Norman** Mailer is arguably today's most famous **Norman,** and even he once stabbed a now ex-wife.

Normand (Spanish: variation of **Norman,** "man of the North"). Also, **Normande.**

Normando (Spanish: variation of **Norman,** "man of the North")

Normy (English: variation of **Norman,** "man of the North"). Also, **Normie, Normey.**

Norris (English: a nurse, of the north county). Also, **Norrys.**

North (English: a direction, of the North; variation of **Northam, Northbrook, Northcliff, Northcott**). Also, **Northe.** *Plus:* Not so much a map name as a direction name. This is a good thing. You might get more mileage out of something that is less region specific. *Minus:* Two potential bad things: (1) It'll make geography class hell; (2) Rob Reiner once made a movie called *North* about a kid named **North.** It bombed.

Northam (English: enclosed meadow). Also, **Northem, Northym.** Familiar, **North.**

Northbrook (English: northern stream). Also, **Northbrooke.** Familiar, **North.**

Northcliff (English: northern cliff). Also, **Northclif, Northcliffe.** Familiar, **North, Cliff.**

Northcott (English: northern cottage). Also, **Northcot.**

Norton   (English: northern town). Also, **Norten.** *Plus:* The stately, sound-alike alternative to **Norman.** *Minus:* Nerd city.

Norville   (English: northern village). Also, **Norvil, Norvill, Norvyl, Norvyll, Norvylle.**

Norward   (English: warden or protector of the north). Also, **Norwarde.**

Norwood   (English: northern woods). Also, **Norwoode.**

Novak   (Slavic: stranger, newcomer). Also, **Novac, Novack.**

Nowles   (English: a mound). Also, **Nowls.**

Noyce   (English: walnut tree).

Nuncio   (Spanish: messenger). Also, **Nuncyo.**

Nunzio   (Italian: messenger). Also, **Nunzyo.**

Nye   (Irish: champion; Welsh: honor).

O

CRIB NOTES

Famous Os: Cousin **Oliver** (the unlucky Brady, TV's *The Brady Bunch*); **Omar** Sharif (actor, *Doctor Zhivago*); **Orrin** Hatch (U.S. senator); **Orson** Welles (filmmaker, *Citizen Kane*); **Oscar** the Grouch (Muppet, TV's *Sesame Street*); **Ossie** Davis (actor, *Do the Right Thing*); **Owen** Salinger (the littlest Salinger, TV's *Party of Five*); **Ozzie** Smith (ex–baseball player); **Ozzy** Osbourne (heavy-metal head)

Pocket Ts: Oliver, Oscar, Owen

Trendy suspenders: No pick here. No such thing as a trendy O. Every choice is a bit left of mainstream.

Think long, think hard: Odin (A name on steroids. Dubbing your son in honor of the ancient Norse god of gods is a bold move—bordering on the extreme.); **O.J.** (Think we all need a little distance from the trial of the century. Like maybe another century.); **Olaf** (When this book's special edition for eighteenth-century European parents goes to press, we promise to include it among the list of viable choices.); **Opie** (Remember: *The Andy Griffith Show* ended before **Opie** reached manhood and grew to question what Sheriff Taylor and his late mother were smoking when they hatched **Opie**.); **Otis** (Not in. Not cool. Not nerdy cool. Not retro cool. Just out.); **Otto** (Sounds like a *Hogan's Heroes* heavy.)

Oakes (English: oak trees). Also, **Oaks, Okes.**
Oakley (English: oak woods). Also, **Oakly, Okley, Okly.** *Plus:* Something of a reversible jacket. Its English roots allow it to pass for prep-

pie; its twang allows it to pass for Western. *Minus:* The source of a million "Hey, Annie! . . . Annie **Oakley!**" schoolyard taunts?

Obadiah (Hebrew: worshiper). Also, **Obadia, Obedia, Obediah.**

Oberon (German: noble, bear). Also, **Oberron, Oeberon, Oeberron.**

Ocher (Greek: pale yellow clay). Also, **Oacher.**

Octavio (Latin: eighth).

Octavius (Latin: eighth). Also, **Octavyus.**

Octavo (Latin: eight).

Odam (Hebrew: variation of **Adam,** "the maker"). Also, **Odamm, Odem, Odemm.**

Odell (Scandinavian: wealthy). Also, **Odel, Odelle.**

Ogden (English: oak valley). Also, **Ogdin, Ogdyn.** *Whatever:* Offbeat but possessing an undeniably strong sound.

Ogier (German: rich, spear). Also, **Ogear, Ogeer.**

Ohan (Armenian: variation of **John,** "God is gracious). Also, **Ohann.**

Oland (Scandinavian: island). Also, **Olande.**

Olander (Scandinavian: islander). Also, **Olendar, Olynder.**

Olcott (English: old cottage). Also, **Olcot, Olecot, Olecott.**

Olin (English: to inherit). Also, **Olinn, Olyn, Olynn.**

Oliver (French: olive tree). Also, **Olliver, Ollyver, Olyver.** Familiar, **Ollie.** *Whatever:* Distinctive **Oliver** is a survivor. Like Charles Dickens's plucky orphan of the same name, **Oliver** has had difficulty finding a home. Sometimes it sounds dorky (à la the infamous Cousin **Oliver**), sometimes it sounds preppie (à la Ryan O'Neal's Harvard grad from *Love Story*). But through it all, it has never completely lost it. **Oliver** sounds offbeat but not wrong. It can still hang with the **Michaels,** and refuses to sound Jurassic next to the **Codys. Oliver**— a pocket T.

Oliverio (Spanish: variation of **Oliver,** "olive tree"). Also, **Olliverio, Ollyvero, Olyvero.** Familiar, **Ollie.**

Olivero (Italian: variation of **Oliver,** "olive tree"). Also, **Olliverio, Ollyverio, Olyverio.** Familiar, **Ollie.**

Ollie (French/Italian/Sapnish: variation of **Oliver, Oliverio, Olivero**). Also, **Olley, Olly.** *Plus:* You loved kids' TV show *Kukla, Fran and Ollie. Minus:* You only watched *Kukla, Fran and Ollie* when the other *good* kid shows ended.

Olney (English: lonely field). Also, **Olny.**

Olson (Scandinavian: a relic). Also, **Olesen, Oleson, Olessen, Oles-**

son, Olsen, Olssen, Olsson. *Whatever:* A *Little House on the Prairie* name for boys. Use this entry to pay tribute to the Ingalls' fellow townsfolk, the **Oleson**s. . . . Granted, it's a pick for die-hard fans of the show only.

Oman (Arabic: for Arab nation). Also, **Omann.**

Omar (Arabic: better). Also, **Oamar, Oamarr, Omarr.**

Omri (Hebrew: servant of God). Also, **Omrey, Omry.**

O'Neal (Celtic: from the chief's line). Also, **Oneal, O'Neall, Oneall.**

O'Neil (Celtic: variation of **O'Neal,** "from the chief's line"). Also, **Oneil, Oneill, O'Neill.**

Orel (Latin: listener). Also, **Oril, Oryl.**

Oren (Hebrew: cedar). Also, **Orin, Oryn.**

Ori (Hebrew: my light). Also, **Orie, Ory.**

Oriel (Latin: bay window). Also, **Oriell, Oryel, Oryell.**

Orion (Greek: a star constellation). Also, **Oryon.**

Orlando (Italian: famous). *Whatever:* Hey, it's a map name! (About as quasi-hip as an O gets.)

Orman (German: sailor). Also, **Ormann.**

Ormand (Spanish: variation of **Orman,** "sailor"). Also, **Ormande.**

Ormond (English: spear). Also, **Ormonde, Ormund, Ormunde.**

Orne (Scandinavian: eagle).

Orr (English: variation of **Orrick,** "old oak tree").

Orrick (English: old oak tree). Also, **Orric, Orrik, Orryc, Orryck, Orryk.**

Orris (Greek: an iris). Also, **Orriss, Orrys, Orryss.**

Orsini (Italian: variation of **Orson,** "bearlike"). Also, **Orseeni, Orsyni.**

Orsino (Spanish: variation of **Orson,** "bearlike"). Also, **Orseeno, Orsyno.**

Orson (Latin: bearlike). Also, **Orsen.** *Whatever:* All newborns kind of look like **Orson**s anyway (round, regal, easily moved to displeasure), so why not just concede the obvious?

Orton (English: upper town). Also, **Orten.**

Orville (French: gold town). Also, **Orvil, Orvill, Orvyl, Orvyll, Orvylle.**

Osbert (English: divine, bright). Also, **Osberte, Osburt, Osburte.** Familiar, **Ossie.** *Whatever:* Way too close to comic-strip pencil-pusher "Dilbert" to be anything but a nerd name. Only included here as a way to get to the infinitely more hip nickname, **Ossie.**

Osborn (English: man of God). Also, **Osborne, Osbourn, Osbourne.** Familiar, **Ossie.** *Whatever:* This Thurston Howell III is the safer way to get to **Ossie.**

Oscar (English: god, spear). Also, **Oscer.** *Whatever:* Here's another **Oliver**—a baby name that won't win any popularity contests. Commonly derided from the stuff of **Oscar** the *Sesame Street* grouch and **Oscar** Madison the *Odd Couple* slob, it's a nerdy cool pick here. Offbeat, road-tested, reliable   (when given the chance), and, yes, a pocket T.

Osean (Irish: son of **Sean**). Also, **O'Sean, O'Shaun, Oshaun, O'Shawn, Oshawn, O'Shon, Oshon.**

Osgood (English: a good god). Also, **Osgoode.** Familiar, **Ossie.**

Oshane (Irish: son of **Shane**). Also, **O'Shain, Oshain, O'Shane, O'Shayne, Oshayne.**

Oshea (Irish: son of **Shea**). Also, **O'Shae, Oshae, O'Shay, Oshay, O'Shea.**

Oskar (Scandinavian: variation of **Oscar,** "god, spear"). Also, **Osker.**

Osman (English: man of God). Familiar, **Ossie.**

Osmond (English: sheltering God). Also, **Osmonde, Osmund, Osmunde.** Familiar, **Ossie.**

Ossie (English/Spanish: variation of **Osbert, Osborn, Osgood, Osman, Osmond, Oswald, Oswaldo, Oswell, Oswin**). Also, **Ossey, Ossy.** *Plus:* If **Max** can come back, then so can **Ossie.** *Minus:* Unless, of course, you think **Ossie** sounds like **Max**'s less successful, screw-up younger brother.

Osvaldo (Spanish: variation of **Oswald,** "divine power").

Oswald (English: divine power). Also, **Oswalde.** Familiar, **Ossie.** *Plus:* Another way to get to **Ossie.** *Minus:* The Lee Harvey **Oswald** association.

Oswaldo (Spanish: variation of **Oswald,** "divine power"). Familiar, **Ossie.**

Oswell (English: divine power). Also, **Oswel.** Familiar, **Ossie.**

Oswin (English: divine friend). Also, **Oswyn.** Familiar, **Ossie.**

Overland (English: highland). Also, **Overlande.**

Overton (English: town by the riverbank). Also, **Overten.** *Whatever:* Administered a shot of relevancy, courtesy of TV's *Living Single* (1993–98) and the show's building super, **Overton** Jones.

Owen (English/Wesh: nobility). Also, **Owin, Owyn.** *Whatever:* TV's

Party of Five is shining light on this oft overlooked pocket T. (**Owen** is the name of the youngest member of the picture-perfect Salinger clan.) A name of timeless panache that nicely balances its precious and preppie sides.

Owens (English: variation of **Owen**, "nobility"). Also, **Owins, Owyns.**

Oxford (English: ox crossing by the riverbank). Also, **Oxforde.**

Ozbert (English: variation of **Osbert**, "divine, bright"). Also, **Ozberte, Ozburt, Ozburte.** Familiar, **Ozzie.**

Ozborn (English: variation of **Osborn**, "man of God"). Also, **Ozborne, Ozbourn, Ozbourne.** Familiar, **Ozzie.**

Ozgood (English: variation of **Osgood**, "a good god"). Also, **Ozgoode.** Familiar, **Ozzie.**

Ozman (English: variation of **Osman**, "man of God"). Also, **Ozmen, Ozmyn.** Familiar, **Ozzie.**

Ozmond (English: variation of Osmond, "sheltering God"). Also, **Ozmonde, Ozmund, Ozmund.** Familiar, **Ozzie.**

Ozvaldo (Spanish: variation of **Oswald**, "divine power"). Familiar, **Ozzie.**

Ozwald (English: variation of **Oswald**, "divine power"). Also, **Ozwalde.** Familiar, **Ozzie.**

Ozwaldo (Spanish: variation of **Oswald**, "divine power").

Ozwell (English: variation of **Oswell**, "divine power"). Also, **Ozwel.** Familiar, **Ozzie.**

Ozwin (English: variation of **Oswin**, "divine friend"). Also, **Ozwyn.** Familiar, **Ozzie.**

Ozzie (English/Spanish: variation of **Ozbert, Ozborn, Ozgood, Ozman, Ozmond, Ozvaldo, Ozwald, Ozwaldo, Ozwell, Ozwin**). Also, **Ozzey, Ozzy.** *Plus:* A nickname that fills you with warm-and-fuzzy thoughts of back-patting TV dad **Ozzie** Nelson. *Minus:* A nickname that fills you with disturbing thoughts of bat-biting rocker **Ozzy** Osbourne.

P

CRIB NOTES

Famous Ps: **Parker** Stevenson (Frank Hardy, TV's *The Hardy Boys*); **Payne** Stewart (golfer); **Perry** Farrell (rocker/Lollapalooza founder); **Peter** Jennings (network TV news anchor); **Peyton** Manning (football player); **Pierce** Brosnan (Bond, James Bond); **Preston** Sturges (filmmaker, *The Palm Beach Story*)

Pocket Ts: Patrick, Peter

Trendy suspenders: Parker

Think long, think hard: **Pagan** (Maybe—*maybe*—this works as a girl name.); **Percival** (In an enlightened society **Percivals** would be accepted and embraced, allowed to pursue microbiology or wrestling without prejudice. Meanwhile, here on planet Earth, naming a boy **Percival** is tantamount to taping a KICK ME sign on the kid.); **Percy** (Somehow even worse than **Percival**. The mother of all wuss names.); **Plato** (Well, it certainly gives a kid something to live up to.); **Pride** (A 1970s do-gooder's name. If antihero Billy Jack of *Billy Jack Goes to Washington* fame had a son, he would have named him **Pride**.); **Puffy** (It's hip, it's hop, it's not something you name a baby. Ask Mrs. Combs, who started off her future rap mogul with the more solid-sounding **Sean**.)

Pablo (Spanish: variation of **Paul**, "small").
Pack (Irish: variation of **Patrick**, "nobleman"). Also, **Pac, Pak.**
Packy (Irish: variation of **Patrick**, "nobleman"). Also, **Packey.**
Padden (Irish: **Patrick**, "nobleman"). Also, **Paddin, Paddyn.**
Paddy (Irish: variation of **Patrick**, "nobleman"). Also, **Paddey.** *Plus:*

A fresh, distinctive spin on **Patrick**. *Minus:* Too close to that "Patty cake, patty cake" rhyme for comfort.

Padget (English/French: servant). Also, **Padgett, Padgit, Padgitt, Padgyt, Padgytt.**

Padraic (Irish: variation of **Patrick**, "nobleman"). Also, **Padraick, Padraik, Padrayc, Padrayck, Padrayk.**

Padre (Latin: father). Also, **Padrae, Padray.**

Pall (Scandinavian: **Paul**, "small").

Palmer (English: bearing palm branches). *Whatever:* A pick to click. A not-too-stuffy Thurston Howell III that is the peer of sound-alikes **Parker** and **Patrick.**

Paolo (Italian: variation of **Paul**, "small").

Parish (English: church congregation). Also, **Parrish, Parrysh, Parysh.**

Park (English: a park). Also, **Parke.**

Parker (English: park warden, gamekeeper). *Plus:* A comer. An adorable baby name that morphs into a responsible adult name—no tinkering required. *Minus:* Comedian Rosie O'Donnell talks up the name incessantly on her daytime talk show—**Parker** is her son. Do we have another Kathie Lee/**Cody** backlash in the making? Potential trendy suspenders.

Parkes (English: variation of **Park**, "a park"). Also, **Parks.**

Parkinson (English: variation of **Peter**, "rock"). Also, **Parkinsen, Parkynsen, Parkynson.** *Whatever:* Too diseaselike—as in **Parkinson's** disease.

Parley (French: to speak, with an enemy). Also, **Parly.**

Parnell (Latin: stone). Also, **Parnel.**

Parris (English: from Paris). Also, **Paris, Pariss, Parriss, Parrys, Parryss.** *Plus:* A handsome map name. *Minus:* A wimpy girl name?

Parson (English: a clergyman; variation of **Peter**, "rock"). Also, **Parsen.**

Pass (English: move forward).

Pat (Latin: variation of **Patrick**, "nobleman"). *Whatever:* Julia Sweeney's androgynous "It's **Pat**" character has done this nickname no favors—particularly for boys.

Pate (Scottish: noble; English: head). Also, **Pait, Payte.**

Patek (Slavic: variation of **Patrick**, "nobleman"). Also, **Patec, Pateck.**

Pater (Latin: father).

Paterson (English: son of the father). Also, **Patersen, Paterssen, Patersson.**

Patricio (Spanish: variation of **Patrick,** "nobleman"). Also, **Patricyo.**

Patrick (Latin: nobleman). Also, **Patric, Patrik, Patryc, Patryck, Patryk.** Familiar, **Packy, Paddy, Pat.** *Plus:* A prototypical pocket T. Never out of time, never out of place. Classic and classy. Best of all it's not *too* popular. (Inexplicably, no P really is.) *Minus:* In this age, where we aspire to the "unique," is **Patrick** looking like a bland peanut-butter-and-jelly sandwich? Also, will your school-age boy grow to dread March 17?

Patrizio (Italian: variation of **Patrick,** "nobleman"). Also, **Patrizyo.**

Patterson (Scottish: son of **Patrick**). Also, **Pattersen.** Familiar, **Pat.**

Pattison (English: variation of **Patterson,** "son of **Patrick**"). Also, **Pattisen, Pattysen, Pattyson, Patysen, Patyson.**

Patton (English: variation of **Patrick,** "nobleman"). Also, **Patten.** *Plus:* Wiggle room on **Patrick.** *Minus:* The first step on the road to creating your own little barking general.

Paul (Latin: small). Familiar, **Paulie.** *Plus:* A name that bridges the apostles and the Beatles and beyond. A strong, steady performer. Would qualify as a pocket T . . . *Minus* . . . if it somehow didn't sound vaguely 1970s. Clearly, it's not. But Gen Xers went to school with a lot more **Paul**s than we're producing today, so something's not ringing true. Even more than **Patrick, Paul** has a big peanut-butter-and-jelly sandwich image problem.

Paulie (English: variation of **Paul,** "small"). Also, **Pauley, Pauly.** *Whatever:* Paulie has a big **Pauly** Shore image problem.

Paulin (German: variation of **Paul,** "small"). Also, **Paulyn.**

Paulinus (Latin: very small). Also, **Paulinuss, Paulynus, Paulynuss.**

Paulis (Latin: variation of **Paul,** "small"). Also, **Pauliss, Paulys, Paulyss.**

Pavel (Russian: variation of **Paul,** "small"). Also, **Pavell.**

Pax (Latin: peaceful). Also, **Paxx.**

Paxton (Scottish: **Pack's** town). Also, **Paxten.**

Payne (Latin: of the country; English: villager). Also, **Paine, Pane.** *Plus:* Can be used in a preppie emergency—like, when **Parker** busts out too big. *Minus:* A name rich in potential pun material. Could prove to be a real, *ahem,* pain.

Payton (English: variation of **Patrick,** "nobleman"). Also, **Payten.** *Whatever:* A fine Southern gentleman name. Cultured, classy, and contemporary.

Peale (English: hill). Also, **Peal, Peel, Peele.**

Peat (Latin: moss). Also, **Peate, Peet, Peete.**

Peder (Scandinavian: variation of **Peter, Pederson**).

Pederson (Scandinavian: son of **Peter**). Also, **Pedersen.** Familiar, **Peder.**

Pedro (Spanish: variation of **Peter,** "rock").

Peers (English: variation of **Peter, Peerson**).

Peerson (English: variation of **Pierson,** "son of **Pierce**"). Also, **Peersen.**

Pender (English: caretaker of a pen).

Penn (English: a pen, sheep's quarters).

Pentecost (Greek: fiftieth day). Also, **Penticost, Pentycost.**

Perkin (Welsh: variation of **Peter, Perkinson**). Also, **Perkyn.**

Perkins (English: variation of **Peter,** "rock"). Also, **Perkyns.**

Perkinson (English: son of **Perkin,** "rock"). Also, **Perkinsen, Perkynsen, Perkynson.**

Pernell (Latin: variation of **Parnell,** "stone"). Also, **Pernel.**

Perris (English: variation of **Parris,** "from Paris"). Also, **Peris, Periss, Perrys, Perys.**

Perry (English: of the pear tree). Also, **Perrey.** *Plus:* Overlooked—inexplicably so. **Perry** coolly mixes elements of the preppie and the cuddly bear. *Minus:* Here's a theory: Our parents' generation started the big chill toward this name after convicted killer **Perry** Smith, rendered chillingly in Truman Capote's *In Cold Blood,* rose to infamy in the 1960s.

Pete (Greek: variation of **Peter,** "rock").

Peter (Greek: rock; English: variation of **Peterson,** "son of **Peter**"). Familiar, **Pete, Petey.** *Whatever:* This one's got as much history behind it as **Paul**—no Beatles connection, but a *Brady Bunch* one, if that counts for anything—but is more contemporary sounding than its peer. A pocket T.

Peterson (English: son of **Peter**). Also, **Petersen.** Familiar, **Peter.**

Petey (English: variation of **Peter,** "rock"). Also, **Petie, Pety.**

Petro (Greek: variation of **Peter,** "rock").

Petter (Scandinavian: variation of **Peter,** "rock").

Petya (Russian: variation of **Peter,** "rock").

Peyton (English: variation of **Patrick,** "nobleman"). *Whatever:* It's the name of a budding young sports star (footballer **Peyton** Manning). A good sign. Or . . . a red flag that this baby name is about to bust out.

Phelim (Irish: ever good). Also, **Phelym.**

Phil (Greek: variation of **Phillip,** "lover of horses"). Also, **Phill.**

Philemon (Greek: kiss). Also, **Philimon, Philymon.**

Philip (Greek: lover of horses). Also, **Philipp, Philyp, Philypp.** Familiar, **Flip, Phil, Phillie.** *Plus:* Vintage, stalwart. *Minus:* Victorian, stuffy.

Philippe (French: variation of **Phillip,** "lover of horses"). Also, **Philipe, Philype, Philyppe.**

Phillie (Greek: variation of **Phillip,** "lover of horses"). Also, **Philley, Philly.**

Phineas (Hebrew: serpent's mouth). Also, **Phinyeas.**

Pierce (French: to stab; English: variation of **Peter, Pierson**) *Plus:* Strong, timeless. James Bond actor **Pierce** Brosnan's classy looks and suave accent don't hurt either. *Minus:* A touch *Dynasty.*

Piero (Italian: variation of **Peter,** "rock"). Also, **Pierro.**

Pierre (French: variation of **Peter,** "rock"). Also, **Piere.**

Piers (English: variation of **Peter,** "rock").

Pierson (English: son of **Pierce**). Also, **Piersen.**

Pieter (Scandinavian: variation of **Peter,** "rock").

Pietro (Italian: variation of **Peter,** "rock").

Pilgrim (English: wanderer). Also, **Pilgrym.** *Whatever:* Can't get much more salt of the earth than this. The original flannel shirt.

Pillion (English: jump seat). Also, **Pilion, Pillyon, Pilyon.**

Pilot (English: guider).

Pippin (French: seed). Also, **Pipin, Pippyn, Pipyn.**

Piton (French: spike).

Plash (English: a splash). *Whatever:* Unusual but cool—like a pair of dark black sunglasses.

Plat (English: map, plan). Also, **Platt.**

Pluck (English: courage). *Plus:* Sounds like a character that got left out of *To Kill a Mockingbird* . . . *Minus:* . . . a *girl* character.

Poe (English: peacock).

Pollard (English: end of the pool, small). Also, **Polard, Polerd, Pollerd.**

Pons (Latin: bridge). Also, **Ponse.**

Poole (English: body of water).

Port (English: haven; variation of **Porter,** "carrier, gatekeeper"). Also, **Porte.**

Porter (English: carrier, gatekeeper). Familiar, **Port.** *Whatever:* Not just for railroad-luggage luggers anymore. Now that we're safely in the automobile age, **Porter** sounds cool and preppy. A pick to click.

Powell (Welsh: famous). Also, **Powel.**

Powers (Irish: pauper). *Whatever:* About as close to a superhero name as you can get without crossing that Iron Man line.

Prescott (English: priest's cottage). Also, **Prescot.**

Preston (English: priest's town). Also, **Presten.** *Plus:* Nifty tribute to one of the most individual and respected writer/directors of Hollywood's Golden Age, **Preston** Sturges. *Minus:* Just this side of **Percival.**

Price (Welsh: ardor). Also, **Pryce.** *Whatever:* A sound-alike alternative to the more popular, more common **Bryce.**

Primo (Latin: the first). Also, **Preemo, Prymo.** *Plus:* A jazzy cool way of honoring your number one son. *Minus:* OK, so you name the first kid **Primo**. What do you call the second kid? **Leftover**? Good luck refereeing sibling wars in that household.

Prince (English: son of the king). Also, **Prynce.** *Whatever:* Michael Jackson named his firstborn son, **Prince.** Granted, not exactly the *Good Housekeeping* seal of approval. But it's still a pretty nifty name.

Prinze (Latin: variation of **Prince,** "son of the king"). Also, **Prinz, Prynz, Prynze.**

Proctor (English: supervisor, administrator). Also, **Procter.**

Proust (French: for the novelist Marcel **Proust**).

Pryor (English: before, rank just below abbot in the monastery heirarchy). Also, **Prior.** *Whatever:* A pick to click. Stylish, dashing, with just a hint of that trendy Western flair.

Pullman   (English: railroad sleeping car). Also, **Pulman, Pulmann, Pullmann.**

Putnam   (English: one who lives near a pond). Also, **Putnem.** *Whatever:* Usable, but will your little **Putnam** insist on spending summers in the Hamptons?

Pyre (Greek: fire). Also, **Pire, Pyr.**

Q

CRIB NOTES

Famous Qs: **Quentin** Tarantino (filmmaker); **Quincy** Jones (musician/producer/mogul)

Pocket Ts: We're talking about Q here. Nothing's a slam dunk; everything's a tricky bank shot.

Trendy suspenders: Remember the part about this being Q?

Think long, think hard: **Quigley** (Rhymes with squiggly.)

Qabil (Arabic: able). Also, **Qabeel, Qabyl, Quabeel, Quabil, Quabyl.**
Qadim (Arabic: ancient). Also, **Qadeem, Qadym, Quadeem, Quadim, Quadym.**
Qadir (Arabic: talented, powerful). Also, **Qadeer, Qadyr, Quadeer, Quadir, Quadyr.**
Qaeshon (American: variation of **Sean**, "God is gracious"). Also, **Qaesean, Qaeshaun, Qaeshawn, Qaysean, Qayshaun, Qayshawn, Qayshon.**
Qajon (American: variation of **John**, "God is gracious"). Also, **Qajohn, Qejohn, Qejon.**
Qamar (Arabic: moon). Also, **Qemar, Quamar, Quemar.**
Qashon (American: variation of **Sean**, "God is gracious"). Also, **Qasean, Qashaun, Qashawn, Qesean, Qeshaun, Qeshawn, Qeshon.**
Qawon (American: variation of **John**, "God is gracious"). Also, **Qawan, Qewan, Qewon.**
Qequon (American: variation of **Juan**, "God is gracious"). Also, **Qequan, Qeyquan, Qeyquon.**

Qeyshon (American: variation of **Sean,** "God is gracious"). Also, **Qeysean, Qeyshaun, Qeyshawn.**

Quadry (American: from quad, four). Also, **Quadree, Quadrey.**

Quail (French: a partridge). Also, **Quaile, Quayle.**

Quaker (English: follower of the religion).

Quan (Native American: fragrant). Also, **Quann.**

Quandre (American: variation of **Andre,** "brave"). Also, **Quandrae, Quandray.**

Quantay (American: variation of **Quadry,** "from quad, four"). Also, **Quantae.**

Quarry (Latin: stone quarry). Also, **Quarrey.**

Quarto (Latin: fourth).

Quashon (American: variation of **John,** "God is gracious"). Also, **Quasean, Quashaun, Quashawn.**

Quay (Celtic: a wharf). Also, **Quaye.**

Quemby (Norse: woman's house). Also, **Quembey.** *Whatever:* Is **Quemby** too fancy, even by Thurston Howell III standards? Perhaps, but all Qs have that frilly, powdered-wig feel, so whatever. Your call.

Quenby (Norse: variation of **Quemby,** "woman's house"). Also, **Quenbey.**

Quennell (French: oak tree). Also, **Quenel, Quenell, Quennel.**

Quentin (Latin: fifth). Also, **Quentyn.** *Whatever:* Getting a giant hypo of hip to the heart thanks to leading Gen X filmmaker **Quentin** Tarantino (*Pulp Fiction*). A definite comer. The name that could make Q hot. Or relatively warm.

Quenton (Latin: variation of **Quentin,** "fifth"). Also, **Quenten.**

Quest (English: journey).

Quill (Irish: hazel). Also, **Quille.**

Quillon (Latin: crossing swords; Greek: strong). Also, **Quilen, Quillen, Quilon.**

Quimby (Scandinavian: woman's house). Also, **Quimbey.**

Quinby (Scandinavian: variation of **Quimby,** "woman's house"). Also, **Quinbey.**

Quince (Latin: applelike fruit; Scottish; variation of **Quincy,** "estate"). *Whatever:* An offbeat pick to click. A clean, simple, and cool entry. Think of it as **Quincy** unplugged.

Quincy (Scottish: estate). Also, **Quincey.** Familiar, **Quince.** *Plus:* A versatile performer. Conveys a jazzy cool courtesy of **Quincy** Jones.

Conveys a presidential strength courtesy of John **Quincy** Adams. Conveys a medical examiner's care of detail courtesy of Jack Klugman's *Quincy*. *Minus:* **Quincy** is exactly the sort of prissy, precious name that'll become the title of the next TV sitcom to star a diminutive child actor, à la *Webster*.

Quinlan   (Irish: graceful). Also, **Quindlan, Quindlen, Quindlyn, Quinlen, Quinlyn.** Familiar, **Quinn.** *Whatever:* Wiggle room on the trendier **Cameron** and **Conlan.**

Quinlay   (Irish: variation of **Quinlan**, "graceful"). Also, **Quindlae, Quindlay, Quinlae.** Familiar, **Quinn.**

Quinley   (Irish: variation of **Quinlan**, "graceful"). Also, **Quindley, Quindly, Quinly.** Familiar, **Quinn.**

Quinn   (Irish: bushy-haired, heart; variation of **Quinlan, Quinlay, Quinley**). Also, **Quin.** *Plus:* A classy, no-fuss name for today. *Minus:* The only **Quinn**s you know—assuming you actually know one—are girls.

Quinsy   (Greek: tonsillitis; Scottish: variation of **Quincy**, "estate"). Also, **Quinsey.**

Quint   (Latin: variation of **Quinton**, "fifth"). Also, **Quinte.** *Plus:* **Clint**—with a little something extra. *Minus:* With a name like **Quint,** don't be surprised if inquiring minds ask where the kid's four other siblings are.

Quintay   (American: variation of **Quantay**, "from quad, four"). Also, **Quintae.**

Quintero   (Spanish: five). Also, **Quinterro.**

Quinton   (Latin: variation of **Quentin**, "fifth"). Also, **Quinten.** Familiar, **Quint.**

Quiran   (Irish: black, dark). Also, **Qiran, Qiren, Qiryn, Quiren, Quiryn.**

Quire   (English: set of paper).

Quirin   (Irish: magical). Also, **Qirin, Qiryn, Quiryn.**

Quito   (Spanish: variation of **Quentin**, "fifth"). Also, **Qeeto, Qito, Queeto, Quyto, Qyto.**

Quon   (Chinese: bright). Also, **Quonn.**

R

CRIB NOTES

Famous Rs: **Ralph** Kramden (bus driver, TV's *The Honeymooners*); **Randy** Travis (country singer); **Ray** Bradbury (author, *Fahrenheit 451*); **Redd** Foxx (comedian); **Richard** Pryor (comedian); **Rider** Strong (actor, TV's *Boy Meets World*); **River** Phoenix (actor); **Rock** Hudson (actor); **Rodney** Allen Rippy (TV spokeskid of the 1970s); **Ronald** Reagan (U.S. president); **Rupert** Murdoch (mogul); **Rush** Limbaugh (radio personality)

Pocket Ts: **Reed, Reid, Richard, Robert**

Trendy suspenders: No pick here. About the trendiest thing going is **Ryan** and that's been trendy for some two decades now, a tad long to be considered a fly-by-night.

Think long, think hard: **Regis** (Works well for **Regis** Philbin. And if your boy grows up to cohost a chatty morning talk show, maybe it'll work swell for him too. In the meantime, there are schoolyard bullies to consider.); **Rene** (Unfortunately, schoolyard bullies must be taken into account before selecting many fine names—especially ones that sound best fit for a French chanteuse.); **Ridge** (A dramatically masculine entry. Fit for the daytime soap *The Bold and the Beautiful,* from whence it came.); **Ringo** (Fortunately, there are three other Beatles from which to choose.); **Rock** (The male equivalent of a bimbo name.); **Rocky** (Two words: Yo, Adrian. Two more words: Where's Bullwinkle?); **Romeo** (They still read Shakespeare in junior high, right?); **Roscoe** (Last notable pop-culture figure to model this one was Sheriff **Rosco** Coltrane of TV's *The Dukes of Hazzard.*)

Rad (English: red; variation of **Radcliff, Radford, Radley, Radliff**). Also, **Radd.** *Plus:* Totally tubular! *Minus:* Um, maybe you should start off with one of the root names. No need to downsize needlessly.

Radcliff (English: red cliff). Also, **Radclif, Radcliffe.** Familiar, **Rad.**

Radford (English: red ford, river crossing). Also, **Radforde.** Familiar, **Rad.**

Radley (English: red brook). Also, **Radly.** Familiar, **Rad.**

Radliff (English: variation of **Radcliff,** "red cliff"). Also, **Radlif, Radliffe.** Familiar, **Rad.**

Rafaele (Italian: variation of **Raphael,** "healed by God"). Also, **Rafael.** Familiar, **Raffi.**

Rafe (English/Irish: variation of **Rafferty, Ralph**). Also, **Raife, Rayfe.**

Rafer (Irish: variation of **Rafferty,** "prosperous").

Raff (Irish: variation of **Rafferty,** "prosperous"). Also, **Raf.**

Rafferty (Irish: prosperous). Also, **Rafertey, Raferty, Raffertey.** Familiar, **Raff.**

Raffi (Hebrew: exalted; variation of **Rafaele, Raphael**). Also, **Rafi, Raffy, Rafy.**

Raiment (English: clothing). Also, **Raimint, Raimynt, Rayment, Raymint.**

Rainer (German: mighty counsel). Also, **Rainor, Rayner, Raynor.**

Raines (English: frog, boundary line). Also, **Raynes.** *Whatever:* An ingenious blend of the hippie and the yuppie. You start with *rain* to satisfy the tree-hugger in you, then add the *es* to assure that the name will look sufficiently adultlike on business cards one day.

Rainey (Scottish: judge).

Raj (Indian: ruling government in India; American: variation of **Roger, Rogers**). *Whatever:* Let's play word association. Word: **Raj.** Association: "Hey, hey, hey! . . . *What's Happening!!*"

Raleigh (English: red meadow).

Ralph (English: counselor, wolf). Also, **Ralphe.** Familiar, **Ralphie.** *Whatever:* How out of it is **Ralph** these days? Its most famed current user is actor **Ralph** Fiennes, a guy who refuses to own up to his **Ralph**-ness and instead goes around calling himself "**Rafe.**" The lesson? Plain old **Ralph** is too lunchbox for modern tastes. Will Gen Xers recognize its earnest **Hank**-ness and rescue it from the reject pile? Well, since one of **Ralph**'s other problems is that it's a common college euphemism for the act of vomiting (as in, "to ralph"), probably not. Still, it's ethnic variations are almost uniformly rakish, unique, and—dare we say?—cool.

Ralphie (English: variation of **Ralph,** "counselor, wolf"). Also, **Ralphey, Ralphy.**

Ralston (English: **Ralph**'s town). Also, **Ralsten.**

Ram (English: male sheep; Scottish: variation of **Ramsay, Ramsey**). Also, **Ramm.** *Whatever:* A pick to click. It's strong, it's naturelike (those little horned goats, you know), and, hey—it's of the computer age. It's not every name that allows you to safely and covertly dub your kid in honor of Random Access Memory.

Rame (Hindi: godlike). Also, **Raime, Rayme.**

Ramiro (Spanish: supreme judge). Also, **Ramyro.**

Ramon (Spanish: variation of **Raymond,** "mighty counsel, protector"). Also, **Ramone.**

Ramsay (Scottish: variation of **Ramsey, "Ram**'s isle"). Also, **Ramsae.** Familiar, **Ram.**

Ramsey (Scottish: **Ram**'s isle). Also, **Ramsy.** Familiar, **Ram.** *Plus:* Good option if you're looking for a way to get to **Ram.** *Minus:* Bad option if **Ramsey** makes you think of a top brand of prophylactics.

Rand (English: shield). Also, **Rande.**

Randall (English: variation of **Randolph,** "shield, wolf"). Also, **Randal.** Familiar, **Randy.** *Whatever:* A comfortable, doable peanut-butter-and-jelly sandwich.

Randolf (German: variation of **Randolph,** "shield, wolf"). Also, **Randolfe.** Familiar, **Randy.**

Randolph (English: shield, wolf). Also, **Randolphe.** Familiar, **Randy.**

Randy (Scottish: amorous; English/German: variation of **Randall, Randolf, Randolph**). Also, **Randey.** *Whatever:* A swinger who no longer swings. **Randy** is bellying up to the barfly bar with **Gary** and **Keith.**

Ranger (English: mounted trooper). Also, **Rainger, Raynger.**

Rankin (English: shield, wolf). Also, **Ranken, Rankyn.**

Raoul (French: variation of **Ralph,** "counselor, wolf"). Also, **Raoull.**

Raphael (English/Hebrew: healed by God). Also, **Raphyel.** Familiar, **Raffi.**

Rashad (Arabic: counselor, moral). Also, **Rashaad, Rashadd.**

Rashid (Arabic: moral). Also, **Rasheed, Rashyd.**

Rashim (Arabic: variation of **Rashid,** "moral"). Also, **Rasheem, Rashym.**

Rashon   (American: variation of **Sean,** "God is gracious"). Also, **Rasean, Rashaun, Rashawn, Resean, Reshaun, Reshawn, Reshon.**

Raske (Scandinavian: daring). Also, **Rask.** *Whatever:* A perfect choice for spelunkers who want names that are so unique they don't sound like names at all. **Raske?** What's a **Raske?** Who cares? Sounds kinda cool, doesn't it?

Rathburn   (English: reedy stream). Also, **Rathbern, Rathberne, Rathburne.**

Rathe (Irish: fort). Also, **Raithe, Raythe.**

Raul (French: variation of **Ralph,** "counselor, wolf"). Also, **Raull.**

Rawley (English: variation of **Raleigh,** "red meadow"). Also, **Rawly.**

Rawlins   (English: variation of **Raleigh,** "red meadow"). Also, **Rawlyns.**

Ray   (French: king; English/French/German/Scottish: variation of **Rayburn, Rayford, Raymond, Raynard**). *Whatever:* A receding hairline. How far has this name slipped? When it turned up on the alleged arbiter of hip, *Beverly Hills, 90210,* it was used as the moniker of Tori Spelling's dull and abusive boyfriend, played by Jamey Walters.

Rayburn   (Scottish: fierce stream). Also, **Raybern, Rayberne, Rayburne.** Familiar, **Ray.**

Rayford (English: river crossing). Also, **Rayforde.** Familiar, **Ray.**

Raymond   (German: mighty counsel, protector). Also, **Raymonde, Raymund, Raymunde.** Familiar, **Ray.** *Whatever:* Like **Randall,** a perfectly serviceable, if unchallenging, peanut-butter-and-jelly sandwich.

Raynard   (French: variation of **Raymond,** "mighty counsel, protector"). Also, **Raynarde.** Familiar, **Ray.**

Rayshon (American: variation of **Sean,** "God is gracious"). Also, **Raesean, Raeshaun, Raeshawn, Raeshon, Raysean, Rayshaun, Rayshawn.**

Reade (Old English: to counsel; English: to read). Also, **Read.**

Reagan (Celtic: little king). Also, **Reagen.** *Whatever:* Back when parents named their kids after the president of the United States, **Reagan** might have been kind of hot. But Gen Xers being notoriously apolitical—note, not *un*political—Reagan is just kinda there. Still, if you're in the mood to pay tribute to our fortieth prez, **Reagan** is the contemporary pick—over **Ronald.**

Rebus (Latin: by things). Also, **Reebus, Rebuss.**

Red (English: red-haired, ruddy; variation of **Redding, Redford, Redman, Redmond**). Also, **Redd.** *Plus:* Your loving tribute to *Sanford and Son*'s **Redd** Foxx. *Minus:* Are you having a baby, or a tobacco-chewing, .236-hitting, minor-league shortstop?

Redding (English: clearing at the red meadow). Also, **Reddyng.** Familiar, **Red.** *Whatever:* If you love **Red,** try **Redding** or **Redman.** In case your kid hates the shorter version, he's got a more formal-sounding name to fall back on.

Redford (English: red river crossing). Also, **Redforde.** Familiar, **Red.**

Redman (English: red-headed man). Also, **Redmann.** Familiar, **Red.**

Redmond (English: variation of **Raymond,** "mighty counsel, protector"). Also, **Redmonde, Redmund, Redmunde.** Familiar, **Red.** *Whatever:* Baby boomers Farrah Fawcett and Ryan O'Neal caught a baby name trend on the upswing when they dubbed their son, born in 1984, **Redmond,** striking a blow for the now ubiquitous craze; the use of an Anglo-Saxon last name as a first name.

Reece (Welsh: enthusiastic).

Reed (Old English: ruddy, red; English: slender blade of grass). Also, **Reede.** *Plus:* A fine, strong, gentlemanly name that's immensely adaptable. It's at home on the ranges of the West or the concrete jungles of the East. A pocket T. *Minus:* Watch out: If the girls start taking over this uncommonly classy name, it's over for **Reed** as a viable boy name.

Reeder (English: variation of **Reed,** "ruddy, red").

Reese (Celtic: prince). *Plus:* The sound-alike alternative to **Reed.** *Minus:* Those inevitable **Reese's** Pieces schoolyard taunts.

Reeves (English: supervisor).

Reilly (Irish: combative). Also, **Reiley, Reilley, Reily.**

Reg (English: variation of **Reginald,** "powerful, mighty"). Also, **Regg.**

Regan (German: counsel; Celtic: little king). Also, **Reegan, Reegen, Regen.** *Plus:* The nonpartisan alternative to **Reagan.** *Minus:* The girl from *The Exorcist.*

Reggie (English: variation of **Reginald,** "powerful, mighty"). Also, **Reggey, Reggy.**

Reginald (English: powerful, mighty). Also, **Regynald.** Familiar, **Reg, Reggie.**

Reid (English: variation of **Reed,** "ruddy, red"). Also, **Reide.** *Whatever:* With **Reed,** a pocket T.

Rem (English: dream state). Also, **Remm**. *Whatever:* For die-hard Michael Stipe and R.E.M. fans only.

Remington (English: border home). Also, **Remingten**. *Whatever:* True, a bit Thurston Howell III, but it sure looked good on Pierce Brosnan in TV's *Remington Steele* (1982–87).

Ren (German/Scottish: variation of **Renfred, Renfrow**). Also, **Renn**.

Renfred (German: counsel, mighty, peace). Familiar, **Ren, Rennie**.

Renfrow (Scottish: brook). Also, **Renfro, Renfrowe**. Familiar, **Ren, Rennie**. *Whatever:* At first glance, a prime example of the last-name-as-first-name trend gone awry. But if you pare the name to **Ren,** you have yourself a nifty, unique pick.

Rennie (English: variation of **Renfred, Renfrow**). Also, **Renney, Renny**.

Reno (Spanish: reindeer). Also, **Reeno**. *Plus:* A grown-up lil' cow-poke—**Cody** with hard edges. *Minus:* The perfect moniker for a budding 1970s TV private detective.

Reuben (Hebrew: behold a son). Also, **Reubin, Reubyn**. Familiar, **Rube**. *Whatever:* Dave Madden played band manager **Reuben** Kincaid on TV's *The Partridge Family* (1970–74).

Revere (English: hold in esteem; Latin: to fear again). Also, **Reveer, Reveere**.

Rex (Latin: king; English: variation of **Rexford,** "king's river crossing"). Also, **Rexx**. *Whatever:* As far as names of the crown go, this one's better than **Duke** or **King,** but it's still most likely to turn up in conversations that go like this: "Here, **Rex**! Here, **Rex**! . . . Sit! Sit! Sit! . . . That's a good boy!"

Rexford (English: king's river crossing). Also, **Rexforde**. Familiar, **Rex**.

Rey (Spanish: king; Scottish/English: variation of **Reyburn, Reyford**).

Reyburn (Scottish: variation of **Rayburn,** "fierce stream"). Also, **Reybern, Reyberne, Reyburne**. Familiar, **Rey**.

Reyford (English: river crossing). Also, **Reyford**. Familiar, **Rey**.

Reynold (English: powerful, mighty).

Reynolds (English: variation of **Reynold,** "powerful, mighty").

Rhett (English: stream). Also, **Ret, Rett, Rhet**. *Plus:* A fine Southern gentleman name with a hint of scoundrel to keep it interesting. *Minus:* The Southern **Romeo**. You get double helpings of emotional baggage when you name your boy after one of fiction's leading romantic figures, à la *Gone With the Wind*'s **Rhett** Butler.

Rhine   (German: for the European river **Rhine**). Also, **Rhyne.** *Whatever:* Potential sound-alike fodder for **Ryan.**

Rhodes   (Greek: roses; English: roadside). Also, **Rhoades, Rhoads.** *Whatever:* A pick to click. Very strong, very cool.

Rhone   (French: for the European river **Rhone**). Also, **Rhoan, Rhoane.**

Rhys   (English: variation of **Reece,** "enthusiastic").

Ric   (German: variation of **Ulric,** "wolf, ruler").

Ricardo   (Spanish: variation of **Richard,** "hard, stern ruler"). Familiar, **Ricky.**

Rice   (Welsh: ardor; Celtic: prince). Also, **Ryce.** *Plus:* A solid pick for those who subscribe to the Gen X ethos. What is more down-to-earth than one of our staple foods? *Minus:* One word: Minute. Three words: Uncle Ben's Converted.

Rich   (English: wealthy; variation of **Richard, Richards, Richardson, Richart, Richfield, Richland, Richmond, Ritchard**).

Richard   (English: hard, stern ruler; variation of **Richardson,** "son of **Richard**"). Also, **Richerd.** Familiar, **Rich, Richie, Rick, Ricky.** *Plus:* A no-baggage, slam-dunk pocket T. Dependable—from the Revolutionary War to the post-Cold War. *Minus:* "Boooring," you say. And your friends agree. This peanut-butter-and-jelly sandwich is doing the slow fade in popularity. (Of course, maybe this qualifies as a plus for your spelunking cause.)

Richards   (English: variation of **Richard,** "hard, stern ruler"). Also, **Richerds.** Familiar, **Rich, Richie, Rick, Ricky.**

Richardson   (English: son of **Richard**). **Also,** Richardsen, Richerdsen, Richerdson. Familiar, **Rich, Richard, Richie, Rick, Ricky.** *Whatever:* The way to dress up **Richard.**

Richart   (German/Scandinavian: variation of **Richard,** "hard, stern ruler"). Also, **Richardt.** Familiar, **Rich, Richie, Rick, Ricky.**

Richfield   (English: ruler's field). Also, **Richfielde.** Familiar, **Rich, Richie, Rick, Ricky.** *Whatever:* Along with **Richland** and **Richmond,** this is a fancy-schmancy, nonboring alternative to **Richard.**

Richie   (English: variation of **Richard, Richards, Richardson, Richart, Richfield, Richland, Richmond, Ritchard**). Also, **Richey, Richy.**

Richland (English: ruler's land). Also, **Richlande.** Familiar, **Rich, Richie, Rick, Ricky.**

Richmond (English: high mountain). Also, **Richmonde, Richmund, Richmunde.** Familiar, **Rich, Richie, Rick, Ricky.**

Rick (English: mighty; variation of **Richard, Richards, Richardson, Richart, Richfield, Richland, Richmond, Ritchard**). Also, **Ric, Rik.** *Whatever:* Doesn't rhyme with *slick* for nothing. A perennial, if clichéd, cool name.

Ricky (English: variation of **Ricardo, Richard, Richards, Richardson, Richart, Richfield, Richland, Richmond, Ritchard**). Also, **Rickie, Rickey.**

Rider (English: mounted police). Also, **Ryder.** *Whatever:* A worthy lil' cowpoke peer to the likes of **Cody** and **Dakota.**

Riddick (Irish: smooth field). Also, **Riddic, Riddik, Riddyck.**

Riddock (Irish: variation of **Riddick,** "smooth field"). Also, **Riddoc, Riddok.**

Ridley (German: reedy meadow). Also, **Ridly.**

Rieger (German: fame, spear). Also, **Reeger.**

Riggs (Scottish: mountain ridge). Also, **Rigs, Rygs, Ryggs.**

Riley (Irish: variation of **Reilly,** "combative"). Also, **Rily.**

Rill (Scandinavian: little stream).

Rind (English: hard outer layer). Also, **Rinde, Rynd, Rynde.**

Riobard (Irish: variation of **Robert,** "bright, fame"). Also, **Riobarde, Ryobard, Ryobarde.**

Riordan (Irish: royal poet). Also, **Riorden, Riordyn, Ryordan, Ryorden.** *Familiar:* A pick to click. Handsome, strong, with a safely hidden romantic side.

Ripley (English: narrow meadow). Also, **Riply.**

Ritchard (English: variation of **Richard,** "hard, stern ruler"). Also, **Rytchard.** Familiar, **Rich, Richie, Rick, Ricky.**

River (English: a river). Also, **Ryver.** *Whatever:* Had actor **River** Phoenix lived, he could have made this tree-hugging hippie name safe for our times. But he died—and he died young—and no one's looking for that kind of name association.

Roades (English: roades). Also, **Roads.**

Roald (Scandinavian: variation of **Ronald,** "powerful, mighty"). Also, **Roalde.**

Roan (English: colored black with white speckles). Also, **Rone.**

Roarke (Irish: famous ruler). Also, **Roark, Rork, Rorke, Rourk, Rourke.** *Plus:* Mr. **Roarke** was the wise master of TV's *Fantasy Island* (1978–84, 1998–99). *Minus:* The guy wore a white suit—June or December. How wise could he possibly be?

Rob (English: variation of **Robers, Robert, Roberto, Robertson, Robeson, Robin, Robins, Robinson, Robson**). Also, **Robb.**

Robby (English: variation of **Robers, Robert, Roberto, Robertson, Robeson, Robin, Robins, Robinson, Robson**). Also, **Robbey, Robby.**

Robers (French: variation of **Robert,** "bright, fame"). Familiar, **Rob, Robby.**

Robert (English: bright, fame; variation of **Robertson,** "son of **Robert**"). Also, **Robbert.** Familiar, **Bob, Bobby, Rob, Robby.** *Plus:* A pocket T. But you knew that. And, really, we're feeling guilty if you bought this book to validate your selection of **Robert.** So, please, read on. Get your money's worth. *Minus:* You don't want your son to fall victim to the **Jennifer/Michael** syndrome. You want a name that sounds like it took some effort to find. You want a name that says something—*anything*—besides, you know, **Jennifer, Michael,** or, in this case, **Robert.**

Roberto (Spanish: variation of **Robert,** "bright, fame"). Familiar, **Rob, Robby.**

Robertson (English: son of **Robert,** "bright, fame"). Also, **Robertsen.** Familiar, **Rob, Robby, Robert.**

Robeson (English: variation of **Robson,** "son of **Rob**"). Also, **Robesen.** Familiar, **Rob, Robby.**

Robin (English: variation of **Robert,** "bright, fame"; variation of **Robinson,** "son of **Robin**"). Also, **Robbin, Robbyn, Robyn.** Familiar, **Rob, Robby.** *Whatever:* Maybe because girls started using this one, **Robin** has become a less attractive option for boys. But get over it—this is a pick to click. It's the sensitive, distinctive alternative to **Robert.**

Robins (English: variation of **Robert,** "bright, fame"). Also, **Robbins, Robbyns, Robyns.** Familiar, **Rob, Robby.**

Robinson (English: son of **Robin;** variation of **Robert,** "bright, fame"). Also, **Robinsen, Robynsen, Robynson.** Familiar, **Rob, Robin, Robby.**

Robson (English: son of **Rob;** variation of **Robert,** "bright, fame"). Also, **Robbsen, Robbson, Robsen.** Familiar, **Rob, Robby.**

Rockford (English: rocky river crossing). Also, **Rockforde.** *Whatever:* A yuppie-friendly choice that feels downtown, too, thanks to its connection to 1970s TV private detective show *The Rockford Files.*

Rockland (English: rocky land). Also, **Rocklande.**

Rocklin (English: variation of **Rockland,** "rocky land"). Also, **Rocklyn.**

Rod (English: scepter; English/German; variation of **Roderick, Rodman, Rodney**). Also, **Rodd.** Familiar, **Roddy.**

Roddy (English/German: variation of **Rod, Roderick, Rodman, Rodney**). Also, **Roddey.** *Whatever:* Kicky, cool, and underused.

Roderick (German: famous ruler). Also, **Roderic, Roderich, Roderik.** Familiar, **Rod, Roddy.**

Rodin (French: spear). Also, **Rodyn.**

Rodman (English: famed protector). Also, **Rodmann.** Familiar, **Rod, Roddy.** *Plus:* A hipper way to get to **Rod** than the usual, ho-hum **Rodney** route. *Minus:* Look for Dennis **Rodman**'s soon-to-be-tired act drag down both parts of his name—first *and* last.

Rodney (English: male deer). Also, **Rodny.** Familiar, **Rod, Roddy.**

Rodolfo (Spanish: variation of **Rudolph,** "fame, wolf").

Roe (English: small deer).

Roebuck (English: male deer). Also, **Robuck, Robuk, Roebuk, Rowbuck, Rowbuk.** *Whatever:* One word: Sears.

Rog (English: variation of **Roger,** "fame, spear").

Roger (English: fame, spear; German: praise). Also, **Rodger.** Familiar, **Raj, Rog.** *Plus:* A perfect name for a necklace-wearing, swingin' single of the 1960s and 1970s. *Minus:* The party's over. Get **Roger** a table next to **Randy, Gary,** and **Keith.**

Rogers (English: variation of **Roger,** "fame, spear"). Also, **Rodgers.** Familiar, **Raj, Rog.**

Roland (German: fame, land). Also, **Roeland, Roelande, Rolande.** Familiar, **Follie, Rollo.**

Rolando (Spanish: variation of **Roland,** "fame, land"). Familiar, **Rollie, Rollo.**

Rolf (German: variation of **Ralph,** "counselor, wolf"). Also, **Rolfe.**

Rollie (English/Spanish: variation of **Roland, Rolando, Rowland**). Also, **Rolley, Rolly.**

Rollo (English: variation of **Roland, Rolando, Rudolph**). Also, **Rolo.**

Roman (English/Scottish: four crossroads; Latin: a Roman). *Whatever:* Sure, the empire fell, but the name? Hey, ain't nothing broke here. Try it on for size. A pick to click.

Romney (Welsh: bending river). Also, **Romny.**

Ron (English/Scottish: variation of **Ronald, Ronaldo, Rondel**). Also, **Ronn.** *Whatever:* Total peanut-butter-and-jelly sandwich.

Ronald (Scottish: powerful, mighty). Familiar, **Ron, Ronnie.** *Whatever:* Some names have the misfortune of being associated with red-haired clowns who hawk hamburgers. **Ronald** has a long enough track record to overcome **Ronald** McDonald, but will your little **Ronald** have the stamina to overcome **Ronald** Mcdonald taunts?

Ronaldo (Spanish: variation of **Ronald,** "powerful, mighty"). Familiar, **Ron, Ronnie.**

Ronan (Irish: little seal). Also, **Ronen, Ronyn.**

Rondel (French: short poem). Also, **Rondell, Rondelle.** Familiar, **Ron, Ronnie.**

Ronel (Scandinavian: variation of **Ronald,** "powerful, mighty"). Also, **Ronell, Ronelle.**

Ronen (Hebrew: song and joy). Also, **Ronin, Ronyn.**

Roney (Irish: hero). Also, **Rony.**

Ronnie (English: variation of **Ronald, Ronaldo, Rondel**). Also, **Ronney, Ronny.**

Roone (Irish: variation of **Rooney,** "red-haired"). Also, **Roon.**

Rooney (Irish: red-haired). Also, **Roony.**

Roosevelt (Scandinavian: field of roses). Also, **Roosivelt, Roosyvelt.** Familiar, **Rosey.** *Whatever:* Another presidential name that's slumped in these politician-bashing times. But remember: Sometimes you can find pretty cool stuff in the basement.

Rory (Irish: red). Also, **Rorey.**

Ross (Scottish: peninsula; English: horse). *Whatever:* Another name that *Friends* wrought. David Schwimmer's puppy-dog **Ross** Geller boosts the profile of this easy-on-the-ears, reliable performer.

Roswell (English: horse spring). Also, **Roswel, Rozwel, Rozwell.** *Whatever:* Trendy hip in our UFO-obsessed times? Or just trendy-kitschy weird? It's definitely the most off-beat map name out there.

Roth (German: red-haired, fame).

Rowan (Irish: mountain ash). Also, **Rowen, Rowyn.** *Whatever:* If your only exposure to **Rowan** as a first name is *Mr. Bean*'s **Rowan** Atkinson, you may not necessarily associate it with a happening baby name. But look again—it's pretty nifty.

Rowe (Irish: red-haired). Also, **Row.**

Rowel (English: small wheel at the end of a spur).

Rowell (English: stream for the deer). Also, **Rowelle.**

Rowland (German: variation of **Roland,** "fame, land"). Also, **Rowlande.** Familiar, **Rollie.**

Roy (Irish: red; French: king; English: variation of **Royston,** "Roy's town"). *Plus:* A name that possesses a **Hank**-like authenticity. *Minus:* A name that possesses a **Gary**-like dorkiness.

Royal (Latin: regal). Also, **Royale.** *Plus:* Finally, a crown name that hasn't been usurped by the dog kingdom! Rest assured, nobody names a pooch **Royal.** *Minus:* Not many people name their sons **Royal** either.

Royce (English: royal).

Royse (English: rose, horse).

Royston (English: Roy's town). Also, **Roysten.** Familiar, **Roy.**

Rube (Hebrew: variation of **Reuben, Ruben**).

Ruben (Hebrew: alternative to **Reuben,** "behold a son"). Also, **Rubin, Rubyn.**

Rudd (Scandinavian: ruddy). Also, **Rud.**

Rudolf (Scandinavian: variation of **Rudolph,** "fame, wolf"). Also, **Rudolfe.** Familiar, **Rudy.**

Rudolfo (Spanish: variation of **Rudolph,** "fame, wolf"). Familiar, **Rudy.**

Rudolph (German: fame, wolf). Familiar, **Rollo, Rudy.** *Whatever:* If you intend to use the full **Rudolph** for everyday use, you might want to be advised of a little holiday song.

Rudolphe (French: variation of **Rudolph,** "fame, wolf"). Familiar, **Rudy.**

Rudolpho (Italian: variation of **Rudolph,** "fame, wolf"). Familiar, **Rudy.**

Rudy (English/French/Italian/Spanish: variation of **Rudolf, Rudolfo, Rudolph, Rudolphe, Rudolpho**). Also, **Rudie.** *Whatever:* A pair of comfortable shoes in our wingtip and/or cowboy-boot world. While these two factions fight for style supremacy, the **Rudy**s of the world will live fat off the middle ground.

Rune (German: mythical poem, song).

Rupert (English/German: variation of **Robert,** "bright, fame"). Also, **Ruppert.**

Rush (German/Scandinavian: elm tree, excitable).Also, **Rush.** *Plus:* You have "The **Rush** Limbaugh Show" call-in number on speed-dial. *Minus:* You have "The **Rush** Limbaugh Show" call-in number on call-block.

Rusk (French: red-haired). Also, **Ruske.**

Ruskin (French: variation of **Rusk,** "red-haired"). Also, **Ruskyn.**

Russ (English/French: variation of **Russell,** "red"). Also, **Rus.** *Whatever:* Candidate for the **Ross** Less Traveled.

Russell (French: red; English: fox). Also, **Russel, Russyl, Russyll.** Familiar, **Russ, Rusty.** *Whatever:* **Russell** is a candidate for nerdy cool. There's something appealing about a name that sounds like a name—and not a family crest.

Rusty (English: coated with rust; variation of **Russell,** "red"). Also, **Rustey.**

Rutger (Scandinavian: variation of **Roger,** "fame, spear").

Rutherford (Scottish: river crossing by the castle). Also, **Rutherforde.**

Rutland (English: red lake, pool). Also, **Rutlande, Ruttland, Ruttlande.**

Rutledge (English: red ledge). Also, **Rutlege, Ruttledge, Ruttlege.**

Ryan (Irish: little king). Also, **Ryen, Ryun.** *Whatever:* The cuddly bear surname that's made the biggest splash in the first-name biz. Building in popularity since the 1980s, **Ryan** is now a monster, surpassing even its stalwart R cousins, **Robert** and **Richard.** Look for it to cool as more girls move into the **Ryan** market.

Rye (English: a cereal grass).

Ryne (Irish: variation of **Ryan,** "little king"). Also, **Rine.**

Ryno (Irish: variation of **Ryan,** "little king"). Also, **Rino.**

S

CRIB NOTES

Famous Ss: **Samuel** L. Jackson (actor, *Pulp Fiction*); **Savion** Glover (dancer, Broadway star); **Scott** Weiland (rocker, Stone Temple Pilots); **Sean** Penn (actor); **Shaquille** O'Neal (basketball player); **Sherman** Hemsley (George Jefferson, TV's *The Jeffersons*); **Stephen** King (horrormeister); **Stone** Phillips (network TV news-mag anchor); **Stu** Sutcliffe (the "fifth" Beatle); **Sylvester** Stallone (*Rocky/Rambo* icon).

Pocket Ts: Sam, Samuel, Saul, Seth, Stephen, Steven

Trendy suspenders: Shane, Spencer

Think long, think hard: Schneider (Once a super on *One Day at a Time,* never a baby name.); **Shaq** (Buy the guy's shoes. Drink the guy's soda. But get a grip before you give your son his unwieldy moniker. Besides, what if your little **Shaq** can't play a lick of ball?); **Sherlock** (It's elemental, Watson. Cross this one off your list.); **Sigfried** (Two words: and Roy.); **Sigmund** (Four words: And the sea monsters.); **Simba** (It's OK to love *The Lion King*. It's debatable whether it's OK to live *The Lion King*.); **Skippy** (For dog-food or peanut-butter labels only.); **Slacker** (Not even as an ironic statement.); **Slate** (Soap Opera City.); **Socrates** (Poses the same dilemma as **Shaq**. What if your kid doesn't display a flair for philosophical theory?); **Steele** (*See* **Slate**.); **Storm** (*See* **Steele**.); **Stiv** (May the 1980s never come so far back that outrageously ostentatious nicknames once again seep into our vernacular.)

Saber (Slavic: heavy sword). Also, **Sabre.**
Sadler (English: saddle-maker).

Safar (Arabic: to journey). Also, **Safer, Safyr.**

Sage (Latin: wise). Also, **Saige, Sayge.** *Plus:* Tough-guy Sylvester Stallone has a son named **Sage.** *Minus:* Others associate **Sage** with a girl name.

Sager (English: sea spear). Also, **Sayger.**

Saith (English: to speak). Also, **Saithe, Saythe.**

Sal (Latin: salt; Spanish/Latin: variation of **Salvador, Salvator**). Also, **Sall.** *Whatever:* Comfortable and real—like a flannel shirt.

Salvador (Spanish: variation of **Salvator**, "savior"). Also, **Salvadore.** Familiar, **Sal.**

Salvator (Latin: savior). Also, **Salvatore.** Familiar, **Sal.**

Sam (Hebrew: variation of **Sampson, Samson, Samuel, Samuele, Samvel**). Also, **Samm.** *Whatever:* Nothing projects honest-to-goodness back-to-basics like **Sam.** (Unless you're talking about its cousins, **Hank** and **Jack.**) A flannel shirt *and* a pocket T.

Samir (Arabic: entertainer). Also, **Sameer, Samyr.**

Sammon (Arabic: grocer). Also, **Sammen.**

Sammy (English: variation of **Sampson, Samson, Samuel, Samuele, Samvel**). Also, **Sammey.**

Sampson (Hebrew: variation of **Samson**, "sunny"). Also, **Sampsen.** Familiar, **Sam, Sammy.**

Samson (Hebrew: sunny). Also, **Samsen.** Familiar, **Sam, Sammy.** *Plus:* The **Samuel** Less Traveled. *Minus:* Well, actually **Samuel** isn't that well-worn of a road. You might be breaking needless ground with this strong-man moniker.

Samuel (Hebrew: asked of God). Also, **Samuell.** Familiar, **Sam, Sammy.** *Plus:* Old-fashioned qualities make **Samuel** an endearing, enduring pocket T. *Minus:* Defiled and belittled on TV's *Saved by the Bell.* **Samuel** is the given name of that Screech creature.

Samuele (Italian: variation of **Samuel**, "asked of God"). Also, **Samuelle.** Familiar, **Sam, Sammy.**

Samvel (Slavic: variation of **Samuel**, "asked of God"). Also, **Samvell, Samvelle.** Familiar, **Sam, Sammy.**

Sanborn (English: sandy stream). Also, **Sanborne, Sanbourn, Sanbourne.** Familiar, **Sandy.**

Sandberg (English: sandy mountain). Also, **Sandburg.** Familiar, **Sandy.**

Sanders (Scottish: variation of **Alexander**, "protector, defender"; English: variation of **Sanderson**, "son of **Sanders**"). Familiar, **Sandy.**

Sanderson   (English: son of **Sanders,** "protector, defender"). Also, **Sandersen.** Familiar, **Sanders.**

Sandy   (English: sandy; Greek: variation of **Alexander,** "protector, defender"; English/Scottish: variation of **Sanborn, Sandberg, Sanders, Sanford**). *Whatever:* Where have you gone, **Sandy** Koufax? A name that coulda been a contender to **Kevin'**s cute, sensitive boy throne is wilting from neglect. Blame it on Olivia Newton-John. To Gen Xers, the most notable **Sandy** is John's good-*girl* **Sandy** from *Grease.* Time for us to get over it. **Sandy** is an untapped mine where boy names are concerned. A pick to click.

Sanford   (English: sandy river crossing). Also, **Sanforde.** Familiar, **Sandy.**

Santiago   (Spanish: saint).

Santino   (Italian: saint). Also, **Santeeno, Santyno.**

Sargent   (English: army officer). Also, **Sargeant.** *Plus:* **Sargent** Shriver was the JFK staffer who oversaw the foundation of the Peace Corps. *Minus:* Two things: (1) The military isn't your bag; (2) The military *is* your son's bag. He enlists. Rises through the ranks. Becomes Sargent **Sargent.** Life grows as confusing as Joseph Heller's *Catch-22.*

Sasha   (Greek: variation of **Alexander,** "protector, defender"). Also, **Sashah.**

Saul   (Hebrew: desired). Also, **Saull.** *Plus:* **Saul** is chock-full of lovable stodginess. An offbeat pocket T. *Minus:* Doesn't sound right to your ears unless there's an "Uncle" in front of it.

Savion   (African: new house). Also, **Savien, Savyen, Savyon.** *Whatever:* This name should ride Broadway star **Savion** Glover's tap shoes to a tidy level of respectability and popularity.

Saxon   (English: short sword). Also, **Saxen.**

Saxton   (English: from the town of Saxons). Also, **Saxten.**

Sawyer   (English: axman). *Whatever:* A pick to click. Charming and rakish, à la picket-fence con artist Tom **Sawyer.**

Sayer   (English: victory of the people). Also, **Sayre.**

Schae   (American: variation of **Shea,** "learned"). Also, **Schay.**

Scott   (English: from Scotland; Irish: tattooed). Also, **Scot.** *Whatever:* When Gen Xers were of middle-school age, **Scott** was one of the hottest sensitive, cute boys around. Today, it doesn't seem classic or hip enough. It's still serviceable, of course—a peanut-butter-and-jelly sandwich is hard to kill. (Or digest.)

Scully (Irish: scholar). Also, **Sculley.**

Seamus (Irish: variation of **Shamus,** "following after").

Sean (Irish: variation of **John,** "God is gracious"). *Whatever:* A solid alternative to the ubiquitous **John.**

Seaton (English: town by the sea). Also, **Seaten, Seeten, Seeton.**

Seaver (English: grave). Also, **Seever.**

Sebastian (Greek: reverend). Also, **Sebastien, Sebastyan, Sebastyen.**

Sedge (English: course plant).

Seely (English: happy, blessed). Also, **Sealy, Sealey, Seeley.**

Seger (English: sea warrior). Also, **Seager, Seeger.**

Serge (Latin: servant). Also, **Serg.**

Sergio (Italian/Spanish: variation of **Serge,** "servant"). Also, **Sergyo.**

Seth (Hebrew: the appointed). *Whatever:* **Seth** easily travels in the same social circles as the sensitive, cute boys **Justin** and **Joshua**. It's also got the goods—a simple, clean, nontrendy feel—to bear up under repeated washings. A pocket T.

Severence (English: a parting). Also, **Severince, Severynce.**

Sewell (English: victory at sea). Also, **Seawell, Seawel, Sewel.**

Seymour (English: black sea). Also, **Semore, Semour, Seymore.** Familiar, **Sy.**

Shakir (Arabic: thankful). Also, **Shakeer, Shakyr.**

Shakur (Arabic: variation of **Shakir,** "thankful"). Also, **Shakurr.**

Shale (English: a rock). Also, **Shaile, Shayle.**

Shamus (Irish: variation of **James,** "following after"). Also, **Schaemus, Schamus, Shaemus.** *Plus:* **James** with a difference. *Minus:* That *shame* part leaves a big opening for schoolyard taunts.

Shanahan (Irish: shrewd, wise). Also, **Shanihan, Shanyhan.** *Whatever:* The **Shannon** that the girls *didn't* steal.

Shane (German: handsome; Irish: variation of **John,** "God is gracious"). Also, **Shaine, Shayne.** *Plus:* Like **Sean, Shane** is the undercover **John.** *Minus:* **Shane** owes its current popularity to two—count 'em two!—trendy trends. It's a name that (1) shows its Irish roots, and (2) qualifies as a lil' cowpoke. (Remember the Western *Shane*?) Beware, a potential pair of trendy suspenders.

Shannon (Irish: venerable, wise). Also, **Shanen, Shannen, Shanon.**

Whatever: If you can get past the fact that this one has been usurped by the girls, **Shannon** makes a nifty, handsome-sounding boy pick.

Shante (French: singer). Also, **Shantae, Shantay.**

Shaun (Irish: variation of **Sean**, "God is gracious"). Also, **Shaunn.** *Whatever:* Every time you see this name you see your bedroom wall, circa 1978, and all the **Shaun** Cassidy posters that memory entails.

Shaw (Scottish: small wood). Also, **Shawe.**

Shawn (Irish: variation of **Sean**). Also, **Shawnn.**

Shea (Irish: learned). Also, **Shay.** *Plus:* Gets you wiggle room on **Sean** and **Shane**. *Minus:* You fear people will assume you named your son after the New York Mets' **Shea** Stadium.

Sheehan (Irish: peaceful). Also, **Sheahan, Sheahen, Sheehen.**

Sheen (English: bright; Irish: variation of **Sheehan**, "peaceful"). Also, **Shean, Sheane, Sheene.**

Shel (Yiddish: variation of **Hershel**, "deer").

Shelby (English: home by the ledge). Also, **Shelbey.**

Sheldon (English: flat hill). Also, **Shelden.**

Shelton (English: flat town). Also, **Shelten.**

Shep (English: variation of **Shepherd**, "a shepherd"). Also, **Shepp.** *Whatever:* Sounds like the lost member of the Rat Pack. Swingin'.

Shepherd (English: a shepherd). Also, **Shepard, Sheperd, Shephard.** Familiar, **Shep.** *Whatever:* A pick to click. A fancy-pants name that endorses the manual-labor work ethic. What's more noble than naming your son in honor of humble sheep herders?

Sheridan (Irish: peaceful). Also, **Sherydan.**

Sherman (English: wool shearer).

Sherrick (Scottish: clear bay). Also, **Sherric, Sherrik, Sherryc, Sherryck, Sherryk.**

Shire (English: a county). Also, **Shyre.**

Shon (American: variation of **Sean**, "God is gracious"). Also, **Shonn.**

Sid (English: variation of **Sidney, Sydney**). Also, **Sidd, Syd, Sydd.** *Whatever:* **Sid** is **Max** minus the attendant hoopla. A nerdy cool entry.

Sidney (English: conqueror). Also, **Sidny.** Familiar, **Sid.** *Whatever:* Whereas **Shannon** can still be saved from the girls, **Sidney** is all but gone. The last notable male **Sidney** of the Gen X era was found in the 1980s Tony Randall sitcom, *Love, Sidney*. That said, the name's included here because nickname **Sid** still has potential.

Sidus (Latin: star). Also, **Sydus.**

Silas (Latin: of the trees). Also, **Sylas**. *Plus:* You loved reading *Silas Marner* in high school. *Minus:* You loathed reading *Silas Marner* in high school.

Simeon   (French: variation of **Simon,** "obedient"). Also, **Simion, Simyon.**

Simmons (English: son of **Simon**). Also, **Simens, Simmens, Simons.**

Simms   (English: gracious; Hebrew: son of **Simon**). Also, **Sims, Symms, Syms.**

Simon (Hebrew: obedient). Also, **Simen, Symen, Symon.** *Plus:* A usable moldy oldie that conjures the go-go 1960s: Roger Moore, skinny ties, **Simon** Templar, aka "the Saint." *Minus:* An unusual moldy oldie that conjures: (a) nerds; (b) Val Kilmer's *The Saint;* and/or (c) **Simon** Legree of *Uncle Tom's Cabin.*

Sinclair (Scottish: bright). Also, **Sinclare, Synclair, Synclare.** *Plus:* A sound-alike that gets you wiggle room on the trendier **Spencer.** *Minus:* A girl name.

Skeet (Scandinavian: projectile). *Whatever:* If actor **Skeet** Ulrich (*Scream*) can popularize this dark-horse candidate, he'll be two miracles short of sainthood.

Skip (English: ricochet, bounce). Also, **Skipp.** *Plus:* Upbeat. *Minus:* Downright silly.

Skylar (Dutch: to shelter). Also, **Skyler, Skylerr, Skylur, Skylurr.**

Slade (English: valley). Also, **Slaide, Slayde.**

Slater (English: roofer). Also, **Slaiter, Slayter.**

Sloan (Irish: fighter). Also, **Sloane, Slone.** *Whatever:* Strong and distinctive, **Sloan** is ready for its own private-detective TV show.

Sly (Scandinavian: cunning; English: variation of **Sylvester,** "of the forest"). Also, **Slye.** *Plus:* Cool. *Minus:* Affected.

Smith (English: metalworker; variation of **Smithson,** "son of **Smith**"). Also, **Smithe, Smyth, Smythe.** Familiar, **Smitty.** *Plus:* Smith—as a first name?!? Sure thing. It's as common and adaptable as **John** or **Michael** but sounds positively exotic because we're used to seeing it pull the caboose. *Minus:* You already have a **Smith**—for a *last* name.

Smithson   (English: son of **Smith**). Also, **Smithsen, Smythsen, Smythson.** Familiar, **Smith.**

Smitty (English: variation of **Smith,** "metalworker"). Also, **Smittey.** *Plus:* Reminds you of American in simpler times. *Minus:* Like before indoor plumbing.

Sol (Latin: sun; Hebrew: variation of **Solomon,** "peacemaker"). Also, **Soll.** *Whatever:* The in-touch-with-nature **Saul.**

Solomon (Hebrew: peacemaker). Also, **Solomen.** Familiar, **Sol.** *Whatever:* About as touch and go as naming your boy **Socrates.** It's included here if you like **Sol** but want the birth certificate to contain a couple more syllables.

Spaulding (English: a surname). Also, **Spalding, Spaldying, Spauldyng.**

Spence (English: variation of **Spencer,** "steward").

Spencer (English: steward). Also, **Spenser.** Familiar, **Spence.** *Whatever:* **Spencer** used to be as nerdy as a pair of busted glasses. Now this nouveau cuddly bear is being deployed as baby name material by members of *Baywatch* (*see* Gena Lee Nolin) and "Tool Time Girls" from *Home Improvement* (*see* Debbe Dunning). *Minus:* When Hollywood starts latching on to a name (i.e., **Dakota**), it's over. The name is no longer a find. It's a moniker that's going to be mimicked by hundreds, maybe thousands, of the star's fans. Include **Spencer** in the list of trendy suspenders.

Sperry (English: spear). Also, **Sperrey.**

Spike (Dutch: a spiker; English: long nail). *Plus:* Cute and kicky. *Minus:* A potential Madonna, thanks to filmmaker **Spike** Lee.

Stace (English: variation of **Eustace,** "stable") Also, **Stayce.**

Stacy (English: variation of **Eustace,** "stable"). Also, **Stacey.** *Whatever:* This one's in the same rough waters as **Sandy** or **Tracy.** It's a cute, sensitive boy struggling to assert his manhood.

Stadler (German: barn). Also, **Stadtler.**

Stan (English: variation of **Standish, Stanley, Stanton**). *Whatever:* A possible flannel shirt peer of **Jack, Gil,** or **Hank.** Key word: *possible.* It's also *possible* people will get their jollies making "**Stan** the Man" rhymes. Your call.

Standish (English: rocky park). Also, **Standysh.** Familiar, **Stan.**

Stanley (English: stony meadow). Familiar, **Stan.** *Whatever:* Tough call. **Stanley** is virtual pop-culture shorthand for pocket-calculator punchers. But . . . can **Stan** save it? Hedge your bets. Go for one of the fancier alternatives—**Standish** or **Stanton.**

Stanton (English: stony house). Also, **Stanten.** Familiar, **Stan.** *Whatever:* The contemporary **Stanley.**

Steadman (English: farmer). Also, **Stedman.**

Stefan (Scandinavian: variation of **Stephen**, "crown"). Also, **Stefen, Stefyn.**

Stefano (Italian: variation of **Stephen**, "crown").

Stepan (Russian: variation of **Stephen**, "crown"). Also, **Stepen, Stepyn.**

Stephen (Greek: crown). Also, **Stephin, Stephyn.** Familiar, **Steve, Stevie.** *Whatever:* A wily pocket T. Has avoided the fate that befell its swingin' 1960s peers **Gary, Roger, Keith,** etc. with the help of two little letters. The **Stephen** (*ph*) option dresses up the **Steven** (*v*) version. Heck, if you want to get fancy, you can even pretend the thing is pronounced "Steh-fen."

Sterling (English: true). Also, **Sterlyng, Stirling, Stirlyng.** *Whatever:* A very classy, doable Thurston Howell III.

Stern (English: strong, austere). Also, **Stearn, Stearne, Sterne.**

Steve (English: variation of **Stephen, Steven**). *Whatever:* Along with **Doug, Gary,** and **Keith, Steve** is a studly boy name of Gen X's youth whose best swingin' days are behind it. Doable but only in a peanut-butter-and-jelly sandwich sort of way.

Steven (Greek: variation of **Stephen**, "crown"). Also, **Stevin, Stevyn.** Familiar, **Steve, Stevie.** *Whatever:* The preferred speling among the **Stephen/Steven** contingent. A pocket T.

Stevie (English: variation of **Stephen, Steven**). Also, **Stevey, Stevy.**

Stewart (English: variation of **Stuart**, "steward"). Also, **Stewert.** Familiar, **Stu.**

Stieran (English: to guide, steer). Also, **Steeran, Steeren, Steeryn, Stieren, Stieryn.**

Stoat (English: large coat). Also, **Stoate, Stote.**

Stocker (English: true). *Plus:* A comer. **Stocker** rhymes with **Walker** and looks like **Spencer.** *Minus:* You work in the supermarket industry. This name is about as appealing as **Cashier.**

Stockton (English: town by the tree stumps). Also, **Stockten.**

Stoddard (English: one who cares for horses). Also, **Stodderd.**

Stone (English: rock). Also, **Stoane.** Familiar, **Stony.** *Whatever:* It helps to have a champion. Were it not for NBC News's **Stone** Phillips, this rock hard name would be right down there with **Slate.** But thanks to Phillips, **Stone** almost makes sense. Almost.

Stony (English: full of stones; variation of **Stone**, "rock"). Also, **Stoney.** *Plus:* Cool. *Minus:* Spacey.

Stowe   (English: to pack away). Also, **Stow.**

Strother   (English: marshy meadow).

Stu   (English: variation of **Stewart, Stuart**). *Plus:* A worthy, low-key peer of **Hank.** *Minus:* Sounds like something you eat for dinner.

Stuart   (English: steward). Also, **Stuwart.** Familiar, **Stu.** *Whatever:* Remarkably consistent—a name that has been around (seemingly) forever, yet has never quite captured the American imagination. This is not a bad thing. **Stuart** is historical enough never to sound wrong, tepid enough never to be considered trendy.

Sullivan   (Irish: black-eyed). Also, **Sulivan, Sullyvan, Sulyvan.** Familiar, **Sully.**

Sully   (Irish: variation of **Sullivan,** "black-eyed"). Also, **Sulley.**

Sumner   (English: summoner).

Sutter   (English: shoemaker).

Sutton   (English: southern home). Also, **Sutten.**

Sy   (English: variation of **Seymour,** "black sea"). *Whatever:* **Sy**'s root name, **Seymour,** ain't remotely happening. But **Sy?** How decent does that sound? The unplugged **Seymour** is something that elemental-lovin' Gen Xers can embrace. A pick to click.

Sydney   (English: the Australian city; variation of **Sidney,** "conqueror"). Also, **Sydny.** Familiar, **Sid.**

Sylvester   (Latin: of the forest). Also, **Silvester, Silvestor, Sylvestor.** Familiar, **Sly.** *Whatever:* Star power can only go so far. More than twenty years after **Sylvester** Stallone barged his way into our lives, **Sylvester** remains baby name challenged. Sounds like that spittle-spewing Warner Bros. animated cat. Consider for family reasons only.

T

CRIB NOTES

Famous Ts: **Theodore** Roosevelt (U.S. president); **Thurman** Munson (late New York Yankees captain); **Thurston** Howell III (millionaire castaway, *Gilligan's Island*); **Tiger** Woods (golfer); **Tom** Cruise (über movie star); **Tommy** Bradford (1970s hunk ideal, TV's *Eight Is Enough*); **Travis** Tritt (country singer); **Treat** Williams (actor); **Trent** Dilfer (football player); **Troy** Aikman (football player); **Truman** Capote (author, *Breakfast at Tiffany's*)

Pocket Ts: Terence, Thomas, Timothy

Trendy suspenders: No pick here. Trendy faves **Tanner, Taylor, Travis,** and **Tyler** will inevitably flatten out under the weight of their own popularity, but each is staid enough to avoid sounding, well, silly once their day passes.

Think long, think hard: **Thor** (Maybe the boy should get his feet wet in kindergarten before you go comparing him to the Norse god of thunder.); **Thurston** (A role model for preppie names, but virtually off-limits itself. For castaway use only.); **Tito** (Best left to the Jackson family.); **Treat** (The Golden Rule, Parts XVI and XVII: No snacking between meals. No baby naming during snacking, lest you become unduly influenced.)

Tad (Hebrew: variation of **Taddeus**, "wise"). Also, **Tadd.** *Plus:* The slightly hipper **Todd.** *Minus:* Rhymes with cad.

Taddeus (Hebrew: variation of **Thaddeus**, "wise"). Also, **Taddius, Taddyus.** Familiar, **Tad.**

Tadeo (Slavic: variation of **Thaddeus**, "wise").

Taeshon (American: variation of **Sean,** "God is gracious"). Also, **Tae-sean, Taeshaun, Taeshawn, Taysean, Tayshaun, Tayshawn, Tayshon.**

Taft (English/Irish: yard). Also, **Tafte.**

Tal (Hebrew: morning dew; Irish: variation of **Talley,** "peaceful"). Also, **Tall.** *Whatever:* A nifty, almost un-name name. So pared down, so sparse, it's positively aerodynamic—fit for space travel, even. ("Sitting in for Mr. Sulu on navigation controls tonight—it's **Tal!**") A strong candidate for perfect name of the new millennium.

Tale (English: fiction). Also, **Taile, Tayle.**

Talley (Irish: peaceful). Also, **Tally.** Familiar, **Tal.**

Tam (Irish: for tam-o'-shanter). Also, **Tamm.**

Tanner (English: one who tans leather). Also, **Tannor.** *Whatever:* A sensitive, cute boy that conjures dreams of straight teeth, college degrees, and cuddly bear souls. It's no wonder that this entry is giving established T talent—**Thomas, Timothy,** etc.—solid competition for supremacy in the letter's power rankings.

Tarian (American: variation of **Darian,** "daring"). Also, **Tarien, Taryan, Taryen.**

Taro (Polynesian: tropical plant). Also, **Tarro.**

Tarrell (American: variation of **Darrell,** "brave, bold"). Also, **Tarrel, Tarryl, Tarryll.**

Tarrique (American: variation of **Derrick,** "ruler"). Also, **Tariqe, Tarique, Tarriqe, Tarryque, Taryqe, Taryque.**

Tashon (American: variation of **Sean,** "God is gracious"). Also, **Tasean, Tashaun, Tashawn, Tesean, Teshaun, Teshawn, Teshon.**

Tate (English: cheerful). Also, **Taite, Tayte.**

Tawon (American: variation of **John,** "God is gracious"). Also, **Tawan, Tewan, Tewon.**

Taylor (English: a tailor). Also, **Tayler.** *Whatever:* **Taylor**'s riding the same wave with **Tanner**—with one exception: Girls are starting to latch on to this one, likely hastening a drop in its usability and popularity as a boy name.

Teague (Irish: variation of **Tighe,** "poet"). Also, **Teegue.**

Teandre (American: variation of **Andre,** "brave"). Also, **Teandrae, Teandray.**

Ted (English: variation of **Edward, Tedmond, Theodore**). Also, **Tedd.** *Whatever:* Sounds more fitting for one of your dad's business associates than your newborn?

Teddy (English: variation of **Edward, Tedmond, Theodore**). Also, **Teddey.**

Tedmond (English: protector). Also, **Tedmonde, Tedmund, Tedmunde.** Familiar, **Ted, Teddy.** *Whatever:* The Thurston Howell III way to get to **Ted.**

Tempus (Latin: time). Also, **Tempuss.**

Tenney (English: variation of **Dennis,** "fighter, warrior"). Also, **Tenny.**

Teodoro (Spanish: variation of **Theodore,** "gift from God").

Terence (latin: tender). Also, **Terance, Terrance, Terrence.** Familiar, **Terry.** *Plus:* This one's a peer of trendy **Tanner** with the track record of classic **Thomas.** A pocket T. *Minus:* Not happening in the popularity polls.

Tern (English: seagull). Also, **Terne.**

Terrell (English: strong). Also, **Terrel, Terril, Terrill, Terryl, Terryll.**

Terrick (American: variation of **Derrick,** "ruler"). Also, **Terric, Terrik, Terryc, Terryck, Terryk.**

Terry (English: ruler of the people; variation of **Terence,** "tender"). Also, **Terrey.** *Whatever:* Here's an example of what happens when a sensitive, cute boy gets clocked by the girls—the name gets stolen, and it doesn't come back. Even if it's a handsome entry like this one.

Thad (Hebrew: variation of **Thaddeus,** "wise"). Also, **Thadd.**

Thaddeus (Hebrew: wise). Also, **Thaddius, Thaddyus.** Familiar, **Thad.** *Plus:* **Thaddeus** is outrageously formal but somehow—magically—not terribly wussy. *Minus:* You happen to think it sounds terribly wussy.

Thane (English: prosperous gentleman). Also, **Thaine, Thayne.** *Whatever:* The usable **Blane,** if only because it wasn't the one lampooned in *Pretty in Pink.*

Thatch (English: roof of straw; variation of **Thatcher,** "roofer"). Also, **Thatche.**

Thatcher (English: roofer). Familiar, **Thatch.**

Thayer (English: army of the people). Also, **Thayor.**

Theion (Greek: brimstone). Also, **Theyon.**

Theo (German/Greek: variation of **Theobold, Theodore**). *Whatever:* Theodore is in mothballs, **Ted** and **Teddy** are over, but **Theo**? That cooks. A jazzy little number woefully underused, except on *The Cosby Show.* A pick to click.

Theobold   (German: people, bold). Also, **Theobald, Theobalde, Theobolde.** Familiar, **Theo.**

Theodore   (Greek: gift from God; English: ruler of the people). Also, **Theodor.** Familiar, **Ted, Teddy, Theo.**

Theos   (Greek: a god).

Thoma   (German: variation of **Thomas**, "twin").

Thomas   (Greek/Hebrew: twin; English: variation of **Thomason**, "son of **Thomas**"). Also, **Thomass.** Familiar, **Tom, Tommy.** *Plus:* A no-sweat, no-brainer pocket T. **Thomas** is **Thomas** is **Thomas.** People have long accepted it as something you name a boy. You can get fancy with **Thoma** and such, but chances are the boy ends up plain old (dependable) **Tom.** *Minus:* No challenge, say the spelunkers. A big-time peanut-butter-and-jelly sandwich.

Thomason   (English: son of **Thomas**, "twin"). Also, **Thomasen.** Familiar, **Thomas, Tom, Tommy.**

Thompson   (English: variation of **Thomson**, "son of **Tom**"). Also, **Thompsen.**

Thomson   (English: son of **Tom**). Also, **Thomsen, Thomssen, Thomsson.** Familiar, **Tom, Tommy.**

Thorndyke   (English: river by the thorn bushes). Also, **Thorndike, Thornedike, Thornedyke.** Familiar, **Thorne.**

Thorne   (English: a thorn; variation of **Thorndyke, Thornton**). Also, **Thorn.** *Whatever:* Very *Dynasty,* but doable.

Thornton   (English: town of thorn bushes). Also, **Thorneten, Thorneton, Thornten.** Familiar, **Thorne.**

Thorold   (Norwegian: god of thunder, strength). Also, **Thorrold.**

Thorpe   (English: farm). Also, **Thorp.**

Thorsen   (Norse: son of **Thor**, god of thunder). Also, **Thorson, Thorsyn.** Familiar, **Thor.** *Whatever:* If you're absolutely committed to **Thor,** at least give the kid an extra syllable with which to soften the impact of this heavy-duty hero name.

Thurman   (English: protector; variation of **Thor,** god of thunder). Also, **Thurmann.**

Thurmond   (English: of **Thor,** god of thunder). Also, **Thurmonde, Thurmund, Thurmunde.**

Tibald   (Latin: variation of **Theobold**, "people, bold"). Also, **Tybald.**

Tiger   (Greek: big, striped cat). Also, **Tyger.** *Whatever:* Will we *all* be **Tigers** by the year 2525? Don't bet on it knocking **Michael** from its perennial number one slot anytime soon, but monster personality **Tiger** Woods can't help but lead a mini-popularity surge of this off-beat moniker.

Tighe (Irish: poet). Also, **Teege.** *Whatever:* **Tiger**-esque without being nearly so literal. A comer.

Tiller (Latin: weaver's beam).

Tilson (German: good son). Also, **Tilsen, Tillsen, Tillson.**

Tim (Greek: variation of **Timothy,** "respect of God"). Also, **Timm, Tym, Tymm.** *Whatever:* Your little **Tim** will rarely make it through the Christmas season without hearing at least one Tiny **Tim** crack.

Timmy (English: variation of **Timothy,** "respect of God"). Also, **Timmey.**

Timoteo (Spanish: variation of **Timothy,** "respect of God"). Also, **Tymoteo.**

Timothy (Greek: respect of God). Also, **Timothey.** Familiar, **Tim, Timmy.** *Whatever:* Another pocket T (or peanut-butter-and-jelly sandwich, depending on your perspective). Not much more counsel can a baby name book provide on an entry like **Timothy.** Just one proviso: The name has been on a slow, steady trip *down* the popularity charts during the last quarter-century.

Titus (English: safe). Also, **Tituss, Tytus, Tytuss.** *Whatever:* An off-beat pick to click. A strong, manly name that doesn't make a spectacle of its testosterone, à la **Rock,** of "think long, think hard" infamy.

Tobey (Hebrew: variation of **Tobiah, Tobias**). Also, **Tobie, Toby.** *Whatever:* Works as a worthy lil' cowpoke peer of **Cody.**

Tobiah (Hebrew: variation of **Tobias,** "God is good"). Also, **Thobia, Thobiah, Tobia.** Familiar, **Tobey.**

Tobias (Hebrew: God is good). Also, **Thobias.** Familiar, **Tobey.** *Whatever:* Yet another pick to click. For parents who like the idea of **Joshua** but not its celebrity.

Todd (English: fox). Also, **Tod.** *Whatever:* This great jock name of Gen Xer's wonder years has lost much of its muscle tone since the 1970s. Today, it's as squishy as a peanut-butter-and-jelly sandwich.

Toddy (Hindi: a whiskey drink; variation of **Todd,** "fox"). Also, **Toddie, Toddey.**

Tom (English: variation of **Thomas, Thomasson, Thomson**). Also, **Thom, Thomm, Tomm.** *Whatever:* Plain, dull? Perhaps. But über movie star **Tom** Cruise ensures this peanut-butter-and-jelly sandwich features an extra dash of flavor.

Toma (Russian: variation of **Thomas,** "twin").

Tomas (Spanish: variation of **Thomas,** "twin").

Tomasso (Italian: variation of **Thomas,** "twin"). Also, **Tomaso.**

Tomey (Irish: variation of **Thomas,** "twin"). Also, **Tomy.**

Tommy (English: variation of **Thomas, Thomasson, Thomson**). Also, **Tommey, Tommie.**

Tony (Greek: variation of **Anthony,** "priceless"). Also, **Toney.** *Plus:* Established enough to go it as a stand-alone. *Minus:* Common enough to seem positively, well, *common* against the likes of **Brandon** or **Zachary.**

Torrance (Scottish: little hills). Also, **Torance, Torence, Torrence.**

Towne (English: village). *Whatever:* If you're dead set on naming your kid after a collective dwelling community, **Towne** is the pick here over the likes of **Urban.**

Townsend (English: town's end). Also, **Townesend.** *Whatever:* The private detectives of TV's *Charlie's Angels* worked for Charles **Townsend** Associates.

Trace (English: to sketch, trace; variation of **Tracy,** "balcony"). Also, **Trayce.**

Tracy (English: balcony). Also, **Tracey.** Familiar, **Trace.** *Plus:* An alternative to the more trendy **Spencer.** (That is, if your supreme objective is to pay tribute to actor Spencer **Tracy.**) *Minus:* A name that's falling between the cracks in this precious age of lil' cowpokes and cuddly bears. That **Tracy** is now mostly thought to be the domain of girls doesn't help.

Travers (English/French: crossroads). *Whatever:* An entry that offers wiggle room on the more trendy, popular **Travis.**

Travis (English: binding, uniting). Also, **Traviss, Travys, Travyss.** *Whatever:* One of the best lil' cowpoke names going. **Travis** may be a flavor of the month (or the decade), but at least it'll wear well. You can picture a **Travis** at age five or thirty-five, unlike the **Cody/Coby/Cory** bunch.

Traynor (Irish, strong, champion). Also, **Traener, Traenor, Trayner.**

Trent (English: trespass; variation of **Trenton,** "Trent's town"). *Whatever:* Pro football quarterback **Trent** Dilfer makes this charming, sophisticated entry safe for jocks. Take that, **Todd.**

Trenton (English: Trent's town). Also, **Trenten.** Familiar, **Trent.**

Trev (Celtic: variation of **Trevor,** "judicious"). Also, **Trevv.**

Trevor (Celtic: judicious). Also, **Trever.** Familiar, **Trev.** *Whatever:* There's not a lot of downside to **Trevor**—unless you're a spelunker who is worried that's it's no longer the cool find it once was. This long-time Brit favorite now regularly charts on top fifty lists in the States.

Trey (English: three). Also, **Trae, Tre.** *Whatever:* A pick to click. This one's usually assigned as a nickname for the boy whose name comes attached with the Roman numeral accessory "III." But it works as a stand-alone too. Think of it as the hip version of **Tracy.**

Trip (English: three). Also, **Tripp, Tryp, Trypp.** *Plus:* Plucky. *Minus:* One word: Linda.

Tris (English: variation of **Tristam, Tristan, Tristian**). Also, **Triss, Trys, Tryss.**

Tristam (French: variation of **Tristan,** "sad"). Also, **Tristem, Tristym, Trystam, Trystem.** Familiar, **Tris.**

Tristan (Celtic: din; French: sad). Also, **Tristen, Tristyn, Trystan, Trysten.** Familiar, **Tris.** *Plus:* A **Kevin** sound-alike that's got **Kevin** potential as a defining sensitive, cute boy. Immortalized in the opera, *Tristan and Isolde,* it was a *soap*-opera actor (*General Hospital*'s **Tristan** Rogers) who brought the name into the 1980s. Now, it's charging up the top fifty charts. *Minus:* Poses the same dilemma as **Trevor:** How do you know when a pick is about to break out and become the new **Joshua** or **Justin**? You don't.

Tristian (Celtic: variation of **Tristan,** "din"). Also, **Tristien, Tristyan, Tristyen, Trystian, Trystien.** Familiar, **Tris.**

Trotter (Scottish: runner, messenger).

Troy (French: from the city of Troyes).

Tru (English: true; variation of **Truman,** "truc man, faithful servant"). Also, **True.**

Truman (English: true man, faithful servant). Also, **Trueman, True-mann, Trumann.** Familiar, **Tru.** *Plus:* There's something endearingly nerdy cool about **Truman** . . . *Minus:* . . . Unless, of course, the name strikes you as unabashedly nerdy.

Tucker (English: a cloth cleaner). *Whatever:* Morally opposed to names that honor the leather trade? Try the all-cloth **Tucker**—the vegan alternative to **Tanner.**

Turlough (Irish: like **Thor,** god of thunder). Also, **Turlow, Turlowe.**

Turner (English: spun).

Twain (English: two). Also, **Twaine, Twayne.**

Ty (English: enclosed pasture; variation of **Tyler, Tyrone, Tyson**). Also, **Tye.**

Tyler (English: a tile layer). Also, **Tiler.** Familiar, **Ty.** *Whatever:* This one's the new prince of the Ts, making **Thomas** and **Timothy** look tired by comparison. **Tyler** is today's quintessential sensitive, cute boy.

Tyndall (English: burning light). Also, **Tindall.**

Tyrone (Greek: independent, unsurpassed). Also, **Tirone.** Familiar, **Ty.**

Tyson (English: son of **Ty**). Also, **Tysen.** Familiar, **Ty.**

U

CRIB NOTES

Famous Us: **Ulysses** (ancient hero guy, *The Iliad*); **Upton** Sinclair (slightly more recent writer guy, *The Jungle*)

Pocket Ts: Us are Us. They're in the alphabet to keep Qs company. Other than that, we don't think about them much. And we certainly don't dream up a lot of baby names for them. So, no. No suggested pocket Ts here.

Trendy suspenders: Uh, no.

Think long, think hard: **Urban** (This is not an elitist slam. **Suburb** and **Township** are also discouraged as baby names. Why? *Because babies are people, not subdivisions*); **Uzi** (A classic Hebrew name, meaning "my strength." Unfortunately, it's better known today as Modern Disgruntled American for "my automatic weapon.")

Ualtar (Irish: army ruler). Also, **Ualtarr.**
Uben (German: practice). Also, **Ubin, Ubyn.**
Ubrig (German: other). Also, **Ubrigg, Ubryg, Ubrygg.**
Ubrigens (German: besides). Also, **Ubrigins, Ubrigyns.**
Ubrigs (German: variation of **Ubrig,** "other"). Also, **Ubriggs, Ubryggs, Ubrygs.**
Uchtred (Old English: counsel). Also, **Uchtrid, Uchtryd, Uctred, Uctrid, Uctryd, Uktred, Uktrid.**
Udall (English: variation of **Udell,** "valley of yew, evergreen trees"). Also, **Udahl, Udahll, Udal.**
Udell (English: valley of yew, evergreen trees). Also, **Udel, Udelle.**

Whatever: The list of usable, workable U names for modern boys is small. This one sounds more usable and workable than most.

Ufer (German: river).

Uhr (German: clock).

Uilleac (Irish: variation of **Uilleog**, "small defender"). Also, **Uilleack, Uilleak, Uilliac, Uilliack, Uilliak, Uillyac, Uillyack, Uillyak.**

Uilleog (Irish: small defender). Also, **Uilliog, Uillyog.**

Ulan (African: firstborn twin). Also, **Ulann.**

Uland (German: noble country). Also, **Ulande.**

Ulf (German: wolf). Also, **Ulff.**

Uli (Hebrew/Irish/German/Latin: variation of **Ulick, Ulriah, Ulric, Ulysses**). Also, **Uley, Ulie, Uly.**

Ulick (Irish: variation of **Ulysses,** "wrathful"). Also, **Ulic, Ulik, Ulyc, Ulyck, Ulyk.** Familiar, **Uli.** *Whatever:* A name that sounds like an unusual request. If you're so entranced, you might want to side with its sound-alike cousin **Ulric.**

Ulman (German: elm trees, landlord). Also, **Ulmann, Ullman, Ullmann.**

Ulriah (Hebrew: light). Also, **Ulria, Ulrya, Ulryah.** Familiar, **Uli.** *Whatever:* Earnest and sober, **Ulriah** fits well with today's **Jacob**s and **Elijah**s.

Ulric (German: wolf, ruler). Also, **Ulrick, Ulrik, Ulryc, Ulryck, Ulryk.** Familiar, **Uli, Ric.**

Ulster (English: heavy coat).

Ultar (Irish: variation of **Ualtar,** "army ruler"). Also, **Ultarr.**

Ulysses (Latin: wrathful). Also, **Ulisses.** Familiar, **Uli.** *Plus:* A strong boy's name in the tradition of some of our grandest epic heroes, **Ulysses.** *Minus:* A superstar name in the tradition of Madonna.

Umar (Arabic: bloom). Also, **Umaar, Umarr.**

Umbard (English: variation of **Umber,** "reddish brown"). Also, **Umbarde.**

Umber (English: reddish brown).

Umberto (Italian: variation of **Humbert,** "giant, bright").

Umed (Hindi: desire).

Umher (German: around, about).

Unser (German: our).

Unten (German: beneath). Also, **Untenn.**

Unus (Latin: one). Also, **Unuss.**

Unwin (English: foe). Also, **Unwyn.**

Upjohn (Welsh: son of **John**). Also, **Upjon.**

Upshaw (English: upstream). Also, **Upshawe.** *Whatever:* A name that's fit for an English professor. But until graduate school looms, be prepared for the inevitable "upchuck" jibes.

Upton (English: elevated, higher). Also, **Upten.** *Whatever:* In the same boat as **Upshaw.**

Upwood (English: elevated forest. Also, **Upwoode.**

Uri (Hebrew: light; Hebrew/Welsh: variation of **Uriah, Urian, Uriel, Urien**). Also, **Urey, Urie, Ury.**

Uriah (Hebrew: light). Also, **Uria, Urya, Uryah.** Familiar, **Uri.**

Urian (Welsh: fortunate). Also, **Urien, Uryan, Uryen.** Familiar, **Uri.**

Uriel (Hebrew: light). Also, **Uriell, Uryel, Uryell.** Familiar, **Uri.**

Urien (Hebrew: light). Also, **Uryen.** Familiar, **Uri.**

Ursan (Latin: bear). Also, **Ursen, Ursyn.**

Urteil (German: judgment). Also, **Urteel, Urtiel.**

Usama (Arabic: lion). Also, **Usaama.**

Usher (Latin: doorkeeper).

Uthman (Arabic: bird). Also, **Uthmann.**

Uwe (German: variation of **Ulric,** "wolf, ruler").

Uziah (Hebrew: God is my strength). Also, **Uzia, Uzya, Uzyah.**

Uziel (Hebrew: powerful). Also, **Uziell, Uzyel, Uzyell.**

V

CRIB NOTES

Famous Vs: Val Kilmer (ex-Bat actor); **Victor** Hugo (author, *The Hunchback of Notre Dame*); **Vin** Scully (sportscaster); **Vince** Vaughn (actor, *Swingers*); **Vincent** van Gogh (artist); **Vincente** Minnelli (filmmaker)

Pocket Ts: Vaughan, Victor, Vincent

Trendy suspenders: None

Think long, think hard: Valentino (Great lovers are made not born.); **Vern** (That damn Ernest and his incessant, "Hey, **Vern!**" ruined *everything*.); **Verrill** (Like **Valentino,** a mucho manly man name that gives a boy a lot to live up to.); **Virgil** (A very modest, decent-sounding moniker . . . that is utterly not of this age.); **Vulcan** (OK, this is how it works: You watch *Star Trek*. You don't live *Star Trek*.)

Vajon (American: variation of **John,** "God is gracious"). Also, **Vajohn, Vejon, Vejohn.**

Val (French/Latin/Scandinavian: variation of **Valborg, Valdemar, Valentine, Valere, Valerian, Valmont**). *Plus:* A blast of cool. Maybe it's the succinct three-letters-and-out thing. Maybe it's the **Val** Kilmer *Batman* thing. Whatever, **Val** is a pair of black jeans—cool enough to do the stand-alone thing on the birth certificate. *Minus:* Uh-huh, you say—**Val** is a *girl* name.

Valborg (Scandinavian: great mountain). Also, **Valborge, Valbourg.** Familiar, **Val.**

Valdemar (Scandinanvian: strong ruler). Also, **Valdimar, Valdymar.** Familiar, **Val.**

Vale (English/Scottish: valley). Also, **Vail, Vaile, Vayle**. *Whatever:* A stealthy map name. Less obvious than **Dakota**. Less populated than **Brooklyn**. (Permanent population of **Vail**, Colorado, circa 1996: 3,716.)

Valentine (Latin: strong). Also, **Valintine, Valyntine**. Familiar, **Val**. *Whatever:* Handsome, graceful. Still, you might want to opt for **Val** in everyday use. Otherwise things could get brutal every February 14.

Valere (Latin: strong). Familiar, **Val**.

Valerian (Latin: strong). Also, **Valerien, Valeryan, Valeryen**. Familiar, **Val**. *Whatever:* Way too fancy. Simply included here as another way to get to **Val**.

Vallis (French: Welshman). Also, **Valliss, Vallys, Vallyss**. *Whatever:* A slightly hipper sound-alike version of **Wallace**.

Valmont (French: powerful guardian). Also, **Valmonte**. Familiar, **Val**. *Plus:* Another way to get to **Val**. *Minus:* Way too *Dangerous Liaisons*.

Van (Armenian: town; Dutch: variation of **Vandyke**, "the dam"). Also, **Vann**. *Whatever:* About the hippest guy to wear this name this century was actor **Van** Johnson. (Note: Even at his peak, Johnson wasn't what you'd call hip.) Still, this is a nifty, underused name. *Minus:* It's underused because it's about as delicate as naming a kid **Pickup Truck**.

Vance (English/Dutch: small hill). *Whatever:* A pick to click. **Vance** is the with-it **Lance**.

Vandan (Hindi: salvation). Also, **Vandann**. *Whatever:* A name for a future movie action hero: "Wham, bam, thank you, **Vandan**."

Vander (Dutch: variation of **Vandyke**, "the dam").

Vanders (Dutch: variation of **Vandyke**, "the dam").

Vandyke (Dutch: the dam). Also, **Vandike, VanDike, VanDyke**. Familiar, **Van**. *Plus:* Cool daddy-O. This beatnik-worthy name serves as apt tribute to the goatee (read: **Vandyke** beard), *the* facial-hair choice of the Gen X era. *Minus:* Too hip for the classroom?

Vanya (Russian: variation of **John**, "God is gracious").

Varden (French: green mountain).

Varick (Scandinavian: sea drift). Also, **Varic, Varik**.

Vartan (American: giver of roses). Also, **Vartann**.

Vashon (American: variation of **Sean**, "God is gracious"). Also, **Vasean, Vashaun, Vashawn, Vesean, Veshaun, Veshawn, Veshon**.

Vasil (Slavic: royal). Also, **Vasill, Vasyl, Vasyll**.

Vasin (Hindi: ruler). Also, **Vasyn.**

Vaughan (Welsh: little). Also, **Vaughen, Vaughn.** *Whatever:* A pocket T. It's understated class wears well in any region, anytime.

Vayshon (American: variation of **Sean,** "God is gracious"). Also, **Vaesean, Vaeshaun, Vaeshawn, Vaeshon, Vaysean, Vayshaun, Vayshawn.**

Veitel (German: variation of **Vitalis,** "life"). Also, **Veitell.**

Ver (Latin: spring). Also, **Verr.**

Vere (Latin: true). Also, **Verre.**

Verner (French/English: protecting army). Also, **Vernor.**

Vernon (French/English: birth-tree grove). Also, **Vernen.** *Whatever:* Thankfully, that Ernest guy isn't formal. He has yet to ruin **Vernon,** a sturdy, down-home entry.

Vic (Latin/Slavic/Spanish: variation of **Victor, Victorio, Viktor**). Also, **Vick, Vik.**

Victor (Latin: conqueror). Also, **Victer.** Familiar, **Vic.** *Plus:* A long track record helps **Victor** weather the down times and still end up sounding fit for a king. A pocket T. *Minus:* **Victor** is soap-opera shorthand for dark and sinister.

Victorio (Spanish: variation of **Victor,** "conqueror"). Also, **Victorrio, Victorryo, Victoryo.** Familiar, **Vic.**

Vidor (Scandinavian: powerful god).

Vijay (Hindi: victorious). Also, **Veejay, Vejay.**

Viktor (Slavic: variation of **Victor,** "conqueror"). Familiar, **Vic.**

Vilem (Slavic: variation of **William,** "will, helmet"). Also, **Vilim, Villem, Villim, Villym, Vilym.**

Vilhelm (German: variation of **William,** "will, helmet"). Also, **Vilhem.**

Vilmos (German: variation of **William,** "will, helmet").

Vin (English/Latin: variation of **Vincent, Vincente, Vincenzio, Vincenzo, Vinson, Vinton**). Also, **Vinn, Vyn, Vynn.** *Plus:* Lots of nifty stuff going on in the Vs. Here's another **Van** or **Vaughan.** Unique, unfettered, and (almost) too hip for the room, **Vin** is a nickname that's strong enough to stand alone. *Minus:* It's probably not as cool-sounding if your interest in baseball, and legendary announcer **Vin** Scully, is little to none.

Vinay (Hindi: polite). Also, **Vinae.**

Vince (Latin: variation of **Vincent, Vincente**)

Vincent (Latin: conqueror). Also, **Vincint, Vincynt.** Familiar, **Vin, Vince, Vinnie.** *Whatever:* An entry that's uptown *and* downtown. Consider its most famed namesake, **Vincent** van Gogh. He's an artist (uptown). He's a loon (downtown). Time to get in on this pocket T's action.

Vincente (Spanish: variation of **Vincent,** "conqueror"). Also, **Vincinte, Vincynte.** Familiar, **Vin, Vince, Vinnie.**

Vincenzio (Italian: variation of **Vincent,** "conqueror"). Also, **Vincenzyo.** Familiar, **Vin, Vinnie.**

Vincenzo (Italian: variation of **Vincent,** "conqueror"). Familiar, **Vin, Vinnie.**

Vinnie (English/Latin: variation of **Vince, Vincent, Vincente, Vincenzo, Vinson, Vinton**). Also, **Vinney, Vinny.** *Whatever:* A name that's been done irreprarable harm by one too many buffoonish, brutish portrayals in Hollywood.

Vino (Italian/Spanish: wine). Also, **Veeno, Vyno.**

Vinson (English: son of **Vin**). Also, **Vinsen.** Familiar, **Vin, Vinnie.**

Vinton (English: village by the stream; Latin: life). Also, **Vinten.** Familiar, **Vin, Vinnie.**

Viscount (English: nobleman). Also, **Viscounte.**

Vitalis (Latin: life). Also, **Vitalys.** *Plus:* A strong boy name . . . *Minus:* . . . usurped by a hair gel.

Vitel (English: variation of **Vitalis,** "life"). Also, **Vitell.**

Vitis (Latin: vine). Also, **Vitys.**

Vito (Italian: variation of **Victor, Vittorio**).

Vittorio (Italian: variation of **Victor,** "conqueror"). Also, **Vitorio, Vitorrio, Vitoryo, Vittoryo.** Familiar, **Vito.**

Vitya (Russian: variation of **Victor,** "conqueror").

Vlad (Russian/Slavic: variation of **Vladimir,** "famous prince"). Also, **Vladd.** *Whatever:* The fifteenth-century Transylvanian prince known as **Vlad** the Impaler is believed to be author Bram Stoker's inspiration for *Dracula.*

Vladimir (Russian/Slavic: famous prince). Also, **Vladymir.** Familiar, **Vlad.**

Voigt (German: steward). Also, **Vogt, Voight, Voyt.**

Volker (German: defender of the people). Also, **Volkker, Vollker.** *Whatever:* The **Walker** sound-alike for parents who think **Walker** is too, well, literal.

Volney (German: spirit of the people). Also, **Volny.**

Von (Scandinavian: hope). Also, **Vonn.** Familiar, **Vonnie.** *Plus:* Worried about **Vaughan** looking too fancy? Try **Von.** *Minus:* Yeah, but will it make the kid sound like an extra on *Hogan's Heroes*?

Vonnie (Scandinavian: variation of **Von,** "hope"). Also, **Vonney, Vonny.**

Vyell (English: variation of **Vitalis,** "life"). Also, variation of **Vyel.**

CRIB NOTES

Famous Ws: Walt Disney (father of Mickey Mouse); **Waylon** Jennings (country singer); **Whit** Stillman (filmmaker, *The Last Days of Disco*); Prince **William** (British royalty); **Willem** Dafoe (actor, *Platoon*); **Willis** Jackson (big brother, TV's *Diff'rent Strokes*); **Wilt** Chamberlain (basketball legend); **Winston** Churchill (British prime minister); **Woody** Harrelson (actor; *Natural Born Killers*); **Wynton** Marsalis (jazz musician)

Pocket Ts: William, Wyatt

Trendy suspenders: Walker

Think long, think hard: Waldo (Where's **Waldo**? Missing in action. Last seen in the nineteenth century.); **Webster** (We watched far too many half hours of *Webster* as impressionable youths. Don't think we need to waste any more time on this one.); **Wilbur** (To Gen X fans of E. B. White's *Charlotte's Web*, **Wilbur** is once and forever a *pig*.); **Wilfred** (Irreparably nerdy.); **Willard** (**Willard** Scott aside, this name's biggest claim to fame is the 1970s rat movie *Willard*. True, **Willard** wasn't one of the rodents, but big deal, he was the social misfit who befriended them.); **Wink** (The game-show rule: Good for watching; bad for baby naming.); **Winthrop** (Sounds like "with cough drop." One of its many issues.)

Wade (English: shallow river crossing). Also, **Waid, Waide, Wayde.** *Plus:* Perfect Southern gentleman fodder. *Minus:* Yes, but which South—*Gone With the Wind* or *Deliverance*?

Waede (English: garment).

Waggoner (English: wagon maker). Also, **Waggener.**

Wagner (English: wagon maker). Also, **Waggner.**

Wainwright (English: wagon maker). Also, **Wainwrighte, Wane-wright, Wanewrighte, Waynewright, Waynewrighte.**

Waite (English: castle watchman). Also, **Wate, Wayte.**

Wakely (English: watcher by the meadow). Also, **Wakeley.**

Wakeman (English: watchman).

Wakemond (English: variation of **Wakeman,** "watchman"). Also, **Wakemonde, Wakemund, Wakemunde.**

Walden (English: little forest). Also, **Waldin, Waldyn.** *Whatever:* The map name with literary aspirations. It's a pond. It's Henry David Thoreau. It's two—two!—cool references in one baby name.

Walder (English: forest guard).

Walker (English: a tanner). *Plus:* Very today. **Walker** is the grown-up lil' cowpoke, evoking soft-spoken cowboys strolling the range. *Minus:* Evokes Chuck (*Walker, Texas Ranger*) Norris. And, beware: **Walker** is so much of its time—with all its affected uniqueness—that it may have trouble playing in other decades. A potential pair of trendy suspenders.

Wallace (Scottish: foreigner). Also, **Wallece, Wallyce.** Familiar, **Wally.** *Whatever:* A solid, fundamentally sound boy name.

Waller (English: wall builder). Also, **Whaller.** *Plus:* Offers wiggle room on the more trendy **Walker.** *Minus:* It's just as affected as our home-on-the-range friend.

Wallin (Scandinavian: untended land). Also, **Wallyn.**

Walling (English: foreigner). Also, **Wallyng, Whalling, Whallyng.**

Wallis (English: variation of **Wallace,** "foreigner"). Also, **Walliss, Wallys, Wallyss.** Familiar, **Wally.**

Walls (English: wall, spring, stream). Also, **Wals, Whalls, Whals.**

Wally (Scottish: variation of **Wallace,** "foreigner"). Also, **Walley.** *Plus:* Perfectly good flannel shirt material (if you can get past the **Wally** Cleaver thing). *Minus:* You can't get past the **Wally** Cleaver thing.

Walsh (Irish: from Wales, foreigner). Also, **Walshe.**

Walt (Welsh/German: variation of **Walter, Walters**). Also, **Walte.**

Walter (Welsh/German: army leader). Also, **Walther.** Familiar, **Walt.** *Plus:* Evokes decency and honor. *Minus:* Evokes **Walter** Cronkite and other octogenarians.

Walters (English: variation of **Walter**, "army leader"). Also, **Walthers.** Familiar, **Walt.**

Walton (English: woods). Also, **Walten.** *Whatever:* The contemporary **Walter.** Scores in that important contemporary category: Being a baby name that doesn't sound like a baby name, but rather a little-person name.

Ward (English: to guard; variation of **Wardell, Wardley, Wardman**). Also, **Warde.** *Whatever:* Another *Leave It to Beaver* moniker, **Ward** projects the same good-guy feel of a **Ben** or **Jacob.**

Wardell (English: watchman on the hill). Also, **Wardel, Wardelle.** Familiar, **Ward.**

Warder (English: watchman).

Wardley (English: guard by the meadow). Also, **Wardly.** Familiar, **Ward.**

Wardman (English: watchman). Familiar, **Ward.**

Ware (English: protecting dam). Also, **Waire.** *Plus:* A pick to click. It's handsome, unique, robust. *Minus:* You object to the practice of scrambling letters ("Let's see, 'wear' . . . Move that *a* here . . . **Ware!**") to make a baby name.

Warfield (English: field by the dam). Also, **Warfielde.**

Waring (English: variation of **Ware**, "protecting dam").

Warner (English/French: protector, guardian). *Plus:* Contemporary. Strong. Unique. *Minus:* A predicable last-name-as-first-name ploy. When is enough enough? Trust this, future civilizations are going to look back and wonder if we suffered from baby name dyslexia.

Warners (English: variation of **Warner**, "protector, guardian").

Warren (English: protector, watchman). Also, **Warrin, Warryn.** *Plus:* **Warren** used to seem humdrum. Now it's so rare it's a virtual act of rebellion when used. A nerdy cool pick. *Minus:* Platitudes are nice. The bottom line: This is nerd city.

Warrick (English: variation of **Warwick**, "farm by the dam"). Also, **Warric, Warrik, Warryc, Warryck, Warryk, Wharric, Wharrick, Wharrik, Wharryc, Wharryck, Wharryk.**

Warton (English: riverbank). Also, **Warten, Wharten, Wharton.** *Plus:* Hey, this is why last names are hot. They just kinda work. *Minus:* They make all newborns sound like Oxford undergrads.

Warwick (English: farm by the dam). Also, **Warwic, Warwik, War-**

wyc, **Warwyck, Warwyk, Wharwic, Wharwick, Wharwik, Wharwyc, Wharwyck, Wharwyk.**

Washer (English/German: washer of cloth). *Plus:* If **Walker,** why not **Washer**? *Minus:* It's all wet.

Washington (English: town by the water). Also, **Washyngton.** *Plus:* Great source material—the, uh, president guy. *Minus:* Gen Xers, astute or no, are about as apolitical as they come. Naming kids after presidents was another trend for another time.

Watson (English: son of **Watt**). Also, **Watsen, Wattsen, Wattson.**

Watt (English: ruler of the people). Also, **Watte.**

Watts (English: variation of **Watt,** "ruler of the people"). Also, **Wats.**

Waylon (English: land by the road). Also, **Waylen.** *Whatever:* Country legend **Waylon** Jennings performed the theme song to TV's *The Dukes of Hazzard* (1979–85).

Wayne (English: wagon). Also, **Wain, Waine, Wane.** *Whatever:* Looking for **Wayne**? He's hanging with **Gary, Glen,** and **Randy**—in baby name exile.

Weaver (English: cloth weaver). Also, **Weever.** *Whatever:* Hey, spelunkers, can you get any more elemental, any more salt-of-the-earth than this—a *weaver*? A pick to click.

Webb (English: sword blade; German: variation of **Webber,** "weaver"). Also, **Web.**

Webber (German: weaver). Also, **Weber.** Familiar, **Webb.** *Plus:* The doable **Webster**. *Minus:* The sandwich-bread thing.

Weeb (English: variation of **Webber,** "weaver"). Also, **Weebe.**

Wegener (English: variation of **Wagner,** "wagon maker"). Also, **Weggener, Wegginer, Weggyner, Weginer, Wegyner.**

Welch (Welsh: variation of **Welsh,** "a person from Wales"). Also, **Welche.**

Weldon (English: hill by a stream). Also, **Welden, Whelden, Wheldon.**

Welkin (English: vault of the sky). Also, **Welkyn.**

Weller (English: welder). Also, **Wheller.** *Whatever: See* **Weaver.**

Welles (English: natural springs; variation of **Wellesley, Wellsley**). Also, **Wells, Whelles, Whells.** *Whatever:* A nifty tribute to *Citizen Kane* auteur, Orson **Welles.**

Wellesley (English: western meadow; city in Massachusetts). Also, **Wellesly, Whellesley, Whellesly.** Familiar, **Welles.** *Whatever:* Workable in this age of map names and **Walkers,** but, come on, it's time to ask yourself: Are you naming a future human being or christening an ivy-covered institution of higher learning?

Wellsley (English: variation of **Wellesley,** "western meadow"). Also, **Whellsley, Whellsly.** Familiar, **Welles.**

Welsh (Welsh: a person from Wales). Also, **Welshe.**

Werner (German: variation of **Warner,** "protector, guardian"). Also, **Wernor.**

Wes (English: variation of **Wesly,** "western meadow"). Also, **Wess.**

Wesly (English: western meadow). Also, **Wesley.** Familiar, **Wes.** *Whatever:* The "Stop the madness!" version of **Wellesley.**

West (English: a direction, from the west; variation of **Westbrook, Westcott, Westford, Westgate, Westley, Weston, Westwood**). Also, **Weste.** *Whatever:* More a location name than a map name, but it still works.

Westbrook (English: western stream). Also, **Westbrooke.** Familiar, **West.**

Westcott (English: western cottage). Also, **Westcot.** Familiar, **West.**

Westford (English: western stream crossing). Also, **Westforde.** Familiar, **West.**

Westgate (English: western gate). Also, **Westgaite, Westgayte.** Familiar, **West.**

Westley (English: variation of **Wesly,** "western meadow"). Also, **Westly.** Familiar, **West.**

Weston (English: western town). Also, **Westen.** Familiar, **West.** *Whatever:* Sounds like "Wesson." This makes it more of a cooking-oil name than a location name.

Westwood (English: western wood). Also, **Westwoode.** Familiar, **West.**

Whalley (English: hillside home). Also, **Whally.** *Plus:* The preppie **Wally.** *Minus:* If it sounds like **Wally,** sorta looks like **Wally,** it's **Wally.**

Wheat (English: fair-complected, a grain; variation of **Wheaton,** "where the grain grows"). Also, **Weat, Weate, Wheate.** *Plus:* A pick to click. **Wheat** is elemental, basic, and unpretentious— **Walker** unplugged. *Minus:* It's the freakin' stuff that's in bread. Get a grip.

Wheaton (English: where the grain grows). Also, **Weaten, Weaton, Wheaten.** Familiar, **Wheat.** *Whatever:* The dressed-up, socially acceptable **Wheat.**

Wheeler (English: wheel maker). Also, **Weeler**. *Plus:* Swifter than **Walker**. *Minus:* Reminiscent of fluff-head Bobby **Wheeler** from TV's *Taxi*.

Whip (Scandinavian: to swing). Also, **Whipp, Wipp.**

Whit (English: light-complected; variation of **Whitfield, Whitman**). Also, **Whitt, Witt.** *Whatever:* A pick to click.

Whitey (English: light-complected; variation of **Whitfield, Whitman**). *Whatever:* A name that seems to work best on grizzled, gray-haired baseball managers.

Whitfield (English: white field). Also, **Whitfielde, Whittfield, Whittfielde, Witfield, Witfielde, Wittfield, Wittfielde.** Familiar, **Whit, Whitey.**

Whitman (English: fair-complected). Also, **Whittman, Witman, Wittman.** Familiar, **Whit, Whitey.** *Whatever:* A boy version of a *Little House on the Prairie* name. So 1800s, so honest, so distinctively nerdy cool.

Wiatt (French: variation of **Wyatt**, "little battler"). Also, **Wiat.**

Wilde (English: wild; variation of **Wilder**, "forest, army"). Also, **Whild, Whilde, Wild, Wyld, Wylde.**

Wilder (English: forest, army).

Wiley (English: clever, beguiling). Also, **Wily.**

Will (English: will; variation of **Willem, William, Williams, Williamson, Willis**). Also, **Wil, Wyl, Wyll.**

Willem (German: variation of **William**, "will, helmet"). Also, **Wilem, Wilim, Willim.** Familiar, **Will, Willie.**

William (English: will, helmet; variation of **Williamson**). Also, **Wiliam, Wiliem, Williem, Wilyam, Wilyem.** Familiar, **Bill, Billy, Will, Willie.** *Whatever:* A big-time pocket T. Not trendy popular, not hot, not cold—always just right. This is a boy's boy name, from the eleventh century to today. Two provisos: (1) **William** is also a peanut-butter-and-jelly sandwich, with all the inventiveness and distinctiveness of that meal; (2) Its fortunes as a contemporary name may rest with the popularity, or lack thereof, of royal heir Prince **William**. In the short run, look for young **Wills** to be a big champion of this blue-blood classic.

Williams (English: variation of **William**, "will, helmet"). Also, **Wiliams, Wiliems, Williems.** Familiar, **Will, Willie.**

Williamson (English: son of **William**). Also, **Wiliamsen, Wiliemson,**

Williamsen, Williemsen, Williemson, Willyamson, Wilyemsen, Wilyemson, Wilyemssen, Wilyemsson. Familiar, **Will, William, Willie.**

Willie (English: variation of **Willem, William, Williams, Williamson, Willis**). Also, **Willey, Willy.** *Plus:* Popularized by the *Free Willy* whale movies. *Minus:* Popularized by the *Free Willy* whale movies.

Willis (English: son of **Will**). Also, **Willys.** Familiar, **Will, Willie.** *Plus:* The distinctive twist on **William** you want. *Minus:* The *Diff'rent Strokes* association you don't want.

Wills (English: variation of **Will**, "will"). Also, **Wils, Wylls, Wyls.**

Wilson (English: son of **Will**). Also, **Wilsen, Wilssen, Wilsson.**

Wilt (German: determined, brave; English: variation of **Wilton**, "town by the willows"). Also, **Wilte.**

Wilton (English: town by the willows). Also, **Wilten.** Familiar, **Wilt.**

Wim (Dutch: variation of **William**, "will, helmet"). Also, **Whim, Whimm, Wimm.**

Windham (English: hamlet by the meadow). Also, **Whindam, Whindham, Whindhem, Windam, Windem, Windhem.**

Winston (English: from the town). Also, **Winsten, Wynsten, Wynston.**

Winter (English: the season; German: wind, army). Also, **Wynter.** *Plus:* More macho than **Spring** or **Summer.** *Minus:* Another twenty years of nonnames like **Winter,** and we're gonna get big-time nostalgic for **Bob.**

Winters (English: variation of **Winter**, "the season"). Also, **Wynters.**

Wolf (German: a wolf, predator; variation of **Wolfgang**, "gang of wolves"). Also, **Wolfe, Wolff.** *Plus:* A name so strong it snarls. Championed in recent years by CNN correspondent **Wolf** Blitzer. *Minus:* A name that will launch a thousand bad woof-woof jokes.

Wolfgang (German: gang of wolves). Also, **Wolfegang.** Familiar, **Wolf, Wolfie.** *Whatever:* Not just for Amadeus anymore. Celeb couple Valerie Bertinelli and Eddie Van Halen named their son **Wolfgang**. Further proof that *anything* can be done provided you possess the vision, or myopia, depending on your feelings about **Wolfgang** and other offbeat monikers.

Wolfie (German: variation of **Wolfgang**, "gang of wolves"). Also, **Wolfey, Wolfy.**

Wood (English: the forest; variation of **Woodman, Woodrow, Wood-**

son, **Woodward**). Also, **Woode.** *Whatever:* A thought on the **Wood** names: They're all relatively timeless and doable. They just all seem like they'd be relative burdens for your average teenage boy on his quest to survive the locker room, ego intact.

Woodman (English: lumberjack). Also, **Woodeman.** Familiar, **Wood, Woody.**

Woodrow (English: row of trees). Familiar, **Wood, Woody.**

Woodson (English: son of **Wood**). Also, **Woodesen, Woodeson, Woodsen.** Familiar, **Wood, Woody.**

Woodward (English: forest ranger). Also, **Woodeward, Woodewarde, Woodwarde.** Familiar, **Wood, Woody.**

Woody (English: variation of **Wood,** "the forest"). Also, **Woodey.**

Worth (English: estimable; variation of **Wortham,** "enclosed property"). Also, **Worthe, Wurth, Wurthe.** *Whatever:* Neat, different, and laudable.

Wortham (English: enclosed property). Also, **Worthem, Worthym, Wurtham, Wurthym.** Familiar, **Worth.**

Wray (German: isolated). Also, **Wraye.** *Whatever:* The today **Ray.**

Wren (Irish: spear). Also, **Wrenn.**

Wright (English: carpenter). Also, **Wrighte.** *Plus:* A pick to click. So simple, so in tune with the times. *Minus:* So open for bad puns.

Wyatt (French: little battler). Also, **Wyat.** *Whatever:* A pocket T. Sure, maybe it hasn't been hot since the days of Sheriff **Wyatt** Earp, but it's hung in there, waiting for its time to come around again. The time is now. **Wyatt** is the grown-up **Cody.**

Wyeth (Scottish: brave). Also, **Wieth, Wyith.**

Wylie (English: variation of **Wiley,** "clever, beguiling"). Also, **Wiley, Wily, Wyle, Wyley.** *Whatever:* It's the surname of *ER* resident Noah **Wyle.** Is that enough to rescue this cool number from Mr. Post, the World War II aviator?

Wynne (Scottish: meadow; English: friend). Also, **Winn, Wyn, Wynn.** *Whatever:* Another **Whit.** Maybe even more accessible. A win-**Winn** baby name.

Wynton (English: town by the willows). Also, **Winten, Winton, Wynten.** *Whatever:* Got a great booster in young jazz great **Wynton** Marsalis.

X

CRIB NOTES

We interrupt Famous Xs, Pocket Ts, Trendy suspenders, and Think long, think hard, to bring you this special message:

This is what Americans think of the letter X: It's an eight-point Scrabble tile. A game-breaker. An albatross. The letter that leaves you praying for an open *a* on the board, so you can spell "ax" and be done with it.

In short, we don't know what to do with X. We know it makes car models sound faster, secret formulas more mysterious, and generations cooler. But baby names? There, we're clueless. It's all Greek to us. Appropriate, considering the usual list of baby X names reads like a phone book for ancient Athens. Honestly, **Xystus**? Who names a kid **Xystus**? But because we promised you the entire alphabet, and because it's your right to award a baby name you're not even sure how to pronounce, we present—with the above provisos—the letter X.

Xan (Greek: variation of **Alexander,** "protector, defender"; variation of **Xantho, Xanthos, Xanthus**). Also, **Xann, Xanne.** *Plus:* Kind of kicky. *Minus:* Kind of Wondertwins-esque.

Xandar (Greek: variation of **Alexander,** "protector, defender").

Xander (Greek: variation of **Alexander,** "protector, defender").

Xanthin (Greek: yellow-colored). Also, **Xanthyn.**

Xantho (Greek: yellow). Familiar, **Xan.**

Xanthos (Greek: yellow). Familiar, **Xan.**

Xanthus (Greek: variation of **Xanthos,** "yellow"). Also, **Xanthous, Xanthuss.** Familiar, **Xan.**

Xat (Native American: totem pole). Also, **Xatt.**

Xaver (German: variation of **Xavier,** "bright"). Also, **Xaiver, Xayver.**

Xaverius (Greek: brilliant). Also, **Xaverious, Xaveryus.**

Xavier (Arabic: bright; Spanish: new house). Also, **Xavyer.** *Whatever:* Erstwhile New Kids on the Block member Donnie Wahlberg has a son named **Xavier.**

Xavion (African: new house). Also, **Xavien.** *Whatever:* The sound-alike to **Savion,** as in **Savion** *"Bring In 'Da Noise, Bring In 'Da Funk"* Glover.

Xebec (English: ship). Also, **Xebeck, Xebek.**

Xenik (Greek: stranger). Also, **Xenic, Xenick, Xenyc, Xenyck, Xenyk.**

Xeno (Greek: alien, guest). Also, **Xeeno, Xino, Xyno.**

Xenon (Greek: a gas).

Xenophon (Greek: strange voice). Also, **Xenofon, Xenofone, Xeno-phone.**

Xenos (Greek: stranger).

Xerarch (Greek: dry place). Also, **Xerarche.**

Xeres (Spanish: older). Also, **Xeris, Xerys.**

Xerxes (Greek: lion king). Also, **Xerxis, Xerxys.**

Xhosan (African: variation of **Xhosas,** "South African tribe"). Also, **Xhosen, Xhosyn.**

Xhosas (African: South African tribe). Also, **Xhoses, Xhosys.**

Ximen (Spanish: dutiful). Also, **Ximin, Ximyn.**

Ximena (Spanish: variation of **Ximenes,** "obedient"). Also, **Xymena.**

Ximenes (Spanish: obedient). Also, **Xymenes.**

XL (English: extralarge). *Whatever:* Heck, why not? It's about as colloquial as the rest of these "names." Besides, this letter combo sounds cool on cars, why not babies?

Xuthus (Greek: from Greek mythology, husband of Creusa—whoever that was). Also, **Xuthous.**

Xylo (Greek: wood).

Xylon (Greek: forest). Also, **Xilon.** *Whatever:* Toner cartridges not in-cluded.

Xyst (Greek: a garden). Also, **Xist.**

Xystum (Greek: variation of **Xystus,** "promenade"). Also, **Xistoum, Xistum, Xystoum.**

Xystus (Greek: promenade). Also, **Xistus.**

CRIB NOTES

Famous Ys: Yanni (New Age musician); **Yaphet** Kotto (actor); **Yancy** Thigpen (football player); **Yul** Brynner (bald guy, *The King and I*).

Pocket Ts: Yale

Trendy suspenders: The way it works is, the alphabet starts running out of steam at U, briefly revives at W, and then peters out for the stretch drive to Z. In short, there's not a lot of Y material to begin with here, and certainly nothing that parents have glommed on to.

Think long, think hard: Yanni (If you must pay tribute to an easy-listening guru, think **John** Tesh. At least then your son can pretend he was named after somebody else.); **Yeoman** (Let him enlist on his own time.); **Yoda** (Rent the movies. Dress up like a stormtrooper for Halloween. Name your first three kids, **Luke, Leia,** and **Han**. Do whatever you have to do to get *Star Wars* out of your system before you even *think* of going down the dark alley that is dubbing a boy *Yoda*.)

Yaegar (German: hunter). Also, **Yager, Yeager.** *Whatever:* Evokes *The Right Stuff* images of rough-and-ready test pilot Chuck **Yeager.**

Yaeshon (American: variation of **Sean,** "God is gracious"). Also, **Yaesean, Yaeshaun, Yaeshawn, Yaysean, Yayshaun, Yayshawn, Yayshon.**

Yale (English: nook). Also, **Yael, Yaele, Yaile, Yayle.** *Plus:* OK, admittedly, this is a pocket T made of stretch fabric—because this pick is stretching it. You've likely never known any man named **Yale,** never heard of any parent naming a baby **Yale.** But maybe you heard it once in a movie (say, Woody Allen's *Manhattan*) and it sounded sort of nifty—bookish, but not prissy. *Minus:* You went to Harvard.

Yamil (Arabic: handsome). Also, **Yameel.**

Yance (Frency: variation of **Yancy,** "from England").

Yancy (French: from England). Also, **Yancey.** *Plus:* If a **Yancy** can make it to the NFL then your **Yancy** can make it to the schoolyard. *Minus:* Rhymes with "fancy."

Yank (Dutch: stranger). Also, **Yanke.** *Plus:* A **Hank** sound-alike. *Minus:* You live in the South.

Yankee (English: a U.S. citizen). Also, **Yankey.** *Plus:* Patriotic. *Minus:* Two words: Doodle dandy.

Yaphet (Hebrew: handsome). Also, **Yaphett, Yaphit, Yaphitt.**

Yardley (English: enclosed meadow). Also, **Yardly.** *Whatever:* A lovable Thurston Howell III. Or as lovable as a Thurston Howell III can get.

Yared (Hebrew: variation of **Jared,** "descending"). Also, **Yarid, Yaryd.** *Whatever:* Sound-alike for popular **Jared.**

Yashon (American: variation of **Sean,** "God is gracious"). Also, **Yasean, Yashaun, Yashawn, Yesean, Yeshaun, Yeshawn, Yeshon.**

Yasin (Arabic: prophet). Also, **Yaseen, Yasyn.**

Yasir (Arabic: prosperous). Also, **Yaseer, Yassir.**

Yates (English: enclosed meadow). Also, **Yaites, Yaytes.**

Yeardley (English: variation of **Yardley,** "enclosed meadow"). Also, **Yeardly.**

Yeats (English: enclosed meadow). Also, **Yeates, Yeetes, Yeets.** *Whatever:* Attention former literature majors: This name makes for an acceptable tribute to Nobel Prize–winning Irish poet William Butler **Yeats**.

Yisa (Hebrew: variation of **Isaiah,** "God is helper"). Also, **Yeesa, Yeesah, Yisah.**

Yisaac (Hebrew: variation of **Isaac,** "laughter"). Also, **Yisaak, Yisac, Yisak.**

Yismael (Arabic: variation of **Ishmael,** "God will hear"). Also, **Yismail, Yismale, Yismayle.**

Yisrael (Hebrew: variation of **Israel,** "wrestling with God"). Also, **Yisreal, Yisreel.**

Yitzak (Hebrew: variation of **Itzak,** "laughter"). Also, **Yitzac, Yitzaac, Yitzaak.**

Yizaac (Hebrew: variation of **Izaac,** "laughter"). Also, **Yizaak, Yizac, Yazak.**

Yizaiah (Hebrew: variation of **Izaiah,** "God is helper"). Also, **Yizaia, Yizaya, Yizayah.**

Yizaias (Hebrew: variation of **Izaias,** "God is helper"). Also, **Yizayas.**

Yizrael (Hebrew: variation of **Izrael,** "wrestling with God"). Also, **Yizreal, Yizreel.**

Yoaquim (Hebrew: variation of **Joaquim,** "God judges"). Also, **Yoaqueem, Yoaqym.**

Yoaquin (Hebrew: variation of **Joaquin,** "God judges"). Also, **Yoaqueen, Yoaqyn.**

Yoel (Hebrew: variation of **Joel,** "Jehovah is God").

Yohanan (German/Hebrew: variation of **John,** "God is gracious"). Also, **Yohanen, Yohanyn.**

Yohann (German: variation of **John,** "God is gracious"). Also, **Yohan.**

Yon (Hebrew: variation of **John,** "God is gracious"). Also, **Yonn.**

Yonah (Hebrew: variation of **Jonah,** "dove"). Also, **Yona.**

Yonas (Welsh: variation of **Jonas,** "God is gracious"). Also, **Yonahs.**

Yonathan (Hebrew: variation of **Jonathan,** "God gave"). Also, **Yohnathan, Yohnathon, Yohnathyn, Yohnethan, Yohnethen, Yohnethon, Yonathen, Yonathon, Yonethan, Yonethen, Yonethon.**

Yordan (Hebrew: variation of **Jordan,** "down-flowing river;" English: variation of **Yordison,** "son of **Jordan**"). Also, **Yorden, Yordyn.** Also, **Yordy, Yory.**

Yordane (Hebrew: variation of **Jordane,** "down-flowing river"). Also, **Yordaine, Yordayne.** Familiar, **Yordy, Yory.**

Yordison (English: variation of **Jordison,** "son of **Jordan**"). Also, **Yordisen, Yordysen, Yordyson.** Familiar, **Yordan, Yordy, Yory.**

Yordy (Hebrew: variation of **Yordan, Yordane, Yordison**). Also, **Yordie, Yordey.**

Yorick (Danish: farmer). Also, **Yoric, Yorik, Yoryc, Yoryck, Yoryk.** *Plus:* A sly *Hamlet* tribute. *Minus:* **Yorick** is the skull in the play—the *skull.*

York (English: yew tree). Also, **Yorke.** *Plus:* Revolutionary War–tested. *Minus:* Will well-intended wits refer to your son as "New" **York**?

Yory (Hebrew: variation of **Yordan, Yordane, Yordison**). Also, **Yorey, Yorie.**

Yosef (German: variation of **Josef,** "increaser, God will add"). Also, **Yoseff.** *Whatever:* Your own private Joseph.

Yoseph (Hebrew: variation of **Joseph,** "increaser, God will add").

Yosephe (French: variation of **Josephe,** "increaser, God will add").

Yosha (Sanskirt: variation of **Josha,** "satisfying").

Yoshua (Hebrew: variation of **Joshua,** "God saves"). Also, **Yoshuah.**

Yosiah (Hebrew: variation of **Josiah,** "God supports"). Also, **Yosia.**

Yotham (Hebrew: variation of **Jotham,** "God is perfect"). Also, **Yothem, Yothym.**

Young (English: young; English/German/Scandinavian: variation of **Youngblood,** "hunter"). Also, **Younge.**

Youngblood (Scandinavian/German: hunter). Also, **Youngbloode.** Familiar, **Young.**

Younger (English: fresh, youth). Also, **Yunger.**

Yovan (Slavic: variation of **John,** "God is gracious"). Also, **Yovann.**

Yovanni (Slavic: variation of **John,** "God is gracious"). Also, **Yovani, Yovanie, Yovannie.**

Ysaiah (Hebrew: variation of **Isaiah,** "God is helper"). Also, **Ysaia, Ysaya, Ysayah.**

Ysaias (Hebrew: variation of **Isaias,** "God is helper"). Also, **Ysayas.**

Yul (Chinese: beyond the horizon). *Whatever:* A pick to click. Two reasons: (1) Namesake **Yul** Brynner was the Michael Jordan of his day, making baldness an acceptable fashion statement); (2) It sounds like Christmas! (And it's a lot less obvious than, say, **Eggnog.**)

Yule (English: Christmas).

Yuri (Japanese: lily; Russian: variation of **George,** "farmer"). Also, **Youri, Yourie, Yurie, Yury.** *Plus:* An exotic cuddly bear. *Minus:* Harkens back to **Yuri** Andropov's dreary two years as leader of the Soviet Union in the early 1980s. Also, in the spirit of full disclosure, let it be noted that **Yuri** is a hop, skip, and jump away from *urinate.*

Yves (French: evergreen).

Z

CRIB NOTES

Famous Zs: Zac Hanson (the littlest member of "MmmBop" boys, Hanson); **Zachary** Taylor (U.S. president); **Zane** Grey (Western author); **Zeus** (Greek god)

Pocket Ts: Zachary, Zeke

Trendy suspenders: It's Z, people. Ain't no trends starting here.

Think long, think hard: Zen (The song may tell us "Everything's Zen," but trust this: *not baby names*.); **Zeus** (Mythical Greek gods eat ambrosia; real-life little boys eat Cookie Crisp. Just so we make that distinction clear before you go getting any big ideas.); **Zoltan** (Hungarian for "life"—fabulous. Problem is, it sounds outerspace for "arch enemy of Space Ghost."); **Zorba** (Leave the dancing to Anthony Quinn.)

Zac (Hebrew: variation of **Zachariah, Zacharias, Zachary**). Also, **Zach, Zack, Zak.** *Whatever:* The pick here for the new, cuter **Max.**

Zachariah (Hebrew: God is reknown). Also, **Zacaria, Zacariah, Zacharia, Zackaria, Zackariah, Zakaria, Zakariah.** Familiar, **Zac.** *Whatever:* Slight, *slight* wiggle room on the more popular **Zachary.**

Zacharias (Hebrew: variation of **Zachariah,** "God is reknown"). Also, **Zacarias, Zackarias, Zakarias.** Familiar, **Zac.**

Zachary (Hebrew: pure, may God remember). Also, **Zacarey, Zacary, Zacharey, Zackarey, Zackary, Zakarey, Zakary.** Familiar, **Zac.** *Plus:* This is a pocket T enjoying a big-time revival. It fits in nicely with the cuddly bears, while possessing arguably more substance and staying power than **Cody** and **Coby**. Heck, even the seventeenth-century Puritans liked **Zachary**—and the Puritans didn't like anything! *Minus:* Approaching very, *very* popular status. (Example: The number four boys name in Kansas.) In danger of oversaturation.

Zafir (Arabic: victor). Also, **Zafeer, Zafyr.**

Zaire (African: the nation).

Zale (Greek: wave). Also, **Zaile, Zayle.** *Whatever:* Usable, doable—just sounds like a jewelry store.

Zamil (Arabic: variation of **Jamil,** "handsome"). Also, **Zameel, Zamyl.**

Zamir (Hebrew: song bird). Also, **Zameer, Zamyr.**

Zan (Chinese: praise). Also, **Zann.** *Whatever:* Usable, doable—just kind of sounds like one of the Wondertwins from *Superfriends*. In fact, it *is* a member of the Wondertwins.

Zandar (Greek: variation of **Alexander,** "protector, defender").

Zander (Greek: variation of **Alexander,** "protector, defender").

Zane (Hebrew: grace of God). Also, **Zaine, Zayne.** *Whatever:* A pick to click. **Zane** works on a number of levels—it sounds handsome, looks dignified, and projects decency. Call it **Hank** with a Z.

Zaquan (American: variation of **John,** "God is gracious"). Also, **Zaquon, Zequan, Zequon.**

Zared (Hebrew: luxurious). Also, **Zarid, Zaryd.** *Whatever:* A sound-alike alternative to **Jared.**

Zavier (Spanish: variation of **Xavier,** "bright"). Also, **Zavyer.**

Zavion (African: new house). Also, **Zavien.**

Zawon (American: **John,** "God is gracious"). Also, **Zawan, Zewan, Zewon.**

Zeandre (American: variation of **Andre,** "brave"). Also, **Zeandrae, Zeandray.**

Zeb (Hebrew: variation of **Zebediah, Zebulon**). Also, **Zebb.** *Whatever:* Cut from the same flannel shirt as **Zed** and **Zeke.** It's comfortable, understated, sturdy, and—dare we say?—real.

Zebediah (Hebrew: bestowed). Also, **Zebedia, Zebedya, Zebidia, Zebidiah, Zebydia, Zebydiah.** Familiar, **Zeb.**

Zebulon (Hebrew: dwelling). Also, **Zebulonn.** Familiar, **Zeb.** *Whatever:* Another way to get to **Zeb.**

Zechariah (Hebrew: variation of **Zachariah,** "God is reknown"). Also, **Zecaria, Zecariah, Zecharia, Zeckaria, Zeckariah, Zekaria, Zekariah.**

Zed (Hebrew: variation of **Zedediah,** "bestowed"). Also, **Zedd.** *Whatever:* Now playing on a *Pulp Fiction* video or soundtrack near you: "**Zed**'s dead, baby. **Zed**'s dead."—Butch the boxer

Zedediah (Hebrew: variation of **Zebediah,** "bestowed"). Also, **Zededia, Zedidia, Zedidiah.** Familiar, **Zed.**

Zeeman (Dutch: seaman). Also, **Zeaman.** *Plus:* The coolest name you've never heard: It's literally the Z-man! Gotta love that. *Minus:* Sounds like semen.

Zeke (Hebrew: variation of **Ezekiel,** "who sees God"). Also, **Zeek.** *Plus:* A prototypical Gen X pocket T. So decent, so fundamental, so . . . **Ben.** *Minus:* No matter what this book says, *you* think **Zeke** sounds like a stagehand from *Hee Haw.*

Zel (Persian: cymbal). Also, **Zell.**

Zeth (American: variation of **Seth,** "the appointed"). Also, **Zethe.**

Zev (Hebrew: variation of **Zevediah, Zevulon**). Also, **Zevv.** *Whatever:* Even niftier than Zeb.

Zevediah (Hebrew: variation of **Zebediah,** "bestowed"). Also, **Zevedia, Zevidia, Zevidiah.** Familiar, **Zev.**

Zevulon (Hebrew: dwelling). Also, **Zevulonn.** Familiar, **Zev.**

Zimran (Arabic: praise).

Zion (Hebrew: good sign). Also, **Zyon.**

Ziv (Hebrew: to shine). Also, **Zivv, Zyv, Zyvv.**

Zivan (Slavic: lively). Also, **Zyvan.**

Zowie (Greek: life). Also, **Zowey, Zowy.** *Plus:* A little hippie-dippie but refreshingly loose in the era of the ever-noble **Joshua**s and **Zachary**s. *Minus:* This entry is a player in one of the darkest hours of the Gen X baby name era (i.e., when *we* were the babies). In 1971, pop star David Bowie and his then-wife exercised the decade's anything-goes attitude and dubbed a son **Zowie** Bowie. This was really cute. All the way up until the day **Zowie** changed his name. To **Joey.**

A

CRIB NOTES

Famous As: **Alanis** Morissette (irony-obsessed singer); **Alfre** Woodard (actor, *Miss Evers' Boys); Alicia* Silverstone (actor, *Clueless*); **Ally McBeal** (postmodern feminist and/or simpering drag, TV's *Ally McBeal*); **Angela** Bassett (actor, *Waiting to Exhale*); **Anita** Baker (singer); **Annette** Bening (actor/Mrs. Warren Beatty); **Annie** Lennox (singer); **Aretha** Franklin (Queen of Soul); **Ashley** Judd (actor, *A Time to Kill*); **Audrey** Hepburn (*Breakfast at Tiffany's* icon)

Pocket Ts: Abigail, Amelia, Anne, Audrey

Trendy suspenders: Alexandra, Alexis, Amanda, Ashley

Think long, think hard: **Adelaide** (Total museum piece.); **Adeline** (Best left to barbershop quartets); **Agatha** (In its next life, **Agatha** should put in a request to rhyme with anything *but* "hag."); **Agnes** (**Agnes** might want to fill out that paperwork too.); **Alberta** (Map name, schmap name. Looks like the untouchable **Bertha**.); **Antigone** (Reserve the agony bit for tragic Greek heroines who get stoned to death in the final act.); **Augusta/Augustine** (As far as strong girl names go, **Xena** would look more at home on today's business letterhead.); **Atilla** (Makes **Augusta** seem wimpy by comparison.)

Abby   (English: church; Hebrew: variation of **Abigail,** "father's joy"). Also, **Abbee, Abbey, Abbi, Abbie.** *Whatever:* This sporty, peppy nickname is **Abigail's** built-in irrelevancy protector.
Abigail   (Hebrew: father's joy). Also, **Abigale, Abigayle, Abygail, Abygale, Abygayle.** Familiar, **Abby.** *Whatever:* Right at home in the

Little House on the Prairie world of **Emily, Sarah,** and **Elizabeth.** A reliable pocket T.

Abrianna (American: variation of **Brianna,** "strong"). Also, **Abriana, Abryana, Abryanna.**

Ada (African: first daughter; Scottish: happiness).

Adair (Scottish: of the oak tree). Also, **Adare.**

Adanna (Scottish: variation of **Ada,** "hapiness"). Also, **Adana.**

Addison (Hebrew: variation of **Adam,** "the maker"). Also, **Addisen, Adisen, Adison, Addysen, Addyson.**

Adela (German: noble). Also, **Adella.**

Adrian (Greek: brave). Also, **Adrien, Adryan, Adryen.** *Plus:* No fuss. No mess. Just pretty, and neatly unisex. *Minus:* Pray the little boys of the twenty-first century don't get their hands on a *Rocky* video until they're past the age of thinking "Yo, **Adrian!**" is high comedy.

Adriana (Greek: variation of **Adrian,** "brave"). Also, **Adrianna, Adryana, Adryanna.**

Adriene (Greek: variation of **Adrian,** "brave"). Also, **Adrienne, Adryene, Adryenne.**

Aida (Arabic: reward). Also, **Ayda.**

Aidan (Irish: fire). Also, **Aiden, Aidyn.**

Aileen (Irish: variation of **Helen,** "the bright one"). Also, **Aileene, Aleen, Aleene.** *Plus:* A hearty, underused Irish lass. *Minus:* Underused because it's stale. Could use the boost of a modern champion, à la **Audrey** Hepburn.

Aimee (French: variation of **Amy,** "beloved"). Also, **Aimi, Aimie, Aimey.**

Aine (French: eldest; Latin: fire). Also, **Ayne.**

Aisha (African: life). Also, **Aaisha, Aaysha, Aysha.**

Akala (Hebrew: shrub). Also, **Akalla.**

Akasha (Indian: the ether).

Ala (Italian: wing). Also, **Alla.**

Alana (Irish: traveler). Also, **Alanna.** *Plus:* An elegant, contemporary pretty girl. *Minus:* Evokes images of a champagne-swilling divorcée.

Alanis (Irish: variation of **Alana,** "traveler"). Also, **Alaniss, Alannis, Alannys, Alanys.** *Plus:* Isn't it ironic how one singer can take a name from relative obscurity to a tidy level of popularity in nothing flat? *Minus:* No! That's *not* irony. That's called How the Baby Name Biz Works. But beware: The faster they rise, the faster they fall. Watch out before you swallow this potentially jagged, little pill.

Alba (Italian: dawn).

Albina (Latin: white). Also, **Albyna.**

Alda (German: old).

Aleshia   (English: variation of **Alicia,** "noble). Also, **Aleeshia, Aleeshya, Aleshya, Alyshia, Alyshya.**

Alejandra (Spanish: variation of **Alexandra,** "protector, defender"). Also, **Alijandra, Alyjandra.** Familiar, **Ally.**

Alejandria (Spanish: variation of **Alexandra,** "protector, defender"). Also, **Alijandria, Alijandrya, Alyjandria, Alyjandrya.** Familiar, **Ally.**

Alesandra (Italian: variation of **Alexandra,** "protector, defender"). Also, **Alisandra, Alysandra.** Familiar, **Ally.**

Alesandria (Italian: variation of **Alexandra,** "protector, defender"). Also, **Alisandria, Alisandrya, Alysandria, Alysandrya.** Familiar, **Ally.**

Aletta (French: support column). Also, **Aleta.**

Alette   (French: variation of **Aletta,** "support column"). Also, **Alet, Alete, Alett.**

Alex (Greek: variation of **Alexandra, Alexandria**). Also, **Alix, Alyx.**

Alexa (Greek: variation of **Alexandra,** "protector, defender"). Also, **Alixa, Alyxa.**

Alexandra (Greek: protector, defender). Also, **Alixandra, Alyxandra.** Familiar, **Alex, Ally, Sandy.** *Plus:* What the grandest little princesses are wearing this season. A power name of almost overpowering beauty. *Minus:* When the commoners—let's say, an uprising of **Jane**s and **Susan**s—start storming the castle, here's betting grand old **Alexandra** gets her trendy suspenders snapped first. She's too big a target.

Alexandria (Greek: variation of **Alexandra,** "protector, defender"). Also, **Alixandria, Alixandrya, Alyxandria, Alyxandrya.** Familiar, **Alex, Allie.**

Alexi   (Greek: variation of **Alexandra,** "protector, defender"). Also, **Alexie, Alexy, Alixi, Alixie, Alixy, Alyxi, Alyxie.**

Alexis (Greek: helper). Also, **Alexys.** *Plus:* The *Dynasty* version of **Alexandra**. Very happening. *Minus:* The thing about soaps is, once we stop watching them, we stop watching them—the numbers fall off, pronto. If the same is true about soap names, we've got a pair of trendy suspenders on our hands here.

Alfre (English: genius of the people). Also, **Alfree, Alfrey, Alfri, Alfrie, Alfry.**

Ali (Arabic: higher). Also, **Aly.**

Alice (English: noble). Also, **Alyce.** Familiar, **Ally.** *Whatever:* A comer. Parents who want that **Emily** magic without the requisite crowds might be wise to give **Alice** a look. Its variations (**Alicia, Alisa,** etc.) have sounded more vital in recent years, but the real deal *is* the real deal.

Alicia (English: variation of **Alice,** "noble"). Also, **Aleecia, Alycia.** Familiar, **Ally.** *Whatever:* Conventional wisdom says **Alicia** and **Alisa** are the doable **Alice**s of today. And they are. Both are *very* today, *very* now. Which one's *better*? Whichever one floats your boat. Although, beware: The future of **Alicia** may very well be tied to the future of its recent champion, **Alicia** Silverstone. A couple more turns in stuff like *Batman and Robin,* and **Alicia** may start looking like *Excess Baggage.*

Alina (Latin: variation of **Alice,** "noble"). Also, **Aleena, Alyna.**

Aline (Latin: variation of **Alice,** "noble"). Also, **Aleene, Alyne.**

Alisa (English: variation of **Alice,** "noble"). Also, **Alissa, Alysa, Alyssa.** Familiar, **Ally.**

Alisha (English: variation of **Alice,** "noble"). Also, **Aleesha, Alysha.** Familiar, **Ally.**

Aliya (American: variation of **Alicia,** "noble"). Also, **Aleeya, Alya.**

Allison (English: variation of **Alice,** "noble"). Also, **Alisen, Alison, Allysen, Allyson, Alysen, Alyson.** Familiar, **Ally.** *Plus:* **Alicia** Silverstone movies may bomb, today's spunk may become tomorrow's **Buffy,** but **Allison** endures. Also, major Gen X cred, thanks to the former Billy and **Alison** tandem on TV's *Melrose Place.* (Not to mention the current Billy and **Ally** tandem on TV's *Ally McBeal.*) *Minus:* A touch on the stuffy side.

Ally (English: variation of **Alejandra, Alejandria, Alesandra, Alesandria, Alice, Alicia, Alisa, Alisha, Allison**). Also, **Allee, Alleigh, Alley, Alli, Allie.** *Plus: Ally McBeal* makes you laugh. *Minus: Ally McBeal,* her stupid pajamas, and that creepy dancing baby all combine to make you cringe.

Alma (Latin: kind).

Altea (Greek: variation of **Althea,** "wholesome"). Also, **Alteea.**

Althea (Greek: wholesome). Also, **Altheea.** *Whatever:* **Althea** Gibson was the first black American woman to win the Wimbledon and U.S. Open tennis championships in 1957 and 1958.

Amanda (Latin: beloved). Familiar, **Mandy.** *Plus:* A hot name that's three—three!—trends in one: It's a pretty girl, a cuddly bear, and a *Little House on the Prairie* resident. This top ten performer will leave its mark on many a cheerleading squad of the future. *Minus:* A **Kimberly** waiting to happen? **Amanda** sounds cute as a button today, but overuse could weaken its appeal. Potential trendy suspenders.

Amber (English: orange-yellow). *Plus:* The color of honey, the byproduct of the diligent bee. *Minus:* The bimbo-fied name of centerfolds and go-go dancers, diligent though they may be.

Amelia (Greek: melodious). Also, **Ameelia, Ameelya, Amelya.** *Whatever:* The grown-up **Amanda.** Just as pretty, just as contemporary (if you think **Emily**), but with an older, wiser feel. Maybe it's the gutsy foremother thing (**Amelia** Earhart). No matter, a pocket T.

Amoretta (French: variation of **Amorette,** "love"). Also, **Amoreta, Amorreta, Amorretta.**

Amorette (French: love). Also, **Amorrette.**

Amy (French: beloved). Also, **Amee, Amey, Ami, Amie.** *Plus:* Reliable. *Minus:* Rusty.

Anastace (English: variation of **Anastasia,** "resurrection"). Also, **Anastayce, Anestace, Anestayce, Anystace, Anystayce.** Familiar, **Stacy.**

Anastasia (Greek: resurrection). Also, **Anastasya, Anestasia, Anestasya, Anystasia, Anystasya.** Familiar, **Anya.** *Plus:* Watch this one give **Alexandra** a run for her tiara. It's every bit the little princess—even has the backing of an animated feature, 1997's *Anastasia. Minus:* Your baby is, understandably, your crowned jewel. But do you have to, or want to, be so literal?

Anastice (French: variation of **Anastasia,** "resurrection"). Also, **Anasteece, Anesteece, Anestice, Anysteece, Anystice.** Familiar, **Stacy.**

Anaysis (Armenian: from the ancient Armenian goddess). Also, **Anaysys.**

Ander (German: another).

Andes (Greek: variation of **Andrea,** "brave"). Also, **Andee.**

Andie (English: variation of **Andrea,** "brave"). Also, **Andey, Andi, Andy.**

Andrea (Scottish: brave). Also, **Andraea, Andraya, Andria, Andrya.** Familiar, **Andie.** *Whatever:* A nice, but nowhere name that was reborn in the 1990s as class-brain fodder for *Beverly Hills, 90210* ex-resident **Andrea** Zuckerman.

Andreana (Italian: variation of **Andrea,** "brave"). Also, **Andreanna, Andriana, Andrianna, Andryana, Andryanna.**

Andree (English: variation of **Andrea,** "brave"). Also, **Andre.**

Ange (French: variation of **Angel,** "messenger").

Angel (Greek: messenger). Also, **Angil, Angyl.**

Angela (Latin: angelic). Also, **Angila, Angyla.** Familiar, **Angie.** *Whatever:* Will *Touched by an Angel* mania give this heavenly entry a lift?

Angelica (Greek: variation of **Angel,** "messenger"). Also, **Angelyca, Angilica, Angilyca, Angylica.** Familiar, **Angie.**

Angelika (German: variation of **Angelica,** "messenger"). Also, **Angelyka, Angilika, Angilyka, Angylika.** Familiar, **Angie.**

Angelina (Italian: variation of **Angela,** "angelic"). Also, **Angeleena, Angelyna, Angileena, Angilina, Angilyna, Angyleena, Angylina.** Familiar, **Angie, Gina.**

Angeline (English: variation of **Angela,** "angelic"). Also, **Angeleene, Angelyne, Angileene, Angiline, Angilyne, Angyleene, Angyline.** Familiar, **Angie.**

Angelique (French: variation of **Angela,** "angelic"). Also, **Angelyque, Angilique, Angylique.** Familiar, **Angie.** *Whatever:* Très *Dynasty.*

Angie (English: variation of **Angela, Angelica, Angelika, Angelina, Angeline, Angelique**). Also, **Angee, Angey, Angi, Angy.** *Whatever:* A name to make Donna Pescow proud. (And other fans of the obscure 1970s TV sitcom *Angie.*)

Anisha (Arabic: variation of **Anissa,** "friendly"). Also, **Aneesha, Anysha.**

Anissa (Arabic: friendly). Also, **Anisa, Anysa, Anyssa.**

Anita (Spanish: grace). Also, **Aneeta, Anyta.**

Anna (Italian: variation of **Anne,** "gracious"). Also, **Ana.** *Whatever:* This dressed-up version of **Anne** is pulling a neat trick—trending up without becoming trendy.

Annabella (Italian: combination of **Anna** and **Bella**). Also, **Anabela, Anabella, Annabela.**

Annabelle (Italian: combination of **Anna** and **Belle**). Also, **Anabell, Anabelle, Annabell.**

Anne (French: gracious). Also, **Ann.** Familiar, **Annie.** *Plus:* A pocket T that doubles as the ultimate can do no wrong. It's a name that can look refined (**Anne**), or spunky (**Annie**). Also, it goes with absolutely everything—the eighteenth century, the nineteenth century. In the England of the 1700s, it virtually *was* everything—14 percent of all girls were named **Anne**. (Even today's top names barely register in single digits.) *Minus:* Perceived plainness could be cutting into its viability.

Annemarie (French: combination of **Anne** and **Marie**). Also, **Annmarie, Ann Marie, Anne Marie.**

Annette (French: variation of **Anne**, "gracious"). Also, **Annete, Annett.** *Whatever:* Doable but still not fully recovered from the sweater-girl set running rampant with it in the real-time *Grease* era.

Annie (English: variation of **Anne**, "gracious"). Also, **Annee, Anney, Anni, Anny.**

Antoinette (French: variation of **Antonia**, "priceless"). Also, **Antwonette.** Familiar, **Toni.** *Whatever:* The **Alexandra** Less Traveled.

Antonetta (French: variation of **Antonia**, "priceless"). Also, **Antoneta.** Familiar, **Toni.**

Antonia (Latin: priceless). Also, **Antonya.**

Antonine (French: variation of **Antonia**, "priceless"). Also, **Antonyne.**

Anya (Greek: variation of **Anastasia**, "resurrection").

April (English: fourth month of year). Also, **Apryl.**

Arabella (Latin: easy to be entreated). Also, **Arabela.**

Arabelle (Latin: variation of **Arabella**, "easy to be entreated"). Also, **Arabell.**

Arden (Latin: ardent). Also, **Ardin, Ardyn.**

Aretha (Greek: virtue). Also, **Areetha.** *Whatever:* A Madonna. Use at your own risk.

Ari (Hebrew: lion; variation of **Ariana, Ariel, Ariella**). Also, **Aree, Arey, Arie, Ary.**

Aria (Italian: air). Also, **Arya.**

Ariadne (Greek: character from Greek mythology). Also, **Aryadne.**

Ariana (Persian: honored). Also, **Arianna, Aryana, Aryanna.** Familiar, **Ari.** *Whatever:* A *power* little princess. This is a force to be reckoned with.

Ariel (Hebrew: lioness of God). Also, **Ariell, Arielle, Aryel, Aryell, Aryelle.** Familiar, **Ari.** *Whatever:* A landmark. **Ariel** is the namesake of the little princess in *The Little Mermaid,* the 1989 film that reignited Disney's animation studio, and set girl names aspiring to a higher plane. After this cartoon, Barbies—the doll, the name—would not be sufficient. The new generation wants to be **Ariel**—queendom and all.

Ariella (Hebrew: variation of **Ariel,** "lioness of God"). Also, **Ariela, Aryela, Aryella.** Familiar, **Ari.**

Arin (Hebrew: exalted; Irish: variation of **Erin,** "peace, from Ireland"). Also, **Aryn.**

Arlen (Irish: vow). Also, **Arlin, Arlyn.**

Arlene (Irish: oath). Also, **Arleen, Arlyne.**

Ash (English: ash; variation of **Ashby, Asher, Ashley, Ashlin, Ashton**). Also, **Ashe.**

Asha (African: life). Also, **Aasha.**

Ashby (English: ash trees). Also, **Ashbee, Ashbey, Ashbi, Ashbie.** Familiar, **Ash.** *Whatever:* A way to get wiggle room on the more ubiquitous **Ashley.**

Asher (Hebrew: happy). Familiar, **Ash.**

Ashla (American: variation of **Ashley,** "meadow by the ash trees").

Ashley (English: meadow by the ash trees). Also, **Ashlee, Ashleigh, Ashli, Ashlie, Ashly.** Familiar, **Ash.** *Plus:* **Ashley** is what's happening. It's the number one girl name in Florida, New York, and Texas. A reigning little princess. *Minus:* Kindergartens are busting at the coatrooms with little **Ashley**s. If it climbed the charts fast, will it fall down them faster? Also, like other little princess names, it's a bit on the adult-challenged side. **Ashley** will look great on a perky, seventeen-year-old high school senior. How about a thirty-seven-year-old congressional candidate? Trendy suspenders fodder.

Ashlin (English: land of the ash trees). Also, **Ashlinn, Ashlyn, Ashlynn.** Familiar, **Ash.**

Ashton (English: town by the ash trees). Also, **Ashten.** Familiar, **Ash.** *Whatever:* Commonly a boy name, author John Jakes awarded **Ashton** to **Ashton** Main, the femme fatale of his *North and South* Civil War saga.

Aspasia (Greek: welcome). Also, **Aspasya.**

Aspen (English: for the city, **Aspen,** Colorado). Also, **Aspin, Aspyn.**

Asta (Italian: spear).

Astrid (Persian: beautiful). Also, **Astridd, Astryd, Astrydd.** *Whatever:* German photographer **Astrid** Kircher (and her scissors) gave the Beatles their famous "Beatle cuts" in the early 1960s.

Aube (French: dawn).

Aubrey (Scottish: wealthy). Also, **Aubree, Aubri, Aubrie, Aubry.** *Whatever:* Another common boy name that's swiped, on occasion, by the girls.

Auburn (English: reddish brown). Also, **Aubern, Auberne, Auburne.**

Audrey (English: noble counselor). Also, **Audree, Audri, Audrie, Audry.** *Whatever:* Retro Gen X icon **Audrey** Hepburn instills the would-be stale with something approaching classic status. Color this one a pocket T.

Austin (Scottish: famous; Italian: venerable). Also, **Austen, Austyn.** *Whatever:* **Ashley** was not enough. **Austin** is the next one the girls are gonna steal from the boys.

Autumn (English: the fall season). Also, **Autum, Autumm.**

Ava (Latin: bird). *Whatever:* A comer, thanks to the Gen X icon Heather Locklear. The *Melrose Place* miniskirt maven and her husband, rocker Richie Sambora, christened their own daughter, born in 1997, **Ava.** We've known Ms. Locklear since *Dynasty* and *T. J. Hooker*. We trust her. We may just follow her lead on this old-time movie star classic, à la **Ava** Gardner.

Averil (English: boar, favor). Also, **Averill, Averyl, Averyll.**

Avery (English: ruler). Also, **Averee, Averey, Averi, Averie.** *Whatever:* The name of Murphy Brown's TV mom. (She passed down this moniker to her son.)

Aves (Latin: birds).

Azriella (Hebrew: strength from God). Also, **Azriela, Azryela, Azryella.**

Azure (French: blue). Also, **Azur, Azurre.**

B

CRIB NOTES

Famous Bs: Barbra Streisand (über celebrity); **Bea** Arthur (one of those *Golden Girls*); **Belinda** Carlisle (ex-Go-Go); **Bernadette** Peters (actor/singer); **Betty** Rubble (TV 'toon, *The Flintstones*); **Billie** Holliday (jazz singer); **Blanche** DuBois (tragic heroine, *A Streetcar Named Desire*); **Blythe** Danner (actor/Gwyneth Paltrow's mom); **Bonnie** Barrow (gun moll); **Brandy** Norwood (pop star/TV star, *Moesha*); **Brett** Butler (comedian); **Bridget** Fonda (actor, *Singles*)

Pocket Ts: Becca, Belle, Bridget

Trendy suspenders: Brianna, Brittany, Brooke

Think long, think hard: Bambi (Easily misread as *Bimbo*. Coincidence? No.); **Barbarella** (Rent another movie. Like maybe *Emma*.); **Barbie** (Solid choice if you're giving birth to a plastic doll.); **Bertha** (**Bertha** didn't deserve it, but some smart aleck put a *Big* in front of her name and that was all she wrote.); **Bessie** (*See* **Bertha**.); **Betsy, Betty, Bitsy** (Three quarters of a country-club tennis doubles match, circa 1962.); **Blanche** (Game over.); **Bobbi** (The perfect name . . . for your high school principal's fiftysomething secretary.); **Buffy** (Too little, too late. Not even TV's *Buffy, the Vampire Slayer* can give weight to this airhead.)

Bailey (English: overseer of the estate). Also, **Bailee, Baileigh, Bailie, Baylee, Bayleigh, Baylie.** *Whatever:* Sounds like current fave **Hayley** but not as ubiquitous. A win-win.
Bairn (Scottish: child). Also, **Bairne.**

Baize (Latin: brown cloth). Also, **Bayze, Baze.**

Barbara (Latin: stranger, foreign). Also, **Barbra, Barbera.** *Plus:* **Barbra** Streisand's sheer force of personality can make the name seem magical even today. *Minus:* Minus La Streisand, it's merely a leftover from World War II–era victory gardens.

Barrett (German: bear, ruler). Also, **Baret, Barett, Barit, Baritt, Barret, Barrit, Barritt, Barryt, Barrytt, Baryt, Barytt.**

Barrie (Irish: spear). Also, **Barree, Barrey, Barri, Barry.** *Whatever:* On a boy, it feels hackneyed. On a girl, it feels lyrical.

Barrow (English: hill). Also, **Barow.**

Bay (English: laurel tree). Also, **Bae.**

Baye (African: straightforward).

Baylor (English: horse trainer). Also, **Bayler.**

Bea (English: variation of **Beatrice, Beatrix**). Also, **Bee.**

Beatrice (Latin: blessing). Also, **Beatryce, Beetrice, Beetryce.** Familiar, **Bea, Bebe.** *Plus:* Enough with **Kayla** and **Caitlyn**! Your daughter's going to be called something adultlike! *Minus:* A name that's buried in the same victory garden with **Barbara.**

Beatrix (Spanish: variation of **Beatrice**, "blessing"). Also, **Beatryx, Beetrix, Beetryx.** Familiar, **Bea, Bebe.**

Bebe (English: variation of **Beatrice, Beatrix**). Also, **Beebee, Bibi.**

Becca (Hebrew: familiar for **Rebecca**, "faithful, beauty, noose"). Also, **Beca, Becka, Beka, Bekka.** *Whatever:* Rooted in another pocket T, **Becca** is one in its own right—contemporary, pretty, perky, and thankfully not as cheerleaderesque as **Becky.** Popularized on TV's *Life Goes On* (1989–93), with Kellie Martin as Everyteen, **Becca** Thatcher.

Becky (English: variation of **Rebecca**, "faithful, beauty, noose"). Also, **Beckee, Beckey, Becki, Beckie, Bekkee, Bekkey, Bekki, Bekkie, Bekky.**

Beige (English: tan). Also, **Bayge.**

Belinda (German: serpent). Also, **Belynda.**

Bella (Latin: beautiful). Also, **Bela.** *Plus:* A contemporary pretty girl. *Minus:* A **Bela** Lugosi fright fest.

Belle (French: beautiful). Also, **Bell.** *Whatever:* A pocket T. This literal translation of beauty does not disappoint. It's ready-to-wear on both girl and woman. Repopularized in recent years by the Disney 'toon and stage show, *Beauty and the Beast.*

Berit (German: water source). Also, **Beritt, Beryt, Berytt.**

Berkeley (English: birch wood). Also, **Berkelee, Berkeleigh, Berkeli, Berkelie, Berkely, Berklee, Berkleigh, Berkley, Berkli, Berklie, Berkly.**

Berlin (German: for the city, **Berlin**). Also, **Berlyn.**

Berlynn (German: bear). Also, **Berlin, Berlinn, Berlyn.** *Whatever:* Uncommon, classy.

Bernadette (French: brave little bear). Aslo, **Bernadete, Bernadett, Bernidete, Bernidett, Bernidette.** Familiar, **Bernie.**

Bernadine (German: brave as a bear). Also, **Bernadeene, Bernadyne, Bernideene, Bernidine, Bernydeene, Bernydine.** Familiar, **Bernie.**

Bernie (English: variation of **Bernadette, Bernadine, Bernita**). Also, **Bernee, Berney, Berni, Berny.** *Plus:* Spry. *Minus:* Fried.

Bernita (Spanish: variation of **Bernadine,** "brave as a bear"). Also, **Berneeta, Bernyta.** Familiar, **Bernie.**

Berry (English: a juice fruit). Also, **Berree, Berrey, Berri, Berrie.**

Beryl (German: precious stone). Also, **Beril, Berill, Beryll.**

Bess (English: variation of **Elizabeth,** "God's oath"). Also, **Bes.**

Beth (English: variation of **Bethann, Bethany, Elizabeth**).

Bethann (English: combination of **Beth** and **Ann**). Also, **Bethanne, Beth Ann, Beth Anne.**

Bethany (Hebrew: worships God). Also, **Bethanee, Bethaney, Bethani, Bethanie, Bethenee, Betheney, Betheni, Bethenie, Betheny.** Familiar, **Beth.** *Whatever:* Bethany is today's way to dress up wallflower **Beth.**

Bette (English/Scandinavian: variation of **Elisabet, Elizabeth**).

Bettina (German: variation of **Elizabeth,** "God's oath"). Also, **Betina, Bettyna, Betyna.**

Bev (English: variation of **Beverly,** "beaver meadow").

Beverly (English: beaver meadow). Also, **Beverlee, Beverleigh, Beverley, Beverli, Beverlie.** Familiar, **Bev.** *Plus:* Slightly more today than **Barbara.** *Minus:* Slightly less today than **Beatrice.**

Bianca (Italian: white). Also, **Bianka, Byanca, Byanka.**

Billi (English: variation of **William,** "will, helmet"). Also, **Billee, Billey, Billie, Billy.** *Plus:* Spunky. *Minus:* "I hate spunk." —Lou Grant, *The Mary Tyler Moore Show.*

Billi Jo (American: combination of **Billi** and **Jo**). Also, **Billee Jo, Billey Jo, Billie Jo, Billy Jo.**

Birgitta   (Scandinavian: variation of **Bridget,** "strength"). Also, **Birgeeta, Birgeetta, Birgita, Birgyta, Birgytta.**

Birgitte   (Scandianvian: variation of **Bridget,** "strength"). Also, **Birgite, Birgitt, Birgyte, Birgytt, Birgytte.**

Blade   (English: leaf). Also, **Blaide, Blayde.**

Blair   (Scottish: cleared plain). Also, **Blare, Blaire.** *Whatever:* A 1980s power name of weakening strength, losing ground against the likes of **Brooke** and **Madison.** One problem: It's forever linked in the Gen X mind with snobby **Blair** Warner of TV's *The Facts of Life* (1979–1988).

Blake   (English: fair-haired). Also, **Blaike, Blayke.** *Plus:* The no-baggage **Blair.** *Minus:* You watched *Dynasty.* This name does *too* have baggage.

Blakely   (English: fair meadow). Also, **Blaklee, Blakeley, Blakeli, Blakelie.**

Blaze   (English: bright fire). Also, **Blaize, Blayze.** *Plus:* A name that can't help but stand apart. *Minus:* A name that can't help but stand apart.

Bliss   (English: happiness). Also, **Blis, Blys, Blyss.**

Blossom   (English: to bloom). *Plus:* Let 'em laugh. You liked *Blossom* (1991–95). And you thought the show made for a nifty name. *Minus:* They won't be laughing at *you.* . . . **Blossom** isn't so much ridiculous as it is so 1990s. And, remember the law of mass-media recyclables says pop-culture icons of the 1990s won't seem cheesy cool until at least 2010.

Blythe   (English: free spirit). Also, **Blithe.** *Whatever:* Elegant and, um, well, blithe.

Bonnie   (Irish: cheerful). Also, **Bonnee, Bonney, Bonni, Bonny.** *Plus:* An underexploited standard. *Minus:* It's underexploited because it's been supplanted by supposedly more sophisticated Irish lasses such as **Caitlin** and **Megan.**

Booth   (English: hut). Also, **Boothe.**

Boston   (English: town near the shrubs). Also, **Bosten.**

Brady   (Irish: spirited). Also, **Bradee, Bradey, Bradi, Bradie.**

Brandy   (Dutch: distilled wine). Also, **Brandee, Brandey, Brandi, Brandie.** *Plus:* And so we come to one of the most popular name sounds of our time: *Bruh.* From **Brandon** and **Brendan** for boys, to **Brandy** and **Brooklyn** for girls, we're mad about *Bruh.* **Brandy,** used as a stand-alone name by the star of TV's *Moesha,* will satisfy this craving in a pinch. Sounds very today. *Minus:* So did **Mindy.** Once.

Braxton (English: badger, town). Also, **Braxten.**

Bree (Scottish: broth). Also, **Bre.**

Breena (Irish: palace).

Brena (Irish: raven). Also, **Brenna.**

Brenda (Irish: aflame). *Plus:* Wins karma points from popular boy name **Brendan.** *Minus:* Loses karma points for the Shannen Doherty–inspired "I Hate **Brenda**" campaign.

Brett (French: from Britain). Also, **Bret.** *Whatever:* The picture of a strong Hemingway heroine, i.e., Lady **Brett** Ashley from *The Sun Also Rises.*

Brianna (Celtic: strong). Also, **Breeana, Breeanna, Briana, Briannah, Bryana, Bryanna, Bryannah.** *Whatever:* A reigning little princess—pink and cute and popular. So scrumptious you almost forget what it's going to sound like when your pink and cute baby runs for Congress. Sometimes it takes strength to swear off the temptations of trendy suspenders.

Bridged (Irish: variation of **Bridget,** "strength"). Also, **Bridgid, Briged, Brigid.**

Bridget (Irish: strength). Also, **Bridgett, Bridgit, Bridgitt, Briget, Brigett, Brigit, Brigitt.** *Plus:* The defiant adult among trendy Irish lasses. Robust, striking, and confident, **Briget** is *in* even when it's not really *in.* A pocket T. *Minus:* Rhymes with **Gidget.**

Brie (French: a cheese). Also, **Bri.** *Plus:* Feels like a cool breeze—sprightly, refreshing. *Minus:* Sounds like a cheese wheel.

Brigida (Spanish: variation of **Bridget,** "strength"). Also, **Brigeeda.**

Brigitta (French: variation of **Bridget,** "strength"). Also, **Brigeeta, Brigeetta, Brigita.**

Brigitte (French: variation of **Bridget,** "strength"). Also, **Brigeete, Brigeette, Brigite.**

Brindle (English: a color). Also, **Bryndle.**

Brine (English: saltwater). Also, **Bryne.**

B'rinna (Hebrew: joyful). Also, **B'rinnah.**

Brinna (Yiddish: brown). Also, **Brina, Brinah, Brinnah, Bryna, Brynah, Brynna, Brynnah.**

Brit (English: from Britain). Also, **Britt, Bryt, Brytt.**

Britta (English: variation of **Brittany,** "from **Britain**"). Also, **Brita,**

Bryta, Brytta. *Plus:* This one's for parents who really like **Brittany** but can't bear the thought of throwing their girl's lot into that mass of humanity. *Minus:* Reminds you of a water filter.

Brittany (English: from Britain). Also, **Brittanee, Brittaney, Brittani, Brittanie, Brittenee, Britteney, Britteni, Brittenie, Britteny.** Familiar, **Britty.** *Plus:* If *Heathers* were remade to feature the Class of 2013, it would have to be called **Brittanys.** This is an inescapable baby name of our era. A cute-as-a-button little princess. *Minus:* Names that are inescapable in an era are unable to escape *from* an era. Potential trendy suspenders.

Brittney (English: variation of **Brittany,** "from Britain"). Also, **Britnee, Britney, Britni, Britnie, Britny, Brittnee, Brittni, Brittnie, Brittny.** Also, **Britty.**

Britty (English: variation of **Brittany, Brittney**). Also, **Britee, Britey, Briti, Britie, Brittee, Brittey, Britti, Brittie, Brity.**

Brody (Scottish: steep, overhanging rock). Also, **Brodee, Brodey, Brodi, Brodie.**

Bronwen (Welsh: white beast). Also, **Bronwin, Bronwyn.** *Whatever:* A popular power name. Overbearing and yet vaguely alluring.

Brooke (English: stream). Also, **Brook.** *Plus:* It's a water name. Can't get more elemental or basic than that. *Minus:* It's a little princess that doubles as a power name. Can't get more trendy suspenders than that.

Brooklyn (English: stream). Also, **Brooklin, Brooklinn, Brooklynn.** *Plus:* Here's an urban center map name to take place alongside the Great West **Austins, Dakota**s, and **Montanas. Brooklyn** doesn't seem like it should work, but it sort of does. *Minus:* Would you name the kid **Staten Island?** That's where this map name thing is taking us, you know. One day we'll run out of "good" cities and states (they'll get too popular), and move on to the B list. Which is where **Staten Island** Smith comes in. Stop the madness now.

Brynn (Welsh: of the hill). Also, **Brin, Brinn, Bryn.**

Burgundy (French: wine). Also, **Burgundee, Burgundey, Burgundi, Burgundie.**

Burkeley (English: variation of **Berkeley,** "birch wood"). Also, **Burkelee, Burkeleigh, Burkeli, Burkelie, Burkely, Burklee, Burkleigh, Burkley, Burkli, Burklie, Burkly.**

Butte (French: mound).

C

CRIB NOTES

Famous Cs: Calista Flockhart (actor, TV's *Ally McBeal*); **Cameron** Diaz (actor, *There's Something About Mary*); **Candice** Bergen (actor, TV's *Murphy Brown*); **Carnie** Wilson (ex-member, Wilson Phillips); **Caroline** Kennedy (JFK's kid); **Carolyn** Bessette (JFK Jr.'s wife); **Carly** Simon (singer/songwriter); **Cassidy** Gifford (talk-show hostess's daughter); **Celine** Dion (pop diva); **Chelsea** Clinton (first daughter); **Cher** (Sonny and **Cher** survivor); **Chynna** Phillips (another ex-member, Wilson Phillips); **Christa** McAuliffe (teacher/*Challenger* astronaut); **Christina** Applegate (*Married . . . with Children* alum); **Claire** Danes (actor, TV's *My So-Called Life*); **Coco** Chanel (designer).

Pocket Ts: Caroline, Catherine, Clare

Trendy suspenders: Caitlin, Carissa, Cassidy

Think long, think hard: Candy (Three words: Exotic dancer city.); **Charity** (Better as a concept.); **Chastity** (One of those hippie-dippie names Gen Xers got tagged with in the 1960s. No reason to dredge up our unfortunate past.); **Cher** (Do not be fooled by *Clueless*. The glitteratti are *not* naming their daughters **Cher**. This is the domain of one-name celebrities only.); **Cherry** (Uh, no.); **Christmas** (In *Three's Company* **Chrissy** Snow's given name was **Christmas**. This hints at the sitcom's true subtext: **Chrissie** wasn't stupid; she merely was trying to live *down* to her ditzy name.); **Clarabell** (Suffers from an unfortunate clown association.); **Coco** (Belongs in a mug with melting marshmallows, or on a designer clothing label.); **Cleopatra** (The ancient Egyptian version of a Madonna name.)

Caden (English: little warrior). Also, **Cadin, Cadyn.**

Cady (Scottish: little warrior). Also, **Cadee, Cadey, Cadi, Cadie.** *Whatever:* A fresh spin on **Cathie** or **Katie.**

Caia (Latin: mistress). Also, **Caiya.**

Caitlin (Irish: variation of **Cathleen,** "pure"). Also, **Caitlinn, Caitlyn, Caitlynn, Catelin, Catelinn, Catelyn, Catelynn, Caytlin, Caytlinn, Caytlyn, Caytlynn.** Familiar, **Caty.** *Plus:* Pretty. Popular. Well-adjusted. *Minus:* Didn't that sort of kid bug you in school? Potential trendy suspenders.

Cali (Greek: beautiful; variation of **Calista,** "most beautiful"). Also, **Calee, Caley, Calie, Caly.** *Whatever:* A comer. **Cali** is unique and elegant and fit for today.

Calista (Greek: most beautiful). Also, **Calysta.** Familiar, **Cali.** *Whatever:* A funny-sounding name that's not so funny-sounding anymore thanks to rising star **Calista** Flockhart of TV's *Ally McBeal.*

Cally (Greek: beautiful).

Cameron (Scottish: crooked nose). Also, **Cameren, Camerin, Cameryn, Camiron, Camren, Camron, Camryn, Camyron.** *Whatever:* Here's another comer. Strong girl names need no longer be watered down. **Cameron** is there for the taking.

Cami (Italian/French: variation of **Camilla, Camille**). Also, **Camee, Camey, Camie, Camy.** *Plus:* Nice 'n' sporty. *Minus:* Sounds like *clammy;* rhymes with *hammy.*

Camilla (Italian: white). Also, **Camila, Camyla, Camylla.** Familiar, **Cami.**

Camille (French: white). Familiar, **Cami.** *Whatever:* A delicate museum piece. To be exposed to light (or to babies) only in the right conditions—preferably the 1880s.

Candace (Greek: variation of **Candice,** "brilliant, fair"). Also, **Candaice, Candayce.**

Candice (Greek: brilliant, fair). Also, **Candyce.** *Whatever:* A pocket T classic. **Candice** possesses a beauty unlikely to fade. It also rakes in the good karma points from its famed current champion, the elegant **Candice** Bergen.

Cappa (Latin: cape). Also, **Capa.**

Capri (Italian: variation of **Caprice,** "fanciful"). Also, **Capree, Caprey, Caprie, Capry.** *Plus:* You love *capri* pants. *Minus: Capri* pants make you look thick around the middle.

Caprice (Italian: fanciful). Also, **Capryce**. Familiar, **Capri**.

Cara (Irish: friend; Greek: variation of **Catherine**, "pure"). Also, **Carra**. *Whatever:* A couple notches lower on the cuddly bear scale than **Carissa**. Also, not as ubiquitous.

Carina (Greek: variation of **Catherine**, "pure"). Also, **Careena, Careenna, Carinna, Caryna, Carynna**.

Carissa (Latin: artful). Also, **Carisa, Carrisa, Carrissa, Carrysa, Carryssa, Carysa, Caryssa**. *Plus:* Very today. Pretty, precious, with appropriate vowel action. It's the fashionable thing to do. *Minus:* **Carissa** is a cuddly bear that's so cuddly it evokes greeting-card company mascots the Care Bears. Can anything this cute possibly last? Trendy suspenders.

Carla (Latin: variation of **Caroline**, "valiant, strong").

Carlin (Irish: little champion). Also, **Carlinn, Carlyn, Carlynn**.

Carlita (Spanish: variation of **Carla**, "valiant, strong"). Also, **Carleeta, Carlyta**.

Carlota (Italian: variation of **Charlotte**, "valiant, strong"). Also, **Carlotta**.

Carly (Italian: feminine). Also, **Carlee, Carley, Carli, Carlie**.

Carmen (Latin: song). Also, **Carmin, Carmyn**. *Whatever:* As long as divas keep singing Bizet's opera, this one's not going anywhere as a classic heroine tag.

Carmina (Latin: rosy). Also, **Carmeena, Carmyna**.

Carmita (Italian: variation of **Carmina**, "rosy"). Also, **Carmeeta, Carmyta**.

Carnie (Hebrew: horn). Also, **Carnee, Carney, Carni, Carny**. *Whatever:* **Carnie** Wilson tried her darndest to take this one back from the circus folk with her work in Wilson Phillips and her self-titled (and short-lived) TV talk show. Didn't quite work.

Carol (Irish: champion; English: valiant, strong). Also, **Carole, Caroll, Carolle, Carrol, Carrole, Carroll, Carrolle**. Familiar, **Carrie**. *Whatever: Brady Bunch* reruns are guaranteed to keep this one alive and on our lips for at least a couple more decades. A good or bad thing, depending on your tolerance for the sitcom.

Carolina (Italian: variation of **Caroline**, "valiant, strong"). Also, **Carolyna**.

Caroline (English: valiant, strong; French: woman). Also, **Carolyne**. Familiar, **Carrie**. *Plus:* A real little princess—used by the Kennedys of America and the royal family of Monaco. A pocket T. *Minus:* If there's gridlock among royalty for dibs on this name, imagine what it's like among the masses.

Carolyn (English: variation of **Caroline,** "valiant, strong"). Also, **Carolin, Carolinn, Carolynn.** Familiar, **Carrie.**

Carr (English: marsh).

Carrie (English/Irish: variation of **Carol, Caroline, Carolyn, Caryl**). Also, **Carree, Carrey, Carri, Carry.** *Whatever:* Time for some free association: **Carrie.** Sissy Spacek. Prom night. Pig's blood.

Carson (English: son of **Carr**). Also, **Carsen.** *Whatever:* A pick to click. This one's better known as a last name, but try it on for size. (Author **Carson** McCullers did.) It's sturdy like **Bronwen** without sounding so, well, like **Bronwen.**

Cary (Irish: dark-complected; Welsh: castle). Also, **Carey.** *Plus:* A good example of how much our experiences influence our name choices. This entry is a **Carrie** sound- and look-alike, except **Cary** works on a totally different level mainly because there's no Stephen King baggage. Instead **Cary** comes across as classic and sporty. *Minus:* Blah, blah, blah. People hear "**Cary,**" they think **"Carrie"**— our little telekinetic outcast.

Carya (Greek: walnut tree).

Caryl (English: variation of **Carol,** "champion"). Also, **Carryl.** Familiar, **Carrie.**

Caryn (Greek: variation of **Catherine,** "pure").

Casey (Irish: vigilant). Also, **Casee, Casi, Casie, Casy.**

Casia (Greek: variation of **Catherine,** "pure"). Also, **Casya.**

Cass (English: maker of copper pots; Greek: variation of **Cassandra, Cassaundra**).

Cassandra (Greek: prophet, helper of man). Also, **Casandra.** Familiar, **Cass, Cassie.** *Whatever:* Very wily, this one. An evening-gown name in a dress-casual world, **Cassandra** maintains its viability by passing itself off as a little princess.

Cassaundra (Greek: variation of **Cassandra,** "prophet, helper of man"). Familiar, **Cass, Cassie.**

Cassidy (Irish: curly-haired). Also, **Casidey, Casidy, Cassydy.** *Plus:* A prototypical of-the-moment name. **Cassidy** is solidly suburban, unabashedly girlie and lil' cowpoke-ish. *Minus:* If you buy the theory that you grow into a name, this is one you're going to grow into at about age eight. At eight, it'll be perfect. Every eight-year-old girl should be named **Cassidy**. (Or **Ashley** or **Brittany**.) The question is, what happens at nine, or twenty-nine? Trendy suspenders.

Cassie   (Greek: variation of **Cassandra, Cassaundra**). Also, **Cassee, Cassey, Cassi, Cassy**.

Casta   (Latin: chase).

Cat   (English: feline; Italian/Slavic: variation of **Catarina, Catrina**). Also, **Catt**.

Catarina   (Italian: variation of **Catherine**, "pure"). Also, **Catareena, Cataryna, Catereena, Caterina, Cateryna, Catyreena, Catyrina**. Familiar, **Cat**.

Cate   (English: variation of **Cathleen**, "pure"). Also, **Caite, Cayte**.

Catherine   (Latin: pure). Also, **Catharine, Catharyn, Catharyne, Catherin, Catheryn, Cathyrin, Cathyrine**. Familiar, **Cathy**. *Whatever:* Doesn't get much more pocket T than this. **Catherine** is a name that just works—any region, any time.

Cathleen   (Irish: variation of **Catherine**, "pure"). Also, **Cathlean, Cathlene**. Familiar, **Cate, Cathy, Caty**.

Cathrine   (English: variation of **Catherine**, "pure"). Also, **Cathrin, Cathryn, Cathryne**. Familiar, **Cathy**.

Cathy   (Irish/Latin: variation of **Catherine, Cathleen, Cathrine**). Also, **Cathee, Cathey, Cathi, Cathie**.

Catrina   (Slavic: variation of **Catherine**, "pure"). Also, **Catreena, Catryna**. Familiar, **Cat**.

Caty   (Irish/Latin: variation of **Caitlin, Catherine, Cathleen**). Also, **Catee, Catey, Cati, Catie**.

Catya   (Russian: variation of **Catherine**, "pure").

Cay   (Scottish: serenity). Also, **Cae**.

Cayla   (Yiddish: laurel crown; variation of **Catherine**, "pure"). Also, **Caylah**.

Ceara   (Irish: ruddy). Also, **Caera, Ciara**. *Plus:* An Irish lass that hasn't yet been mass-produced. *Minus:* A name that begs to be mispronounced. (It's *Share-ah*, not *See-air-ah*.) Your daughter will forever be correcting and respelling.

Cecilia   (Latin: blind, gray-eyed). Also, **Cecillia**. Familiar, **Cissy**. *Plus:* Sufficiently modern. Simon and Garfunkel sang of "**Cecilia**" more than thirty years ago, and the name's *still* workable. *Minus:* Plain and prissy.

Cecille (French: variation of **Cecilia,** "blind, gray-eyed"). Also, **Ceceele, Ceceelle, Cecile.**

Cein (Irish: jewel).

Celeste (Latin: heavenly). *Whatever:* Graceful, often overlooked classic. The **Caroline** Less Traveled.

Celestia (Latin: variation of **Celeste,** "heavenly"). Also, **Celestya.**

Celestine (French: variation of **Celeste,** "heavenly"). Also, **Celesteen, Celesteene, Celestyne.**

Celia (Scandinavian: variation of **Cecilia,** "blind, gray-eyed"). Also, **Celya.**

Celina (Greek: variation of **Selena,** "the moon"). Also, **Celeena, Celyna.**

Celine (Greek: variation of **Selena,** "the moon"). Also, **Celeen, Celeene, Celyne.** *Whatever:* Canadian singer **Celine** Dion is the perfect celebrity type to popularize a name—she's VH-1 pleasant, pretty, and safe.

Cella (Italian: cell dweller). Also, **Cela.**

Chaise (French: carriage). Also, **Chaize.**

Chance (English: luck; variation of **Channing,** "wise").

Chanda (Sanskirt: goddess who battles evil).

Chandra (Sanskrit: moon).

Channing (English: wise). Also, **Channyng.**

Chantae (French: variation of **Chantal,** "song"). Also, **Chantay.**

Chantal (French: song). Also, **Chantall.**

Chapel (English: church). Also, **Chapell.**

Charley (English: variation of **Charles,** "man, valiant, strong"). Also, **Charlee, Charli, Charlie, Charly.**

Charlotte (English: valiant, strong). Also, **Charlote.** *Plus:* Can't go wrong with a Brontë sisters tribute. *Minus:* **Emily** is the hot Brontë, not **Charlotte.**

Charma (Greek: joy, delight).

Chase (French: hunter). Also, **Chaise, Chayse.** *Plus:* Sleek, direct. *Minus:* Theatrical, a touch *Dynasty.*

Chelsea (English: seaport). Also, **Chelsee, Chelsey, Chelsi, Chelsie, Chelsy.** *Plus:* A first kid takes this one to the White House and does well by it. The name gods are smiling on **Chelsea.** *Minus:* Know how many girls were named after then–first kid **Caroline** Kennedy in the 1960s? Beware a crowded market.

Cherilynn (English: combination of **Cheryl** and **Lynn**). Also, **Cherilyn, Cherylin, Cherylinn.**

Cherokee (Native American: Cherokee tribe). Also, **Cheroki.**

Cheryl (French: beloved). Also, **Cherryl, Cherryll, Cheryll.** *Whatever:* **Cheryl** Ladd played Chris Munroe on TV's *Charlie's Angels.*

Cheyenne (Native American: Cheyenne tribe). Also, **Cheyene.**

China (English: the country, **China;** the porcelain dinnerware). Also, **Chyna, Chynna.** *Whatever:* **Chynna** was the name of choice among flower children rockers in the 1970s—both Michelle Phillips (the Mamas and Papas) and Grace Slick (Jefferson Airplane) dubbed their daughters thusly.

Chloe (Greek: blooming). Also, **Cloe.** *Whatever:* A pick to click. The **Candice** Less Traveled.

Chris (Greek: variation of **Christian, Christina, Christine**). Also, **Cris.**

Chrissie (Greek: variation of **Christian, Christina, Christine**). Also, **Chrissi, Chrissie, Chrissy, Crissi, Crissie, Crissy.**

Christa (German: variation of **Christian,** "follower of Christ"). Also, **Chrysta, Crista, Crysta.**

Christian (Greek: follower of Christ). Also, **Cristian.** Familiar, **Chris.**

Christina (Greek: variation of **Christine,** "follower of Christ"). Also, **Christeena, Christyna, Cristeena, Cristina, Cristyna.** Familiar, **Chris, Chrissie, Christy.**

Christine (Greek: follower of Christ). Also, **Christeene, Christyne, Cristeene, Cristine, Cristyne.** Familiar, **Chris, Chrissie, Christy.** *Plus:* Sterling silver doesn't tarnish. This one's a pocket T. *Minus:* Even sterling silver collects dust every once in a while.

Christy (English: variation of **Christina, Christine**). Also, **Christi, Christie, Cristi, Cristie, Cristy.**

Cicely (English: variation of **Cecelia,** "blind, gray-eyed"). Also, **Cicily, Cicyly.**

Cilla (English: variation of **Priscilla,** "long life"). Also, **Cila.**

Cindy (English: variation of **Cynthia,** "lofty"). Also, **Cindee, Cindey, Cindi, Cindie, Cyndee, Cyndey, Cyndi, Cyndie, Cyndy.**

Cire (French: wax). Also, **Cyre.**

Cissy (English: variation of **Cecilia,** "blind, gray-eyed"). Also, **Cissee, Cissey, Cissi, Cissie.** *Whatever:* It's hard to make a girl name sound *too* wussy. **Cissy** comes pretty close.

Clara (Latin: variation of **Clare,** "clear light"). Also, **Clarra.**

Clare (Latin: clear light; Irish: flatland). Also, **Clair, Claire.** *Plus:* A delicate flower that's deceptively strong, **Clare** qualifies for pocket T status. *Minus:* A name more associated with the first half of the twentieth century than the latter half.

Clarice (French: clear light). Also, **Clareece, Claryce.** *Whatever:* Jodie Foster's FBI agent in *Silence of the Lambs* gave this museum piece a shot of adrenaline, not to mention relevance. Still a rarity, but an old fogey no more.

Clarina (Spanish: variation of **Clarice,** "clear light"). Also, **Clareena, Claryna.**

Clarine (French: variation of **Clarice,** "clear light"). Also **Clareene, Claryne.**

Clarissa (Latin: clear light). Also, **Clarisa, Clarysa, Claryssa.** *Whatever:* Popularized by the Nickelodeon comedy series, *Clarissa Explains It All.*

Claudia (Latin: lame). Also, **Claudea, Claudya.** *Plus:* It's getting clunky, yes, but **Claudia** smacks of too much dignity to be entirely dismissed. Being featured on TV's *Party of Five* doesn't hurt, either.

Clio (Greek: glorious, renowned). Also, **Cleeo, Cleo, Clyo.**

Coda (Italian: end).

Cody (English: cushion; helper, assistant). Also, **Codee, Codey, Codi, Codie.** *Whatever:* Here's more of what Kathie Lee Gifford has wrought. **Cody** is a boy cuddly bear that's doing the crossover thing. Not even the threat of cootie taunts can cut into its appeal.

Colby (English: dark). Also, **Colbee, Colbey, Colbi, Colbie.**

Coletta (Italian: variation of **Nicole,** "victory of the people"). Also, **Coleta.**

Colette (French: variation of **Nicole,** "victory of the people"). Also, **Colete, Colett.** *Plus:* Evokes images of a French pixie. *Minus:* Evokes images of a French chambermaid.

Conall (Irish: high, mighty). Also, **Conal.**

Concessa (Latin: granted). Also, **Concesa.**

Concetta (Italian: bright thought). Also, **Conceta.**

Connie (English: variation of **Constance,** "constant"). Also, **Connee, Conney, Conni, Conny.**

Connor (Irish: desired). Also, **Conner.** *Whatever:* A pick to click. Understated refinery.

Connors (Irish: variation of **Connor,** "desired"). Also, **Conners.**

Constance (Latin: constant). Also, **Constence, Constynce.** Familiar, **Connie.** *Plus:* **Constance** is pretty . . . *Minus:* . . . pretty drab next to today's **Clarissa**s.

Coquette (French: a flirt). Also, **Coqete, Coqett, Coqette, Coquete, Coquett.** *Whatever:* The literal little princess.

Cora (Greek: maiden). Also, **Corra.**

Coral (Greek: yellowish red; a piece of coral).

Corina (Spanish: little maiden). Also, **Coreena, Coryna.**

Corinth (Greek: region of Greece). Also, **Corinthe, Corynth, Corynthe.** *Whatever:* There's a fine line between classic and Jurassic. **Corinth** is fancier sounding than **Corrine,** and therefore a touch more grannylike.

Cornelia (Latin: enduring). Also, **Cornelya.**

Corrine (Greek: hummingbird; variation of **Cora,** "maiden"). Also, **Corine, Corryne, Coryne.**

Cory (Irish: hollow). Also, **Coree, Corey, Cori, Corie.** *Plus:* **Cory** is the cuddly bear cousin of **Cody**—every bit as spirited and lively. *Minus:* Nearly as ubiquitous.

Cosette (French: pet lamb). Also, **Cosete, Cosett.** *Plus:* A must for *Les Miserables* fans. *Minus:* Yeah, there's nothing more inspiring than naming your kid after literature's famed French orphan.

Courtnay (French/Irish: variation of **Courtney,** "drinking cup"). Also, **Cortnae, Cortnay, Courtenae, Courtenay, Courtnae.**

Courtney (French: court; Irish: drinking cup). Also, **Cortnee, Cortney, Cortni, Cortnie, Cortny, Courteney, Courteny, Courtnee, Courtni, Courtnie, Courtny.** *Whatever:* The *Melrose Place* factor: **Courtney** Thorne-Smith played heroine Alison Parker, she of the Alison-Billy tandem, from 1992–97 on the Gen X–era prime-time soap.

Crystal (Latin: ice). Also, **Christal, Chrystal, Cristal, Cristel, Crystel.** *Whatever:* **Crystal** doesn't shatter easily. It's still going full-blast as a popular, pretty girl name.

Cynthia (Greek: lofty). Also, **Cinthia, Cinthya, Cynthya.** Familiar,

Cindy. *Whatever:* A standard that's starting to wheeze. As far as Gen Xers are concerned, its *Brady Bunch* connection hurts more than helps. **Cindy** was rarely confused for the cool Brady.

Cyra (Greek: lady).

D

CRIB NOTES

Famous Ds: **Daisy** Fuentes (model/TV personality); **Danica** McKellar (TV's Winnie, *The Wonder Years*); **Danielle** Steel (romance author); **Daphne** Zuniga (former *Melrose Place* resident); **Daryl** Hannah (actor, *Splash*); **Debbie** Gibson (teen singer); **Deborah** Gibson (adult Broadway star); **Della** Reese (TV angel, *Touched by an Angel*); **Demi** Moore (demi-icon, *Striptease*); Princess **Diana** (beloved British royalty); **Dianne** Feinstein (U.S. senator); **Dinah** Washington (jazz singer); **Dionne** Warwick (singer/psychic friend); **Dolly** Parton (wig lady/country superstar); **Doris** Day (*Pillow Talk* gal); **Dorothy** Parker (writer/wit); **Drew** Barrymore (recovering child actor, *The Wedding Singer*)

Pocket Ts: **Diana, Diane**

Trendy suspenders: **Dakota, Desiree, Dylan**

Think long, think hard: **Darling** (That's what wolf-hound guys call girls when they can't remember their names).; **Davida** (Sounds like you were really married to **David** and opted to slap an *a* on the end when a girl popped out.); **Decima** (Means "tenth." Most Gen Xer parents won't require the services of anything higher than *dos*.); **Destiny** (A concept, not a name.); **Dolly** (For toy bins or Grand Ole Opry performers only. Not a lot of wiggle room in between.); **Dolores** (A borderline call. It's exotic and pretty. Unfortunately, women who proved this name's mettle are drawing Social Security.); **Dora** (Blame Gene Rayburn and *The Match Game* for ruining **Dora**. Rayburn: "Dumb **Dora** is so dumb . . ."); **Dorene** (The ship has sailed. Wave good-bye.); **Duana** (**Duane** needs more than an *a* to defuse the nerd factor.)

Dace (French: earthy). Also, **Daice, Dayce.**

Daeshawna (American: variation of **Shawna,** "God is gracious"). Also, **Daeseana, Daeshauna, Daeshona, Dayseana, Dayshauna, Dayshawna, Dayshona.**

Daisy (English: a flower, day's eye). Also, **Daisee, Daisey, Daisi, Daisie, Daysee, Daysey, Daysi, Daysie, Daysy.** *Plus:* A spry, flighty name given weight by the literary world (Henry James's *Daisy Miller,* *The Great Gatsby*'s **Daisy** Buchanan). *Minus:* Until onetime MTV maven **Daisy** Fuentes arrived, the name was sounding a little less than contemporary.

Dajuana (American: variation of **Juana,** "God is gracious"). Also, **Dawana, Dawona, Dejuana, Dewana, Dewona.**

Dakota (Sioux: Great Plains region). Also, **Dakoda, Dakodah, Dakotah.** *Plus:* No old-hat **Sarah**s or **Emma**s for your daughter—she's going to have a name as wide open as the big, blue sky. *Minus:* The big, blue sky needs an air-traffic controller because lots of **Dakota**s are circling. And while there's safety in numbers, will the **Dakota**s of 2025 be stranded by only-in-the-'90s names? Trendy suspenders potential.

Dale (Scottish: bushy valley). Also, **Daile, Dayle.**

Daley (Irish: a gathering). Also, **Dalee, Dali, Dalie, Daly.**

Dalia (Hebrew: branch). Also, **Daliah, Dalya, Dalyah.** *Whatever:* A pick to click. **Dalia** is technically as out of fashion as, say, **Dalila,** but it sorts works for today's ears.

Dalila (Hebrew: hair). Also, **Dalilah, Delila, Delilah.**

Dallas (Scottish: place on the plain). Also, **Dalas.**

Dana (Celtic: darling).

Daneta (Hebrew: variation of **Danita,** "the Lord is just"). Also, **Danetta.**

Dani (Hebrew/Italian: variation of **Daniella, Danielle, Danita**). Also, **Danee, Daney, Danie, Dany.**

Danica (Slavic: morning star). Also, **Danicka, Danika, Danyca, Danycka, Danyka.** *Whatever:* Here's a pretty girl for our time—frilly, feminine and full of vowel action.

Daniella (Italian: variation of **Danielle,** "the Lord is just"). Also, **Daniela, Danyela, Danyella.** Familiar, **Dani.**

Danielle (Hebrew: the Lord is just). Also, **Daniele, Danyel, Danyele, Danyell, Danyelle.** Familiar, **Dani.** *Whatever:* Go figure. **Danielle** is more popular than **Danica** or **Dana,** and it's got *no* vowel action. What's up? One theory: It's been around longer, being tied to old (and still) favorite **Daniel.** This is a trendy name that's proving it may just be trend-proof.

Danita (Hebrew: variation of **Danielle,** "the Lord is just"). Also, **Daneeta, Danyta.** Familiar, **Dani.**

Daphne (Greek: morning dew). Also, **Daphnee, Daphney, Daphni, Daphnie, Daphny.** *Plus:* This name is sported by two Gen X pop-culture notables—**Daphne** Zuniga of *Melrose Place* and **Daphne** (no last name given) of *Scooby-Doo.* *Minus:* With regards to *Scooby-Doo,* **Velma** was the brains of the Mystery Machine; **Daphne** was just sort of there to get scared.

Dara (Hebrew: wisdom). Also, **Darah, Darra, Darrah.** *Whatever:* Very today. Pretty and hard-edged, **Dara** is a little princess who wears Doc Martens. A very cool pick to click.

Darby (English: free; Scandinavian: deer settlement). Also, **Darbee, Darbey, Darbi, Darbie.**

Darcy (French: stronghold). Also, **Darcee, Darcey, Darci, Darcie, D'Arcy.** *Plus:* Some letter combos just *work.* Right now, *Dar* is one of them. You come up with a name that begins with *Dar* and you probably have a name that'll do your daughter well in the first grade. *Minus:* Can't vouch for how well *Dar*s are going to hold up. Other than **Darby** and **Darian,** they're not exactly road-tested.

Dareh (Persian: wealthy). Also, **Darreh.**

Daria (Hebrew: variation of **Dara,** "wisdom"). Also, **Dariah, Darria, Darriah, Darrya, Darryah, Darya, Daryah.** *Whatever:* A pick to click, this name's hip credentials were confirmed in the MTV animated series *Daria* about a dryly witty **Janeane** Garofalo–type teen.

Darian (Greek: darling). Also, **Darien, Daryan, Daryen.** *Plus:* Very today and very versatile, **Darian** sounds like a Riot Grrl who riots in Ann Taylor blazers. *Minus:* **Darian** sounds like a disaffected youth from an old Bret Easton Ellis novel.

Darius (Persian: to preserve). Also, **Darrius, Darryus, Daryus.** *Whatever:* Isn't this a boy name? Well, yeah, sorta. But so were **Taylor** and **Sydney,** once. As possible girl names go, **Darius** is, yes, a weaker pick than **Taylor,** but a stronger one than **Bob.**

Darla (English: darling). Also, **Darlah.** *Whatever:* Got the *Dar* sound going for it, but not much else. Not happening.

Darlene (English: variation of **Darla,** "darling"). Also, **Darleen, Darleene, Darlyne.**

Daryl (English: brave, bold). Also, **Darryll, Daryll.** *Whatever:* Interesting—on a boy this sounds hayseedish (no small thanks to *Newhart's* Larry, **Darryl,** and **Darryl** contingent); on a girl it passes for elegant (no small thanks to movie star **Daryl** Hannah).

Dashawna (American: variation of **Shawna,** "God is gracious). Also, **Daseana, Dashauna, Dashona, Deseana, Deshauna, Deshawna, Deshona.**

Dawn (English: break of day). *Plus:* Hopeful, sunny. *Minus:* Tony Orlando and you-know-what.

Dawna (English: variation of **Dawn,** "break of day").

Deana (Latin: divine). Also, **Deanna, Deeana, Deeanna.** *Whatever:* Like its cousin **Dina,** this is a name that hasn't aged well. It's still plugging away, hoping its vowel action will convince parents of its vitality.

Deandrea (American: variation of **Andrea,** "brave"). Also, **Deandraea, Deandraya, Deandria, Deandrya.**

Deb (English: variation of **Debra, Deborah**). Also, **Debb.**

Debbie (English: variation of **Debra, Deborah**). Also, **Debbee, Debbey, Debbi, Debby.**

Debra (English: variation of **Deborah,** "soft-spoken"). Also, **Debrah.**

Deborah (Hebrew: soft-spoken). Also, **Debera, Deberah, Debora.** Familiar, **Deb, Debbie.** *Whatever:* If **Debbie** Gibson's parents had started her off with **Debbie** instead of **Deborah,** she would have had nowhere to go once her career as the perky singer of "Electric Youth" was over. But by allowing her the **Deborah** option, Ms. Gibson was able to reroute her name and pursue a life in the theater. Let this be a lesson to us all.

Dedra (English: variation of **Deirdre,** "sorrowful"). Also, **Dedre.**

Dee (English: dark water; Irish: good luck). Also, **Dea.** *Plus:* **Dee** was the name of Raj's little sister on TV's *What's Happening!!* Pay tribute as you wish. *Minus:* The *Dee* sound *isn't* happening—**Deana, Deena, Didi,** etc. This can't be explained, no more than it can be explained why "Dar" *is* happening. Just trust your inner baby name detector. It knows.

Dee Dee (Irish: variation of **Dee,** "good luck"). Also, **Deedee.**

Deidre (Irish: variation of **Deirdre,** "sorrowful"). *Plus:* Classic Irish lass fare . . . *Minus:* . . . lacking a notable American champion. (Unless you count daytime soap star **Deidre** Hall.)

Deirdre (Irish: sorrowful). Also, **Deirdra, Deirdrah.**

Delaney (Irish: challenger). Also, **Delanee, Delani, Delanie, Delany.**

Della (English: noble). Also, **Dela.** *Whatever:* If a name's not going to be hip—and **Della**'s *not* hip—the least it can do is be free of extraneous baggage. **Della** obliges. It's innocuous and pleasant.

Delta (Greek: fourth). *Whatever:* Extraneous baggage: The 1970s. Helen Reddy. "**Delta** Dawn."

Dema (English: judge). Also, **Demma.**

Demi (Greek: half, lesser). Also, **Deme, Demee, Demie, Demy.** *Plus:* Classically structured for today—pretty, feminine, vowel-friendly. *Minus: Striptease, The Scarlet Letter, Disclosure.*

Deni (English: variation of **Denise,** "from Dionysus, god of wine"). Also, **Denee, Deney, Denie, Deny.**

Denise (Greek: from Dionysus, god of wine). Also, **Denice, Deniece, Deniese, Denyce, Denyse.** Familiar, **Deni.** *Plus:* Gen Xers were weaned on this peanut-butter-and-jelly sandwich. It feels familiar and safe. *Minus:* Gen Xers are in for culture shock: **Denise** is not keeping up with **Ashley** and her fellow pretty girls. It's starting to sound like a quaint anachronism of the 1970s.

Denisha (American: variation of **Denise,** "from Dionysus, god of wine"). Also, **Daneesha, Danisha, Danysha, Deneesha, Denysha.**

Denver (English: green valley).

Deonne (Greek: variation of **Dionne,** "godlike"). Also, **Deon, Deone.**

Deseret (French: variation of **Desiree,** "desire"). Also, **Deserett, Desiret, Desirett, Desyret, Desyrett.**

Desira (Spanish: variation of **Desiree,** "desire"). Also, **Desyra.**

Desire (English/French: desire). Also, **Desyre.**

Desiree (Latin/French: desire). Also, **Desirae, Desiray, Desyrae, Desyray, Desyree.** *Plus:* The latest in pretty girl wear. *Minus:* Right or wrong, **Desiree** sounds like a Fleetwood Mac groupie, circla 1976. Potential trendy suspenders.

Devin (Celtic: poet). Also, **Devyn.**

Devra (Hebrew: variation of **Debra,** "soft-spoken"). Also, **Devrah.**

Devorah (Hebrew: variation of **Deborah,** "soft-spoken"). Also, **Devora.**

Dezeret (American: variation of **Deseret**, "desire"). Also, **Dezerett, Deziret, Dezirett, Dezyret, Dezyrett.**

Dezira (American: variation of **Desira**, "desire"). Also, **Dezyra.**

Deziree (American: variation of **Desiree**, "desire"). Also, **Dezirae, Deziray, Dezyrae, Dezyree.**

Dharma (Sanskrit: divine law). Also **Darma, Darmah.** *Plus:* It's fancy. It's free. It's one with nature. *Minus:* It's been co-opted by a sitcom.

Di (English: variation of **Diana, Dyana**). *Whatever:* Princess **Di**'s untimely death didn't do her already morbid nickname any favors.

Diamond (English: precious stone). Also, **Diamonde, Diamund, Diamunde.** *Whatever:* For future cast members of a *Dynasty* revival only.

Diana (Greek: divine one; Roman: goddess of the moon and the forest). Also, **Dianna.** Familiar, **Di.** *Plus:* The ancient Greeks can't be wrong! The classy and strong **Diana** is a name fit for a princess or a wonder woman. (Wonder Woman, in fact, did use it. **Diana** Prince was WW's civilian identity.) A true-blue pocket T.

Diane (Latin: bright, like the moon). Also, **Dian, Dianne.** *Whatever:* Timeless sophistication. Another pocket T.

Diarra (African: gift). Also, **Diara, Diera, Dierra, Dyara, Dyarra, Dyera, Dyerra.** *Whatever:* What today's little princess needs—a pretty name that rhymes with "tiara."

Didi (Hebrew: beloved). Also, **Deedee.**

Dillon (Welsh: variation of **Dylan**, "ocean"). Also, **Dilen, Dillen, Dilon.**

Dina (Hebrew: judgment). Also, **Deena, Dena.**

Dinah (Hebrew: judgment). Also, **Dyna, Dynah.** *Plus:* Cool, like jazz great **Dinah** Washington. *Minus:* Dated, like entertainer **Dinah** Shore.

Dionne (Greek: godlike). Also, **Dion, Dione, Dyon, Dyone, Dyonne.** *Plus:* Refined, sophisticated, and adaptable enough to work in jeans or taffeta. *Minus:* Namesake of the Psychic Friends Network's chief spokeswoman.

Diva (Latin: prima donna). Also, **Deeva, Dyva.** *Plus:* The late rock iconoclast Frank Zappa branded his youngest daughter with this moniker. *Minus:* The Zappa clan also sports a **Moon Unit** and a **Dweezil,** so consider the source.

Divan (Persian: low couch).

Dixie (French: tenth). Also, **Dixee, Dixey, Dixi, Dixy.** *Whatever:* A regional map name. Don't know how well **Dixie** would play in, say, Seattle.

Dominica   (Spanish: variation of **Dominique,** "born on Sunday"). Also, **Dominicka, Dominika, Domynica, Domynicka, Domynika.**

Dominique   (Latin: born on Sunday). Also, **Dominiqe, Domyniqe, Domynique.** *Whatever:* This *Dynasty*-borrowed moniker is a nice fit for the Age of **Alexandria.** Scooting along at a tidy level of popularity.

Donata   (Latin: gift). Also, **Donatta.**

Donna   (Latin: lady). Also, **Dona.** *Whatever:* Tori Spelling and *Beverly Hills, 90210* combined haven't convinced us that **Donna** is anything but a name that saw its day pass in the 1960s.

Donovan   (Irish: brown, poet). Also, **Donoven, Donovyn.**

Dorat   (French: a gilder). Also, **Doratt.**

Doria   (Greek: God's gift). Also, **Dorria, Dorrya, Dorya.** *Whatever:* Amazing—one well-placed *i,* and suddenly **Dora** is as contemporary as **Daria.**

Doris   (Greek: gift of the ocean). Also, **Doriss, Dorys, Doryss.** *Whatever:* Pretty, but ultimately **Doris** is a World War II relic that needs some help.

Dorit   (Hebrew: variation of **Doris,** "gift of the ocean"). Also, **Doritt, Doryt, Dorytt.**

Dorn   (English: stronghold). Also, **Dorne.**

Doro   (English: variation of **Dorotea, Dorothea, Dorothy**). Also, **Dorro.**

Dorotea   (Italian: variation of **Dorothy,** "God's gift"). Also, **Dorotaea.** Familiar, **Doro.**

Dorothea   (Greek: variation of **Dorothy,** "God's gift"). Also, **Dorothia, Dorothya.** Familiar, **Dot, Dotty.**

Dorothy   (Greek: God's gift). Also, **Dorothee, Dorothey, Dororthi, Dorothie.** Familiar, **Dot, Dotty.** *Plus:* If **Abigail** can be revived, why not **Dorothy**? It's a throwback to the glamour days of **Dorothy** Parker and the Algonquin Round Table. *Minus:* The majority of the nation's current **Dorothy**s are holding it together with support hose.

Dorthea   (Greek: variation of **Dorothea,** "God's gift"). Also, **Dorthia, Dorthya.** Familiar, **Dot, Dotty.**

Dorthy   (Greek variation of **Dorothy,** "God's gift"). Also, **Dorthee, Dorthey, Dorthi, Dorthie.** Familiar, **Dot, Dotty.**

Dory   (French: golden). Also, **Doree, Dorey, Dori, Dorie, Dorrie.**

Dot (English: a dot; variation of **Dorothea, Dorothy, Dorthea, Dorthy,** "God's gift"). Also, **Dott.** *Whatever:* Unfortunately, **Dorothy** doesn't get any more contemporary in nickname form.

Dotty (English: variation of **Dorothea, Dorothy, Dorthea, Dorthy,** "God's gift"). Also, **Dottee, Dottey, Dotti, Dottie.**

Drachma (Greek: ancient monetary unit). Also, **Drackma, Dracma, Drakma.**

Drew (English: wise; Scottish: brave). *Whatever:* A solid Gen X name—simple, unembellished, adaptable.

Dru (English: variation of **Drucilla,** "strong"). Also, **Drue, Druw.**

Drucilla (Latin: strong). Also, **Drucila, Druscila, Druscilla, Drusila, Drusilla.** Familiar, **Dru.** *Plus:* Popuarlized on top-rated daytime soap, *The Young and the Restless. Minus:* Soap characters aren't exactly life's supreme role models.

Dulce (Latin: agreeable).

Dyan (Latin: variation of **Diane,** "bright, like the moon"). Also, **Dyane, Dyanne.**

Dyana (Greek: variation of **Diana,** "divine one, goddess of the moon and forest"). Also, **Dyanna.** Familiar, **Di.**

Dylan (Welsh: ocean). Also, **Dylen, Dyllan, Dyllen, Dylon, Dyllon.** *Whatever:* Unlike **Donna,** here's an entry that *Beverly Hills, 90210* did help popularize—for boys *and* girls. For this very reason, we should approach **Dylan** with caution. *90210* is fabulous fast-food entertainment, but should we expect any trends that emerge from it to be anything but fleeting? Label this one trendy suspenders.

E

CRIB NOTES

Famous Es: **Eartha** Kitt (singer/TV's Catwoman); **Eleanor** Roosevelt (legendary U.S. first lady); **Ella** Fitzgerald (jazz great); **Elle** Macpherson (model); **Ellen** DeGeneres (comedian); **Erica** Kane (fictional soap diva, TV's *All My Children*); **Erin** Moran (TV's Joanie, *Happy Days*); **Etta** James (singer); **Eve** Plumb (TV's Jan, *The Brady Bunch*).

Pocket Ts: Elizabeth, Ellen, Emily, Emma, Eva

Trendy suspenders: Erica

Think long, think hard: **Edwina** (A badly disguised boy name.); **Effie** (Sort of cute, mostly bovine-esque.); **Elektra** (Way too Freudian.); **Elsie** (*See* **Effie**.); **Elvira** (Best known as the name of a catchy country-music song and a busty fright-queen. Either way, off-limits for baby use.); **Enid** (Too old-fashioned.); **Ernestine** (Played for laughs on *Laugh-In*—thirty years ago. The situation hasn't improved.); **Evita** (The Madonna name of 1940s Agentina. Still off-limits for use by mere mortals.)

Eartha (English: of the earth). Also, **Ertha**. *Whatever:* Jazzy **Eartha** Kitt, arguably the coolest of all the big- and little-screen Catwomen, is so happening, even in her seventies, she makes this rarity a winner.
Easter (English: for Easter Sunday). *Plus:* You really like **Esther** but are afraid it sounds too old lady. So you try to get yourself some wiggle room with sound-alike, look-alike **Easter**. It's not dated, you tell yourself. It's today! It's a name that refuses to bow to the usual rules of what can and cannot be a first name! Holidays, regions, cities—

they're all fair game. Your daughter is **Easter**. Hear her roar! *Minus:* Get a grip.

Eaves (English: edges). Also, **Eves.**

Ebony (Greek: black wood). Also, **Ebonee, Eboney, Eboni, Ebonie.** *Whatever:* Now that Paul McCartney and Stevie Wonder's "**Ebony** and Ivory" has been buried by time, this one's probably safe from provoking a thousand poorly sung comments.

Echo (Greek: to repeat).

Eddy (English: a water current; variation of **Edward,** "wealthy guardian"). Also, **Eddee, Eddey, Eddi, Eddie.** *Plus:* No **Edwina** this one. **Eddy** is cute and spunky. *Minus:* Potential therapy bill alert—it still sounds like you had your heart set on an **Edward.**

Eden (Hebrew: delight). Also, **Edin, Edyn.** *Plus:* Biblical—as natural and unadorned as a fig-leaf wardrobe. *Minus:* Dramatic—as subtle as a soap-opera diva.

Edie (English: variation of **Edith,** "happy warrior"). Also, **Edee, Edey, Edi, Edy, Eydee, Eydey, Eydi, Eydie, Eydy.** *Whatever:* Fit for the swingin' lounge life, à la Steve and **Eydie.**

Edith (English: happy warrior). Also, **Edithe Edyth, Edythe.** Familiar, **Edie.** *Plus:* **Emily** used to be the domain of blue hairs, too. Her underappreciated peer **Edith** just needs a little love. *Minus:* Hope your kid likes it out there in the wilderness. For better or worse, **Edith** is not a modern-day pretty girl.

Edna (German: mind). *Whatever:* In the same straits as **Edith.**

Eileen (Irish: variation of **Helen,** "the bright one"). Also, **Eileene.** *Plus:* A dependable Irish lass. *Minus:* Get ready for a million "I lean" jokes.

Elaine (French: variation of **Helen,** "the bright one"). Also, **Elane, Elayne.** Familiar, **Ellie, Laney.** *Whatever:* Interesting case study: Do the whiners of *Seinfield, the* sitcom of the 1990s, make for good baby name role models?

Elana (Hebrew: oak tree). Also, **Elanah, Elanna, Elannah.** *Whatever:* The hip, pretty girl version of **Elaine.** Very today.

Eleanor (Hebrew: God of my youth; variation of **Helen,** "the bright one"). Also, **Elenor, Elinor, Elynor.** Familiar, **Ellie.** *Plus:* Stately and sturdy. *Minus:* Bidding for old-lady status if it doesn't get a modern champion, pronto. **Eleanor** Roosevelt can take this one only so far. And, frankly, she's never going to make it seem graceful, frothy, or elegant—key components of contemporary girl names.

Eleni (Greek: variation of **Elaine,** "the bright one"). Also, **Elenee, Eleney, Elenie, Eleny.**

Elenora (Italian: variation of **Eleanor,** "God of my youth"). Also, **Elenorra, Elinora, Elynora.** Familiar, **Ellie.**

Elenore (Scandinavian: variation of **Eleanor,** "God of my youth"). Also, **Elinore, Elynore.** Familiar, **Ellie.**

Eliana (Hebrew: God has answered me). Also, **Elianah, Elianna, Eliannah, Elyana.**

Elina (Greek: variation of **Elaine,** "the bright one"). Also, **Eleena, Elyna.**

Elisa (Spanish: variation of **Elizabeth,** "God's oath"). Also, **Eleesa, Elysa.** *Whatever:* Like **Eliana** and **Elana, Elisa** is a showroom model of the prototypical modern-day pretty girl—pink, girlie, and vowel-friendly.

Elisabet (Scandinavian: variation of **Elizabeth,** "God's oath"). Also, **Elisabett, Elisabette, Elysabett, Elysabette.** Familiar, **Bette.**

Elise (English: variation of **Elizabeth,** "God's oath"). Also, **Elice, Elyce, Elyse.** *Whatever:* **Elyse** Keaton was the matriarch of TV's *Family Ties* clan (1982–89).

Elisha (Hebrew: to whom God is savior). Also, **Elishah, Elysha, Elyshah.**

Eliza (English: variation of **Elizabeth,** "God's oath"). Also, **Elyza.** Familiar, **Liza.** *Whatever:* Another entry with a vaunted Audrey Hepburn connection. Hepburn starred as grammar-challenged **Eliza** Doolittle in the beloved musical *My Fair Lady.*

Elizabeth (Hebrew: God's oath). Also, **Elizebeth, Elizibeth, Elizybeth.** Familiar, **Bess, Beth, Bette, Lib, Libbie, Liz, Lizzie.** *Whatever:* Time was, in the early seventeenth century, when 25 percent of all baby girls born in England were dubbed **Elizabeth.** Overkill? Agreed. Today, the name has receded to a manageable level of popularity. As an added bonus, it still projects the regal beauty and elegance that made it the rage of the Renaissance. A pocket T.

Ella (German: all; English: noble). *Whatever:* Namesake **Ella** Fitzgerald makes this an always classy, timeless selection.

Elle (French: beauty). *Plus:* Approved by fashion magazines and supermodels alike. *Minus:* A name that's *too* stylish? There's a lot to live up to here: the pages of *Elle* magazine, *and* the résumé of **Elle** Macpherson.

Ellen (English: variation of **Helen,** "the bright one"). Also, **Ellin, Ellyn.** Familiar, **Ellie, Laney.** *Plus:* A pocket T. **Ellen** is a levelheaded pretty girl name that always wears well. *Minus:* Potential *Ellen* backlash?

Ellie (English/French/Italian/Hebrew: variation of **Elaine, Eleanor, Elenora, Elenore, Ellen**). Also, **Ellee, Elley, Elli, Elly.**

Eloisa (French: famous warrior; Latin: wide). Also, **Eloysa.**

Elsa (German/Spanish: noble).

Elysia (Latin: from Elysium, mythical home of the blessed). Also, **Eleesia, Eleesya, Elisia, Elisya.**

Em (English: variation of **Emily, Emma, Emme**). Also, **Emm.** *Plus:* Pert. *Minus:* Best used as a companion with "Auntie."

Emerald (English: jewel). Also, **Emeralde.** *Plus:* Pretty, like the proverbial jewel. *Minus:* Precious, like **Krystle.**

Emery (German: ruler). Also, **Emerey.**

Emila (English: variation of **Emily,** "graceful"). Also, **Emilla, Emyla, Emylla.**

Emilia (English: variation of **Emily,** "graceful"). Also, **Emeelia, Emeelya, Emilya.**

Emily (Greek: graceful). Also, **Emilee, Emiley, Emili, Emilie.** Familiar, **Em, Emmy.** *Plus:* This is the back-to-basics bomb. A number one or top five pick nationwide. Why? It's got what Gen Xers crave: Simple, elemental grace. (The taint of **Emily** Litella, Gilda Radner's lovably loopy *Saturday Night Live* character of the 1970s, is finally gone). There may be a ton o' **Emily**s graduating from the Class of 2016, but they'll have good company. A pocket T. *Minus:* You're a recovering **Jennifer**. You know the pain of having to use your last initial to distinguish yourself from a homeroom full of clones.

Emily Ann (English: combination of **Emily** and **Ann**). Also, **Emilyann, Emily Anne, Emilyanne.**

Emma (German: whole, universal). Familiar, **Em.** *Whatever:* The recent Jane Austen revival has boosted **Emma**. A rediscovered pocket T.

Emme (French: variation of **Emma,** "whole, universal").

Epi (Greek: upon). Also, **Epee, Epey, Epie, Eppee, Eppey, Eppi, Eppie, Eppy, Epy.**

Erica (Latin: heath). Also, **Ericka, Erika, Eryca, Erycka, Eryka.** *Plus:* A pretty girl that looks like a million bucks. *Minus:* Beware deflation. *Dynasty* names—or, in this case, an *All My Children* name—

are not long-term investments. Soap operas, after all, are about big emotions and rash, trendy suspenders decisions.

Erin (Irish: peace, from Ireland). Also, **Erinn, Eryn, Erynn.** *Plus:* Can't get more Irish lass than the isle itself. *Minus:* Hotter in the 1970s and 1980s. Getting buried by the daintier pretty girls.

Ery (Latin: place). Also, **Eree, Erey, Eri, Erie, Ery.**

Esha (African: variation of **Asha,** "life").

Esmerelda (Spanish: emerald). Also, **Esmerilda, Esmerylda.**

Esperanza (Spanish: hopeful).

Este (Persian: star).

Estefani (Spanish: variation of **Stephanie,** "crown"). Also, **Estefanee, Estefaney, Estefanie.**

Estella (Spanish: variation of **Estelle,** "star of the East"). Also, **Estela.**

Estelle (Persian: star of the East). Also, **Estel, Estele, Estell.**

Esther (Persian: star). Also, **Ester.**

Eta (Greek: seventh letter of the Greek alphabet).

Ethel (English: noble). Also, **Ethil, Ethyl.** *Plus: I Love Lucy*'s **Ethel** Mertz was a great friend. *Minus:* Mrs. Mertz, however, was not a great enough champion to keep this name afloat in the age of the little princesses.

Etta (English/German: little). *Whatever:* Another great jazz singer name—this one enlivened by **Etta** James.

Eugenia (Greek: variation of **Eugene,** "noble"). Also, **Eugenya.** Familiar, **Genie.** *Plus:* An offbeat little princess, **Eugenia** is grand-sounding in the tradition of **Erica,** with none of the attendant trendiness. *Minus:* The name's got no grip on modern-day fashions either.

Eugenie (Greek: variation of **Eugenia,** "noble"). Also, **Eugenee, Eugeney, Eugeni, Eugeny.** Familiar, **Genie.**

Eunice (Greek: good victory). Also, **Eunyce.**

Eva (Hebrew: life-giving). *Whatever:* A gem. **Eva** is a pretty, contemporary and vowel-friendly name with a track record that should make the likes of **Brittany** jealous. Best of all, there's still time to get in on the ground floor of this pocket T. . . . Oh, wait, Gen X icon Heather Locklear named her first child sound-alike **Ava.** The rush is officially on.

Evangalista (Italian/Spanish: variation of **Evangeline,** "messenger of good news"). Also, **Evangalysta, Evangelista, Evangelysta.**

Evangaliste (French: variation of **Evangeline,** "messenger of good news"). Also, **Evangalyste, Evangeliste, Evangelyste.**

Evangeline (Greek: messenger of good news). Also, **Evangeleen, Evangileen, Evangiline, Evangilyne.** *Plus:* This *Dynasty*-friendly entry should ensure your daughter at least one grand entrance atop a stairwell. *Minus:* A bit much if your girl ends up favoring flats over heels.

Eve (Hebrew: life-giving). *Whatever:* The resurgence of a Bible stalwart like **Rebecca** bodes well for the most stalwart of them all.

Evelyn (French: hazelnut). Also, **Evelin, Evilin, Evilyn, Evylin, Evylyn.** *Whatever:* A nice name that's just kind of there. Not hot, not cold. Not today, not yesterday. Just nice.

Evonne (French: young archer). Also, **Evonn.**

Eyrie (English: aerie). Also, **Eyree, Eyrey, Eyri, Eyry.**

Esmerelda (Spanish: variation of **Esmerelda,** "emerald"). Also, **Ezmerilda, Ezmerylda.**

CRIB NOTES

Famous Fs: **Faith** Hill (country singer); **Farrah** Fawcett (actor/ex-Angel); **Fawn** Hall (footnote, Iran-Contra scandal); **Fiona** Apple (singer, "Criminal"); **Flannery** O'Connor (short-story specialist, "A Good Man Is Hard to Find"); **Frances** Bean Cobain (Kurt Cobain and Courtney Love's kid).

Pocket Ts: Faith

Trendy suspenders: Felicia

Think long, think hard: **Fancy** (Sounds like a whacked-out heroine from a Tennessee Williams play.); **Fanny** (More colloquial than, say, **Posterior,** but in the end it's all the same.); **Fawn** (**Bambi**'s spiritual bimbo cousin.); **Fedora** (Best worn as a hat.); **Fern** (Best worn by a plant); **Fifi** (Frou-frou); **Flo** (Three words: Kiss. Ma. Grits.); **Flossie** (One word: Moo.); **Flower** ("Excuse me, could I see that with a pair of love beads?")

Faith (English: belief). Also, **Fathe, Faythe.** *Whatever:* No minuses in **Faith,** presuming you have one—religious or otherwise. The name's classic Gen X fodder: It's straightforward, road-tested, and blessed with simplicity—a pocket T.

Falice (Latin: variation of **Felice,** "happy"). Also, **Faleece, Falyce.**

Falicia (Latin: variation of **Felicia,** "happy"). Also, **Faleecia, Faleecya, Faleesha, Faleeshya.**

Fallon (Irish: ruler). Also, **Falen, Fallen, Falon.** *Plus:* Devastatingly strong. It stands apart, in a good way. *Minus:* Very 1980s. Very *Dynasty.*

Farrah (English: beautiful one). Also, **Fara, Farah, Farra.** *Plus:* The **Heather** of its day. *Minus:* This is not its day. **Farrah** is very 1970s, very *Charlie's Angels.* For die-hard fans only.

Fatima (Arabic: daughter of Mohammed). Also, **Fatimah, Fatyma, Fatymah.** *Whatever:* Your religion may inspire you to select this exotic beauty. Fine choice, just be warned—not even a name of holy origin will prevent some bully from calling your daughter "Fatty **Fatima.**"

Faun (Latin: from Roman mythology, half person, half goat).

Fauna (Latin: animals).

Fay (English: fair). Also, **Faye, Fey, Feye.** *Plus:* A low-rent **Faith.** All the simplicity . . . *Minus:* . . . not much of the elegance. Not by today's ears anyway.

Felice (Latin: happy). Also, **Feleece, Felyce.** *Whatever:* This is a name that satisfies yuppie needs for a power name, while appeasing the no-B.S. sensibility of Xers. Best of all, it's yours for a ground-floor price. Hasn't caught fire. Yet.

Felicia (Latin: happy). Also, **Feleecia, Feleecya, Feleesha, Feleeshya.** *Plus:* More popular than **Felice,** thanks to long-standing exposure on daytime soap *General Hospital. Minus:* This pair of trendy suspenders lacks the clean lines of **Felice.** Its extra syllables hang like costume jewelry.

Felicity (English: variation of **Felice,** "happy"). Also, **Felicitee, Felicitey, Feliciti, Felicitie.**

Fen (English: marsh). Also, **Fenn.** *Whatever:* The safest way to do fen-phen.

Fenella (Irish: of the white shoulders). Also, **Fenela, Fenila, Fenilla, Fenyla, Fenylla.**

Fernanda (Spanish: variation of **Fernando,** "brave adventurer"). Also, **Fernenda, Fernynda.**

Findley (Scottish: variation of **Finley,** "fair hero"). Also, **Findlay, Findlee, Findli, Findlie, Findly.**

Finley (Scottish: fair hero). Also, **Finlee, Finleigh, Finli, Finlie, Finly.**

Finn (Irish: fair). Also, **Fin, Fyn, Fynn.**

Fiona (Irish: fair, white). Also, **Fionna, Fyona, Fyonna.** *Whatever:* If her career doesn't flame out, twentysomething singer/songwriter **Fiona** Apple will help popularize this British Isles thing of delicacy.

Flannery (Irish: red eyebrows). Also, **Flanary, Flanerey, Flanery,**

Flannary. *Whatever:* A pick to click. This is a strong Southern concoction with good bones and good genes, neatly linked with dark gothic writer **Flannery** O'Connor. Belles need not apply.

Flavia (Latin: blond). Also, **Flavya.** *Plus:* Musical. Unique. *Minus:* It's hard to come up with a girl's name that's too out there, but this might be a candidate. Whatever it used to signify, today it sounds like a bone near your shoulder.

Flax (English: blue-flowered plant). Also, **Flaxx.**

Flay (English: critical). Also, **Flaye.**

Fletcher (English: arrow maker). *Whatever:* A popular boy name that can work on a girl too.

Flora (Latin: flower). Also, **Florra.** *Whatever:* Sort of like **Flavia,** except not quite as out of it. This is a name we *should* think of as beautiful but often don't.

Florence (Latin: blooming). Also, **Florince, Florynce.** *Plus:* Classic. *Minus:* Borderline Jurassic. Not happening today.

Florencia (Spanish: variation of **Florence,** "blooming"). Also, **Florencya, Florincia, Florincya.**

Flynn (Irish: child of the red-haired man). Also, **Flin, Flinn, Flyn.**

Fran (English: variation of **Frances, Francesca, Francessa, Francine**). Also, **Frann.**

Frances (Welsh/French: free; Latin: of France). Familiar, **Fran, Francie, Frankie.** *Whatever:* A name that can project both dignity and, because of volatile actress **Frances** Farmer, rebellion. Coincidence that the first child of grunge—daughter of Kurt Cobain and Courtney Love—is **Frances** Bean Cobain?

Francesca (Italian: variation of **Frances,** "free"). Familiar, **Fran, Frannie.**

Francessa (Italian: variation of **Frances,** "free"). Also, **Francesa.** Familiar: **Fran, Frannie.**

Francie (English: variation of **Frances,** "free"). Also, **Francee, Francey, Franci, Francy.** *Whatever:* The name of one of Barbie's doll friends.

Francine (English: variation of **Frances,** "free"). Also, **Franceene, Francyne.** Familiar, **Fran, Frannie.**

Françoise (French: variation of **Frances,** "free").

Frankie (English: variation of **Frances,** "free"). Also, **Frankee, Frankey, Franki, Franky.**

Frannie (English: variation of **Frances, Francesca, Francessa,**

Francine). Also, **Frannee, Franney, Franni, Franny.** *Whatever:* For buffs of J. D. Salinger's *Franny and Zooey.*

Freda (Welsh: white wave). Also, **Freeda, Freida, Frieda.**

Freddie (English: variation of **Frederica,** "peaceful ruler"). Also, **Freddee, Freddey, Freddi, Freddy.**

Frederica (German: variation of **Frederic,** "peaceful ruler"). Also, **Fredereeca, Frederyca.** Familiar, **Freddie.**

Frida (Spanish: variation of **Frederica,** "peaceful ruler"). Also, **Freeda, Fryda.** *Plus:* Shares namesake with en-vogue Mexican painter **Frida** Kahlo. *Minus:* **Frida** sounds like one of Archie Andrews's peers, circa 1974, not a peer of a **Brittany,** circa 2004.

Frith (English: peace). Also, **Frithe, Fryth.**

Fuchsia (English: purple red). Also, **Fushia, Fushya.**

Fury (Latin: rage). Also, **Furi, Furie.** *Whatever:* A splendid *Dynasty* name for a spitfire of a character—perhaps **Sammy Jo**'s cousin.

G

CRIB NOTES

Famous Gs: **Gabrielle** Reece (volleyball player); **Gaby** Hoffmann (teen star, *Volcano*); **Gail** Sheehy (author, *Passages*); **Geena** Davis (Thelma in *Thelma and Louise*); **Genie** Francis (Laura, of Luke and Laura soap fame); **Gertrude** Stein (author, author, author); **Gilda** Radner (*Saturday Night Live* alum); **Gillian** Anderson (Agent Scully, TV's *The X-Files*); **Glenn** Close (actor, *The Big Chill*); **Golda** Meir (pioneering Israeli prime minister); **Goldie** Hawn (actor, *Private Benjamin*); **Grace** Kelly (actor/princess); **Gracie** Allen ("Say goodnight, Gracie" namesake); **Gwen** Stefani (rocker, No Doubt); **Gwyneth** Paltrow (actor/Brad Pitt's ex-girlfriend)

Pocket Ts: Grace

Trendy suspenders: Geneva, Gwyneth

Think long, think hard: **Gennifer** (President Clinton's lady friend **Gennifer** Flowers speaks volumes for "misspelled" first names.); **Geraldine** (Not going to recover in our lifetimes from being most notably worn by a man—Flip Wilson—playing a woman.); **Gerdie** (Rhymes with "sturdy"—you know, like a coffee thermos or a hard hat.); **Gertrude** (Admiration for **Gertrude** Stein is the only thing keeping this name alive—and barely so. A washout is a washout is a washout.); **Gigi** (Fabulous musical. Frou-frou name.); **Ginger** (Once a castaway, always a castaway.); **Godiva** (Fabulous chocolates. Heavy-baggage name. Something about a streaker.); **Gretel** (Hansel and guess who?); **Griselda** (Makes you think of one of Cinderella's crabby stepsisters. Not that **Cinderella**'s a million-dollar name either, mind you.)

Gable (German: farmer). Also, **Gabel.**

Gabriella (Italian: variation of **Gabrielle,** "God is my strength"). Also, **Gabriela, Gabryela, Gabryella.** Familiar, **Gaby.**

Gabrielle (Hebrew: God is my strength). Also, **Gabriele, Gabryele, Gabryelle.** Familiar, **Gaby.** *Whatever:* A formal gown that's not too dainty for these times. This one still works.

Gaby (English: variation of **Gabriella, Gabrielle**). Also, **Gabi.** *Plus:* About the best spunk offered today. *Minus:* Pray the kid's a talker.

Gale (Celtic: brave). Also, **Gail, Gaile, Gayle.** *Plus:* Nice. A nice name. *Minus:* Nice names get buried.

Galen (Greek: speaker). Also, **Galin, Galyn, Gaylen, Gaylin, Gaylyn.**

Galienna (Latin: lofty). Also, **Galiena, Galyena, Galyenna.**

Garland (French: flower wreath). Also, **Garlande.**

Garlynn (French: variation of **Garland,** "flower wreath"). Also, **Garlin, Garlinn, Garlyn.**

Garnet (English: little protector). Also, **Garnett.**

Gavit (Hebrew: garden). Also, **Gavitt, Gavyt, Gavytt.**

Gavriella (Hebrew: variation of **Gabriella,** "God is my strength"). Also, **Gavriela, Gavrielah, Gavriellah.**

Gavrielle (Hebrew: variation of **Gabrielle,** "God is my strength"). Also, **Gavriele, Gavryele, Gavryelle.**

Gay (English: happy). Also, **Gae, Gaye.** *Whatever:* Someday **Gay** will lose its power to evoke giggles among the not quite mature. This isn't that day.

Geary (Irish: hunting dog). Also, **Gearee, Gearey, Geari, Gearie, Geeree, Geerey, Geeri, Geery.**

Gelsey (English: of unknown meaning). Also, **Gelsee, Gelsey, Gelsi, Gelsie, Gelsy.** *Whatever:* Wiggle room for **Chelsea**. It's got all that name has to offer at (roughly) half the trendiness and popularity.

Gemma (Italian: a gem). Also, **Gema.**

Genesis (English: beginning). Also, **Genesys, Genisis, Genisys, Genysis, Genysys.**

Geneva (German/French: spirit, a Swiss city). Also, **Geneeva, Genyva.** *Plus:* The European **Dakota,** dahlings. *Minus:* Sounds like the name for an over-the-top, bratty kid character on a sitcom. Trendy suspenders time.

Genevieve (Celtic: white wave). Also, **Geneveeve, Geniveeve, Genivieve, Genyveeve, Genyvieve.** Familiar, **Genny.** *Plus:* Another

Gabrielle, this elaborate piece of work wears well today. *Minus:* It's still on the fancy side. The familiar **Genny** or **Ginny** might be best bets for actual everyday use.

Genie   (English: supernatural being; Greek: variation of **Eugenia,** "noble"). Also, **Geenee, Geeney, Geeni, Geenie, Geeny, Genee, Geney, Geni, Geny.** *Whatever:* If you think the family can put up with the garage-door-opener jibes and the inevitable *I Dream of* "Guess Who" comparisons, it's a safe, if increasingly vanilla, choice.

Genna   (Arabic: small bird). Also, **Gena.**

Genny   (English: variation of **Genevieve,** "white wave"). Also, **Genney, Genni, Gennie.**

Georganna   (English: combination of **George** and **Anna**). Also, **Georgana, Georgeana, Georgeanna.**

Georganne   (English: combination of **George** and **Anne**). Also, **Georgann, Georgeann, Georgeanne.**

Georgene   (English: variation of **Georgia,** "farmer"). Also, **Georgeene, Georgyne.**

Georgette   (French: variation of **Georgia,** "farmer"). Also, **Georgett, Georgitt, Georgitte.**

Georgia   (Greek: variation of **George,** "farmer"). Also, **Georgya.** Familiar, **Georgie.** *Whatever:* As map names go, **Dakota** and **Montana**—even **Brooklyn**—have it all over **Georgia** right now. But never count out the South to rise again. TV's *Ally McBeal,* with its legal eagle **Georgia,** is doing its part to boost this fading entry.

Georgie   (English: variation of **Georgia,** "farmer"). Also, **Georgee, Georgey, Georgi, Georgy.** *Plus:* Cute. *Minus:* A washed-up bobby-soxer.

Germaine   (English: blood relative). Also, **Germane, Germayne.**

Gia   (Greek: dark flower). Also, **Gya.** *Whatever:* Perfectly charming, perfectly current. *Minus:* Not at all common. Will people confuse it for a designer handbag label or a certain economy-class car?

Gianna   (Italian: variation of **Gianni,** "God is gracious"). Also, **Giana, Gyana, Gyanna.**

Gila   (Hebrew: joy). Also, **Gilla, Gyla, Gylla.**

Gilda   (English: golden, gilded). Also, **Gylda.** *Whatever:* Good-natured **Gilda**s probably sold lots of war bonds back in WWII—about the last time this vintage entry was really hot. And yet . . . it's not so far off from **Sadie** or **Sophie,** two other turn-of-the-nineteenth-century names seeing mini-revivals in our own turn-of-the-century.

Gillian (English: youthful). Also, **Gilian, Gilien, Gillien, Gillyan, Gillyen, Gilyan, Gilyen.** *Whatever:* Everything's falling into place for **Gillian**. It's pretty, feminine, and dressy. It's also got a chic champion, **Gillian** Anderson of TV's *The X-Files*. If it had a little vowel action, it'd be perfect. A comparable alternative to the ubiquitous **Katherine** or **Caitlyn.**

Gina (Hebrew: garden; Japanese: silvery; Italian: variation of **Angelina, Regina**). Also, **Geena, Gena, Gyna.** *Whatever:* If this book was written in the 1960s, this would have been a pick *not* to click— something that would fade and sound anachronistic. But it wasn't, and it hasn't. Admirable resiliency. Outnumbered in this Brave New **Brianna** World, it's resisting irrelevancy.

Ginerva (Italian: variation of **Guenevere,** "fair wife"). Also, **Gynerva.**

Ginevieve (Celtic: variation of **Genevieve,** "white wave"). Also, **Gineveeve, Giniveeve, Ginivieve, Ginyveeve, Ginyvieve.** Familiar, **Ginny.**

Ginny (English: variation of **Ginevieve, Regina**). Also, **Ginnee, Ginney, Ginni, Ginnie.**

Gisella (Spanish: variation of **Giselle,** "pledge"). Also, **Gisela.**

Giselle (French/German: pledge). Also, **Gisel, Gisele, Gisell.**

Githa (Scandinavian: war). Also, **Gytha.**

Giva (Hebrew: hill). Also, **Givah, Gyva, Gyvah.**

Gizella (Spanish: variation of **Gisella,** "pledge"). Also, **Gizela.**

Gizelle (French/German: variation of **Giselle,** "pledge"). Also, **Gizel, Gizele, Gizell.**

Gladys (Welsh: lame). Also, **Gladis, Gladiss, Gladyss.** *Whatever:* If there was any hope for this name among Gen Xers, it was ruined by the crabby **Gladys** Kravitz of *Bewitched* infamy. It's included here because if *Mad About You* can bring back **Mabel** (or try to), then you gotta figure this one is just as deserving of a shot at redemption.

Glenn (Welsh: valley). Also, **Glen.** *Plus:* This is a strong name that holds its own against **Madison** and **Morgan.** *Minus:* Too big a pain to overcome the perception that this is a boy name?

Glenna (Irish: valley). Also, **Glena.**

Glenys (Welsh: beautiful). Also, **Glenis, Gleniss, Glenyss.** *Whatever:* A pick to click—solid, pretty, today.

Gloria (Latin: glory, fame). Also, **Glorya.** *Plus:* A safe choice. **Gloria** is too rooted in Christian liturgy to ever become profoundly unfashionable. *Minus:* Laura Branigan's **"Gloria"** *will* become the running soundtrack of your life.

Glory (English: glory). Also, **Gloree, Glorey, Glori, Glorie.**

Glynis (Welsh: variation of **Glenys,** "beautiful"). Also, **Glyniss, Glynys, Glynyss.**

Glynn (Welsh: variation of **Glenn,** "valley"). Also, **Glin, Glinn, Glyn.**

Glynna (Irish: variation of **Glenna,** "valley"). Also, **Glina, Glinna, Glyna.**

Golda (Yiddish: golden). Familiar, **Goldie.**

Goldie (English: variation of **Golda,** "golden"). Also, **Goldee, Goldey, Goldi, Goldy.** *Plus:* A less ordinary alternative to **Gracie.** *Minus:* A Madonna—this one being owned by **Goldie** Hawn, if not **Goldilocks**.

Grace (Latin: beautiful, elegant). Also, **Graice, Grayce.** Familiar, **Gracie.** *Whatever:* A perennial for good reason—it's literally full of grace. Other little princess seem wanna-bes compared to the brilliance of the real thing. A classic pocket T.

Graceanne (English: combination of **Grace** and **Ann**). Also, **Graceann, Graiceann, Graiceanne, Grayceann, Grayceanne.**

Gracie (Latin: variation of **Grace,** "beautiful, elegant"). Also, **Gracee, Gracey, Graci, Gracy.** *Whatever:* Even **Grace**'s nickname manages to be spunky in a tasteful, noncutesy way.

Gracilia (Latin: slender). Also, **Gracillia, Gracillya, Gracilya.**

Grady (Irish: noble). Also, **Gradee, Gradey, Gradi, Gradie.** *Whatever:* If **Avery** can be a girl name, why not this prep-school candidate?

Grainne (Irish: variation of **Grace,** "beautiful, elegant"). Also, **Graine, Grayne, Graynne.**

Greer (Scottish: watchful). Also, **Greere, Grear, Greare, Grier.** *Plus:* A pick to click that projects all the ageless class of **Grace**. *Minus:* Lacks the feminine and contemporary feel of **Grace**.

Greta (German: variation of **Margaret,** "pearl"). Also, **Gretta.** *Whatever:* If you love **Gretel** but wish your daughter to emerge from kindergarten emotionally sound, then **Greta** is the way to go. This pick's distinctive and untainted by the Brothers Grimm.

Gretchen (German: variation of **Margaret,** "pearl"). Also, **Grechen, Grechin, Grechyn, Gretchin, Gretchyn.**

Guadalupe (Spanish: valley, wolf). Also, **Guadelupe, Guadylupe.**

Guenevere (Celtic: fair wife). Also, **Gueneveere, Gueniveere, Guenyveere.** Also, **Gwen.**

Guenna (Italian: variation of **Guenevere,** "fair wife"). Also, **Guena.**

Gwen (English: variation of **Guenevere, Gwendolyn, Gwenevere**). Also, **Gwenn.**

Gwenda (English: variation of **Gwendolyn,** "crescent moon"). Also, **Guenda.**

Gwendolyn (Celtic: crescent moon). Also, **Gwendolin, Gwendolinn, Gwendolynn.** Familiar, **Gwen.** *Whatever:* A pretty girl to the max. This name is defiantly girlie. Good thing it keeps **Gwen** around as a built-in balance.

Gwenevere (Celtic: variation of **Guenevere,** "fair wife"). Also, **Gweneveere, Gweniveere, Gwenyveere.** Familiar, **Gwen.**

Gwenna (English: variation of **Gwenevere,** "fair wife"). Also, **Gwena.**

Gwyn (English: variation of **Gwyneth,** "fair"). Also, **Gwin, Gwinn, Gwynn.**

Gwyneth (Celtic: fair). Also, **Gwynethe, Gwynith, Gwynithe, Gwynyth, Gwynythe.** Familiar, **Gwyn.** *Whatever:* Pocket T **Gwyneth** is too pretty and well-structured to be a fly-by-night. But beware any name that makes the headlines on the coattails of the next hot young thing. Will **Gwyneth** Paltrow be Meryl Streep in ten years? Or will she be Mariel Hemingway? Nothing wrong with either **Meryl** or **Mariel,** but because of circumstances beyond their names' controls, one sounds more contemporary than the other. (Hint: It's not **Mariel.**)

H

CRIB NOTES

Famous Hs: **Halle** Berry (actor, *Boomerang*); *Harriet the Spy* (children's novel); **Harper** Lee (author, *To Kill a Mockingbird*); **Hayley** Mills (actor, *The Parent Trap*); **Hedy** Lamarr (screen siren); **Helen** Hunt (TV/movie star); **Hester** Prynne (heroine, *The Scarlet Letter*); **Hillary** Clinton (U.S. first lady)

Pocket Ts: Hope

Trendy suspenders: Harley, Hayley, Heather

Think long, think hard: **Happy** (A little restraint, please.); **Hazel** (Let's play word association. Word: **Hazel**. Association: Sitcom star Shirley Booth in support hose and a maid's uniform.); **Heaven** (Oh, yeah? Wait 'til you change her first diaper.); **Heidi** (Borderline. Clearly, a classic. Also clearly associated with "Hollywood Madam" **Heidi** Fleiss, not to mention any number of XXX-rated "actresses." Your call.); **Helga** (Sorry, just not an attractive-sounding name to our modern ears.); **Heloise** (Here's a hint: This one's stale.); **Hilda** (*See* **Helga.**); **Henrietta** (Somehow, vaguely hippo-esque.); **Honey** (Leave it to the bees.)

Hadley (English: landowner). Also, **Hadlee, Hadleigh, Hadli, Hadlie, Hadly.** *Whatever:* A solid alternative to **Hayley.** It's got vowel action going for it, it's got a *Dynasty* feel going for it. It just doesn't have the popularity.

Haldana (Scandinavian: half Danish). Also, **Haldanna.**

Haldayne (Scandinavian: half Danish). Also, **Haldaine, Haldane.**

Halden (Scandinavian: variation of **Haldayne,** "half Danish"). Also, **Haldin, Haldyn.**

Halena (Greek: variation of **Helen,** "the bright one"). Also, **Haleena, Halyna.**

Halene (Greek: variation of **Helene,** "the bright one"). Also, **Haleen, Haleene, Halyne.**

Hali (Hebrew: necklace). Also, **Halli.**

Halina (African: gentle; Russian: variation of **Helen,** "the bright one"). Also, **Haleena, Halyna.**

Halle (English: head of house). Also, **Hallee, Halleigh, Halley, Halli, Hallie, Hally.** *Plus:* Wiggle room on the ubiquitous **Hayley.** *Minus:* Not different enough.

Hamida (Arabic: praiseworthy). Also, **Hameeda, Hamyda.**

Hana (Japanese: flower). Also, **Hanna.**

Hannabelle (English: combination of **Hannah** and **Belle**). Also, **Hannabell, Hannahbell, Hannahbelle.**

Hannah (Hebrew: gracious). Also, **Hana, Hanah, Hanna.** *Plus:* A monster that's storming the popularity charts as a costar in *The Revenge of the Little House on the Prairie Gals,* with **Emily** and **Sarah.** It's a name with deep enough roots to avoid looking silly when the heat cools. *Minus:* Came out of nowhere—*nowhere*—in the 1990s. If we'd forgotten about **Hannah** so completely before, could we do it again?

Harita (Hindi: wind). Also, **Hareeta, Haryta.**

Harlan (English: messenger). Also, **Harlen, Harlyn.**

Harley (English: deer hunter). Also, **Harlee, Harleigh, Harli, Harlie, Harly.** *Plus:* The anti-**Hannah.** This is a name that dares to sound unrelentingly *today! Minus:* What will it sound like tomorrow? Potential trendy suspenders.

Harlow (English: meeting place). Also, **Harlowe.**

Harmony (Latin: accord). Also, **Harmonee, Harmoney, Harmoni, Harmonie.** *Whatever:* This book's stance on anything that smacks remotely of hippiness has been consistent: Don't. But . . . this one's not as embarrassingly tie-dyed as, say, **Freedom. Harmony** is a name of hope that doesn't sound too naive.

Harper (English: harp player). *Whatever:* **Harper** Lee wrote the classic Gen X term-paper assignment, *To Kill a Mockingbird.*

Harrah (English: frosty). Also, **Hara, Harah, Harra.**

Harriet (English: variation of **Henry,** "head of house"). Also, **Harriett, Harryet, Harryett.** Familiar, **Hattie.** *Whatever:* Outmoded, yes. But it wins points for being the namesake of the beloved Gen X–era kids' book *Harriet the Spy.*

Hart (English: red deer). Also, **Harte.** *Whatever:* Preppie but not overtly so, like, say, **Muffy.**

Hartley (English: meadow where the deer are). Also, **Hartlee, Hartleigh, Hartli, Hartlie, Hartly.**

Hattie (English: variation of **Harriet,** "head of house"). Also, **Hati, Hattee, Hattey, Hatti, Hatty, Haty.** *Whatever:* A long shot that's got spunk. **Hattie** shouldn't look too out of place in a class picture populated by **Hannah**s, **Sarah**s, and **Emily**s. Definite *Little House on the Prairie* material.

Havana (Spanish: for the city **Havana,** Cuba). Also, **Havanna.** *Whatever:* A map name with political intrigue.

Haven (English: port). Also, **Havin, Havyn.**

Hayden (Irish: hill). Also, **Haydin, Haydyn.**

Hayley (English: hallway; Norwegian: heroine). Also, **Hailey, Haili, Hailie, Haily, Haylee, Hayleigh, Hayli, Haylie, Hayly.** *Plus:* Meet the new, improved **Kimberly. Hayley** is today's leading pretty girl. *Minus:* Remember how many **Kimberly**s were in your junior-high homeroom? We're about three minutes away from **Hayley** backlash. When it hits, watch out—trendy suspenders time.

Heather (English/Scottish: heather, flowery shrubs). Also, **Hether.** *Plus:* This is another pretty girl that's helping **Hayley** obliterate the likes of **Karen** and **Michelle.** Don't hate her because she's popular. *Minus:* Yeah, don't hate her. Fear her. Beware the curse of **Jennifer**— the ubiquitous pretty girl of Gen X's formative years. **Heather** is strapping on those very same trendy suspenders.

Hedley (English: landowner). Also, **Hedlee, Hedleigh, Hedli, Hedlie, Hedly.**

Hedy (English: warrior). Also, **Heddi, Heddie, Heddy, Hedi, Hedie.** *Whatever:* Perfect for a budding spitfire.

Helen (Greek: the bright one). Also, **Helin, Helyn.** *Plus:* A nice, safe, peanut-butter-and-jelly sandwich, with an appealing modern-day celeb namesake, Oscar-winner **Helen** Hunt. *Minus:* Is it too old-fashioned for infants of the new millennium?

Helena (Greek: variation of **Helen,** "the bright one"). Also, **Heleena, Helyna.**

Helene (Greek: variation of **Helene,** "the bright one"). Also, **Heleene, Helyne.**

Helice (Greek: fields). Also, **Heleece, Helyce.**

Hera (Greek: from mythology, Zeus's wife). Also, **Herra.**

Hesper (Greek: variation of **Esther,** "star").

Hester (German: beech tree; English: variation of **Esther,** "star). Also, **Hesther.** Familiar, **Hettie.** *Plus:* It also came from *Little House on the Prairie.* **Hester** is the proper-sounding, underutilized peer of **Hannah.** *Minus:* Things could get rough when your daughter's class reads *The Scarlet Letter.*

Hettie (English: variation of **Hester,** "beech tree"). Also, **Hettee, Hettey, Hetti, Hetty.** *Whatever: See* **Hattie.**

Hiatt (English: variation of **Hyatt,** "high gate"). Also, **Hiat.**

Hillary (Latin: cheery). Also, **Hilari, Hilarie, Hilary, Hileri, Hilerie, Hilery, Hillari, Hillarie, Hilleri, Hillerie, Hillery.** *Whatever:* Hillary Clinton's popularity may not rival that of, say, a **Jacqueline** Onassis, but a U.S. first lady is still a trendsetter, even in this apolitical age. This name's a strong choice without Clinton's help; an even stronger one with it. A pocket T.

Hisa (Japanese: to endure). Also, **Hissa, Hysa, Hyssa.**

Holland (English: the Netherlands, lowlands). Also, **Holand, Holande, Hollande.**

Hollander (English: from the Netherlands). Also, **Holander, Holender, Holynder, Hollender, Hollynder.**

Hollis (English: holly tree). Also, **Holis, Hollis, Holliss, Hollys, Hollyss, Holys, Holyss.** *Whatever:* A pick to click. Sleek and stylish, **Hollis** is a tonier-sounding **Holly.**

Holly (English: berry shrub). Also, **Hollee, Holley, Holli, Hollie.** *Plus:* Sounds like Christmas. *Minus:* Sounds like 1970s merchandising relic **Holly** Hobbie.

Hope (English: a hope, prayer for good). *Whatever:* Kudos to the baby boomers for *thirtysomething,* the TV series that reminded us what a class act **Hope** is. This is a virtue name (e.g., **Charity, Love**) that doesn't preach—it just is.

Hosanna (Hebrew: save now). Also, **Hosana, Hosanah, Hosannah.**

Hoyden (Scandinavian: spunky girl). Also, **Hoydin, Hoydyn.**

Hunter (English: hunter).

Hutton (English: village; German: cottage). Also, **Huten, Huton, Hutten.**

Hyatt (English: high gate). Also, **Hyat.**

I

CRIB NOTES

Famous Is: **Illeana** Douglas (actor, *To Die For*); **Iman** (model); **Ingrid** Bergman (*Casablanca* heroine); **Ione** Skye (actor, *Say Anything*); **Irene** Ryan (Granny Clampett, TV's *The Beverly Hillbillies*); **Isadora** Duncan (dancer); **Ivana** Trump (divorcee)

Pocket Ts: **Isabel**

Trendy suspenders: The Is don't have it where baby names are concerned. There's not a blockbuster name among the bunch—just a bunch of unique, potential supermodel monikers.

Think long, think hard: **Ikea** (Keep it in the living room.); **Imogene** (Not even comedian **Imogene** Coca at the zenith of her *Your Show of Shows* popularity—*forty-plus years ago*—could make this one anything but a flatliner.); **Irma** (Buried in a World War II victory garden.); **Isis** (Works best on plaster busts of ancient Greek goddesses.)

Ianthe (Greek: violet flower). Also, **Ianth.**
Ibis (Egyptian: large bird). Also, **Ibiss, Ibys, Ibyss.**
Ida (Norwegian: labor; Irish: thirst). *Plus:* Think Charlie Brown's Christmas tree. Like that sickly branch, this is a name that just needs a little love to blossom. *Minus:* **Ida**. Ho. . . . **Ida**, ho. . . . **Ida**-ho. . . . Somewhere, sometime, some boy will put the two syllables together and laugh. And laugh. And laugh.
Ide (Italian: variation of **Ida**, "labor").
Idella (Greek: variation of **Idelle**, "happy"). Also, **Idela.**
Idelle (Greek: happy). Also, **Idel, Idele, Idell.**

Ides (Latin: Fifteenth day of the month, like March).

Idola (Latin: idolized). Also, **Idolla**. *Whatever:* Supermodelesque, part I.

Iisha (African: variation of **Aisha**, "life"). Also, **Iysha.**

Ilan (Hebrew: youth; variation of **Ilana**, "oak tree"). Also, **Ilann.**

Ilana (Hebrew: oak tree). Also, **Ilanah, Ilanna, Ilannah.**

Ilea (Greek: variation of **Helen**, "the bright one"). Also, **Ileea, Ilia, Ilya.** *Whatever:* Supermodelesque, part II.

Ilena (Greek: variation of **Helen**, "the bright one"). Also, **Ileena, Ilyna.**

Ilene (Greek: variation of **Helen**, "the bright one"). Also, **Ileene, Ilyne.**

Ilisa (German: variation of **Elizabeth**, "God's oath"). Also, **Ileesa, Ilysa.**

Illiana (Greek: from city of Troy). Also, **Ileana, Ileanna, Iliana, Il- ianna, Illeana, Illeanna, Illiana, Illianna.** *Whatever:* This one's a proper little princess, also, it's arguably more stately than the gaudy likes of **Alexis**.

Ilona (Greek: light). Also, **Ilonna**. *Whatever:* Supermodelesque, part III.

Ilone (Greek: variation of **Ilona**, "light").

Ilsa (German: variation of **Elizabeth**, "God's oath"). Familiar, **Ilsie.** *Plus:* Pretty, different. *Minus:* Perfect for a future member of the Swedish Bikini Team.

Ilse (German: variation of **Elizabeth**, "God's oath"). Familiar, **Ilsie.**

Ilsie (German: variation of **Ilsa, Ilse**). Also, **Ilsee, Ilsey, Ilsi, Ilsy.**

Ilya (Greek: Lord is my God). Also, **Ilia, Illia, Illya.**

Iman (Arabic: faith). Also, **Imann.** *Plus:* A name that projects strength and beauty: *Minus:* Seeing as this moniker is the *real* supermodel deal, you're giving your daughter a lot to live up to.

Imani (Arabic: variation of **Iman**, "faith"). Also, **Imanee, Imaney, Imanie, Imany.**

Ina (Latin: mother; Spanish: strong).

Incencia (Spanish: innocent). Also, **Incencya.**

Incenzia (Italian: innocent). Also, **Incenzya.**

India (English: rear). Also, **Indya.** *Plus:* More colloquial than **Aus- tralia.** *Minus:* Less colloquial than **Dakota.**

Indiana (English: of the Indies). Also, **Indianna, Indyana, Indyanna.** *Plus:* More colloquial than **Ohio.** *Minus:* Less colloquial than **Car- olina.**

Indigo (English: deep violet-blue). Also, **Indygo.** *Plus:* You're banking that Crayolas will inspire the next hot baby name trend. *Minus:* Before you go crazy spelunking, maybe you should keep something like **Sue** as a backup.

Ines (Spanish: pure, chaste). Also, **Inis, Inys.**

Inez (Spanish: pure, chaste). Also, **Iniz, Inyz.**

Inga (Norwegian: variation of **Ingrid,** "hero's daughter"). *Whatever:* Works on the same levels—both plus and minus—as **Ilsa.**

Inge (Norwegian: variation of **Ingrid,** "rider").

Ingrid (Norwegian: hero's daughter; English: meadow). Also, **Ingridd, Ingryd, Ingrydd.** *Whatever:* **Ingrid** Bergman's radiant screen presence keeps this chestnut from turning into the dearly departed **Ida.**

Inigo (Greek: variation of **Ignatius,** "ardent, spirited"). Also, **Inygo.**

Inis (Greek: daughter). Also, **Inys.**

Innis (Irish/Scottish: island). Also, **Inis, Iniss, Innys, Innyss, Inys.**

Inola (Latin: small bell). Also, **Inolla.**

Iola (Welsh: worthy god; Greek: cloud at dawn). Also, **Iolla.** *Whatever:* Supermodelesque, part IV.

Iolo (Welsh: youthful).

Iona (Greek: violet jewel). Also, **Ionna.** *Plus:* Sounds contemporary, not temporary. *Minus:* "**Iona** . . . Isn't that a pretty name?" Your girl will hear this unsolicited commentary a thousand times during her lifetime—mostly as she merely tries to leave a brief telephone message with an office receptionist. This is not a bad thing, just a potentially annoying thing.

Ione (Greek: variation of **Iona,** "violet jewel"). Also, **Ionee, Ioney, Ioni, Ionie, Iony.**

Iram (English: shining bright). Also, **Iramm.**

Ireana (English: variation of **Irene,** "peace"). Also, **Ireanna, Iriana, Irianna, Iryana, Iryanna.**

Ireland (Irish: the country). Also, **Irelande.**

Irene (Greek: peace). Also, **Ireene.** *Plus:* A dear classic . . . *Minus:* . . . that's starting to show its age.

Iris (Greek: rainbow). Also, **Iriss, Irys, Iryss.** *Plus:* "**Iris** . . . That means 'rainbow,' right? How pretty." *Minus:* "Isn't that the eyeball thing?"

Isa (German: iron; Hebrew: God is helper). Also, **Isah, Issa, Issah.**

Isabel (Spanish: variation of **Elizabeth,** "God's oath"). Also, **Isabell, Isabelle, Isebell, Isebelle.** *Plus:* Understated, musical, elegant, exotic.

Isabel is always right and a pocket T. *Minus:* It's something of a purple pocket T. **Isabel** is a name that will stand out because it's not **Ashley, Brittany,** or **Heather**. It's the equivalent of Winona Ryder's **Veronica** in *Heathers*—on the outside looking in.

Isabella (Italian: variation of **Elizabeth,** "God's oath"). Also, **Isabela, Isebela, Isebella.**

Isadora (Latin: gift). Also, **Isadorra, Isedora, Isedorra.**

Isha (Hindi: protector). Also, **Ishah.**

Ishtar (Arabic: for the ancient Babylonian goddess of fertility). *Whatever:* Forget the Dustin Hoffman–Warren Beatty movie (as if you *saw* the thing). This is a little princess with genuine credentials. Stately, unique.

Isis (Egyptian: goddess of fertility). Also, **Isiss, Isys, Isyss.** *Whatever:* Forget the 1970s TV kids' show (as if you can). This is another little princess that's the real thing.

Isla (Scottish: inlet). Also, **Issla.**

Isolda (German: variation of **Isolde,** "ice ruler").

Isolde (German: ice ruler). Also, **Isold.** *Whatever:* Remember, you can take fancy chances with girl names. Don't be afraid to go operatic (*Tristan and* **Isolde**). Besides, here's betting an **Isolde** can hang just fine with a **Vanessa** or **Victoria.**

Isolte (German: variation of **Isolde,** "ice ruler"). Also, **Isolt.**

Issa (Swahili: God is our salvation).

Italy (English: the country of Italy). *Whatever:* None of these provincial, regional map names for you. You're staking a claim for an entire blinkin' country.

Iva (Hebrew: gift from God). Also, **Ivah.**

Ivana (Slavic: variation of **John,** "God is gracious"). Also, **Ivanna.**

Ivanka (Slavic: variation of **Ivana,** "God is gracious"). Also, **Ivanca, Ivancka.**

Ivens (Welsh: young warrior, archer). Also, **Ivins, Ivyns.**

Ivonne (French: young archer). Also, **Ivon, Ivone, Ivonn.**

Ivory (English: white wood). Also, **Ivoree, Ivorey, Ivori, Ivorie,** *Plus:* Dramatic, in an environmental sort of way. *Minus:* Sounds fit for a 1970s daytime soap.

Ivy (English: the climbing vine). Also, **Ivee, Ivey, Ivi, Ivie.** *Plus:* Variations **Ivey, Ivie** and the like hippen-up this **Ida**-ish relic. *Minus:* No matter how you spell it, people still think, "Poison **Ivy.**"

Iye (Native American: smoke).

Izabel (Spanish: variation of **Isabel,** "God's oath"). Also, **Izabell, Iz-abelle, Izebel, Izebell, Izebelle.**

Izabella (Italian: variation of **Isabella,** "God's oath"). Also, **Izabela, Izebela, Izebella.**

Izadora (Latin: variation of **Isadora,** "gift"). Also, **Izadorra, Izedora, Izedorra.**

J

CRIB NOTES

Famous Js: **Jacqueline** Bouvier Kennedy Onassis (Cassini-clad U.S. first lady); **Jackie O.** (shades-wearing private citizen); **Jada** Pinkett Smith (actor/Mrs. Will Smith); **Jane** Pratt (that *Jane* editor girl); **Janet** Jackson (the normal one, the Jackson family); **Janis** Joplin (1960s-era rocker); **Jennifer** Aniston (a friend, TV's *Friends*); **Jewel** (singer/song-writer); **Jodie** Foster (actor/director); **Joely** Fisher (actor, TV's *Ellen*); **Josephine** Baker (American-born French chanteuse); **Josie** Bissett (*Melrose Place* resident); **Juliette** Lewis (actor, *Natural Born Killers*); **Justine** Bateman (Mallory Keaton, TV's *Family Ties*)

Pocket Ts: Jane, Jessica, Julia

Trendy suspenders: Jacinda, Janita, Jasmine, Jordan

Think long, think hard: **Jacoba** (Yes, **Jacob** is a very nifty name. But you should wait for a *boy* to use it.); **Jazz** (Sounds ripped from the pages of a Jackie Collins potboiler.); **Jemima** (Battered by far too many years of unfortunate Aunt **Jemima** stereotypes—no matter how spiffy they try to make her look on syrup bottles these days.); **Jezebel** (Well, it's better than **Hussy**. But not by much.); **Johnette** (The equivalent of a pink toolbox.); **Josie** (Three words: and the Pussycats.)

Jabot (French: shirt ruffle).
Jacey (English: variation of **Jacinda, Jacinta**). Also, **Jacee, Jaci, Jacie, Jacy, Jaycee, Jaycey, Jayci, Jaycie.**
Jacinda (Greek: purple, lily). Also, **Jacynda.** Also, **Jacey.** *Plus:* Kind of wow, kind of now. **Jacinda** is a pretty girl in good standing. *Minus:*

Supermodel-ready names have about as long a shelf life as supermodels themselves. Where are **Sheryl, Christie,** and **Kathy** today? In the back of the closet with the rest of the trendy suspenders.

Jacinta (Spanish: variation of **Jacinda,** "purple, lily"). Also, **Jacynta, Jacey.**

Jackie (English: variation of **Jacqueline,** "following after"). Also, **Jackee, Jackey, Jacki, Jacky, Jacquee, Jacquey, Jacqui, Jacquie, Jacquy.**

Jacklyn (English: variation of **Jacqueline,** "following after"). Also, **Jacklin, Jacqulin, Jacqulyn.**

Jacqueline (French/Hebrew: following after). Also, **Jackeline, Jackelyn, Jackelyne, Jackiline, Jackilyne, Jackyline, Jackylyn, Jackylyne, Jacquelyn, Jacquelyne, Jacquiline, Jacquilyn, Jacquilyne, Jacquyline, Jacquylyn, Jacquylyne.** Familiar, **Jackie.** *Whatever:* Gen Xers have little firsthand knowledge of **Jacqueline** Kennedy Onassis. To us, she was the skinny lady in the dark, round sunglasses. So can she *really* be the reason that this evening gown remains stylish today? There are two other possibles behind the name's appeal: (1) Americans—of any age—aspire to be French, or at least talk like them; (2) Early exposure to the elegant *Charlie's Angels* Angel, **Jaclyn** Smith.

Jacquita (Spanish: girl). Also, **Jackeeta, Jacketa, Jackita, Jackyta, Jacqueeta, Jacquyta.**

Jada (Sanskrit: frigid; Latin: semiprecious stone). Also, **Jaida, Jayda.**

Jade (Latin: semiprecious stone). Also, **Jaide, Jayde.** *Plus:* A take-no-prisoners girl name, full of drama and angles. *Minus:* Probably best reserved for the title of a pulp romance.

Jakarta (English: for the island city). Also, **Jacarta, Jaquarta, Jaqarta.**

Jakayla (American: variation of **Kayla,** "laurel crown"). Also, **Jakaela, Jakaila.**

Jakayli (American: variation of **Kayli,** "laurel crown"). Also, **Jakaylee, Jakayley, Jakaylie, Jakayly.**

Jamie (English: variation of **James,** "following after"). Also, **Jamee, Jamey, Jami, Jamy, Jaimee, Jaimey, Jaimi, Jaimie, Jaimy, Jaymee, Jaymey, Jaymi, Jaymie, Jaymy.** *Plus:* Cute, sporty. *Minus:* About as today as a bottle of Love's Baby Soft perfume.

Jamilla (Arabic: beautiful). Also, **Jamila, Jamyla, Jamylla.**

Jamille (Arabic: variation of **Jamilla,** "beautiful"). Also, **Jameele, Jameelle, Jamyl, Jamyle, Jamyll, Jamylle.**

Jan (Latin: variation of **Janis,** "from Roman god Janus, keeper of the door"). Also, **Jann.** *Whatever:* An overpowering sense of *The Brady Bunch* colors **Jan**. Whatever this name was supposed to signify has long been supplanted by TV reruns and images of a petty, jealous, positively goofy, borderline-disturbed young girl. Even **Jan** Brady fans would be hard-pressed to name their daughters after the patron saint of the persecution complex. But it'd be higher on their lists than **Marcia.**

Jana (Slavic: variation of **Jane,** "God is gracious"). Also, **Janna.** *Whatever:* An exotic spin on **Jane.**

Janda (Slavic: variation of **Jane,** "God is gracious")

Jane (Hebrew/English: God is gracious). Also, **Jain, Jaine, Jayne.** Familiar, **Janie.** *Plus:* Plain wrap is back. **Jane** makes generic seem sublime. It's so . . . *real,* a pocket T. *Minus:* It's as daring as a peanut-butter-and-jelly sandwich.

Janelle (French: little **Jane**). Also, **Janell, Jeanell, Jeanelle.** *Whatever:* The *Ja* sound—as in **Janelle, Janessa**—is where it's happening in little princess names. Hazard to guess that if you stuck *Ja* in front of any letter combo, you'd have yourself an appropriate contemporary selection. Well, maybe not **Jadirt,** but you get the idea.

Janessa (American: variation of **Vanessa,** "butterfly"). Also, **Janesa, Janisa, Janissa, Janysa, Janyssa.**

Janet (Hebrew: variation of **Jane,** "God is gracious"). Also, **Janit, Janyt.** *Plus:* Sunny, spunky. A name for the New Frontier. *Minus:* The New Frontier was in the 1960s.

Janice (English: variation of **Jane,** "God is gracious"). Also, **Janyce.**

Janie (English: variation of **Jane,** "God is gracious"). Also, **Janee, Janey, Jani, Jany.**

Janina (Sanskrit: kind). Also, **Janyna.**

Janine (French: variation of **Jane,** "God is gracious"). Also, **Janeene, Janyne, Jeaneene, Jeanyne.**

Janis (Latin: from Roman god Janus, keeper of the door). Also, **Janiss, Janus, Januss, Janys, Janyss.** Familiar, **Jan.**

Janita (Scandinavian: variation of **Jane,** "God is gracious"). Also, **Janeeta, Janyta.** *Plus:* All the elements of a happening girl name: It's pretty, semisophisticated, and vowel-friendly. **Janita** should be accepted with open arms to the sorority of **Ashley**s and **Brittany**s. *Minus:* The jury's out on the little princess names. Too much, too soon? Beware, trendy suspenders.

Janna (Hebrew: God saves). Also, **Jana, Janah, Jannah.**

Jansen (Dutch: God is gracious). Also, **Jansin, Jansyn.**

Jardine (Scottish/French: garden). Also, **Jardeen, Jardeene, Jardyne.** *Whatever:* A sound-alike alternative to **Jordan.**

Jasmin (Persian: variation of **Jasmine,** "flower"). Also, **Jasminn, Jasmyn, Jasmynn.**

Jasmina (Persian: variation of **Jasmine,** "flower"). Also, **Jasmeena, Jasmyna.**

Jasmine (Persian: flower). Also, **Jasmeene, Jasmyne.** *Plus:* The ultimate little princess—even if it was inspired by the heroine in Disney's *Aladdin,* not *The Little Mermaid.* Dainty, pretty, and popular, **Jasmine** is the new **Michelle** or **Kimberly.** *Minus:* The perfect name for fragrant soap, but for a thirty-five-year-old lawyer? Or a forty-three-year-old astronaut? The Disneyfication of baby names is among the most cloying of today's trends. This one's trendy suspenders.

Jay (English: songbird). Also, **Jaye.**

Jazmin (American: variation of **Jasmin,** "flower"). Also, **Jazminn, Jazmyn, Jazmynn.**

Jazmina (American: variation of **Jasmina,** "flower"). Also, **Jazmeena, Jazmyna.**

Jazmine (American: variation of **Jasmine,** "flower"). Also, **Jazmeene, Jazmyne.**

Jean (French: variation of **Jane,** "God is gracious"). Also, **Jeane, Jeen, Jeene.** Familiar, **Jeannie.** *Whatever:* Does anybody name a baby girl **Jean** anymore? It sure doesn't seem like it. This one's a definite WWII relic—too plain to compete against today's **Jasmine**s and **Courtney**s, not classic enough to get by as a **Jane.** That said, it's a short, succinct number that'll do OK if you're really, really in love with it.

Jeanette (French: variation of **Jean,** "God is gracious"). Also, **Janett, Janette, Jeanett.** *Whatever:* The **Jasmine** of the 1960s, **Jeanette** was a pretty, au courant girl name—for its time. It's got the looks, just not the heat.

Jeannie (English: variation of **Jean,** "God is gracious"). Also, **Jeannee, Jeanney, Jeanni, Jeanny.**

Jen (English: variation of **Jennifer,** "white wave"). Also, **Jenn.**

Jenna (Arabic: small bird). Also, **Jena, Jenah, Jennah.** *Whatever:* Watch TV's *Dharma and Greg* star **Jenna** Elfman help this one take flight.

Jennifer (Celtic: white wave). Also, **Jenifer, Jennyfer, Jenyfer.** Familiar, **Jen, Jenny.** *Plus:* This name has been so common for so long we forget what made it that way in the first place. It's the spirit, stupid. **Jennifer** is hopeful. It's California sunny. It's blithely free of ties to Elizabethan England. It's America, people. *Minus:* Forget "Generation X," our true name is "Generation **Jennifer.**" Starting its climb in the 1960s, **Jennifer** went on to become the most popular girl name of both the 1970s and the 1980s. What began as a good idea, turned into a fanatical obsession. Enough! And that's what Gen X parents are saying. **Jennifer** spent the 1990s slowly—*slowly*—creeping down the charts. (Note: It's still very much a monster performer. It's just not—finally—number one anymore.)

Jenny (English: variation of **Jennifer,** "white wave"). Also, **Jennee, Jenney, Jennie, Jeny.**

Jenson (Dutch: variation of **Jansen,** "God is gracious"). Also, **Jensen.**

Jess (Hebrew: variation of **Jessica,** "God's grace"). Also, **Jes.**

Jessa (Hebrew: variation of **Jessica,** "God's grace"). Also, **Jesa, Jesah, Jessah.**

Jesse (Hebrew: God exists; variation of **Jessica,** "God's grace"). Also, **Jesi, Jessee, Jessey, Jessi, Jessie, Jessy, Jesy.** *Whatever:* With **Dakota, Jesse** is another Old West name that the fashionable lil' cowpoke wears today.

Jessica (Hebrew: God's grace). Also, **Jessika, Jessyca, Jessyka.** Familiar, **Jess, Jesse.** *Plus:* Hot, hot, hot. With **Amanda, Emily,** and **Sarah,** this is a big winner in the *Little House on the Prairie* movement. Rescued from the retirement home and refashioned for the kindergarten, **Jessica** has a lot of appeal to new parents: It's popular but not trendy-sounding. It's old-fashioned but not old lady–sounding. A rediscovered pocket T. *Minus:* Two things: (1) It reminds you of the *Murder, She Wrote* lady; (2) It's very, *very* popular.

Jet (English: an airplane; a lush black). Also, **Jett.**

Jetty (English: a pier). Also, **Jeti, Jettee, Jettey, Jetti, Jettie, Jety.**

Jewel (English: precious stone; French: joy). Also, **Jewele, Jewell, Jewelle.** *Whatever:* Watch twentysomething folk singer **Jewel** Kilcher (just plain old **Jewel** to fans) give this name a good ride.

Jill (English: variation of **Jillian, Jillisa**). Also, **Jil, Jyl, Jyll.** *Whatever:* A peanut-butter-and-jelly sandwich. No baggage. No funny aftertaste. A generic girl name. Works anytime, anywhere. Could be a pocket T except it's a little too cold to be considered *très* fashionable.

Jillian (English: youthful). Also, **Jilian, Jillyan, Jillyen, Jilyan, Jilyen.** Familiar, **Jill, Jillie.** *Whatever:* Think of **Jillian** as the dressy **Jill.** Its extra flair helps make the name seem neatly contemporary. Of course, the renown of *X-Files* star **Gillian** Anderson doesn't hurt either.

Jillie (English: variation of **Jillian, Jillisa**). Also, **Jili, Jillee, Jilley, Jilli, Jilly, Jily.**

Jillisa (English: variation of **Jillian,** "youthful"). Also, **Jilisa, Jillysa, Jilysa.** Familiar, **Jill, Jillie.**

Jinny (English: variation of **Virginia,** "strong"). Also, **Jini, Jinnee, Jinney, Jinni, Jinnie, Jiny.**

Jo (English/Spanish/Italian/French: variation of **Joanna, Joanne, Josefina, Josephina, Josephine**). *Whatever:* From *Little Women* to *The Facts of Life,* **Jo** has represented the ultimate in spunk.

Joal (American: combination of **John** and **Alice**). Also, **Joall.**

Joan (Hebrew: God is gracious). Familiar, **Joanie.** *Whatever:* **Joan** packs more panache than **Jill,** but sounds more old lady–like, too. Bottom line: If your little **Joan** can bear being the odd duck out in the school full of **Ashley**s, she'll learn to love the simple pleasures of her name—around age thirty-five.

Joanie (English: variation of **Joan,** "God is gracious"). Also, **Joanee, Joaney, Joani, Joany.** *Whatever:* Can wall-to-wall *Happy Days* reruns on Nick at Nite give this relic a boost? Here's betting we'll always love it more than **Chachi,** but never quite as much as, say, **Marion.**

Joanna (English: combination of **Jo** and **Anna**). Also, **Joana.** Familiar, **Jo.** *Whatever:* **Joanna**'s not out, per se, it's just not of this time. It's more a name befitting a thirtysomething divorcèe of the late 1960s.

Joanne (English: combination of **Jo** and **Ann**). Also, **Jo Ann, JoAnn, Joann, Jo Anne, JoAnne.** Familiar, **Jo.**

Jocelyn (Latin: supportive; English: just). Also, **Jocelin, Jocilin, Jocilyn, Jocylin, Jocylyn.**

Jocinta (Spanish: variation of **Jocelyn,** "supportive, just"). Also, **Jocynta.**

Joclin (Latin: variation of **Jocelyn,** "supportive, just"). **Joclinn, Joclyn, Joclynn.**

Joda (Latin: playful). Also, **Jodda.**

Jodie (Hebrew: praise). Also, **Jodee, Jodey, Jodi, Jody.** *Plus:* Plucky, game, and, hey, it's got vowel action! *Minus:* Vowels can't cure all ills. This one's trapped in the 1970s.

Joella (Italian: variation of **Joelle**, "God is Lord"). Also, **Joela**.

Joelle (French: God is Lord). Also, **Joele**.

Joely (American: inspired by singer Al Jolson). Also, **Joelee, Joeley, Joeli, Joelie**. *Whatever:* This is the "made-up" name that ex-celeb couple Connie Stevens and Eddie Fisher dreamed up for their daughter, *Ellen* costar **Joely** Fisher.

Johanna (Hebrew/German: variation of **Johann**, "God is gracious"). Also, **Johana, Johanah, Johannah**.

Jojo (African: born on Monday). Also, **Jo Jo, JoJo**.

Jolie (French: pretty). Also, **Jolee, Joley, Joli, Joly**.

Jonina (Hebrew: dove). Also, **Joninah, Jonyna, Jonynah**.

Jonna (English: variation of **John**, "God is gracious"). Also, **Johna, Johnna, Jona**. *Whatever:* The 1990s-style **Joanna** or **Joanne**.

Jordaine (Hebrew: variation of **Jordan**, "down-flowing river"). Also, **Jordane, Jordayne**. Familiar, **Jordy**.

Jordan (Hebrew: down-flowing river). Also, **Jorden, Jordyn**. Familiar, **Jordy, Jory**. *Plus:* Upscale and sophisticated, **Jordan** carries itself with an admirable restraint in this age of the frou-frou little princess. *Minus:* A name championed by yuppified baby boomers. It's not that yuppified baby boomers are bad people, it's just that they thought nouvelle cuisine was really cool once too—and who nibbles on that stuff today? Gen Xers, beware another pair of trendy suspenders.

Jordana (Hebrew: variation of **Jordan**, "down-flowing river"). Also, **Jordanah, Jordanna, Jordannah**. Familiar, **Jordy**.

Jordy (Hebrew: variation of **Jordaine, Jordan, Jordana**). Also, **Jordee, Jordey, Jordi, Jordie**.

Jorna (Spanish: journey).

Jory (Hebrew: variation of **Jordan**, "down-flowing river"). Also, **Joree, Jorey, Jori, Jorie**.

Josefina (Spanish: variation of Joseph, "increaser, God will add"). Also, **Josefeena, Josefyna, Josifeena, Josifina, Josifyna**. Familiar, **Jo**.

Joselyn (Latin: variation of **Jocelyn**, "supportive"). Also, **Joselin, Josilin, Josilyn, Josylyn**.

Josephina (Italian: variation of **Joseph**, "increaser, God will add"). Also, **Josepheena, Josipheena, Josiphina, Josiphyna**. Familiar, **Jo**.

Josephine (French: variation of **Joseph**, "increaser, God will add"). Also, **Josepheen, Josepheene, Josephyne, Josipheen, Josipheene,**

Josiphyne. Familiar, **Jo.** *Whatever:* Pretty but needs a modern champion. It's bordering on becoming a museum piece.

Josinta (Spanish: variation of **Jocinta,** "supportive"). Also, **Josynta.**

Joslin (Latin: variation of **Joselyn,** "supportive"). Also, **Joslinn, Joslyn, Joslynn.**

Jovita (Latin: merry). Also, **Joveeta, Jovyta.**

Joy (English: delight). Also, **Joye.** *Whatever:* Go figure—**Hope**'s a pocket T; **Joy**'s a dishwashing liquid. One theory: **Hope** is hopeful, an admirable trait for these cynical times. **Joy** is outright slaphappy, a potentially foolish trait for these cynical times.

Joyce (Irish: joyful). Also, **Joice, Joyse.** *Whatever:* **Joanna** and **Joyce** were first vice president and second vice president, respectively, at the local PTA, circa 1966.

Juana (Spanish: variation of **Juan,** "God is gracious").

Judd (English: confession). Also, **Jud.**

Jude (Hebrew: praise, variation of **Judith,** "praised;" English: confession). *Whatever:* The hip **Judy.**

Judita (Slavic: variation of **Judith,** "praised"). Also, **Judeeta, Judyta.** Familiar, **Judy.**

Judith (Hebrew: praised). Also, **Judithe, Judyth, Judythe.** Familiar, **Judy.** *Plus:* A stately classic. Refreshingly serious. *Minus:* Too serious for our little princess times.

Juditha (Hebrew: variation of **Judith,** "praised"). Also, **Judytha.** Familiar, **Judy.**

Judy (English: variation of **Judita, Judith, Juditha**). Also, **Judee, Judey, Judi, Judie.** *Whatever:* **Judy** clicked in the 1950s and 1960s. Since then? Well, let's just say she's been taking a really long lunch with **Debbie** and **Muffy.**

Julep (Persian: rosewater). Also, **Julepp, Julip, Julipp, Julyp, Julypp.**

Jules (French: youthful; English: variation of **Julia, Julie**)

Julia (Latin: young). Also, **Julya.** Familiar, **Jules.** *Whatever:* A good baby name rule of thumb is: Can a newborn wear the name as easily as, say, an eightysomething PBS cooking guru? If the answer's yes, you have **Julia**—a moniker possessing a timeless, accessible beauty. A pocket T.

Juliana (English: combination of **Julie** and **Ana**). Also, **Julianna, Julieana, Julieanna, Julyana, Julyanna.** Familiar, **Julie.**

Juliann (English: combination of **Julie** and **Ann**). Also, **Julianne, Julieann, Julieanne, Julyann, Julyanna.** Familiar, **Julie.**

Julie (English: young; variation of **Juliana, Juliann, Juliet, Julietta**).
Also, **Juli**. Familiar, **Jules**. *Plus:* The plucky, dress-casual-Friday
Julia. *Minus: Très* 1960s.

Juliet (French: young). Also, **Juliett, Juliette, Julyett, Julyette**. Familiar, **Julie**. *Whatever:* A little princess in Shakespeare's time. Holding up about as well as his plays.

Julietta (Italian: variation of **Juliet,** "young"). Also, **Julieta, Julyeta,
Julyetta**. Familiar, **Julie**.

Juna (Latin: variation of **June,** "forever young").

June (Latin: forever young). *Whatever:* "I'm worried about the Beaver,
Ward."—**June** Cleaver, about the last notable woman of the twentieth
century to popularize the sixth calendar month as a first name.

Justina (Italian: variation of **Justine,** "honorable, fair"). Also, **Jus-
teena, Justyna**. Familiar, **Tina**.

Justine (English/Latin: honorable, fair). Also, **Justeen, Justeene,
Jusytne**. Familiar, **Tina**.

CRIB NOTES

Famous Ks: **Katarina** Witt (Olympic figure skater); **Katharine** Hepburn (actor/role model/legend); **Katie** Couric (TV news anchor, *Today*); **k. d.** lang (singer); **Keshia** Knight Pulliam (former child star, TV's *The Cosby Show*); **Kellie** Martin (actor, TV's *ER*); **Kirstie** Alley (actor, TV's *Cheers*); **Kylie** Minogue (1980s one-hit wonder, "The Locomotion"); **Kyra** Sedgwick (actor/Mrs. Kevin Bacon).

Pocket Ts: **Kate, Katherine, Kathleen**

Trendy suspenders: **Kaitlyn, Kayla**

Think long, think hard: **Karma** (Yours will not be good if your child spends her teen years demanding to know why you couldn't have settled for **Sue.**); **Kashmir** (Too-too.); **Kiki** (The 1970s retro thing may seem cool now, but by the time your daughter's in middle school the world will be ensconced in the 1980s, making **Kiki** seem more hopelessly outmoded than ever.); **Kitten** (*Father Knows Best?* Oh, really. What was Robert Young's TV dad thinking, pegging his youngest daughter with this pet-only designation?); **Kitty** (Names like this are best left to the assignment of 1950-era sorority sisters.)

The "phony Cs": A note before we begin. Below, you won't find the likes of **Kameron, Karoline, Karissa, Kassidy,** or **Kory.** Names that are commonly Cs—with no popular K variations to be had—are found in the C section (no birthing-procedure pun intended). Again, you are free to spell your baby's name any way you wish. Make **Brittany** into **Obrittany.** ("The *o*'s silent . . . like 'opossum.' "). Just a reminder: You don't get style points for fudging with spelling. **Kassidy** is still **Cassidy.**

Kady   (Scottish: little warrior). Also, **Kadee, Kadey, Kadi, Kadie.** *Whatever:* Sounds sort of like **Katie**—except it's not! Impress friends and family with your clever end run of a hot trend.

Kaelani   (Hawaiian: variation of **Kalani**, "celestial"). Also, **Kaelanee, Kaylanee, Kaylani.**

Kaitlyn   (Irish: variation of **Catherine**, "pure"). Also, **Kaitlin, Katelin, Katelyn, Kaytlin, Kaytlyn.** Familiar, **Katie.** *Plus:* A pretty girl name supreme. This spunky 'n' strong entry is what virtually all the kindergartners on your block will be wearing in five years—well, at least the girls. Très fashionable. *Minus:* You know how **Jennifer** doesn't sound "wrong" today, but it just doesn't sound the way it did when it was being handed out in bulk in 1974? This, too, could be the fate of **Kaitlyn**. Trendy suspenders potential.

Kalani   (Hawaiian: celestial). Also, **Kalanee, Kalanie, Kelanee, Kelani.** *Whatever:* **Kaitlyn,** schmaitlin. Your kid's goin' Hawaiian!

Kali   (Hindu: energy). Also, **Kalli.**

Kalya   (Sanskrit: heavenly). *Whatever:* A quick letter shuffle and *voilà*—spelunkers have **Kayla** that nobody's ever heard of!

Kama   (Sanskrit: wished for). Also, **Kamma.**

Kane   (Japanese: golden; German: warrior; Irish: tribute). Also, **Kaine, Kayne.**

Kanisha   (American: variation of **Aisha**, "life"). Also, **Kaneesha, Kanysha, Keneesha, Kenisha, Kenysha.**

Kara   (Greek: variation of **Katherine**, "pure"). Also, **Karra.**

Karen   (Greek: variation of **Katherine**, "pure"). Also, **Karin, Karyn.** *Plus:* **Karen** is a nice name. Easy to spell. Easy to say. A nice name. Yes, **Karen,** is a *nice* name. *Minus:* **Karen** is the ex-cheerleader you run into at your ten-year high school reunion. The one who once upon a time was voted "Most Popular" but currently spends her days bussing tables at the local greasy spoon wondering where all her adoring minions went. In short, she's not aging well. **Karen**s and **Jennifer**s ruled middle school in the 1970s and 1980s. Their glory days are over. The baby name universe belongs to the **Kaitlyn**s and **Kayla**s now. How do pretty-girl names spend their golden years? Stuffed in a brown paper bag, subexisting as peanut-butter-and-jelly sandwiches.

Karena   (Scandinavian: variation of **Karen**, "pure"). Also, **Kareena, Karyna.**

Karina (Greek: variation of **Katherine,** "pure"). Also, **Kareena, Karyna.**

Karissa (Latin: artful). Also, **Karisa, Karysa, Karyssa.**

Karr (Irish: spear). Also, **Karre.**

Kasey (Irish: vigilant). Also, **Kasee, Kasi, Kasie, Kasy.** *Whatever:* This name would have been perfect for the cutsie 1990s—except it peaked in the 1970s.

Kasia (Greek: variation of **Katherine,** "pure"). Also, **Kasya.**

Kass (German: blackbird; Greek: variation of **Kassandra, Kassaundra**). Also, **Kas.**

Kassandra (Greek: prophet, helper of man). Also, **Kasandra.** Familiar, **Kass, Kassie.**

Kassaundra (Greek: variation of **Kassandra,** "prophet, helper of man"). Also, **Kasaundra.** Familiar, **Kass, Kassie.**

Kassie (Greek: variation of **Kassandra, Kassaundra**). Also, **Kassee, Kassey, Kassi, Kassy.**

Kat (English: variation of **Cat,** "feline;" Italian: variation of **Katarina, Katrina**). Also, **Katt.**

Katarina (Italian: variation of **Katherine,** "pure"). Also, **Katareena, Kataryna, Katereena, Katerina, Kateryna.** Familiar, **Kat.** *Whatever:* Here's another clever baby name ploy. You carve out your own little piece of **Katherine** by opting for this equally elegant variation.

Kate (English: variation of **Kathleen,** "pure"). Also, **Kaite, Kayte.** *Whatever:* This nickname has been so popular for so long, it doesn't need **Katherine** to carry its bags. It can stand alone. **Kate** is a playwright's shorthand for a headstrong, beautiful woman. And it's been this way since Shakespeare's day. A pocket T.

Katherine (Latin: pure). Also, **Katharine, Katharyn, Kathirine.** Familiar, **Katie, Kathy.** *Plus:* Couldn't ask for a better modern champion for this name than screen great **Katharine** Hepburn. She put the spunk in this spunky classic. A slam-dunk pocket T. *Minus:* **Katherine** is the female equivalent of **Michael.** The two are so all-encompassing, it's as if hospitals assign all baby boys **Michael,** all baby girls **Katherine,** and leave it up to parents to change as they see fit.

Kathleen (Irish: variation of **Catherine,** "pure"). Also, **Kathlean, Kathlene.** Familiar, **Kate, Kathy, Katie.** *Whatever:* Pretty and confident-sounding no matter the year. A pocket T.

Kathrine (Latin: variation of **Katherine,** "pure"). Also, **Kathryn, Kathryne.** Familiar, **Katie, Kathy.**

Kathy (Irish/Latin: variation of **Katherine, Kathleen, Kathrine**). Also, **Kathe, Kathee, Kathey, Kathi, Kathie.**

Katie (English: variation of **Kaitlyn, Katherine, Kathleen, Kathrine**). Also, **Katee, Katey, Kati, Katy.**

Katrina (Slavic: variation of **Katherine,** "pure"). Also, **Katreena, Katryna.** Familiar, **Kat.**

Katya (Russian: variation of **Katherine,** "pure").

Kay (English/Scottish: rejoice). Also, **Kae, Kaye.** *Plus:* A classic Gen X name? Well, it *is* short, succinct, and prosaic. *Minus:* Sometimes the rules apply, sometimes they don't. This name is strictly WWII.

Kaya (Native American: older sister).

Kayla (Yiddish: laurel crown; English: variation of **Katherine,** "pure"). Also, **Kaela, Kaelah, Kaylah.** *Plus:* Take that, **Karen.** This is what pretty girls look like today. *Minus:* Feathered bangs used to be considered attractive too. Until proven otherwise, brand this one trendy suspenders.

Kayli (English: variation of **Kayla,** "laurel crown"). Also, **Kaylee, Kayleigh, Kayley, Kaylie, Kayly.**

Kaylyn (English: combination of **Kay** and **Lynn**). Also, **Kaelin, Kaelinn, Kaelyn, Kaelynn, Kaylin, Kaylinn, Kaylynn.** *Plus:* Another sneaky wiggle-room maneuver. **Kaylyn** is **Kaitlyn** without the *t*. *Minus:* That's a little more dubious than the **Kady/Katie** ploy. At least **Kady** has history as a stand-alone. **Kaylyn** sounds like you forgot a letter.

K.C. (American: variation of **Kasey,** "vigilant"). Also, **Kacee, Kacey, Kaci, Kacie, Kacy.**

Keane (Irish: great). Also, **Kean, Keen, Keene.** *Whatever:* A boy name? Yup. But it's no **Mike.** It's got unisex possibilities.

Keely (Irish: falcon's cry). Also, **Keelee, Keeleigh, Keeli, Keelie, Keeley.**

Keilly (Irish: graceful). Also, **Keilee, Keileigh, Keiley, Keili, Keilie, Keillee, Keilleigh, Keilley, Keilli, Keillie, Keily.** *Whatever:* A pick to click with vowel action at half the cloying cuteness. This is how **Kelly** looks today.

Keira (Irish: regal). Also, **Keera.**

Keisha (American: variation of **Aisha,** "life"). Also, **Keesha, Kesha, Keysha, Kisha, Kysha.**

Keita (African: worshiper). Also, **Keeta, Kyta.**

Kelila (Hebrew: victory). Also, **Kelilah, Kelyla, Kelylah.**

Kelly (Irish: warrior). Also, **Kellee, Kelley, Kelli, Kellie.** *Whatever:* A great cheerleader name of the 1970s. Today it's fading, but not as fast for girls as boys.

Kelsay (English: variation of **Kelsey,** "highland marsh"). Also, **Kelsae.**

Kelsey (English: highland marsh). Also, **Kelsee, Kelsi, Kelsie, Kelsy.** *Whatever:* A comer. The **Chelsea** alternative.

Kendall (English: the valley of Kent). Also, **Kendal, Kendel, Kendell, Kendyl, Kendyll.** *Whatever:* A combo power name/pretty girl. Very contemporary.

Kendra (Native American: magical power). *Whatever:* Very today. Another outdoorsy **Montana** or **Dakota** kind of name.

Kenna (Irish: a type of love). Also, **Kena.**

Kennedy (Scottish: armored helmet). Also, **Kenedee, Kenedey, Kenedi, Kenedie, Kenedy, Kennedee, Kennedey, Kennedi, Kennedie.**

Keren (Hebrew: horn). Also, **Kerin, Keryn.**

Kerri (English: captain; Irish: dark-complected). Also, **Keri, Kerree, Kerrey, Kerrie, Kerry, Kery.** *Whatever:* **Kerri** Green costarred in quintessential Gen X coming-of-age teen comedy *Lucas.*

Keshawna (American: variation of **Shawna,** "God is gracious"). Also, **Keseana, Keshauna, Keshona, Keyseana, Keyshauna, Keyshawna, Keyshona.**

Keshia (American: variation of **Aisha,** "life"). **Keshya, Keyshia, Keyshya, Kishia, Kishya, Kyshia, Kyshya.**

Keyne (Irish: jewel).

Kiersten (Greek: variation of **Kirsten,** "anointed"). Also, **Keersten, Keerstin, Keerstyn, Kierstin, Kierstyn.** Familiar, **Kirsti.**

Kiley (Irish: variation of **Keilly,** "graceful"). Also, **Kilee, Kileigh, Kili, Kily.**

Kim (English: variation of **Kimball, Kimberlin, Kimberly**). Also, **Kimm, Kym, Kymm.** *Whatever:* This is a name so basic it makes Dick and Jane books seem avant-garde by comparison.

Kimba (English: variation of **Kimberly,** "ruler"). Also, **Kymba.**

Kimball (English: hill). Also, **Kimbal, Kimbel, Kimbell, Kimble, Kymbal, Kymball, Kymbel, Kymbell, Kymble.** Familiar, **Kim, Kimmy.** *Whatever:* A **Kimberly** for our times.

Kimber (English: variation of **Kimberlin, Kimberly**). Also, **Kymber.**

Kimberlin (English: variation of **Kimberly**, "ruler"). Also, **Kimberlinn, Kimberlyn, Kimberlynn, Kymberlin, Kymberlinn, Kymberlyn, Kimberlynn.** Familiar, **Kim, Kimber, Kimmer, Kimmy.**

Kimberly (English: ruler). Also, **Kimberlee, Kimberley, Kimberli, Kimberlie, Kymberlee, Kymberley, Kymberli, Kymberlie, Kymberly.** Familiar, **Kim, Kimba, Kimber, Kimmer, Kimmy.** *Whatever:* A 1970s pretty girl now relegated to peanut-butter-and-jelly-sandwich status. But the situation for **Kimberly** isn't as bleak as it is for **Karen,** because the old **Kimmer** has one trick left: She's got vowel action! That ought to ensure her entrance into the twenty-first century.

Kimmer (English: variation of **Kimberlin, Kimberly**). Also, **Kymmer.**

Kimmy (English: variation of **Kimball, Kimberlin, Kimberly**). Also, **Kimmi.**

Kin (Japanese: golden; English: family). Also, **Kinn, Kyn, Kynn.** *Plus:* Short, succinct, goes with anything. *Minus:* It's like naming your daughter **Relative**.

Kina (Greek: messenger). Also, **Keena, Kyna.**

Kira (Hindi: light; Slavic: throne). Also, **Kyra.** *Whatever:* A **Kayla** with legs, **Kira** has shown more staying power than your average pretty girl.

Kirby (English: by the church). Also, **Kirbee, Kirbey, Kirbi, Kirbie.** *Whatever:* Nerdy as a boy name, uncommonly classy as a girl name.

Kirsten (Greek: anointed). Also, **Kirstin, Kirstyn.** Familiar, **Kirsti.** *Whatever:* The updated take on **Kristen.**

Kirsti (Greek: variation of **Kiersten, Kirsten**). Also, **Kirstee, Kirstey, Kirstie, Kirsty.** *Whatever:* **Kirsti** walks among the pretty girls, but is not one of them. It's tougher and wilier. And here's guessing it's longer-lasting too.

Kirya (Hebrew: village). Also, **Kiryah, Kyrya, Kyryah.**

Kit (English: Christ-bearer). Also, **Kitt, Kyt, Kytt.** *Whatever:* **Kaitlin,** schmaitlin. Your kid's goin' Western!

Koren (Greek: maiden, womanly). Also, **Korin, Koryn.**

Kris (Greek: variation of **Kristen, Kristina, Kristine**). Also, **Khris, Khrys, Krys.**

Krissy (Greek: variation of **Kristen, Kristina, Kristine**). Also, **Khrissi, Khrissy, Krissee, Krissey, Krissi, Krissie.**

Krista (Greek: variation of **Christian,** "follower of Christ"). Also, **Khrista, Khrysta, Krysta.**

Kristen (Greek: anointed). Also, **Khristen, Khristin, Khristyn, Kristin, Kristyn.** Familiar, **Kris, Krissy, Kristie.** *Whatever:* This is a name that's been hit pretty hard by our penchant for scrambled-egg spellings. We seem dead set on mixing and matching each and every spare vowel to get that "unique" feel—until the poor thing looks like a fifty-point Scrabble word. Here's a suggestion: Let a peanut-butter-and-jelly sandwich sit on the shelf. If we're tired of **Kristen,** move on. There are lots of other names out there. Probably even some we like spelled just the way they are—although we reserve the right to tag an *e* to the end of anything.

Kristie (Greek: variation of **Kristen,** "anointed"). Also, **Khristi, Khristy, Kristee, Kristey, Kristi, Kristy.** *Whatever:* The moniker of Gen X icon (circa 1978), *Family* star **Kristy** McNichol.

Kristina (Greek: variation of **Christine,** "follower of Christ"). Also, **Khristeena, Khristina, Khristyna, Kristeena, Kristyna.** Familiar, **Kris, Krissy, Kristy.**

Kristine (Greek: variation of **Christine,** "follower of Christ"). Also, **Khristeene, Khristine, Khristyne, Kristeene, Kristyne.** Familiar, **Kris, Krissy, Kristie.**

Krystal (English: icelike, a mineral or glass). Also, **Kristal, Kristel, Kristle, Kristyl, Krystel, Krystle, Krystyl.** *Plus:* Better than **Cubic Zirconia.** *Minus: Dynasty* was canceled almost a decade ago. Isn't it time to give up the ghost?

Kyeesha (American: variation of **Aisha,** "life"). Also, **Kieesha, Kiesha.**

Kyle (English: narrow river). Also, **Kile.** *Plus:* The **Kayla** Less Traveled. *Minus:* Inevitable question: "Hey, isn't that supposed to be a boy name?" (Appropriate answer: "Go away.")

Kylie (Australian: a boomerang). Also, **Kylee, Kyleigh, Kyli, Kyly.**

L

CRIB NOTES

Famous Ls: Queen **Latifah** (actor/rapper); **LeAnn** Rimes (country singer); Princess **Leia** (cinnamon-bun-haired space girl, *Star Wars*); **Lena** Horne ("Stormy Weather" survivor); **Lindsay** Wagner (Jaime Somers, TV's *Bionic Woman*); **Liv** Tyler (actor, *Armageddon*); **Liza** Minnelli (entertainer); **Lois** Lane (reporter/Superman's girlfriend); **Loni** Anderson (Burt Reynold's ex-wife); **Loretta** Lynn (country music legend); Jennifer **Love** Hewitt (actor, TV's *Party of Five*); **Lucille** Ball (sitcom innovator, *I Love Lucy*)

Pocket Ts: Lily, Lucy

Trendy suspenders: No pick here. **Lindsay** is the trendiest thing on this front. And it's too preppie to ever feel completely faddish.

Think long, think hard: **Latoya** (Leave it to the Jacksons.); **Laverne** (Mental picture: Brewery company bottle-capper in Milwaukee, circa 1950s.); **Letty** (Doesn't really seem to work without the "Great Aunt" prefix and requisite wrinkles.); **Liberty** (You have every right to name your daughter this. Just please try to use your powers of free will for good not ill.); **Lola** (Viva Las Vegas.); **Lolita** (Uh, no.); **Lolly** (Pop.); **Loni** (*Hollywood Squares* time.); **Lotus** (Went directly from the hippies to the computer programmers—no time for ordinary humans in between.); **Love** (Yes, *Party of Five*'s Jennifer **Love** Hewitt prefers being called **Love** to **Jennifer,** but that's easy for her to say—at least she's got a "real" name to fall back on when she changes her mind and/or turns twenty-five, whichever comes first.); **Lulu** (Uh, no.)

Lacey (Greek: cheerful). Also, **Lacee, Laci, Lacie, Lacy.** *Whatever:* A prototypical name for today, **Lacey** is a vowel-friendly pretty girl—not too popular, not too trendy.

Lakeesha (American: variation of **Aisha,** "life"). Also, **Lakesha, Lakisha, Lakysha.**

Lana (Irish: variation of **Alana,** "traveler"). Also, **Lanna.** *Whatever:* This one used to be a Madonna. But since practically no one watches **Lana** Turner movies anymore, it's probably safe for everyday use again.

Lane (English: fertile land). Also, **Laine, Layne.** *Whatever:* For the sophisticated, career-girl little princess.

Lanetta (French: variation of **Lanette,** "crossing"). Also, **Laneta.**

Lanette (French: crossing). Also, **Lanett.**

Laney (English: variation of **Elaine, Ellen**). Also, **Lanee, Lani, Lanie, Lany.**

Lani (Hawaiian: sky). Also, **Lannee, Lanney, Lanni, Lannie, Lanny.** *Whatever:* The doable **Loni.**

Laqueesha (American: variation of **Aisha,** "life"). Also, **Laqeesha, Laqesha, Laqisha, Laquesha, Laquisha.**

Lara (Latin: famous). *Whatever:* The *Doctor Zhivago* Lesson: That sweeping, 1965 movie romance inspired parents—we're betting the moms—to name their daughters after the heroine, **Lara.** Thirty-plus years later, *Zhivago* is as cold as a Russian winter. Lesson learned: It's tempting to let popular novels, movies, TV shows, and records do the baby name influencing, but it's also a big gamble. **Lara**s got off lucky. At least the name still works.

Laraine (Latin: variation of **Loraine,** "sorrowful"). Also, **Larane, Larayne, Larraine, Larrane, Larrayne.**

Larisa (Greek: cheerful). Also, **Larissa, Larysa, Laryssa.**

Lark (English: a bird, a frolic). Also, **Larke.**

Larkin (English: crowned with laurel). Also, **Larkyn.** *Whatever:* A comer. Here's a preppie power name that soft-pedals its overachieving edge with a lyrical "lark."

Lashawna (American: variation of **Shawna,** "God is gracious"). Also, **Laseana, Lashauna, Lashona, Leseana, Leshauna, Leshawna, Leshona.**

Latifah (Arabic: gentle). Also, **Lateefa, Lateefah, Latifa, Latyfa, Latyfah.** *Whatever:* Queen-approved; commoner-friendly.

Latisha (American: variation of **Aisha,** "life"). Also, **Lateesha, Latysha, Leteesha, Letisha, Letysha.**

Laura (Latin: laurel; Greek: sheltered). Familiar, **Laurie.** *Plus:* Looking for an alternative to the now-ubiquitous likes of **Emily** and **Jessica**? How about **Laura,** namesake of the *Little House on the Prairie* author herself, **Laura** Ingalls Wilder? *Minus:* Its pretty girl days are over. This one's nothing but a peanut-butter-and-jelly sandwich outglammed by the likes of **Alexandra** and **Dominique.**

Laurel (English: the laurel tree). Also, **Lauril, Lauryl.**

Lauren (English: variation of **Laura,** "laurel"). Also, **Laurin, Lauryn.** *Whatever:* With **Laurel,** this one's the popular, contemporary **Laura.**

Laurie (English: variation of **Laura,** "laurel"). Also, **Lauree, Laurey, Lauri, Laury.**

Layla (Arabic/Hebrew: night). Also, **Laela.** *Plus:* Offers wiggle room on **Kayla.** *Minus:* Sounds like Eric Clapton's 1970s hit—the one about obsessive love. Not the world's greatest baby name fodder.

Leah (Hebrew: variation of **Leia,** "weary"). Also, **Lea.**

Leann (English: combination of **Lee** and **Ann**). Also, **LeAnn, LeAnne, Leanne, LeeAnn, LeeAnne.** *Whatever:* A comer. Teen singer **LeAnn** Rimes is exactly the sort of popular, squeaky clean entertainer that will boost a baby name big time.

Lee (English: meadow).

Leeza (English: variation of **Lisa,** "God's oath"). *Plus:* Today's **Lisa.** *Minus:* The big cliché: It Came from a TV Talk Show.

Leia (Hebrew: weary). Also, **Leiah.** *Whatever:* The *Star Wars* Lesson: *Some* novels, movies, TV shows, and records *really* are here to stay. In this age of *Star Wars* rerelease and prequel mania, Princess **Leia**–inspired names are looking to be a pretty good bet.

Leigh (English: variation of **Lee,** "meadow"). *Whatever:* The elegant, refined **Lee.**

Leilani (Hawaiian: heavenly). Also, **Laelani, Laelany, Laylani, Laylany, Leilanee, Leilaney, Leilanie, Leilany.** *Plus:* Pretty, exotic. *Minus:* May not play in the contiguous states.

Lena (English: the bright one). Also, **Leena.** *Whatever:* Jazz greats are timeless. **Lena** Horne infuses this one with grace and beauty.

Leona (Latin: lionlike). Also, **Leonna.**

Leonelle (French: variation of **Leona,** "lion-like"). Also, **Leonell.**

Leonora (Greek: variation of **Eleanor,** "the bright one"). Also, **Leonorra.**

Leonore (Greek: variation of **Eleanor,** "the bright one"). *Whatever:* A museum piece—lovely to look at, near impossible to wear. Only included here if you're looking for someplace bigger to start with for **Lee.**

Lesley (Scottish: garden of holly, gray fort). Also, **Leslee, Lesleigh, Lesli, Leslie, Lesly.**

Letice (Latin: variation of **Leticia,** "joyful"). Also, **Letyce.**

Leticia (Latin: joyful). Also, **Leticya.**

Letitia (Latin: joyful). Also, **Letitya.**

Leva (Latin: rising).

Lexie (Greek: variation of **Alexandra,** "protector, defender"). Also, **Lexee, Lexey, Lexi, Lexy.** *Plus:* The kicky, approachable **Alexis.** *Minus:* Rhymes with "sexy."

Lezley (American: variation of **Lesley,** "garden of holly, gray fort"). Also, **Lezlee, Lezleigh, Lezli, Lezlie, Lezly.**

Li (Chinese: plum).

Lian (Hebrew: joyful). Also, **Liann.**

Liana (Latin: variation of **Liane,** "bond"). Also, **Lianna.**

Liane (Latin: bond; Chinese: willow). Also, **Liann, Lianne.**

Lib (English: variation of **Elizabeth,** "God's oath"). Also, **Libb, Lyb, Lybb.**

Libby (English: variation of **Elizabeth,** "God's oath"). Also, **Libbee, Libbey, Libbi, Libbie.** *Plus:* The epitome of spunk. *Minus:* The epitome of canned food.

Lida (Slavic: people's love). Also, **Leeda, Lyda.**

Lila (Persian: lilac; Hebrew: night). Also, **Lilah, Lyla, Lylah.**

Lilabel (English: combination of **Lila** and **Belle**). Also, **Lilabell, Lilabelle, Lilebell, Lilebelle, Llybel, Lilybell, Lilybelle.**

Lilabeth (English: combination of **Lila** and **Beth**). Also, **Lilebeth, Lilybeth.**

Lilian (Latin: lily). Also, **Lilien, Lillien, Lillyan, Lillyen, Lilyan, Lilyen.** Familiar, **Lily.** *Plus:* The real deal when it comes to style and polish, **Lilian** is a veteran pretty girl that sounds one with the *Little House on the Prairie* likes of **Emily** and **Hanna.** *Minus:* A touch on the old-lady side. Gen Xers' closest brush with a notable **Lilian** was President Jimmy Carter's aged mother, Miss **Lillian.**

Lilith (Hebrew: serpent). Aso, **Lillith, Lillyth, Lilyth.** *Plus:* A comer. Historically strong and recently hip, this entry is the namesake of singer Sarah McLachlan's all-grrl summer concert tour, the **Lilith** Fair. *Minus:* Still best remembered as Frasier Crane's brainy but whacked-out ex-wife, **Lilith** Sternin, of TV's *Cheers* and *Frasier.*

Lily (Latin: bloom; Greek: purity). Also, **Lili, Lillee, Lilley, Lilli, Lillie, Lilly.** *Whatever:* One way to measure the indestructible nature of a name: Give it to a Munster. Let it wear it around for a year. See what happens. In this case, what happens is **Lily** makes even **Lily** Munster look good. This is a graceful pocket T that a ballerina, or a Munster, can wear.

Lilybel (English: combination of **Lily** and **Belle**). Also, **Lilibel, Lilibell, Lilibelle, Lilybell, Lilybelle.**

Lilybeth (English: combination of **Lily** and **Beth**). Also, **Lilibeth.**

Lina (Arabic: palm tree). Also, **Leena, Lyna.**

Linda (Latin: beautiful; German: gentle). Familiar, **Lindy.** *Whatever:* Better get **Linda** a table at the **Karen, Kimberly,** and **Laura** party and order them up a plate of peanut-butter-and-jelly sandwiches. This former popularity queen's been bound for a Wonder Bread coffin since the 1960s.

Lindlay (English: variation of **Lindley,** "blue-flowered plant"). Also, **Lindlae, Lyndlae, Lyndlay.**

Lindley (English: blue-flowered plant). Also, **Lindlee, Lindleigh, Lindli, Lindlie, Lindly, Lyndley, Lyndly.**

Lindsay (English: soft-spoken). Also, **Lindsae.** *Whatever:* Very wow, very now. This pretty girl/cuddly bear is the future best friend of **Brittany**s nationwide.

Lindsey (English: variation of **Lindsay,** "soft-spoken"). Also, **Lindsee, Lindsi, Lindsie, Lindsy.**

Lindy (English: variation of **Linda,** "beautiful"). Also, **Lindee, Lindey, Lindi, Lindie.**

Linnet (Celtic: variation of **Lynett,** "shapely"). Also, **Linet, Linett, Linette, Linnett, Linnette.** Familiar, **Lynn.**

Liona (Latin: lionlike). Also, **Lionna, Lyona, Lyonna.**

Lisa (English: variation of **Elizabeth,** "God's oath"). Also, **Leesa.** *Plus:* Still a pretty girl after all these years. Would be a pocket T . . . *Minus:* . . . except it's showing signs of age. This was the happening pretty girl of the 1960s and 1970s—*was.* Now it's merely another **Linda,** struggling for relevancy in a Brave New **Ashley** World.

Lisann   (English: combination of **Lisa** and **Ann**). Also, **Leesann, Leesanne, Lisanne.**

Lisbet   (Scandinavian: variation of **Elisabet,** "God's oath"). Also, **Lisbett, Lisbette, Lysbet, Lysbett, Lysbette.** Familiar, **Liz, Lizzie.**

Lisetta   (French: variation of **Lisa,** "God's oath"). Also, **Liseta, Lyseta, Lysetta.**

Lisette   (French: variation of **Lisa,** "God's oath"). Also, **Lisett, Lysett, Lysette.**

Lisle   (French: island). Also, **Leesle, Leisle, Liesle.**

Liv   (English: variation of **Olivia,** "olive tree, peace"). Also, **Livv, Lyv, Lyvv.** *Whatever:* Actress **Liv** Tyler (*Armageddon*) is barely into her career and she's already a star. She's got lots of time to make this efficient little number a minor—maybe even a major—favorite. A comer.

Livia   (English: variation of **Olivia,** "olive tree, peace"). Also, **Livya, Lyvia, Lyvya.**

Liz   (English: variation of **Elizabeth, Lizbet**). Also, **Lizz, Lyz, Lyzz.** *Plus:* Fit for movie goddess Elizabeth "**Liz**" Taylor. *Minus:* Elizabeth Taylor *hates* being called **Liz.**

Liza   (English: variation of **Elizabeth,** "God's oath"). *Plus:* Knocks the old-hat Elizabethan era out of **Elizabeth.** *Minus:* Puts it squarely in **Madonna** or **Liza** Minnelli Land.

Lizbet   (Scandinavian: variation of **Elisabet,** "God's oath"). Also, **Lizbett, Lizbette, Lyzbet, Lyzbett, Lyzbette.** Familiar, **Liz, Lizzie.**

Lizle   (French: variation of **Lisle,** "island"). Also, **Leezle, Liezle.**

Lizzie   (English: variation of **Elizabeth, Lizbet**). Also, **Lizzee, Lizzey, Lizzi, Lizzy.** *Plus:* One word: Spunky. *Minus:* One word: Borden.

Logan   (Irish: love). Also, **Logen, Logyn.** *Whatever:* Mark this: This'll be the next trendy entry that the girls steal from the boys. A power name in the tradition of **Morgan.**

Lois   (Greek: good). *Plus:* A must-have for fans of Superman's snooping, plucky girlfriend reporter. *Minus:* **Lois** Lane is the only thing keeping this 1930s relic from being safely stored away as a museum piece.

Lolanda   (English: powerful). *Whatever:* **Lola** with a doable twist.

Loleth   (Sanskrit: flighty). Also, **Lolith, Lolyth.**

Loma   (Spanish: little queen).

Lona   (English: alone). *Whatever:* Spelunkers alert: This is the **Loni** you've never heard of.

London (English: fortress of the moon). Also, **Londen.**

Lora (Slavic: variation of **Laura,** "laurel"). Familiar, **Lori.**

Loraine (Latin: sorrowful). Also, **Lorane, Lorayne, Lorraine, Lorrane, Lorrayne.**

Loren (Latin: lost; English: crowned with laurel). Also, **Lorin, Loryn.** *Whatever:* The **Lauren** Less Traveled.

Lorena (Latin: learned). Also, **Loraena, Lorana, Lorayna, Loreyna.** *Whatever:* Here's a name for our scandal-obsessed times. It's linked to the briefly famous **Lorena** Bobbitt, the I-cut-off-my-husband's-member gal.

Lorene (Latin: variation of **Lorena,** "learned"). Also, **Loreen, Loreene.**

Lori (English: variation of **Lora, Loris**). Also, **Loree, Lorey, Lorie, Lory.**

Loris (Latin: slow; English: crowned with laurel). Also, **Loriss, Lorys, Loryss.** Familiar, **Lori.** *Plus:* **Laura** with a difference. *Minus:* About as close to a nerd name as a girl entry gets.

Lorma (Latin: lash).

Lorna (Latin: lost; English: crowned with laurel). *Whatever:* **Lorna,** not **Liza,** is the doable tribute to the children of Judy Garland. **Lorna** Luft is **Liza** Minnelli's half-sister. She's an entertainer too. Not as widely notable. Sort of like her name.

Lorne (English: bereft; Latin: crowned with laurel). Also, **Lorn.**

Louisa (English: variation of **Louise,** "warrior"). *Whatever:* Ending this variation with an *a,* instead of an *e,* knocks about twenty years off the formal-sounding **Louise.**

Louise (German: warrior). *Whatever:* Louise should be the *Little House on the Prairie* peer of **Jessica.** But instead of experiencing a resurgence, it's buried in a victory garden. Lack of vowel action could be the cause.

Loura (Latin: learned).

Lucette (French: variation of **Lucille,** "light"). Also, **Lucett.**

Lucia (Italian: variation of **Lucille,** "light"). Also, **Lucya.**

Luciana (Italian: variation of **Luciane,** combination of **Lucy** and **Anne**). Also, **Lucianna, Lucyana, Lucyanna.** Familiar, **Lucy.**

Luciane (English: combination of **Lucy** and **Anne**). Also, **Luciann, Lucianne, Lucieane, Lucieann, Lucieanne, Lucyane, Lucyann, Lucyanne.** Familiar, **Lucy.**

Lucille (Latin: light). Also, **Lucile.** Familiar, **Lucy.** *Plus:* Comedian **Lucille** Ball is timeless. You hope her magic rubs off on the name. *Minus:* Hoping will only get you so far. **Lucille** is strictly World War II. Best used as a means to **Lucy.**

Lucy (English: variation of **Luciana, Luciane, Lucille**). Also, **Lucee, Lucey, Luci, Lucie.** *Whatever:* An adorable—dare we say zany?— entry that hasn't worn out its welcome. Perpetual *I Love Lucy* reruns keep it fresh and make it feel established enough to go solo as a given name. One of the cutest pocket Ts around.

Luena (Latin: martial).

Luisa (Spanish: variation of **Louise,** "warrior").

Luisetta (Italian: variation of **Louise,** "warrior"). Also, **Luiseta.**

Luisette (French: variation of **Louise,** "warrior"). Also, **Luisett.**

Luiza (Italian: variation of **Louise,** "warrior").

Luna (Latin: shining, like the crescent moon). *Plus:* Your daughter will be one with nature—with the sun, with the **Luna.** *Minus:* Sure, **Luna**'s nice, but you shouldn't get points for having the good sense *not* to name the baby **Moon.**

Lunetta (Italian: variation of **Lunette,** "little crescent moon"). Also, **Luneta.**

Lunette (French: little crescent moon). Also, **Lunett.**

Lupe (Latin: wolf, bearing good fortune).

Luz (Latin: light). *Whatever:* The *Dynasty* version of **Lucy.**

Luzia (Spanish: variation of **Luz,** "light"). Also, **Luzya.**

Lydia (Greek: woman of ancient Lydia). Also, **Lidia, Lidya, Lydya.** *Whatever:* **Lydia** Cornell played busty sister Sarah on TV's *Too Close for Comfort* (1980–86). That was the high point for **Lydia** in Gen Xers' lifetimes. This sophisticated **Audrey** peer is in need of a modern champion.

Lynda (American: variation of **Linda,** "beautiful").

Lyndell (English: valley of the lime trees). Also, **Lindel, Lindell, Lyndel, Lyndell.** Familiar, **Lynn.**

Lyndsay (English: variation of **Lindsay,** "soft-spoken"). Also, **Lyndsae.**

Lyndsey (English: variation of **Lindsey,** "soft-spoken"). Also, **Lyndsee, Lyndsi, Lyndsie, Lyndsy.**

Lynett (Celtic: shapely). Also, **Lynet, Lynete, Lynette, Lynnet, Lynnete, Lynnett, Lynette.** Familiar, **Lynn.** *Whatever:* A new power name? **Lynette** Woodard is a professional basketball player in the WNBA.

Lynn   (Welsh: lake; English: variation of **Linnet, Lyndell, Lynett**).
Also, **Lin, Linn, Lyn.** *Whatever:* A peanut-butter-and-jelly sandwich—easy to say, easy to spell, easy to like. **Lynn** is the definition of
a nice name. A little plain, not quite a classic, but doable.

Lyra   (Greek: musical instrument).

M

CRIB NOTES

Famous Ms: **Madeline** Albright (U.S. secretary of state); **Madonna** (über icon); **Mariah** Carey (pop diva); **Marie** Osmond (little-bit-country singer); **Mariel** Hemingway (actor, *Manhattan*); **Marlee** Matlin (Oscar-winner, *Children of a Lesser God*); **Martha** Stewart (domestic goddess); **Mary** Tyler Moore (1970s sitcom "It" girl); **Maya** Angelou (poet); **Mayim** Bialik (hat-lovin' plucky teen, TV's *Blossom*); **Meryl** Streep (actor/accent specialist); **Murphy** Brown (Dan Quayle foe).

Pocket Ts: **Maria, Marie, Martha, Meg**

Trendy suspenders: **Madison, Megan, Moesha, Montana, Morgan**

Think long, think hard: **Madge** ("You're soaking in it."); **Madonna** (Let her go superstar on her own time.); **Marge** (One word: Large.); **Marionette** (What, was **Puppet** unavailable?); **Marjorie** (Out.); **Matilda** (Number of supermodels named **Matilda:** None.); **Maude** (Currently enjoying its golden years at the Baby Name Retirement Home. Please do not disturb.); **Mavis** (Stranded on the roadside of life.); **Maxine** (Remember the Andrews Sisters? Didn't think so. Next.); **Medea** (Witches who appeared on *Bewitched* is about as occult as you should get with your little one.); **Mildred** (Has the room next to **Maude.** Likes to watch old movies.); **Minerva** (Works best as a middle name—to complement **Aunt.**); **Myrtle** (Joins **Maude** and **Mildred** for slot-machine tournaments in Vegas.)

Mabel (Latin: beautiful). Also, **Mabil, Mable, Mabyl.** *Whatever:* TV's *Mad About You* broke this museum piece out of its glass. Can the

Buchman baby help lead this musty peer of **Maude, Mildred,** and **Myrtle** into the new millennium? Thought to consider: Stunned silence was the reaction from Paul and Jamie's family to the selection of **Mabel.**

Mackenzie (Scottish: fair, bright). Also, **Mackenzee, Mackenzey, Mackenzi, Mackenzy, Makenzie.** *Plus:* A comer. This is a pretty girl with something extra—a power game. Very today. *Minus:* Very yesterday, if you can't get over the **Mackenzie** Phillips (*One Day at a Time*) connection.

Macy (English: gift of God). Also, **Macee, Macey, Maci, Macie.** *Whatever:* More usable than **Nordstrom.**

Madalena (Spanish: variation of **Madeline,** "high tower"). Also, **Madalayna, Madaleyna, Madelayna, Madelena, Madeleyna.** Familiar, **Maddie.**

Maddie (English: variation of **Madalena, Madeline**). Also, **Maddee, Maddey, Maddi, Maddy.** *Whatever:* This is one of the all-time great, spunky nicknames, next to **Kate.** Cybill Shepherd played model-turned-investigator **Maddie** Hayes on TV's *Moonlighting* (1985–89).

Madeline (Hebrew: high tower). Also, **Madelyn, Madelyne, Madiline, Madilyn, Madilyne, Madyline.** Familiar, **Maddie.** *Whatever:* A regal little princess.

Madison (English: gift of God). Also, **Madisen, Madysen, Madyson.** *Plus:* The great power name of our time—strong, refined, Volvo-esque. *Minus:* The ubiquitous power name of our time. Tag this one trendy suspenders.

Madora (Greek: gift). Also, **Madorra.**

Mae (English: relative). Also, **May.**

Maeli (English: variation of **Mae,** "relative"). Also, **Maelee, Maeley, Maelie, Maely, Maylee, Mayley, Mayli, Maylle, Mayly.**

Maeve (Irish: joyous). Also, **Maive, Mave, Mayve.** *Whatever:* A pick to click. A fine Irish lass alternative to **Megan.**

Magda (Hebrew: tower).

Magdala (Hebrew: variation of **Madeline,** "high tower"). Also, **Magdalla.**

Magdalena (Spanish: variation of **Madeline,** "high tower"). Also, **Magdelena, Magdylena.**

Magdalene (English: variation of **Madeline,** "high tower"). Also, **Magdaline, Magdalyne, Magdelene, Magdelyne.**

Maggie (English: variation of **Margaret,** "pearl"). Also, **Maggi.** *What-*

ever: Along with **Kate** and **Maddie,** *the* great spunky spitfire of our time.

Mahala (Native American: woman).

Mahelia (Native American: variation of **Mahala,** "woman"). Also, **Maheelia, Maheelya, Mahelya.**

Maisie (Scottish: variation of **Margaret,** "pearl"). Also, **Maesee, Maesey, Maesi, Maesie, Maesy, Maisee, Maisey, Maisi, Maisy.**

Maitland (English: meadowlands). Also, **Maitlande, Mateland, Matelande, Maytland, Maytlande.**

Maitlin (English: variation of **Maitland,** "meadowlands"). Also, **Maitlyn, Matelin, Matelyn, Maytlin, Maytlyn.** *Whatever:* Works as wiggle room on sound-alike **Caitlyn.**

Maja (Arabic: splendor).

Malay (English: the official language of Malaysia). Also, **Malae.**

Malene (African: tower). Also, **Maleen, Maleene, Malyne.**

Mali (English: country in Africa). Also, **Malee, Maley, Malie, Maly.**

Malina (Hebrew: tower). Also, **Maleena, Maleenah, Malinah, Malyna, Malynah.**

Mallory (English: unlucky). Also, **Malery, Mallery, Malloree, Mallorey, Mallori, Mallorie, Maloree, Malorey, Malori, Malorie, Malory.** *Whatever:* Justine Bateman played the Valley-gal-esque **Mallory** Keaton on TV's *Family Ties* (1982–89).

Mame (English: variation of **Mary,** "bitterness"). Also, **Maime, Mayme.**

Mamie (English: variation of **Mary,** "bitterness"). Also, **Mamee, Mamey, Mami, Mamy.**

Manda (Latin: commanding).

Mandy (Latin: variation of **Amanda,** "beloved"). Also, **Mandee, Mandey, Mandi, Mandie.**

Manna (Hebrew: divine intervention). Also, **Mana, Manah, Mannah.**

Manuela (Hebrew: variation of **Emmanuel,** "God is with us"). Also, **Manuella.**

Mara (Slavic: variation of **Mary,** "bitterness"). Also, **Marra.** *Whatever:* A **Mary** for spelunkers.

Marcelina (Italian: variation of **Marcella,** "brave warrior"). Also, **Marceleena, Marcelyna, Marcileena, Marcilina, Marcilyna, Marcyleena.** Familiar, **Marcie.**

Marceline (English: variation of **Marcella,** "brave warrior"). Also,

Marceleene, Marcelyne, Marcileene, Marcilyne, Marcyleene. Familiar, **Marcie.**

Marcella (Latin: brave warrior). Also, **Marcela.** Familiar, **Marcie.**

Marcia (Latin: brave warrior). Also, **Marcya.** Familiar, **Marcie.** *Whatever:* "**Marcia! Marcia! Marcia!**" —J. Brady, *The Brady Bunch.* . . . Will Gen Xers *ever* be able to expunge this chant from their memory banks? Until they do, it's unlikely **Marcia** will regain standing as a pretty girl.

Marcie (English: variation of **Marcelina, Marceline, Marcella, Marcia, Marcille**). Also, **Marcee, Marcey, Marci, Marcy.**

Marcille (Latin: brave warrior). Also, **Marcile, Marcyle, Marcylle.** Familiar, **Marcie.**

Maret (English: variation of **Margaret,** "pearl"). Also, **Marett, Marit, Maritt, Maryt, Marytt.**

Margaret (Greek: pearl). Also, **Margarit, Margaryt, Margeret, Margerit, Margeryt.** Familiar, **Maggie, Meg, Peg, Peggy.** *Whatever:* Not just for Dennis the Menace's neighbor friend anymore. **Margaret** belongs in the red schoolhouse with *Little House on the Prairie* peers **Emily** and **Jessica.**

Margarita (Spanish: variation of **Margaret,** "pearl"). Also, **Margareeta, Margaryta, Margereeta, Margerita, Margeryta.** Familiar, **Maggie.**

Margaritte (French: variation of **Margaret,** "pearl"). Also, **Margareete, Margarite, Margereete, Margerite.** Familiar, **Maggie.**

Margaux (French: variation of **Margaret,** "pearl"). *Whatever:* **Margaret**'s feeling positively contemporary compared to this 1970s, Studio 54 relic.

Margot (French: variation of **Margaret,** "pearl"). Also, **Margo.**

Margrita (Slavic: variation of **Margaret,** "pearl"). Also, **Margreeta, Margryta.**

Margueriete (French: variation of **Margaret,** "pearl"). Also, **Margereete, Margeriete, Margeryte, Marguereete.**

Maria (Spanish: variation of **Mary,** "bitterness"). Also, **Mareea.** *Whatever:* A pocket T. **Maria** is a simple name that sings—always in good voice.

Mariah (Italian/Spanish: variation of **Mary,** "bitterness"). Also, **Maryah.** *Whatever:* Almost any variation of **Mary** is hipper than **Mary** itself. This one has a champion in pop singer Mariah Carey. A comer.

Marie (French: variation of **Mary,** "bitterness"). Also, **Maree, Marye.** *Plus:* Another pocket T. Like cousin **Maria, Marie** is an elegant, timeless classic. *Minus:* The whole Donny and **Marie** thing.

Mariel (Hebrew/German: perfect, bitter). Also, **Mariell, Marielle, Maryel, Maryell, Maryelle.**

Mariet (French: church bell; variation of **Mary,** "bitterness"). Also, **Mariett, Mariette, Maryet, Maryett, Maryette.**

Marietta (French: variation of **Mariet,** "church bell"). Also, **Marieta, Maryeta, Maryetta.**

Marigold (English: plant). Also, **Marigolde, Marygold, Marygolde.**

Marika (Slavic: variation of **Mary,** "bitterness"). Also, **Mareeca, Mareecka, Mareeka, Marica, Maricka, Maryca, Marycka, Maryka.**

Marilee (English: variation of **Mary Lee,** "combination of **Mary** and **Lee**"). Also, **Marili.**

Marilu (English: variation of **Mary Lou,** "combination of **Mary** and **Lou**"). Also, **Mariloo, Marilou, Maryloo, Marylou, Marylu.**

Marilyn (Hebrew: of **Mary**'s line). Also, **Marilin, Marilinn, Marilynn, Marylyn, Marylynn.** *Plus:* Forget the little princesses—you want to give your daughter a dose of old-school Hollywood glamour! *Minus:* Try **Vivien** Leigh, or **Ginger** Rogers, or *anybody* else. This moniker is not only a Madonna, it's a moldy-oldie, too.

Marina (Latin: of the sea). Also, **Mareena, Maryna.** Familiar, **Marnie.**

Marion (Greek: variation of **Mary,** "bitterness"). Also, **Marien, Maryen, Maryon.**

Mariposa (Spanish: butterfly). Also, **Maryposa.**

Marissa (Latin: pure). Also, **Marisa, Marysa, Maryssa.**

Marla (English: variation of **Marlene,** "high tower").

Marlee (English: variation of **Marlene,** "high tower"). Also, **Marleigh, Marley, Marli, Marlie, Marly.**

Marlena (Spanish: variation of **Marlene,** "high tower"). Also, **Marleena, Marlina, Marlyna.**

Marlene (Greek: high tower). Also, **Marleen, Marleene, Marline, Marlyne.**

Marlo (English: variation of **Mary,** "bitterness"). Also, **Marloe.** *Plus:* Sounds like today's **Margaux.** *Minus:* Sounds like yesterday's *That Girl,* **Marlo** Thomas.

Marlow (English: hill by the lake). Also, **Marlowe.**

Marna (English: variation of **Marnina,** "rejoice"). Familiar, **Marnie.**

Marnie (English: variation of **Marina, Marna, Marnina**). Also, **Marnee, Marney, Marni, Marny.**

Marnina (Hebrew: rejoice). Also, **Marneena, Marnyna.** Familiar, **Marnie.**

Marsha (Latin: variation of **Marcia,** "brave warrior").

Marta (Slavic: variation of **Martha,** "a lady"). Also, **Marti.**

Martha (Hebrew: a lady). Familiar, **Marti.** *Whatever:* A comer. Or maybe that should be a comebacker. **Martha** is a strong candidate to hop a ride on the covered wagon with her *Little House on the Prairie* peers. The underused **Hannah.**

Marthe (French: variation of **Martha,** "a lady"). Familiar, **Marti.**

Marti (English: variation of **Marta, Martha, Marthe, Martina**). Also, **Martee, Martey, Martie, Marty.**

Martina (Latin: variation of **Martin,** "warrior"). Also, **Marteena, Martyna.** Familiar, **Marti.**

Mary (Hebrew: bitterness). Also, **Maree, Marey, Mari.** *Plus:* Pretty, nice, and pleasant, **Mary** is a salt-of-the-earth girl name. *Minus:* Blah, blah, blah. **Mary** is a *generic* girl name. If this were a boy name, it might win some points for flannel shirt comfort, but it's a girl name, and a selection needs a lot more tools than "comfort" to wing it in the age of the little princess. Mark this one down as a peanut-butter-and-jelly sandwich.

Marya (Sanskrit: mortal, lover).

Maryann (English: combination of **Mary** and **Ann**). Also, **MariAnn, Mariann, MariAnne, Marianne, Mary Ann, MaryAnn, Mary Anne, MaryAnne, Maryanne.**

Marybeth (English: combination of **Mary** and **Beth**). Also, **MariBeth, Maribeth, Mary Beth, Marybeth.**

Maryellen (English: combination of **Mary** and **Ellen**). Also, **Mary Ellen, MaryEllen, MaryEllin, Maryellin, MaryEllyn, Maryellyn.**

Maryjo (English: combination of **Mary** and **Jo**). Also, **MariJo, Marijo, Mary Jo, MaryJo.**

Mary Lee (English: combination of **Mary** and **Lee**). Also, **MaryLee.**

Mary Lou (English: combination of **Mary** and **Lou**). Also, **MaryLou.**

Mattie (German: variation of **Matilda,** "strong warrior"). Also, **Mattee, Mattey, Matti, Matty.**

Maura (Irish: variation of **Mary,** "bitterness").

Maureen (Irish: variation of **Mary,** "bitterness"). Also, **Maurine.** Familiar, **Mo.** *Plus:* Classic Irish lass fare. *Minus:* Tired Irish lass fare. Replaced by **Megan.**

May (English: spring month; variation of **Mary,** "bitterness"). Also, **Mae.**

Maya (Hindu: illusion; Sanskrit: supernatural art and wisdom). *Whatever:* Championed by poet **Maya** Angelou, who in turn has been championed by talk queen Oprah Winfrey. That sort of star power makes this entry a comer.

Mead (English: meadow). Also, **Meade, Meed, Meede.**

Meadow (English: a meadow). Also, **Medow.**

Meara (Irish: merry).

Meg (Irish: variation of **Margaret, Megan, Meghan**). Also, **Megg.** *Whatever:* Its short, unfussy sound and look make this pocket T a versatile performer. **Meg** can hang with the Irish lasses or the *Little House on the Prairie* contingent.

Megan (Irish/Greek: variation of **Margaret,** "pearl"). Also, **Megen, Megyn.** Familiar, **Meg.** *Plus:* Pretty, precious, today. *Minus:* Not as today as it used to be. **Megan** looks to have reached its critical mass in the 1990s. Look for alternative entries like **Ryan** to siphon off its audience, leaving this one a lonely pair of trendy suspenders.

Megha (Sanskrit: cloud). *Whatever:* Offers nifty wiggle room on **Megan.**

Meghan (Welsh: variation of **Megan,** "pearl"). Also, **Meghen, Meghyn.** Familiar, **Meg.**

Meissa (Arabic: proudly marching). Also, **Meisa, Meysa, Meyssa.**

Mel (English/Greek: variation of **Melada, Melana, Melanie, Meleda, Melina, Melinda, Melissa, Mellicent, Melody, Melosa**). Also, **Mell.** *Whatever:* Not just for fry cooks on *Alice* anymore. What's dorky on a boy looks kinda nifty on a girl.

Melada (Greek: honey). Familiar, **Mel, Mellie.**

Melana (Greek: variation of **Melina,** "soft, yellow"). Also, **Melanna.** Familiar, **Mel, Mellie.**

Melanie (Greek: dark-complected). Also, **Melanee, Melaney, Melani, Melany, Meleni, Melenie, Meleny.** Familiar, **Mel, Mellie.** *Whatever:* A doable pretty girl that's stuck in the same lunchbox with **Melissa.** Bland peanut-butter-and-jelly sandwich time.

Meleda (Teutonic: bubbly). Also, **Meleeda, Melida, Melyda.** Familiar, **Mel, Mellie.**

Melia (Greek: ash tree). Also, **Meleea, Melya.** *Whatever:* The **Melinda** for the pretty girl 1990s.

Melina (Greek: soft, yellow). Also, **Meleena, Melyna.** Familiar, **Mel, Mellie.**

Melinda (English: gentle). Also, **Melynda.** Familiar, **Mindy, Mel, Mellie.**

Melissa (Latin: a bee, sweetener). Also, **Melisa, Melysa, Melyssa.** Familiar, **Mel, Mellie, Missy.** *Plus:* An in-crowd name for part of four decades now, this is the durable pretty girl performer **Kimberly** wishes it could have been. *Minus:* Familiarity breeds contempt, at least for spelunkers who are unimpressed by **Melissa**'s commonness.

Mellicent (German: variation of **Millicent,** "work, strong"). Also, **Melicent, Mellycent, Melycent.** Familiar, **Mel, Mellie.**

Mellie (English/Greek: variation of **Melada, Melana, Melanie, Meleda, Melina, Melinda, Melissa, Mellicent, Melody, Melosa**). Also, **Melli, Melly.**

Melody (Greek: song, of musical quality). Also, **Melodee, Melodey, Melodi, Melodie.** Familiar, **Mel, Mellie.** *Plus:* A pretty girl sound-alike alternative to **Melissa.** *Minus:* A hippie-dippie alternative to **Melissa.**

Melosa (Spanish: variation of **Melissa,** "a bee, sweetener"). Also, **Melossa.** Familiar, **Mel, Mellie.**

Mercedes (Spanish: Mary of mercies). *Whatever:* "Next week on *Dynasty*: **Alexis** greets long-lost sister **Mercedes** at the airport. Later, the two duke it out in the estate's garden fountain."

Mercy (Latin: compassion). Also, **Mercee, Mercey, Merci, Mercie.**

Meredith (Irish: coastal guard; Welsh: the sea). Also, **Meredithe, Meredyth, Merydith, Merydithe.**

Merilyn (English: variation of **Marilyn,** of **Mary**'s line"). Also, **Merilin, Merilinn, Merilynn, Merylyn, Merilynn.**

Meris (Latin: pure). Also, **Meriss, Merris, Merrys, Merys.** *Whatever:* A power name peer of **Morgan** and **Madison**—at a fraction of the trendiness.

Merit (Latin: deserving). Also, **Meritt, Meryt, Merytt.**

Merle (Latin: blackbird). Also, **Merl, Murl, Murle.**

Merrill (English: famous). Also, **Merril.**

Merry (English: pleasant). Also, **Meri, Merie, Merree, Merrey, Merri, Merrie, Mery.**

Meryl (Greek: fragrant, like myrrh; Latin: blackbird). Also, **Meryll**. *Whatever:* Champion **Meryl** Streep makes this one an always-classy pick.

Mesha (Hebrew: deliverance). Also, **Meshah**.

Mia (Italian: mine). Also, **Meea, Mya**.

Micala (Hebrew: variation of **Michaela,** "who is like God?"). Also, **Micalah, Michala, Michalah, Mikala, Mikalah, Mycala, Mycalah, Mychala, Mychalah, Mykala, Mykalah**. Familiar, **Micki**.

Michaela (Hebrew: variation of **Michael,** "who is like God?"). Also, **Micaela, Micela, Michela, Mikaela, Mikela, Mycaela, Mycela, Mychaela, Mychela, Mykaela, Mykela**. Familiar, **Micki**. *Whatever:* You'd think we'd get our fill of **Michael** in the boy wing of the nursery, but, no, it's not enough—we have to name the girls **Michael** or **Michaela** too. This is a name of surprising strength and appeal.

Michelle (French: variation of **Michael,** "who is like God?"). Also, **Michell, Mischel, Mischell, Mischelle, Mishell, Mishelle**. *Whatever:* Like **Melissa, Michelle** is a Gen X–era pretty girl that's starting to slump. Guess the Beatles (and "**Michelle**") can only inspire so many millions before their influence wanes.

Micki (English: variation of **Micala, Michaela**). Also, **Mickee, Mickey, Mickie, Micky, Miki, Mikie**. *Plus:* Spunky, spry. *Minus:* Two words of warning: Toni Basil.

Mika (Native American: wise raccoon).

Mila (Latin: lovely). Also, **Milla**.

Millicent (German: work, strong). Also, **Milicent, Millycent, Milycent**. Familiar, **Millie**. *Whatever:* **Millie** might be taking the *Little House on the Prairie* trend to its illogical conclusion. Remember, some names are artfully old-fashioned. Some names are irrevocably old-fashioned. **Millie**'s much closer to the former than the latter.

Millie (English: variation of **Millicent,** "work, strong"). Also, **Mili, Millee, Milley, Milli, Milly**.

Mim (English: variation of **Miriam,** "rebellion"). Also, **Mimm, Mym, Mymm**.

Mimi (French: variation of **Miriam,** "rebellion"). Also, **Meemee**.

Mina (German: variation of **Wilhelmina,** "will, helmet"). Also, **Meena, Myna**.

Mindy (English: variation of **Melinda,** "gentle"). Also, **Mindee, Mindey, Mindi, Mindie, Myndi**.

Minna (German: memory, love). Also, **Mynna.**

Mira (Hebrew: light; Slavic: peace). Also, **Mirah, Mirra, Mirrah.** *Whatever:* A comer. Can Oscar-winning, Gen X–era actor **Mira** Sorvino inspire a sizable number of clones?

Mirabella (Italian: variation of **Mirabelle,** "beautiful"). Also, **Mirabela, Myrabela, Myrabella.** Familiar, **Miri.**

Mirabelle (Latin: beautiful). Also, **Mirabell, Myrabell, Myrabelle.** Familiar, **Miri.**

Miranda (Latin: worthy of admiration). Also, **Myranda.**

Mirella (Italian: variation of **Mirelle,** "wonderful"). Also, **Mirela, Myrela, Myrella.** Familiar, **Miri.**

Mirelle (Latin: wonderful). Also, **Mirell, Myrell, Myrelle.** Familiar, **Miri.**

Miri (Hebrew: variation of **Mary,** "bitterness"; Latin: variation of **Mirabella, Mirabelle, Mirella, Mirelle;** Hebrew: variation of **Miriam,** "rebellion"). Also, **Meeri, Miree, Mirey, Mirie, Miry.** *Whatever:* "**Mlrl**" was the name of an episode on the original *Star Trek* TV series—the one where Kirk et al., beam aboard a planet ruled by children.

Miriam (Hebrew: rebellion). Also, **Miriem, Miryam, Miryem, Myriam, Myriem, Myryam, Myryem.** Familiar, **Mim, Miri.**

Mirit (Hebrew: sweet as wine). Also, **Miritt, Miryt, Mirytt.**

Missy (English: girl; variation of **Melissa,** "a bee, sweetener"). Also, **Missee, Missey, Missi, Missie.**

Misty (English: foggy, misty). Also, **Mistee, Mistey, Misti, Mistie.**

Moesha (Origin unknown). Also, **Moeesha, Moisha, Moysha.** *Whatever:* A modern pretty girl popularized by the **Brandy** Norwood TV sitcom of the same name. Will **Moesha** become another **Samantha** (as seen on *Betwitched*) or another **Fonzie** (as seen on *Happy Days*)? That's a question that will take years to answer. Until then, approach with trendy suspenders caution.

Moina (Celtic: soft). Also, **Moyna.**

Moira (Irish: great; Greek: destiny). Also, **Moyra.** *Whatever:* Another winning, non-**Mary** entry. **Moira** is beautiful and winsome—a pick to click.

Moire (French: a fabric).

Moll (American: slang for gangster girlfriend; Irish: variation of **Molly,** "bitterness"). Also, **Mol.**

Molly (Irish: variation of **Mary**, "bitterness"). Also, **Mollee, Molley, Molli, Mollie.** *Plus:* A cute-as-a-button cuddly bear . . . *Minus:* . . . that's going the way of the canines. Pooch owners are taking over this delightful **Megan** alternative.

Mona (Latin: celibate; Teutonic: solitary).

Monday (English: born on Monday; Latin: moon day). Also, **Mondae.** *Whatever:* Interesting—**Monday** can sound hippie-dippie or power name–packed, depending on your mood.

Monica (Latin: adviser). Also, **Monicka, Monika.** *Plus:* A *Dynasty* name recast as contemporary hip on TV's *Friends*. *Minus:* In fifteen years, *Friends* is going to seem about as contemporary as *Joanie Loves Chachi.*

Monique (French: variation of **Monica**, "adviser"). Also, **Moneeqe, Moneeque, Moniqe.**

Monroe (Celtic: red marsh). Also, **Monro, Monrow, Monrowe.** *Whatever:* The doable way to pay tribute to sex goddess Marilyn **Monroe.**

Montana (Latin: mountain land). *Plus:* Works on three levels: It's a map name, a power name, a *Dynasty* name. *Minus:* Add "It's a pair of trendy suspenders" to that list. Beware any name trading on so many trends.

Mora (Irish: dark-complected).

Moran (Irish: little great one).

Morgan (Welsh: born of the sea, bright). Also, **Morgen, Morgyn.** *Plus:* A **Morgan** will always find friends in **Madison** and **Rhonwen.** *Minus:* Maybe in 2025, the three can band together and establish a power name support group for women who find their trendy suspenders tiring.

Moria (Latin: folly). Also, **Morya.**

Morna (Greek: beloved).

Moya (Irish: variation of **Mary**, "bitterness"). Also, **Moiya.**

Muna (Latin: gifts). Also, **Moona.**

Muriel (Celtic: bright sea). Also, **Muriell, Murielle, Muryel, Muryell, Muryelle.** *Whatever:* A solid pick in its own right, **Muriel** also works as a sound-alike alternative to little princess supreme **Ariel.**

Murphy (Celtic: sea warrior). Also, **Murphee, Murphey, Murphi, Murphie.** *Plus:* The new **Megan** or **Molly.** *Minus:* Its ability to pass for cutting edge has dulled, since its namesake sitcom is headed for the TV afterlife. (Yet anther reason to beware **Moesha.**)

Musa (Latin: song).

Musetta (Italian: variation of **Musette,** "song"). Also, **Museta.**

Musette (French: song). Also, **Musett.**

Myna (Hindi: tropical bird). Also, **Mina.**

Myra (Latin: admirable). Also, **Mira.**

N

CRIB NOTES

Famous Ns: **Nadia** Comaneci (Olympic gymnast); **Naomi** Campbell (model); **Nastassja** Kinski (actor/model); **Natalie** Merchant (singer/songwriter); **Natasha** Henstridge (film baddie, *Species*); **Neve** Campbell (actor, TV's *Party of Five*); **Nichelle** Nichols (Lieutenant Uhura, TV's *Star Trek*); **Nicole** Kidman (actor/Mrs. Tom Cruise); **Nicolette** Sheridan (actor, TV's *Knots Landing*)

Pocket Ts: Natalie, Nina, Nora

Trendy suspenders: Nevada

Think long, think hard: **Nadine** (Sad but true: a name that has been co-opted by Hollywood as shorthand for a gum-smacking, trailer-park denizen.); **Nanny** (You *have* a baby; you *hire* a **Nanny.**); **Nettie/Nessie** (A well-meaning duo that deserves a good home—as in *rest* home.); **Norma** (The name that will forever be remembered as the wallflower that got dumped by Marilyn Monroe, née **Norma** Jean Baker, on her way to sex-goddess-dom.)

Nadia (Russian: hopeful). Also, **Nadeea, Nadya.**
Nan (English: variation of **Nancy, Nannette**). Also, **Nann.** *Whatever:* As far as the **Nancy** name goes, only this preppie-sounding nickname can really cut it today.
Nana (African: mother of earth). Also, **Nanna.** *Plus:* An unfussy beauty. *Minus:* What you called Grandma before you had teeth.
Nance (English: valley). *Whatever:* The sophisticated **Nancy.**
Nancy (English: variation of **Anne,** "gracious"). Also, **Nancee,**

Nancey, Nanci, Nancie. Familiar, **Nan.** *Whatever:* In Gen X history, **Nancy** was **Karen**'s best school friend. Here's hoping the two have stayed in touch—it helps to have company in obscurity. Like **Karen, Nancy** is a peanut-butter-and-jelly sandwich—the tame by-product of the so-called revolutionary 1960s.

Nannette (French: variation of **Anne,** "gracious"). Also, **Nanette, Nannett.** Familiar, **Nan.** *Plus:* A more doable variation of **Nancy.** *Minus:* Its power to sound stylishly European has been usurped by the grander **Alexandra** and **Victoria.**

Naola (Hebrew: charming).

Naoma (Hebrew: variation of **Naomi,** "pleasant"). Also, **Naomah.**

Naomi (Hebrew: pleasant). Also, **Naomee, Naomey, Naomie, Naomy.** *Whatever:* A name that can be successfully worn by an international model (**Naomi** Campbell) and a country singer (**Naomi** Judd) in the same decade has good moves.

Nasia (Hebrew: God's miracle). Also, **Naseea, Naseeah, Nasiah, Nasya, Nsayah.** *Plus:* Here's a qualifier for the ever-elusive "unique" category. *Minus:* Too close to "nasal" for comfort?

Nastassja (German: variation of **Anastasia,** "resurrection"). Also, **Natasja.**

Nat (English: variation of **Natalia, Natalie**). Also, **Natt.**

Natalia (Italian: variation of **Natalie,** "born on Christmas Day"). Also, **Nataleea, Natalya.** Familiar, **Nat.**

Natalie (Latin: born on Christmas Day). Also, **Natalee, Natali, Nataly.** Familiar, **Nat.** *Whatever:* What we learned from *The Facts of Life*: **Natalie** isn't just for movie stars, à la **Natalie** Wood. It's for everyday, insecure teenagers too, à la *Facts* girl **Natalie** Green. Also, it holds up a heck of a lot better than **Jo** or **Tootie.** This classic pocket T is still a top twenty-five pick in California.

Natania (Hebrew: God's gift). Also, **Natanya.**

Natasha (Russian/Slavic: variation of **Natalie,** "born on Christmas Day"). Also, **Natassha.** *Whatever:* How to get fancy on **Natalie.**

Nathalie (French: variation of **Natalie,** "born on Christmas Day"). Also, **Nathalee, Nathaley, Nathali, Nathaly.**

Neal (Irish: variation of **Neil,** "champion"). Also, **Neall.**

Neala (Irish: variation of **Neil,** "champion"). Also, **Neela, Neila.**

Nealy (Irish: variation of **Neiley,** "champion"). Also, **Nealee, Nealey, Neali, Nealie.**

Neary (Irish: happy, prosperous). Also, **Nearee, Nearey, Neari, Nearie, Neeree, Neerey, Neeri, Neerie, Neery.**

Neata (English: neat). Also, **Neeta.**

Neba (Spanish: variation of **Neva,** "snowy"). Also, **Neeba, Niba, Nyba.**

Neda (English: need). Also, **Needa, Nida, Nyda.**

Neema (African: of prosperous times). Also, **Nema, Nima, Nyma.**

Neil (Irish: champion). Also, **Neel, Neell, Neill.**

Neiley (Irish: variation of **Neil,** "champion"). Also, **Neelee, Neeley, Neeli, Neelie, Neely, Neilee, Neili, Neilie, Neily.** *Whatever:* Pop-culture aficionados take note: **Neely** O'Hara was author Jacqueline Susann's plucky rags-to-riches-to-rags performer-type in romance trash classic *Valley of the Dolls.*

Neima (Hebrew: pleasant). Also, **Neyma.**

Neka (Native American: wild goose). Also, **Neca, Necka, Nekka.**

Nell (Greek/Celtic: variation of **Helen,** "the bright one"). Also, **Nel, Nelle.** Familiar, **Nellie.** *Whatever:* This *Little House on the Prairie* selection moves easily in today's **Hannah** and **Jessica** crowd. Wins style points for sound-alike status with classic little princess entry **Belle.**

Nellie (Greek/Celtic: variation of **Nell,** "the bright one"). Also, **Neli, Nellee, Nelley, Nelli, Nelly, Nely.** *Whatever:* **Nellie** Oleson was the "villain" of TV's *Little House on the Prairie.*

Neola (Irish: chieftan). Also, **Neeola, Niola, Nyola.**

Neva (Spanish: snowy; English: new). Also, **Neeva, Niva, Nyva.**

Nevada (Latin: snowy). *Plus:* It's a map name! It's contemporary! It's alive! *Minus:* It's a pair of rhinestone-studded trendy suspenders.

Neve (Latin: snow; Scandinavian: marsh). Also, **Nev.** *Plus:* There's nothing like a burgeoning young actress (**Neve** Campbell) on a trendy TV series (*Party of Five*) to work wonders for a heretofore little-known name. *Minus:* The *Scream* queen isn't the most established of baby name champions. Might want to give Campbell, and **Neve,** a few years.

Nichelle (English: variation of **Michelle,** "who is like God"). Also, **Nichell, Nischell, Nischelle, Nishell, Nishelle.** *Plus:* Freshens up established veteran **Michelle.** And what better testament to its place in the new millenium than to have it modeled by a *Star Trek* crew member (actor **Nichelle** Nichols)? *Minus:* The neighbors will think you're a Trekker.

Nico (Italian: variation of **Nicole,** "victory of the people"). Also, **Neeco, Nyco.**

Nicola (Italian: variation of **Nicole,** "victory of the people"). Also, **Nicolla.** Familiar, **Nicki.**

Nicole (Latin: variation of **Nicholas,** "victory of the people"). Also, **Nichole, Nicholle, Nicolle.** Familiar, **Nicki.** *Whatever:* This is a pretty girl of our youth that we can still recognize in schoolyards today. For a name of such delicate, fair qualities, **Nicole** is proving to have a pretty tough constitution.

Nicolette (French: variation of **Nicole,** "victory of the people"). Also, **Nicolett, Nicollette.** Familiar, **Nicki.**

Nicki (Italian/Latin/French: variation of **Nicola, Nicole, Nicolette**). Also, **Nickee, Nickey, Nickie, Nicky, Niki, Nikkee, Nikkey, Nikki, Nikkie, Nikky, Niky.** *Plus:* A sassy nickname . . . *Minus* . . . charting big as the noms de plume of exotic dancers at airport-area venues.

Niemi (Scandianvian: cape, isle). Also, **Nyemi.**

Nikita (Russian: variation of **Nicole,** "victory of the people"). Also, **Nikeeta, Nikyta.**

Niko (Russian: variation of **Nicole,** "victory of the people"). Also, **Neeko, Nyko.**

Nili (Hebrew: plant). Also, **Nillee, Nilley, Nilli, Nillie, Nilly.** *Plus:* Sprite, bright, appealingly different. *Minus:* Reminds you of **Nilla** Wafers.

Nina (Spanish: girl). Also, **Neena, Nyna.** *Whatever:* Here's a natural beauty that doesn't need makeup, extra syllables, or "Look at me, I'm pretty!" frills to make its points. These kinds of looks don't go out of style. A pocket T.

Ninetta (Slavic: variation of **Ninette,** "grace, beloved daughter"). Also, **Nineta.**

Ninette (French: grace, beloved daughter). Also, **Ninett.**

Nini (African: strong, like stone). Also, **Ninee, Niney, Ninie, Ninnee, Ninney, Ninni, Ninnie, Niny.** *Plus:* A beautiful **Nina** look-alike . . . *Minus:* . . . that doubles as a sound-alike for "ninny."

Ninon (French: variation of **Nina,** "girl"). Also, **Ninen.**

Ninotchka (Russian: variation of **Nina,** "girl"). *Whatever:* Made famous on these shores in the 1939 Great Garbo movie classic of the same name.

Nira (Hebrew: light). Also, **Neera, Nyra.**

Nita (Spanish: God is gracious). Also, **Neeta, Nyta.**

Noa (Hebrew: trembling). *Plus:* Looks—and sounds—very today. A pretty girl for spelunkers. *Minus:* Will it look—and sound—like you really wanted a **Noah** and got a girl instead?

Noami (Arabic: great happiness). Also, **Noamee, Noamey, Noamie, Noamy.**

Noelle (Latin: born on Christmas Day). Also, **Noel, Noell.** *Whatever:* If you name a boy **Noel,** you're asking for Yuletide taunts. If you name a girl **Noelle,** you're still in trouble come the holidays. But because boys—not girls—suffer the most name-razzing, consider this a doable pick for the pigtail set.

Nola (Latin: small bell). *Whatever:* A pick to click. Contemporary—ends with a vowel sound!—and simple enough to avoid feeling too silly once "contemporary" becomes "anachronistic."

Nolan (Irish: noble, famous). Also, **Nolen, Nolyn.**

Nomi (Arabic: variation of **Noami,** "great happiness"). Also, **Nomee, Nomey, Nomie, Nomy.** *Whatever:* Sooner, rather than later, your daughter's male peers will discover this bit of trivia at the video store: **Nomi** is the name of Elizabeth Berkley's topless—and bottomless—dancer in *Showgirls*.

Nona (Latin: ninth).

Noni (African: God's gift). Also, **Nonee, Noney, Nonie, Nony.**

Nora (Irish: beautiful). Also, **Norah, Norra.** *Whatever:* **Nora** feels old-fashioned in a comforting way—as if you know **Nora**s have walked this Earth before and will walk it again. This smart *Little House on the Prairie* number will grow with your daughter. And while it's not happening on the popularity charts, it's a worthy peer of **Sarah** and **Abigail,** which are most definitely happening. A pocket T.

Noreen (Irish: God of my youth). Also, **Norene, Norine, Noryne.**

Nova (Latin: new day). *Whatever:* Nova was Charlton Heston's mute, bikini-clad girlfriend in the 1968 sci-fi movie, *Planet of the Apes*.

Novena (Latin: shine). Also, **Noveena, Novina, Novyna.**

Nowell (Latin: variation of **Noel,** "born on Christmas Day"). Also, **Nowel, Nowele, Nowelle.**

Nuna (Native American: land). Also, **Noona.**

Nyssa (Greek: piercing). Also, **Nissa.** *Whatever:* A unique way to get wiggle room on **Vanessa.**

O

CRIB NOTES

Famous Os: **Odette** (the good swan, *Swan Lake*); **Olivia** Newton-John (the good greaser, *Grease*); **Olympia** Dukakis (Oscar-winner, *Moonlighting*); **Ophelia** (Shakespearean gal-pal, *Hamlet*).

Pocket Ts: Olivia

Trendy suspenders: No pick here. No such thing as a trendy O.

Think long, think hard: Olga (A name for your daughter to grow into—when she's about fifty-five.); **Olympus** (Fit for a mountain.)

Oakley (English: oak woods). Also, **Oaklee, Oakli, Oaklie, Oakly, Oklee, Okley.** *Whatever:* The perfect lil' cowpoke for your budding Annie **Oakley.**

Oba (African: goddess of the river).

Oberon (German: noble, bear). Also, **Oberron, Oeberon, Oeberron.** *Whatever:* Your tribute to *Wuthering Heights* leading lady, Merle **Oberon?**

Ocarina (English: small wind instrument). Also, **Ocareena, Ocaryna.**

Ocean (English: the saltwater sea).

Oceana (Latin: variation of **Ocean,** "the saltwater sea"). Also, **Oceeana, Ociana, Ocyana.**

Oceania (English: for the Pacific Islands). Also, **Oceeania, Ociania, Ocyania.** *Plus:* Here's a map name that doubles as a power name. *Minus:* Or a Jacques Cousteau documentary.

Octavia (Latin: eighth). Also, **Octavya.** *Whatever:* Even grander than a little princess. This one's more like an imposing queen.

Oda (Latin: song).

Odala (German: motherland). Also, **Odalla.**

Ode (Latin: song).

Odelia (Hebrew: praise God). Also, **Odeelia, Odeeliah, Odeliah, Odelya, Odelyah.**

Odell (Scandinavian: wealthy). Also, **Odel, Odelle.**

Odessa (Greek: odyssey). Also, **Odesa.** *Whatever:* **Odessa** was a city of the former Soviet Union. That factoid qualifies this exotic entry for hip map name status.

Odetta (French: "wealthy"). Also, **Odeta.**

Odette (French: "wealthy"). Also, **Odett.** *Whatever:* What little princess worth her crown hasn't wanted to dance lead swan in *Swan Lake?*

Odila (German: motherland). Also, **Odilla.**

Odilia (German: motherland). Also, **Odillia, Odillya, Odilya.**

Ohanna (Armenian: variation of **John,** "God is gracious"). Also, **Ohana.**

Oisha (American: variation of **Aisha,** "life"). Also, **Oaisha, Oeesha, Oysha.**

Okeanas (Greek: the saltwater sea).

Ola (Latin: wave; Hebrew: eternity). Also, **Olla.**

Oliff (English: variation of **Olive,** "olive tree"). Also, **Olif, Olyf, Olyff.**

Olive (Latin: olive tree). Also, **Olyve.** *Plus:* The contemporary of current fave **Abigail.** *Minus:* The namesake of 'toon string bean **Olive** Oyl.

Olivet (French: little olive tree). Also, **Olivett, Olivette, Olyvet, Olyvett, Olyvette.**

Olivetta (Italian: variation of **Olivet,** "little olive tree"). Also, **Oliveta, Olyveta, Olyvetta.**

Olivia (Latin: olive tree, peace). Also, **Oliveea, Olivya, Olyveea, Olyvia, Olyvya.** *Whatever:* A pocket T. Long the symbol of refined elegance, **Olivia** is enjoying a minor revival, pulling midrange numbers on popularity lists in Georgia and Illinois. Now's the time to get in on the ground floor before it becomes the next **Emily.**

Olympia (Greek: heavenly). Also, **Olimpia, Olimpya, Olympya.**

Omaya (American: variation of **Maya,** "illusion").

Onastace (American: variation of **Anastace,** "resurrection"). Also, **Onastayce, Onystace, Onystayce.** Familiar, **Stacy.**

Onastasia (American: variation of **Anastasia,** "resurrection"). Also, **Onastasya, Onystasia, Onystasya.**

Onastice (American: variation of **Anastice**, "resurrection"). Also, **Onasteece, Onysteece, Onystice.** Familiar, **Stacy.**

Ondrea (American: variation of **Andrea**, "brave"). Also, **Ondraea, Ondraya, Ondria, Ondrya.**

Ondreana (American: variation of **Andreana**, "brave"). Also, **Ondreanna, Ondriana, Ondrianna, Ondryana, Ondryanna.**

O'Neal (Celtic: from the chief's line). Also, **Oneal, Oneall, O'Neall.** *Whatever:* The uncommon pretty girl.

O'Neil (Celtic: variation of **O'Neal**, "from the chief's line"). Also, **Oneil, O'Neill, Oneill.**

Oona (Irish: variation of **Una**, "one"). Also, **Oonagh.** *Whatever:* Actress **Uma** Thurman makes this sound-alike safe again for use as a mysterious glamour girl name. (In the 1940s, Charlie Chaplin's wife popularized **Oona** for a different generation).

Ophelia (Greek: helper). Also, **Ofeelia, Ofelya, Opheelia, Ophelya.** *Plus:* Shakespeare's characters, like his plays, are the stuff of classics. *Minus:* But, come on. Would you name a son **Hamlet?**

Oprah (Hebrew: young deer). Also, **Opra.** *Plus:* Thanks to famed namesake **Oprah** Winfrey, this name is a symbol of strength and success. *Minus:* It's also the product of that cloying trend: It Came from a TV Talk Show.

Ora (Hebrew: light). Also, **Orah.**

Oralie (French: golden light). Also, **Oralee, Orali, Oraly.**

Ori (Hebrew: my light). Also, **Oree, Orey, Orie, Ory.**

Oriana (Latin: rising). Also, **Orianna, Oryiana, Oryanna.**

Oriel (German: fire, strife). Also, **Oriell, Orielle, Oryel, Oryell, Oryelle.** *Whatever:* Sounds like hip, little princess favorite **Ariel.** But it's *not* **Ariel.** Could be an individuality saver.

Orla (Hebrew: variation of **Orli**, "light"). Also, **Orlah.**

Orli (Hebrew: light). Also, **Orlee, Orley, Orlie, Orly.**

Orlin (Greek/Latin: golden sunrise). Also, **Orlyn.**

Ornit (Hebrew: lamb). Also, **Ornitt, Ornyt, Ornytt.**

Osanna (Latin: variation of **Hosanna**, "save now"). Also, **Osana.**

Oshea (Irish: offspring of **Shea**). Also, **Oshae, Oshay.**

Ottilia (German: motherland). Also, **Otilia, Otilya, Ottilya.**

Owen (English/Welsh: nobility). Also, **Owin, Owyn.**

Ozul (Hebrew: shadow). Also, **Ozule, Ozull, Ozulle.**

Ozra (Irish: unequaled).

P

CRIB NOTES

Famous Ps: **Pamela** Anderson Lee (ex-*Baywatch* thespian); **Patricia** Arquette (actor, *Flirting with Disaster*); **Patsy** Cline (country singer, "Crazy"); **Penelope** Ann Miller (actor, *The Relic*); **Peggy** Lipton (Julie, TV's *The Mod Squad*); **Pepper** Anderson (TV's *Police Woman*); **Peppermint Patty** ("Peanuts" kid); **Peri** Gilpin (actor, TV's *Frasier*); **Priscilla** Presley (actor/Elvis's ex).

Pocket Ts: **Paige**

Trendy suspenders: **Paloma**

Think long, think hard: **Pandora** (Not a good idea to open this box.); **Pansy** (It's hard to come up with a wussy girl name. This would be an exception.); **Patience** (About the three hundreth time you trudge out of bed in the middle of the night to attend to her crib, you'll realize that you're the one who needs **Patience,** not the kid.); **Peace** (Please.); **Philippa** (If you like **Phillip,** save it for a boy.); **Phyllis** (For every name, for every comedian—oh, say, **Phyllis** Diller—there is a time, there is a place. Sorry, **Phyllis**—the name, the comedian—this is *not* that time.); **Pippi** (Conjures too many bad memories of those weird *Pippi Longstocking* flicks of the 1960s and 1970s.); **Pocahontas** (Read the history book, rent the movie, avoid the baby name.); **Pollyanna** (Uh, no.); **Prissy** (Right down there with **Pansy**.)

Paddy (Irish: variation of **Patrick,** "noble"). Also, **Paddee, Paddey, Paddi, Paddie.** *Whatever:* A boy name that translates into a unique, plucky name for an Irish lass.

Padget (English/French: servant). Also, **Padgett, Padgit, Padgitt, Padgyt, Padgytt.** *Whatever:* Spelunkers alert: Could this be the "unique" **Paige**?

Pagan (Latin: country dweller). Also, **Pagen, Pagyn.** *Whatever:* **Pagan** possesses all the hippie spirit of a **Peace** or **Harmony.** A very un-hippie-like rakishness keeps it contemporary. This is all fine and good, but is it a baby name? Writer **Pagan** Kennedy (author of *'Zine*) seems no worse for it. It's obviously offbeat—and not recommended for the Catholic school bound.

Paget (English/French: variation of **Padget,** "servant"). Also, **Pagett, Pagit, Pagitt, Pagyt, Pagytt.**

Paige (English: attendant). Also, **Page, Payge.** *Plus:* A pocket T. Timelessly distinct and strong, this entry can stand up to the power name likes of **Madison.** *Minus:* Nicolette Sheridan and her pout spent several seasons on TV's *Knot's Landing,* making **Paige** a moniker for the supreme brat.

Paisley (Scottish: fabric design). Also, **Paislee, Paisli, Paislie, Paisly, Payslee, Paysley, Paysli, Payslie, Paysly.**

Pakka (Hindi: ripe). Also, **Paka.**

Pallas (Greek: wise). Also, **Palas.**

Palma (Latin: symbol of victory).

Palmer (English: bearing palm branches). *Whatever:* A pick to click. This is a great, as yet underused power name.

Paloma (Spanish: pigeon). *Plus:* The Euro-style **Dakota.** *Minus:* The Euro-style **Dakota.** Trendy suspenders time.

Pam (English: variation of **Pamela, Pamelia**). Also, **Pamm.** *Plus:* As wholesome as apple pie. *Minus:* Rhymes with "ham." And "Spam." And that brand-name nonaerosol cooking spray.

Pamela (English: gift of the elf). Also, **Pamila, Pamyla.** Familiar, **Pam, Pammie.** *Plus:* A pretty, reliable standby. *Minus:* It's a standby because **Pamela** is nobody's first choice today. This is a name that's feeling very 1950s. Also, it's doubtful that name spokesmodel **Pamela** Anderson is going to help sell this moniker to prospective moms.

Pamelia (English: variation of **Pamela,** "gift of the elf"). Also, **Pameelia, Pameelya, Pamelya.** Familiar, **Pam, Pammie.**

Pammie (English: variation of **Pamela, Pamelia**). Also, **Pammee, Pammey, Pammi, Pammy.**

Panna (Hebrew: grace). Also, **Pana, Panah, Pannah.**

Paola   (Italian: little; variation of **Paula,** "small").

Paris   (English: from Paris). Also, **Pariss, Parris, Parriss, Parrys, Parryss, Parys, Paryss.** *Plus:* "Hey, lookie, it's a map name! Even better, it's Grey Poupon to **Brooklyn**'s spicy brown mustard. *Minus:* Do you think in France they name babies **Sacramento?** Just a thought.

Parker   (English: park warden, gamekeeper). *Whatever:* Another boy name that makes for a doable, classy girl name.

Pascale   (French: born on Easter). Also, **Pascal, Pascall, Pascalle.**

Pasha   (Greek: of the ocean).

Pasquale   (Spanish: variation of **Pascale,** "born on Easter"). Also, **Pasqual, Pasquall, Pasqualle.**

Pat   (English: variation of **Patrice, Patricia, Patrizia**). Also, **Patt.** *Whatever:* Julia Sweeney's gender-bending "It's **Pat**" routine has muddied this nickname for girls and boys.

Patia   (Spanish: leaf). Also, **Pattia, Pattya, Patya.**

Patrice   (French: variation of **Patricia,** "noble"). Also, **Patreece, Patriece, Patryce.** Familiar, **Pat, Patty.**

Patricia   (Latin: variation of **Patrick,** "noble"). Also, **Patrisha, Patrycia, Patrysha.** Familiar, **Pat, Patsy, Patty, Tricia.** *Plus:* Who doesn't like **Patricia?** It's innocuous and inoffensive. A no-baggage peanut-butter-and-jelly sandwich. *Minus:* A name that's just kinda there—no heat.

Patrizia   (Italian: variation of **Patricia,** "noble"). Also, **Patrizya, Patryzia, Patryzya.** Familiar, **Pat, Patty.**

Patsy   (English: variation of **Patricia,** "noble"). Also, **Patsee, Patsey, Patsi, Patsie.**

Patty   (English: variation of **Patrice, Patricia, Patrizia**). Also, **Patti.** *Plus:* You think "Peanuts" character Peppermint **Patty** was a cool, revolutionary feminist. *Minus:* You think Peppermint **Patty** was a weird hippie kid . . . who maybe wasn't even *(gasp)* a girl!

Paula   (French: variation of **Paul,** "small"). Familiar, **Paulie.** *Plus:* The slightly more sophisticated, slightly hipper **Patricia.** *Minus:* World War II–era musty.

Pauletta   (Italian: variation of **Paulette,** "very small"). Also, **Pauleta.** Familiar, **Paulie.**

Paulette   (French: very small; variation of **Paula,** "small"). Also, **Pauletta.** Familiar, **Paulie.**

Paulie   (French/Latin: variation of **Paula, Pauletta, Paulette, Paulina, Pauline**). Also, **Paulee, Pauley, Pauli, Pauly.**

Paulina (Latin: variation of **Paula,** "small"). Also, **Pauleena, Paulyna.** Also, **Paulie.**

Pauline (Latin: variation of **Paula,** "small"). Also, **Pauleene, Paulyne.** Also, **Paulie.**

Payton (English: variation of **Patrick,** "noble"). Also, **Paeten, Paeton, Payten.**

Pearl (English: precious stone). Also, **Pearle, Perl, Perle.** *Whatever:* Here's a good example of how jewelry names (**Diamond, Gem, Jewel, etc.**) tend to devalue over the years. **Pearl**'s feeling pretty old-lady these days.

Pearlie (English: variation of **Pearl,** "precious stone"). Also, **Pearlee, Pearley, Pearli, Pearly, Perli.**

Peg (English: variation of **Margaret,** "pearl"). Also, **Pegg.**

Peggy (English: variation of **Margaret,** "pearl"). Also, **Peggi.**

Penelope (Greek: weaver). Also, **Penilope, Penylope.** Familiar, **Penny.** *Whatever:* Actor **Penelope** Ann Miller again proves that no name is ever really beyond recovery. Parents just have to be savvy enough to find them; their kids, brave enough to wear them. (Reminder: This sort of pioneer spirit is best sublimated when it comes to boy names. The boy equivalents of **Penelope** don't just have to be brave, they have to be armored.)

Penny (English: a coin; variation of **Penelope,** "weaver"). Also, **Penney, Penni, Pennie.** *Whatever:* A hopscotch buddy of **Peg** and **Pearl,** circa 1944.

Pepper (Greek: berry; English: the condiment). *Plus:* Plucky, quirky. *Minus:* TV cops of the 1970s, à la *Police Woman*'s **Pepper** Anderson, are about the only "people" who can carry it off.

Perdita (Latin: lost). Also, **Perdeeta, Perdyta.**

Peri (Hebrew: fruit). Also, **Peree, Perey, Perie, Pery.** *Whatever:* A pick to click. **Peri** has a very happening, very modern feel. It's cute but not frou-frou; simple but not boring.

Perpetua (Latin: perpetual). *Plus:* A unique beauty. *Minus:* A museum piece that should be left under lock and key.

Perry (English: of the pear tree). Also, **Perree, Perrey, Perri, Perrie.**

Persis (German: Persian woman). Also, **Persiss, Persys, Persyss.**

Petra (Greek: rock).

Petrea (Greek: variation of **Petra,** "rock").

Petula (Latin: ready for adventure).

Petunia (English: a flower). Also, **Petunya**. *Whatever:* A borderline museum piece that's relying on vowel action to keep the dust away. Another consideration: **Petunia** is the name of Porky Pig's gal-pal.

Peyton (English: variation of **Patrick**, "noble"). Also, **Peyten**. *Whatever:* Used as a girl name on Aaron Spelling's short-lived prime-time soap, *Savannah*.

Phadra (Greek: bright).

Phaedra (Greek: variation of **Phadra**, "bright"). Also, **Phaydra**.

Philomena (Greek: friend, power). Also, **Philomeena, Philomyna**.

Phoebe (Greek: shining one). Also, **Pheebe, Pheebee, Pheebey, Pheebi, Pheebie, Pheeby, Phoebee, Phoebey, Phoebi, Phoebie, Phoeby**. *Whatever:* Ditzy **Phoebe** character on TV's *Friends* leavens this name's tendency to sound French poodleish.

Pia (Latin: pious, devout). Also, **Pya**. *Plus:* Classic, classy, contemporary. *Minus:* The whole **Pia** Zadora thing.

Piera (Italian: rock). Also, **Pierra, Pyera, Pyerra**.

Pieta (Latin: pity). Also, **Pietta, Pyeta, Pyetta**.

Pietra (Italian: variation of **Petra**, "rock"). Also, **Pyetra**.

Pilar (Latin: tall and strong, pillarlike). Also, **Pillar**. *Whatever:* A power name with a fiery passion. Could it be the exotic **Madison?**

Pillion (English: jump seat). Also, **Pilion, Pillyon, Pilyon**.

Pinna (Latin: feather). Also, **Pina**.

Piper (English: pipe player, strolling musician). Also, **Pyper**. *Whatever: The X-Files* star Gillian Anderson named her daughter **Piper**.

Pippin (French: seed). Also, **Pipen, Pipin, Pippen, Pippyn, Pipyn**.

Pita (Greek/Hebrew: bread). Also, **Peeta, Pyta**. *Plus:* Exotic. *Minus:* Bread-like.

Piton (French: a spike). Also, **Piten**.

Planta (Latin: sole).

Platea (Latin: street). Also, **Plateea, Platia, Platya**.

Pleasance (English/French: pleasant). Also, **Plesance**. *Plus:* A nice thought . . . *Minus:* . . . but is it a name? There are few modern-day examples.

Poe (English: Peacock). Also, **Po**. *Whatever:* A comer. Singer **Poe** ("Angry Johnny") makes it relevant; **Zoe** look-alike status makes it viable.

Poesy (English: poetry). Also, **Poesee, Poesey, Poesi, Poesie, Posee, Posey, Posi, Posie, Posy**.

Polly (Irish: variation of **Molly,** "bitterness"). Also, **Pollee, Polley, Polli, Pollie.** *Plus:* Sunny and simple. *Minus:* As long as kids read pirate books, assume your daughter's school years will be filled with numerous "Wanna cracker?" requests.

Polona (Greek: the sun). Also, **Polonna.**

Porter (English: carrier, gatekeeper).

Powell (Welsh: famous). Also, **Powel.**

Precia (Latin: valuable). Also, **Precya.**

Precious (English: valuable, dear). *Plus:* Southern and sweet and adorable. *Minus: You* know your daughter's precious. You also know she wets her diapers, but you wouldn't call her **Diaper Rash,** would you?

Price (Welsh: ardor). Also, **Pryce.**

Prima (Latin: first). Also, **Preema, Pryma.**

Primrose (English: a flower). Also, **Prymrose.**

Princess (English: royal). Also, **Pryncess.** *Plus:* Accept no imitations—this is the *ultimate* little princess. *Minus: See* **Precious** for thoughts on how literal thinking and baby naming don't mix.

Priscilla (Latin: long life). Also, **Pricila, Pricilla, Priscila, Prisila, Prisilla.** Familiar, **Cilla.**

Pru (English: variation of **Prudence,** "prudent"). Also, **Prue.**

Prudence (Latin: prudent). Also, **Prudince, Prudynce, Pruedence, Pruedince, Pruedynce.** Familiar, **Pru, Prudy.** *Whatever:* Quasi-elegant, mostly prunelike. Then again, if **Mabel** can stage a mini-return, can **Prudence** be far behind?

Prudy (English: variation of **Prudence,** "prudent"). Also, **Prudee, Prudey, Prudi, Prudie.** *Whatever:* There are probably worse things than being subjected to "**Prudy** the Prude" schoolyard taunts. The key word here is "probably."

Puma (English: cougar). Also, **Pooma.**

Pupa (Latin: doll). Also, **Puppa.**

Q

CRIB NOTES

Famous Qs: Quinn Cummings (former child star, TV's *Family, The Goodbye Girl*)

Pocket Ts: Quinn

Trendy suspenders: Guarding unforeseen circumstances, a Q wouldn't be trendy if you stuck a nose ring through it.

Think long, think hard: Queenie (Great for a drama-queen, romance-novel heroine, à la Michael Korda's *Queenie*. A touch much for the rest of us mere mortals.); **Quinella** (A baby named for this racetrack pick should not count on her parents to sock away dough for college.)

Qing (Chinese: blue).
Qaeshawna (American: variation of **Shawna**, "God is gracious"). Also, **Qaeseana, Qaeshauna, Qaeshona, Qayseana, Qayshauna, Qayshawna, Qayshona.**
Qawona (American: variation of **Juana**, "God is gracious"). Also, **Qajuana, Qawana, Qejuana, Qewana, Qewona.**
Quail (French: a partridge). Also, **Quaile, Quale, Quayle.**
Quan (Native American: fragrant). Also, **Quann.**
Quana (Native American: fragrant). Also, **Quanna.**
Quaniqua (American: origin unknown). Also, **Quaneekwa, Quaneequa, Quanikwa, Quanykwa, Quanyqua.**
Quarta (Latin: fourth).
Quashawna (American: variation of **Shawna**, "God is gracious"). Also, **Quaseana, Quashauna, Quashona.**

Quay (Celtic: a wharf). Also, **Quaye.**

Queely (American: variation of **Keely,** "falcon's cry"). Also, **Qeelee, Qeeley, Qeeli, Qeelie, Qeely, Queelee, Queeley, Queeli, Queelie.**

Queen (English: ruler). Also, **Queene.** *Plus:* The über little princess. *Minus:* If you start out a **Queen,** there is no place to go but down.

Quemby (Norse: woman's house). Also, **Quembee, Quembey, Quembi, Quembie.** *Plus:* A preppie stalwart—goes great with a plaid skirt and Top-Siders. *Minus:* Sounds like the name of one of Blair's snobby friends from *The Facts of Life.* Also, beware the **Gumby** factor. The threat of jibes such as, "She was once a little green slab of clay—**Quemby!**" cannot be discounted.

Quenella (French: little oak tree). Also, **Quenela.**

Quill (Irish: hazel: English: feather). Also, **Quil, Quille, Quyl, Quyll, Quylle.**

Quimby (Scandinavian: woman's house). Also, **Quimbee, Quimbey, Quimbi, Quimbie.**

Quince (Latin: applelike fruit). Also, **Quynce.**

Quincy (Scottish: estate of the fifth born). Also, **Quincee, Quincey, Quinci, Quincie.** *Plus:* Every bit the classic preppie equal of **Quemby**—only half as cloying! *Minus:* Go ahead. Name your daugher after a Jack Klugman TV show. See if she cares.

Quinetta (Latin: fifth). Also, **Quineta.**

Quinette (French: fifth). Also, **Quinett.**

Quinlan (Irish: graceful). Also, **Quinlen, Quinlyn.** *Whatever:* It's the rare Irish lass that's underused. This is it. Use it. **Quinlan** offers wiggle room on its trendier, sound-alike cousin **Cameron.**

Quinlay (Irish: variation of **Quinley,** "graceful"). Also, **Quinlae.**

Quinley (Irish: graceful). Also, **Quinlee, Quinleigh, Quinli, Quinlie, Quinly.**

Quinn (Irish: bushy-haired, heart). Also, **Quin, Quyn, Quynn.** *Plus:* A pocket T—simple, elegant, and clean. **Quinn** isn't weighted down with frilly extras (vowels, syllables, accent marks)—the sort of stuff that can take unfashionable turns.

Quinsy (Scottish: variation of **Quincy,** "estate of the fifth born"). Also, **Quinsee, Quinsey, Quinsi, Quinsie.**

Quintessa (Latin: to reap, hunter). Also, **Quintesa.** *Whatever:* It's **Contessa** minus the *Dynasty*-ish look.

Quintina (Latin: fifth). Also, **Quinteena, Quintyna.**

Quiran   (Irish: black, dark). Also, **Qiran, Qiren, Qiryn, Quiren, Quiryn.**

Quirin   (Irish: magical). Also, **Qirin, Qiryn, Quiryn.** *Whatever:* You love **Karen,** but accept that it's a wallflower among today's **Madison**s and **Morgan**s. So, why not try sneaky sound-alike **Quirin?** The exotic Irish lass.

Quisha   (American: variation of **Aisha,** "life"). Also, **Qeesha, Qeysha, Qisha, Queesha, Queysha, Quysha, Qysha.**

Quita   (Spanish: white, five). Also, **Qeeta, Qita, Queeta, Quyta, Qyta.** *Whatever:* Contemporary, cute, and vowel-friendly, **Quita** should wear as well in our Brave New **Brittany** World.

Quon   (Chinese: bright). Also, **Quonn.**

R

CRIB NOTES

Famous Rs: **Raquel** Welch (1960s pinup fodder), **Rose of Sharon** (itinerant farm worker, *The Grapes of Wrath*); **Reba** McEntire (big-haired country singer), **Rebecca** Lobo (basketball player); **Rhea** Perlman (ex-TV barmaid, *Cheers*); **Ricki** Lake (talk-show host), **Rita** Hayworth (screen siren, *Gilda*), **Roma** Downey (heavenly creature, TV's *Touched By an Angel*); **Roseanne** (comedian), **Rosemary** Clooney (singer/George Clooney's aunt); **Rosie** O'Donnell (talk-show host); **Ruth** Bader Ginsburg (U.S. Supreme Court justice)

Pocket Ts: **Rebecca, Rose, Ruth**

Trendy suspenders: **Rachel**

Think long, think hard: **Rain/Rainbow** (Unabashed hippie names.); **Raven** (Best reserved for fictional soap-opera divas.); **Rhonda** (Too sweater-girl-ish; too associated with a cloying Beach Boys tune.); **Rhiannon** (OK, first, it's Welsh for "witch." Second, what if your kid doesn't like Fleetwood Mac? Third, what if she dates some boy who sings the Stevie Nicks–penned tune to her? Are you retching yet? Hope so.); **Romaine** (Too produce-y.); **Royanna** (Too **Roy**.); **Rupaul** (Nothing against Mr. "Supermodel of the World," but please, name your girl **Rupaul** and you're saddling her with more baggage than is allowed on most commercial airline flights.)

Rachel (Hebrew: gentle lamb). Also, **Rachael, Rachil, Rachyl**. *Plus:* The Bible meets "Must See TV." This established veteran's hip quotient has soared thanks to actress Jennifer Aniston, her haircut ("the

Rachel"), and TV's *Friends. Minus:* Is **Rachel** the next **Farrah?** Probably not. It's too ancient to be fly-by-night. Still, the name *is* going to be stuck with the *Friends* taint for quite a while. Might as well stamp it with, "the 1990s." Trendy suspenders potential.

Rachelle (French: variation of **Rachel,** "gentle lamb"). Also, **Rachele, Rachell.**

Racina (Italian: variation of **Racine,** "rose"). Also, **Raceena, Racyna.**

Racine (Latin: rose). Also, **Raceene, Racyne.**

Rae (Scottish: variation of **Ray,** "wise, protector"). *Whatever:* On a boy, **Ray** sounds dated. On a girl, **Rae** sounds positively today. Go figure.

Raeshawna (American: variation of **Shawna,** "God is gracious"). Also, **Raeseana, Raeshauna, Raeshona.**

Rafaela (Spanish: variation of **Raphaela,** "healed by God"). Also, **Rafaella.**

Raga (Sanskirt: color). Also, **Ragga.**

Rainey (Scottish: judge). Also, **Rainee, Raini, Rainie, Rany, Raynee, Rayney, Rayni, Raynie.**

Raisa (Yiddish: rose). Also, **Raisah, Raysa, Raysah.** *Whatever:* Will the impending 1980s retro revival be a boon to this relic of the *glasnost* era? Not even former Soviet Union leading lady **Raisa** Gorbachev knows for sure.

Raiza (Yiddish: variation of **Raisa,** "rose"). Also, **Rayza.**

Raja (Sanskrit: ruler).

Raleigh (English: red meadow). Also, **Ralee, Raley, Rali, Ralie, Raly.**

Ramona (Spanish: mighty). *Whatever:* **Ramona** was the bratty sister in Beverly Cleary's Beezus and **Ramona** children's books series of the 1950s and 1960s.

Ramsay (Scottish: variation of **Ramsey,** "Ram's isle"). Also, **Ramsae.**

Ramsey (Scottish: Ram's isle). Also, **Ramsee, Ramsi, Ramsie, Ramsy.**

Rand (English: shield, wolf). Also, **Rande.**

Randall (English: shield, wolf). Also, **Randal, Randel, Randell, Randyl, Randyll.** Familiar, **Randi.**

Randi (English: variation of **Randall,** "shield, wolf"). Also, **Randee, Randey, Randie, Randy.** *Whatever:* **Randi** Oakes played Officer Bonnie Clark on TV's *CHiPs* from 1979–82.

Ranita (Hebrew: song, joy). Also, **Raneeta, Raneetah, Ranitah, Ranyta, Ranytah.**

Rankin (English: variation of **Randolph,** "shield, wolf"). Also, **Rankinn, Rankyn, Rankynn.**

Raphaela (Hebrew: variation of **Raphael,** "healed by God"). Also, **Raphaella.**

Raquel (French: variation of **Rachel,** "female lamb"). Also, **Racquel, Racquell, Racquelle, Raquell, Raquelle.** *Plus:* The unique, wiggle room alternative to **Rachel.** *Minus:* Conjures images of cavewomen in bikinis, à la **Raquel** Welch's 1966 demi-classic, *One Million Years B.C.*

Rara (Latin: strange).

Rashawna (American: variation of **Shawna,** "God is gracious"). Also, **Raseana, Rashauna, Rashona, Reseana, Reshauna, Reshawna, Reshona.**

Raven (English: a crow). Also, **Ravin, Ravyn.**

Rawleigh (English: red meadow). Also, **Rawlee, Rawley, Rawli, Rawlie, Rawly.**

Ray (Scottish: wise, protector). Also, **Raye.**

Rayna (Yiddish: pure, clean). Also, **Raynah.**

Rayshawna (American: variation of **Raeshawna,** "God is gracious"). Also, **Rayseana, Rayshauna, Rayshona.**

Rea (English: river). Also, **Ree.**

Readey (English: variation of **Reedey,** "by the reeds"). Also, **Readee, Readi, Readie, Ready.**

Reagan (Celtic: little king). Also, **Raegan, Raygan, Raygen, Raygyn, Reagen, Reagyn.**

Reba (Hebrew: peacemaker). Also, **Reeba, Reebah, Rebah.** *Whatever:* Popularized by appealingly earnest country singer **Reba** McEntire.

Rebecca (Hebrew: faithful, beauty, noose). Also, **Rebeca, Rebecah, Rebeccah, Rebecka, Rebeckah, Rebeka, Rebekah, Rebekka, Rebekkah, Ribecca, Rybecca, Rybecka, Rybekka.** Familiar, **Becca, Becky.** *Plus:* Road-tested through the centuries, **Rebecca** is aging gracefully—*very* gracefully. A slam-dunk pocket T. *Minus:* Booming popularity makes this a less-than-attractive option to spelunkers.

Reece (Welsh: enthusiastic). *Whatever:* Here's another boy name that a girl can wear well.

Reed (English: ruddy, red). Also, **Reede.** *Whatever:* Most often a boy name but used to nice effect on TV's *Sisters,* where Ashley Judd played **Reed** Halsey from 1991–94.

Reedey (English: by the reeds). Also, **Reedee, Reedi, Reedie, Reedy.**

Reese (Celtic: prince; Welsh: enthusaistic). Also, **Rees.**

Regan (Irish: little king; German: counselor). Also, **Reegan, Reegen, Reegyn, Regen, Regyn.** *Plus:* A perfect power name for a future lady of the manor. *Minus:* **Regan** MacNeil was the kid who spit green slime in *The Exorcist.*

Regatta (Italian: boat race). Also, **Regata.**

Reggie (English: powerful, mighty; variation of **Regina,** "queen"). Also, **Reggee, Reggey, Reggy, Regi.**

Regina (Latin: queen). Also, **Regeena, Regyna.** Familiar, **Gina, Ginny, Reggie.**

Reid (English: variation of **Reed,** "ruddy, red"). Also, **Reide.**

Reidey (English: variation of **Reedey,** "by the reeds"). Also, **Reidee, Reidi, Reidie, Reidy.**

Reilly (Irish: combative). Also, **Reilee, Reileigh, Reiley, Reili, Reilie, Reillee, Reilleigh, Reilley, Reilli, Reillie, Reily.**

Reina (Latin: queen). Also, **Reyna.**

Remy (French: champagne). Also, **Remee, Remey, Remi, Remie.** *Whatever:* Here's a *très* cool pick to click. Evokes images of an elegant, smoky-voiced, expatriate cabaret singer in Paris.

Ren (Japanese: water lily). Also, **Renn.** Familiar, **Rennie.** *Whatever:* A pick to click. Simple, clean lines, elegant.

Rena (Hebrew: song, joy). Also, **Renah, Renna, Rennah.**

Renata (Latin: variation of **Renee,** "born again"). Also, **Renatta.**

Renee (French: born again). Also, **Renae, Renay, Renaye.**

Reni (Japanese: variation of **Ren,** "water lily"). Also, **Reney, Renie, Reny.**

Renita (Latin: resist). Also, **Reneeta, Renyta.**

Reno (Spanish: reindeer). Also, **Reeno, Ryno.** *Plus:* As far as Nevada gambling outposts go, **Reno** is a much more suitable first name than, say, **Las Vegas.** *Minus:* Not so much a baby name as the perfect moniker for a brand of sequin-covered blue jeans.

Resina (Italian: resin). Also, **Resena, Resyna.**

Reva (Hebrew: dreamer). Also, **Reeva, Revah, Riva, Rivah.**

Reyna (Greek: peaceful). Also, **Raena.**

Rhea (Greek: mother of Zeus). Also, **Rheah.**

Rhine (German: for the European river Rhine). Also, **Rhyne, Rine, Ryne.** *Whatever:* Sound-alike fodder for **Ryan.**

Rho (Greek: seventeenth letter of the Greek alphabet; English: variation of **Rhoda,** "rose"). Also, **Rhoe.**

Rhoda (Greek: rose). Also, **Roda.** Familiar, **Rho, Rhodi, Rodi.** *Plus:* You worship the rerun temple of *The Mary Tyler Moore Show* but identify more with her acerbic neighbor, **Rhoda** Morgenstern. *Minus:* World War II–era musty.

Rhodi (Greek: variation of **Rhoda,** "rose"). Also, **Rhodee, Rhodey, Rhodie, Rhody.** *Whatever:* The fresh take on **Rhoda.**

Rhone (French: for the Eruopean river Rhone) Also, **Rhoan, Rhoane, Roan, Roane, Rone.**

Rhonwen (Welsh: fair, slender). Also, **Rhonwin, Rhonwyn, Ronwen, Ronwyn.** *Whatever:* A power name so supremely yuppie it ought to come free with the purchase of a Volvo.

Richelle (American: variation of **Michelle,** "who is like God?"). Also, **Richell, Rischell, Rischelle, Rishell, Rishelle.**

Ricki (English: variation of **Richard,** "hard, stern ruler"). Also, **Rickee, Rickey, Rickie, Ricky, Rikkee, Rikkey, Rikki, Rikkie, Rikky.** *Plus:* Pom-pom girl peppy. *Minus:* Tainted by **Ricki** Lake's sometimes sleazy talk show.

Rider (English: a rider, mounted police). Also, **Ryder.** *Whatever:* A girl version of a lil' cowpoke, à la **Cody.** Although, thankfully, much lower on the precious scale.

Riley (Irish: variation of **Reilly,** "combative"). Also, **Rilee, Rileigh, Rily.** *Whatever:* The **Ryan** Less Traveled.

Rima (English: border). Also, **Reema, Ryma.**

Rina (Hebrew: cry). Also, **Rinah, Rinna, Rinnah.** Familiar, **Rini.**

Rini (Hebrew: variation of **Rina,** "cry"). Also, **Rinie, Riny, Rinnee, Rinney, Rinni, Rinnie, Rinny.**

Rio (Spanish: river). Also, **Ryo.** *Whatever:* A *Dynasty* name a-go-go.

Ripley (English: narrow meadow). Also, **Riplee, Ripleigh, Ripli, Riplie, Riply.** *Whatever:* Suggested by one of our era's greatest kick-butt screen heroines, Ellen **Ripley,** from the *Alien* flicks. Hear her roar.

Rita (Sanskrit: brave; Greek: variation of **Margaret,** "pearl"). Also, **Reeta, Ryta.**

River (English: a river). Also, **Ryver.**

Ro (Irish: variation of **Rowan,** "mountain ash).

Roberta (English: variation of **Robert,** "bright, fame"). Familiar,

Bobbi. *Plus:* Stout, hearty . . . *Minus:* . . . like your battle-ax of a great-aunt. Sorry, this is just not a happening name.

Robin (English: the bird; variation of **Robert,** "bright, fame"). Also, **Robbin, Robbyn, Robyn.** *Whatever:* From **Robin** Hood to "The Howard Stern Show" sidekick **Robin** Quivers—this is a name with longevity and adaptability. Possibly tough to tag a boy with **Robin** right now, thanks to the *Batman* movies. But for girls, this is a solid choice.

Rocky (English: rocky). Also, **Rockee, Rockey, Rocki, Rockie, Rokkee, Rokkey, Rokki, Rokkie, Rokky.** *Whatever:* Absurdly macho on a boy, **Rocky** looks spunky on a girl.

Rodi (Greek: variation of **Rhoda,** "rose"). Also, **Rodee, Rodey, Rodi, Rodie, Rody.**

Roe (English: small deer). Also, **Ro.**

Rolanda (German: famous). Also, **Rholanda.** *Whatever:* This is another talk-show host name. Better than **Regis,** worse than **Leeza.**

Roma (Latin: gypsy).

Rona (Hebrew: joyful song). Also, **Ronah.**

Ronan (Irish: little seal). Also, **Ronyn.**

Ronen (Hebrew: song and joy). Also, **Ronin, Ronyn.**

Roney (Irish: hero). Also, **Ronee, Ronie, Rony.**

Roni (Hebrew: variation of **Rona,** "joyful song"). Also, **Ronee, Ronie, Rony.**

Ronnie (Latin: variation of **Veronica,** "true image"). Also, **Ronnee, Ronney, Ronni, Ronny.** *Plus:* In "Archie" comics, Veronica seems more humanized when Archie calls her **Ronnie.** *Minus:* Unless you think your girl has a shot at becoming a 1940s gossip columnist, this one's pretty much in mothballs.

Rory (Irish: red). Also, **Roree, Rorey, Rori, Rorie.** *Whatever:* Cute and vowel-friendly, **Rory** is the **Kelly** for our times.

Rosa (Spanish: rose). Familiar, **Rosie.**

Rosabell (Spanish: beautiful rose). Also, **Rosabelle.** Familiar, **Rosie.**

Rosabella (Spanish: beautiful rose). Also, **Rosabela.** Familiar, **Rosie.**

Rosalie (English: rose meadow). Also, **Rosalee, Rosaleigh, Rosali, Rosaly, Roselee.** Familiar, **Rosie.**

Rosalinda (Spanish: pretty rose; German: horse, serpent). Also, **Rosalynda.** Familiar, **Rosie.**

Rosalyn (Spanish: pretty rose; German: horse, serpent). Also, **Rosalin, Rosalind, Rosalinn, Rosalynd, Rosalynn.** Familiar, **Rosie.**

Rosarita (Spanish: rose, pearl). Also, **Rosareeta, Rosaryta.** Familiar, **Rosie.**

Rose (Latin: rose, horse). Familiar, **Rosie.** *Whatever:* This is a can't-go-wrong pocket T—popular but not too popular; old-fashioned but not outmoded. Simple, elegant, clean.

Roseanna (English: combination of **Rose** and **Anna**). Also, **Rosana, Rosanna, Roseana.** Familiar, **Rosie.**

Roseanne (English: combination of **Rose** and **Anne**). Also, **Rosann, Rosanne, Rose Ann, Roseann, RoseAnn, Rose Anne, Rose Anne.** Familiar, **Rosie.** *Whatever:* Can you separate **Roseanne,** the baby name, from **Roseanne,** the screeching comedian? No? Do you think it'll be different for anybody else, save TV-free members of the Amish community?

Rosemary (English: dew of the sea, herb; combination of **Rose** and **Mary**). Also, **Rosemaree, Rosemarey, Rosemari, Rosemarie, Rose Mary, RoseMary.** Also, **Rosie.**

Rosetta (Italian: little rose). Also, **Roseta.**

Rosette (French: little rose). Also, **Rosett.**

Roshawna (American: variation of **Shawna,** "God is gracious"). Also, **Rhoseana, Rhoshauna, Rhoshawna, Rhoshona, Rhoeseana, Rhoeshauna, Rhoeshawna, Rhoeshona, Roseana, Roshauna, Roshona, Roeseana, Roeshauna, Roeshawna, Roeshona.**

Rosie (English: pink, bright; Spanish/Italian: variation of **Rosa, Rosabell, Rosabella, Rosalie, Rosalinda, Rosalyn, Rosarita, Rose, Roseanna, Roseanne, Rosemary, Roslyn**). Also, **Rosee, Rosey, Rosi, Rosy.** *Whatever:* The best talk-show moniker going today. Sunny, sassy—and benefitting from all sorts of good vibes from "the Queen of Nice," **Rosie** O'Donnell.

Roslyn (Spanish: pretty rose; German: horse, serpent). Also, **Roslin, Roslinn, Roslynn.** Familiar, **Rosie.**

Rota (Latin: wheel).

Rowan (Irish: mountain ash). Also, **Rhowan, Rhowen, Rhowyn, Rowen, Rowyn.** Familiar, **Ro.**

Rowe (Irish: red-haired). Also, **Row.**

Rowena (Celtic: white blossom; Welsh: fair). Also, **Roweena, Rowina, Rowyna.**

Rox (Persian: variation of **Roxanne,** "dawn"). Also, **Roxx.**

Roxanne (Persian: dawn). Also, **Roxann.** Familiar, **Rox, Roxie.** *Plus:*

Historically the fair object of Cyrano's desire in *Cyrano de Bergerac*. *Minus:* Currently, a good name for a movieland sex kitten.

Roxie (Persian: variation of **Roxanne,** "dawn"). Also, **Roxee, Roxey, Roxi, Roxy.** *Whatever:* **Roxie** Roker (the late mother of rocker Lenny Kravitz) played Weezy's best gal-pal Mrs. Willis on TV's *The Jeffersons* (1975–85).

Royce (English: royal).

Royse (English: rose, horse).

Roz (American: variation of **Rozlyn,** "pretty rose, horse, serpent"). *Whatever:* **Roz** Kelly played Fonzie's former girlfriend Pinky Tuscadero on TV's *Happy Days*.

Rozlyn (American: variation of **Roslyn,** "pretty rose, horse, serpent"). Also, **Rozlin, Rozlinn, Rozlynn.** Familiar, **Roz.**

Ruby (English: precious stone). Also, **Rubee, Rubey, Rubi, Rubie.**

Rue (German: famous). Also, **Ru.**

Rune (German: mythical poem, song).

Ruta (Hawaiian: friend).

Ruth (Hebrew: friendship). Also, **Ruthe.** Familiar, **Ruthie.** *Plus:* Classic and biblical, **Ruth** is a reliable pocket T. *Minus:* By today's ears, an old-sounding name for a young-looking baby?

Ruthann (English: combination of **Ruth** and **Ann**). Also, **Ruth Ann, RuthAnn, Ruth Anne, RuthAnne, Ruthanne.** Familiar, **Ruthie.**

Ruthie (English/Hebrew: variation of **Ruth, Ruthann**). Also, **Ruthee, Ruthey, Ruthi, Ruthy.**

Ryan (Irish: little king). Also, **Ryen, Ryun.** *Whatever:* Borderline trendy suspenders. Yes, it's a faddish, popular pick. But it's also an established vet. The bottom line: **Ryan** is a pretty girl that's unlikely to fade.

Ryne (Irish: variation of **Ryan,** "little king"). Also, **Rine.**

Rynne (English: river channel).

S

CRIB NOTES

Famous Ss: **Samantha** Stevens (good witch, TV's *Betwitched*); **Sarah** McLachlan (singer/Lilith Fair founder); **Scarlett** O'Hara (heroine, *Gone With the Wind*); **Sean** Young (actor, *No Way Out*); **Selena** (Tejano music legend); **Shannon** Doherty (*Beverly Hills, 90210* exile); **Sigourney** Weaver (*Alien* slayer); **Stockard** Channing (Rizzo, *Grease*); **Summer** Sanders (Olympic swimmer); **Susan** Olsen (Cindy Brady, TV's *The Brady Bunch.)*

Pocket Ts: Sarah, Simone, Sonya, Sophia

Trendy suspenders: Samantha, Savannah, Shelby, Sierra

Think long, think hard: **Sable** (It's no coincidence that this melo-dramatic number did a turn on *Dynasty.*); **Satin** (Could have been cast as **Sable**'s sister.); **Seven of Nine** (Maybe it sounds cool on *Star Trek: Voyager,* but remember two things: (1) **Seven of Nine** is a cyborg; and (2) *It's just a TV show!*); **Shasta** (Keep the soda pop in the fridge.); **Sheena** (Queen of the jungle; loser in the city); **Shirley** (Past its expiration date.); **Silver** (Precious metals look like costume jewelry on new-borns.); **Snow** (No better than **Sleet**.); **Star** (Too-too.); **Stormy** (For those who believe **Troubled Teenager** is too literal. . . . Also, for what it's worth, we've known one **Stormy** in our life. She committed suicide in the ninth grade.); **Sunshine** (Love beads, included.)

Sabina (Latin: from the **Sabine** clan in ancient Rome). Also, **Sabeena,** **Sabyna.** *Whatever:* Pretty, contemporary—plus, gets you wiggle room on **Sabrina** or **Samantha.**

Sabine (Latin: from the **Sabine** clan in ancient Rome). Also, **Sabeene, Sabyne.**

Sabrina (Latin: princess). Also, **Sabreena, Sabryna.** *Whatever:* A comer. This is the pick here to become the new **Samantha.** Like its mega-popular, sound-alike cousin, it's the moniker of a good-hearted TV witch, in this case *Sabrina, the Teenage Witch.* Can the **Sabrina** baby name boom be far behind? Time to get in on the ground floor—pronto.

Sachi (Japanese: blissful girl). Also, **Sachee, Sachey, Sachie, Sachy.**

Sadie (American: variation of **Sarah,** "princess"). Also, **Sadee, Sadey, Sadi, Sady.** *Plus:* **Sadie** is a popular **Sarah** spinoff that's strong enough to stand alone. It's benefitting from the same nostalgia kick that has breathed life into turn-of-the-century faves like **Sophie.** *Minus:* Troublesome "Sexy **Sadie**" taunts?

Sage (Latin: wise, the healing plant). Also, **Saige, Sayge.**

Sahara (Arabic: desert). Also, **Saharra.** *Whatever:* **Sahara** is so melodramatic it would easily qualify for a think long, think hard nomination, save for one thing: It's the **Sierra** Less Traveled. If we're going to insist on making a star of the outdoorsy **Sierra,** then we're going to need a like alternative. This is it.

Sally (Hebrew: peaceful, princess). Also, **Sali, Sallee, Salley, Salli, Sallie.**

Samantha (Hebrew: asked of God). Familiar, **Sam, Sami.** *Plus:* What the cheerleaders of the class of 2015 will be named. **Samantha** is an always-there name that has achieved wide popularity in the 1990s. *Minus:* A trendy suspenders name likely revived through Nick at Nite's endless diet of **Betwitched** reruns. Fear for our future if Nick ever starts running *The Facts of Life* in prime time. (The most popular girl name of 2005: **Tootie**?)

Sandra (Greek: variation of **Alexandra,** "protector, defender"). Familiar, **Sandy.**

Sandy (English: sandy, like the beach; variation of **Alexandra, Sandra**). Also, **Sandee, Sandey, Sandi, Sandie.** *Whatever:* To Gen Xers, this moniker belongs to Olivia Newton-John's goodie-goodie Pink Lady in the 1978 movie musical, *Grease.*

Santana (Spanish: saint). *Whatever:* Exotic, dramatic—and total *Dynasty.*

Sapphire (Greek: gemstone). Also, **Safire, Saphire.** *Whatever:* A quintessential little princess. Pretty, precious, and acceptably popular.

Sarah (Hebrew: princess). Also, **Sara, Sarra, Sarrah.** Familiar, **Sadie.** *Plus:* Baby boomers rescued this one from *Little House on the Prairie* obscurity in the 1980s. Now it's a perennial resident of top ten lists. Even in its downtime, **Sarah** had too much history going for it to be totally "out." In the Bible, **Sarah** is the wife of Abraham. A slam-dunk pocket T. *Minus:* Not exactly the find of the year for spelunkers.

Sari (Arabic: noble). Also, **Saree, Sarey, Sarie, Sarree, Sarrey, Sarri, Sarrie, Sarry, Sary.**

Sarit (Arabic: variation of **Sari,** "noble"). Also, **Saritt, Saryt, Sarytt.**

Sasha (Greek: variation of **Alexandra,** "protector, defender").

Saundra (Greek: variation of **Alexandra,** "protector, defender").

Savannah (English: a treeless plane). Also, **Savana, Savanah, Savanna.** *Plus:* A favorite in the South and West, **Savannah** charts strong in states such as Colorado and Georgia. The now-defunct Aaron Spelling prime-time soap of the same name didn't hurt its cause. Neither does **Savannah**'s combined pretty girl/map name qualities. *Minus:* Too new, too untested to be anything but a suspect for future trendy suspenders status. There's no gauging how it'll hold up. Remember when **Kimberly** was state of the art in the pretty girl name universe?

Savina (Latin: variation of **Sabina,** "from the **Sabine** clan in ancient Rome"). Also, **Saveena, Savyna.**

Sawyer (English: axman).

Sayer (English: victory of the people). Also, **Saer, Sayre.**

Scarlet (English: vivid red). Also, **Scarlett.** *Plus:* The original **Savannah**—not to mention the forerunner for today's pretty girls. Margaret Mitchell's vivid **Scarlett** O'Hara creation helped show America of the 1930s a way out of its **Mary-Betty-Mildred** rut, paving the way for the ascension of **Tiffany,** et al. *Minus:* Two reactions: (1) Swell, but what has **Scarlet** done for us lately?; and (2) Good. Now we know who to blame.

Schae (American: variation of **Shea,** "learned"). Also, **Schay.**

Schylar (Dutch: variation of **Skylar,** "to shelter"). Also, **Schylarr, Schyler, Schylerr, Schylur, Schylurr.** Familiar, **Skye.** *Whatever:* With **Skylar,** a comer.

Scully (Irish: scholar). Also, **Scullee, Sculleigh, Sculley, Sculli, Scullie.** *Whatever:* It'll be no mystery if this surname surges as a girl first name. Look no further than *The X-Files* and Agent **Scully** for an explanation.

Sean (Irish: variation of **John,** "God is gracious").

Seaton (English: town by the sea). Also, **Seaten, Seeten, Seeton, Seten, Seton.**

Seely (English: happy, blessed). Also, **Sealee, Sealey, Seali, Sealie, Sealy, Seelee, Seeley, Seeli, Seelie.**

Selda (German: variation of **Griselda,** "gray battle").

Selena (Greek: the moon). Also, **Seleena, Selina, Selyna.** *Whatever:* Look for slain Tejano singer **Selena**'s remarkable afterlife popularity to champion this contemporary pretty girl.

Selene (Greek: the moon). Also, **Seleene, Seline, Selyne.**

Sella (Latin: resting place). Also, **Sela.**

Selma (Irish: fair). *Plus:* Conjures cozy images of your great grannie— a pleasant trip down memory lane, à la **Sadie** or **Sophie.** *Minus:* When you met your great grannie she was really, really old and couldn't remember your name. You're not looking forward to revisiting that chapter of your life.

Serafina (Hebrew: on fire). Also, **Serafeena, Serafeenah, Serafinah, Serafyna, Serafynah.**

Seraphina (Hebrew: on fire). Also, **Serapheena, Serapheenah, Seraphinah, Seraphyna, Serphynah.**

Serena (Latin: calm, serene). Also, **Sereena, Serina, Seryna.** *Whatever:* Here's the alternative to **Samantha**. Die-hard **Bewitched** fans should take note that **Serena** was **Samantha** Stevens's naughty, look-alike cousin.

Seville (Spanish: from Seville). Also, **Sevill, Sevyll, Sevylle.**

Shakira (Arabic: variation of **Shakir,** "thankful"). Also, **Shakeera, Shakyra.**

Shana (Irish: variation of **John,** "God is gracious). Also, **Shaina, Shayna.**

Shane (Irish: variation of **John,** "God is gracious"). Also, **Shain, Shaine, Shayne.**

Shania (Irish: variation of **Shana,** "God is gracious"). Also, **Shanya, Shenia, Shenya.** *Whatever:* A comer. Watch country/pop singer **Shania** Twain crossover onto the baby name charts with this plucky entry.

Shaniqua (American: origin unknown). Also, **Shaneekwa, Shaneequa, Shanikwa, Shanykwa, Shanyqua, Sheneekwa, Sheneequa, Shenikwa, Sheniqua, Shenykwa, Shenyqua.**

Shannon (Irish: venerable, wise). Also, **Shanen, Shannen, Shanon.**

Plus: A bargain hunter's paradise. Since its heyday as the yuppie companion to **Megan** in the 1980s, **Shannon**'s popularity has cooled. Aesthetically, it's still very workable for an Irish lass. *Minus:* Famed namesake **Shannon** Doherty and her rampage of misadventures in the mid-1990s helped tarnish this one—at least in the short run.

Shante (French: singer). Also, **Shantae, Shantay.**

Shari (Irish: coltish; French: variation of **Sharice, Sharine**). Also, **Sharee, Sharey, Sharie, Sharree, Sharrey, Sharri, Sharrie, Sharry, Shary.**

Sharice (French: cherish). Also, **Shareece, Sharyce.** Familiar, **Shari.**

Sharine (French: variation of **Sharice,** "cherish"). Also, **Shareen, Shareene, Sharyne.** Familiar, **Shari.**

Sharon (Hebrew: plain where roses bloom). Also, **Sharen, Sharren, Sharron.** *Whatever:* Where have all the **Sharon**s gone? Check your old yearbook. Bet you can't turn more than a couple of pages without bumping into a **Sharon.** Today, **Sharon** is being shamed by the more glamorous, supposedly worldly likes of **Sierra** and **Samantha.** Still doable, just looking like a peanut-butter-and-jelly sandwich.

Sharona (Hebrew: variation of **Sharon,** "plain where roses bloom"). Also, **Sharonah, Sharonna, Sharonnah.** *Whatever:* That Knack song. 'Nuff said.

Shaun (Irish: variation of **John,** "God is gracious"). Also, **Shaunn.**

Shauna (Irish: variation of **Shaun,** "God is gracious"). Also, **Shaunna.**

Shawn (Irish: variation of **John,** "God is gracious"). Also, **Shawnn.**

Shawna (Irish: variation of **Shawn,** "God is gracious"). Also, **Shawnna.**

Shay (Irish: learned). Also, **Shaye.**

Shea (Irish: learned). Also, **Schea.**

Sheila (Latin: blind, gray-eyed). Also, **Sheela.**

Shelby (English: estate by the cliff). Also, **Shelbee, Shelbey, Shelbi, Shelbie.** *Plus:* Along with **Madison** and **Morgan,** the Southern-tinged **Shelby** is a power name for our times. *Minus:* Eternal flames do not emerge from *The Bonfire of the Vanities.* Classy as it sounds today, **Shelby** is a potential pair of trendy suspenders in the making.

Sheldon (English: flat hill). Also, **Shelden.** *Whatever:* Nerdy on a boy, doable on a girl.

Shell (English: a seashell). Also, **Shel.**

Shelly (English: shell, meadow). Also, **Sheli, Shellee, Shelleigh, Shelley, Shelli, Shellie.**

Shelton (English: flat town). Also, **Shelten.**

Shepherd (English: a sheep herder). Also, **Shepard, Sheperd, Shephard.**

Sherah (Latin: blind, gray-eyed). Also, **Shera.** *Whatever:* Sound-alike alternative to the more popular **Sarah.**

Shereen (Persian: sweet). Also, **Shereene.** Familiar, **Sheri.**

Sheri (English: variation of **Shereen, Sheryl, Sherylin**). Also, **Sheree, Sherey, Sherie, Shery.**

Sheridan (Irish: peaceful). Also, **Sheriden, Sheridyn, Sherydan, Sheryden, Sherydyn.**

Sherry (English: Spanish wine). Also, **Sherree, Sherrey, Sherri, Sherrie.**

Sheryl (French: beloved). Also, **Sheril, Sherill, Sherryl.** Familiar, **Sheri.** *Whatever:* A doable but tiring pretty girl, **Sheryl** doesn't pack the same winsome punch that it did back in the 1970s and 1980s.

Sherylin (English: combination of **Sheryl** and **Lynn**). Also, **Sherylinn, Sherylyn, Sherylynn.** Familiar, **Sheri.**

Shibhan (Irish: variation of **Siobhan**, "God is gracious"). Also, **Shiban, Shibann, Shibhann.**

Shon (Irish: variation of **John**, "God is gracious"). Also, **Shonn.**

Shona (Irish: variation of **Shon**, "God is gracious"). Also, **Shonna.**

Shoshanah (Hebrew: lily). Also, **Shoshana, Shoshanna.** *Whatever:* How big a shadow did **Seinfeld** cast? We'll soon find out. If one of Jerry Seinfeld's real-life ex-girlfriends—one **Shoshanna** Lonstein— can put oomph into this mouthful of a name just by virtue of her fifteen minutes of tabloid fame, then we can be sure that the Show About Nothing really was *the* show of the 1990s.

Sib (English: variation of **Sibyl**, "God's counsel"). Also, **Sibb.**

Sibyl (Greek: variation of **Sybill**, "God's counsel"). Also, **Sibil, Sibill, Sibyll.**

Sid (English: variation of **Sidney** "conqueror"). Also, **Sidd.**

Sidney (English: conqueror; French: riverside meadow). Also, **Sidnee, Sidni, Sidny.** Familiar, **Sid.**

Sierra (English/Spanish: rugged plains). Also, **Siera, Syera, Syerra.** *Plus:* Encourage your lil' cowpoke to ride the range with this free-wheeling, of-the-moment moniker. *Minus:* Will your lil' cowpoke be

roped in when her trendy suspenders are snapped? Here's guessing
this one's reign ends sooner, rather than later.

Sigournay (English: variation of **Sigourney,** "conqueror"). Also,
Sigournae.

Sigourney (English: conqueror). Also, **Sigournee, Sigourni,
Sigournie, Sigourny.** *Whatever:* Very cool. **Sigourney** is a strong, elegant, non-girlie-girl power name that doesn't have to steal from the
boys. Championed by very cool *Alien* star herself, **Sigourney** Weaver.

Siline (Latin: pink flowers). Also, **Sileen, Sileene, Silyne.**

Sima (Hebrew: gift). Also, **Simah.**

Simone (Hebrew: to hear). Also, **Symone.** *Plus:* An offbeat pocket T,
Simone won't crack anybody's most-popular lineup, but it's a grace-
ful, ageless performer with a **Grace**-like delicacy. *Minus:* It's nerdball
Simon with an *e* tacked on the end.

Sinclair (Scottish: bright). Also, **Sinclare, Synclair, Synclare.**

Siobhan (Irish: God is gracious). Also, **Sioban, Siobann, Siobhann.**
Whatever: If **Shannon** is sounding tired, try out **Siobhan**—an underused gem of an Irish lass.

Sirena (Greek: a siren). Also, **Sireena, Sirina, Siryna.**

Sirene (Greek: a siren). Also, **Sireen, Sireene, Siryne.**

Sivana (Hebrew: from Sivan, ninth month of Hebrew calendar). Also,
Sivanah.

Skye (English: the sky; Dutch: variation of **Schylar, Skylar**). Also, **Sky.**

Skylar (Dutch: to shelter). Also, **Skyler, Skylerr, Skylur, Skylurr.** Familiar, **Skye.** *Whatever:* A comer. A new power name to help ease the
gridlock at the **Madison-Morgan-Taylor** intersection.

Sloan (Irish: fighter). Also, **Sloane, Slone.** *Whatever:* Mia Sara played
Sloane, the game gal-pal in the classic 1980s-era teen movie *Ferris
Bueller's Day Off.*

Sly (English: sly, wily). Also, **Slye.**

Sofia (Slavic: variation of **Sophia,** "wisdom"). Also, **Sofeea, Sofya.**

Sola (Latin: alone).

Soledad (Latin: solitary one). Also, **Solidad, Solydad.** *Whatever:* Not
just for state prisons anymore. MSNBC reporter **Soledad** O'Brien
proves this unique entry worthy of first-name consideration.

Solita (Italian: variation of **Sola,** "alone"). Also, **Soleeta, Solyta.**

Soloma (Persian: peaceable).

Sona (Hindi: gold).

Sondra (Greek: variation of **Alexandra,** "protector, defender").

Sonel (Hebrew: lily). Also, **Sonell.**

Sonja (Scandinavian: variation of **Sonya,** "wise").

Sonya (Slavic: wise). Also, **Sonia.** *Whatever:* A turn-of-the-century throwback that's crossing into yet another century with its regal style intact. That sort of endurance makes it a worthy pocket T.

Sophia (Greek: wisdom). Also, **Sopheea, Sophya.** Familiar, **Sophie.** *Whatever:* Another **Sonya.** Another pocket T.

Sophie (Greek: variation of **Sophia,** "wisdom"). Also, **Sophee, Sophey, Sophi, Sophy.**

Sora (Native American: songbird). Also, **Sorra.**

Sori (Native American: variation of **Sora,** "songbird"). Also, **Soree, Sorey, Sorie, Sory.**

Sosannah (Hebrew: variation of **Susannah,** "rose"). Also, **Sosana, Sosanah, Sosanna.**

Soshana (Hebrew: variation of **Shoshanah,** "lily"). Also, **Soshanah.**

Spaulding (English: a surname). Also, **Spalding.**

Spencer (English: steward). Also, **Spenser.** *Whatever:* A booming boy name that still sounds unique and stately on a girl. In fact, give it a couple years and we'll filch this one from those unsuspecting males, too.

Stacy (Greek: variation of **Anastace, Anastice, Onastace, Onastice**). Also, **Stacee, Stacey, Staci, Stacie.** *Whatever:* A pretty girl doing the fast fade into peanut-butter-and-jelly sandwich territory.

Stefanie (English: variation of **Stephanie,** "crown"). Also, **Stefanee, Stefaney, Stefani, Stefany, Stefenee, Stefeney, Stefeni, Stefenie, Stefeny.** Familiar, **Steffi.**

Steffi (English: variation of **Stefanie, Stephanie**). Also, **Steffee, Steffey, Steffie, Steffy, Stefi.**

Stella (Latin: star). Also, **Stela.**

Stephanie (Greek: variation of **Stephen,** "crown"). Also, **Stephanee, Stephaney, Stephani, Stephany, Stephenee, Stepheney, Stepheni, Stephenie, Stepheny.** Familiar, **Steffi, Stevie.** *Plus:* The new **Kimberly.** Popular, perky, pink—one of the ultimate pretty girls. Another selection that will dominate cheerleader squads of the new millennium. *Minus:* We need a new **Kimberly** because the old one didn't hang around very long. Some pretty girls are faint of heart.

Stevie (English: variation of **Stephanie,** "crown"). Also, **Stevee,**

Stevey, Stevi, Stevy. *Plus:* You like Fleetwood Mac. *Minus:* You don't *live* Fleetwood Mac.

Stockard (English: stockyard).

Suanne (English: combination of **Sue** and **Anne**). Also, **Suann, Sue Ann, SueAnn, Sueann, Sue Anne, SueAnne, Sueanne.**

Sue (English: variation of **Susan, Suzan**). *Whatever:* A peanut-butter-and-jelly sandwich. . . . Make that a double.

Sullivan (Irish: black-eyed). Also, **Sulivan, Sullyvan, Sulyvan.** *Whatever:* Doesn't take much of a stretch to see how this boy name could fit into a **Taylor/Madison/Murphy** unisex world.

Summer (English: a season). *Whatever:* Borderline hippie. But at least it's slightly less trippy than, say, **Sunshine.**

Susan (Hebrew: rose; Irish: radiant). Also, **Susen.** Familiar, **Sue, Susie.** *Whatever:* Tough times for good ol' **Sue.** From the 1950s to 1970s, **Susan** was an all-American baby name staple. Today, it doesn't qualify for either classic or little princess status. Rather, it's a dutiful, generic peanut-butter-and-jelly sandwich.

Susannah (Hebrew: variation of **Susan,** "rose"). Also, **Susana, Susanah, Susanna.** Familiar, **Susie.**

Susette (French: variation of **Susan,** "rose"). Also, **Susett.** Familiar, **Susie.**

Susie (English: variation of **Susan, Susannah, Susette**). Also, **Susee, Susey, Susi, Susy.**

Sutton (English: southern town). Also, **Suten, Sutten, Suton.**

Suzan (American: variation of **Susan,** "rose"). Also, **Suzen.** Familiar, **Sue, Suzi.**

Suzanna (American: variation of **Susannah,** "rose"). Also, **Suzana.** Familiar, **Suzi.**

Suzanne (Hebrew/French: rose). Also, **Suzann.** Familiar, **Suzi.**

Suzette (French: variation of **Susan,** "rose"). Also, **Suzett.** Familiar, **Suzi.**

Suzi (American: variation of **Suzan, Suzanne, Suzette**). Also, **Suzee, Suzey, Suzie, Suzy.**

Syb (English: variation of **Sybill,** "God's counsel"). Also, **Sybb.**

Sybill (Greek: God's counsel). Also, **Sybil, Sybyl, Sybyll.** Familiar, **Syb.** *Whatever:* This could be another **Sonya** or **Sophia** if it wasn't so freakin' synonymous with multiple-personality disorders. (Find *Sybil,* the book, or the Sally Field TV miniseries.)

Syd (English: variation of **Sydney**, "conqueror"). Also, **Sydd.**

Sydney (English: conqueror; French: riverside meadow). Also, **Sydnee, Sydni, Sydny.** Familiar, **Syd.** *Whatever:* Looking good—and thriving even—as a girl selection. A lower voltage power name. *Minus:* **Sydney** Andrews was *Melrose Place*'s resident madam, stripper, and all-around screw-up. Pray the middle school boys don't catch the reruns.

Sylvan (Latin: from the woods). Also, **Silvan, Silven, Silvyn, Sylven, Sylvyn.**

Sylvana (Latin: from the woods). Also, **Silvana, Silvanna, Sylvanna.**

Sylvia (Latin: from the woods). Also, **Silvia, Silvya, Sylvya.** Familiar, **Sylvie.** *Plus:* Just as sophisticated as **Sonya** or **Sophia.** *Minus:* A touch less contemporary than **Sonya** or **Sophia.**

Sylvie (Latin: variation of **Sylvia**, "from the woods"). Also, **Silvee, Silvey, Silvi, Silvie, Silvy, Sylvee, Sylvey, Sylvi, Sylvy.**

Syna (Greek: together). Also, **Sina.**

T

CRIB NOTES

Famous Ts: **Tabitha** Soren (MTV News maven); **Tatum** O'Neal (Oscar-winner, *Paper Moon*); **Tempestt** Bledsoe (former *Cosby Show* kid); **Teri** Hatcher (Lois Lane, TV's *Lois and Clark*); **Tiffany** (1980s teen pop star); **Tipper** Gore (vice-presidential spouse); **Tonya** Harding (figure-skater-gone-bad); **Tori** Spelling (*Beverly Hills, 90210* thespian); **Tyra** Banks (model)

Pocket Ts: Tess, Thea

Trendy suspenders: Taylor, Tiffany

Think long, think hard: Taffy (Perfect . . . if you're expecting a Bengal Toy Leopard, or a carhop waitress.); **Tallulah** (A tad much.); **Temperance** (Do-gooder causes are most appropriately fought with marker pens and poster board, not baby names.); **Tiara** (Pamper your little princess all you want but consider letting her earn her own crown.); **Tipper** (**Tipper** Gore didn't start out a **Tipper,** you know. She was a **Mary Elizabeth.** It's always a good idea to give yourself something to work with—and return to.)

Tabby (English: cat; Hebrew: variation of **Tabitha,** "gazelle"). Also, **Tabbi, Tabbie.** *Plus:* Pleasant. *Minus:* Puh-leeze.

Tabitha (Hebrew: gazelle). Also, **Tabithah, Tabytha, Tabythah.** Familiar, **Tabby.** *Plus:* Here's the **Samantha** Less Traveled. Like **Sam,** the name is tooled for the times—pretty, precious, and vowel-friendly. It's also got its very own *Betwitched* connection. **Tabitha** was **Samantha** Stevens's daughter on the 1964–72 sitcom. *Minus:* It's nickname is about as appealing as a hairball.

Tabla (Arabic: drum).

Tacy (English: silence). Also, **Tacee, Tacey, Taci, Tacie.**

Taeshawna (American: variation of **Shawna,** "God is gracious"). Also, **Taeseana, Taeshauna, Taeshona, Tayseana, Tayshauna, Tayshawna, Tayshona.**

Taft (English/Irish: yard). Also, **Tafte.** *Whatever:* If you're hooked on **Taffy,** try this less cartoony sound-alike. Your future brain surgeon or trial attorney will thank you.

Talia (Hebrew: morning dew). Also, **Taliah, Talya, Talyah.**

Tally (Irish: peaceful). Also, **Tallee, Talley, Talli, Tally, Taly.**

Tam (Vietnamese: heart). Also, **Tamm.**

Tamar (Hebrew: palm tree). Also, **Tamarr.**

Tamara (Hebrew: palm tree; Indian: spice). Also, **Tamarah, Tamarra, Tamarrah, Tamera, Tamerah, Tamerra, Tamerrah.** Familiar, **Tammy.** *Whatever:* This is an example of how the baby name market has gone upscale. When Gen Xers were in school, plain old **Tammy** was the rule; **Tamara** the exception. Now, **Tammy**'s a peanut-butter-and-jelly sandwich and the more formal **Tamara** is the prized little princess. The lesson: Even if you intend to call your kid by her nickname from day one, put the full name on the birth certificate.

Tamia (English: variation of **Tammy,** "palm tree"). Also, **Tameea, Tamya.** Familiar, **Tammy.**

Tammy (Hebrew/Irish: variation of **Tamara, Tamony, Tamra**). Also, **Tami, Tammee, Tammey, Tammi, Tammie, Tamy.**

Tamony (Irish: tympany player). Also, **Tamanee, Tamaney, Tamani, Tamanie, Tamany, Tamonee, Tamoney, Tamoni, Tamonie.** Familiar, **Tammy.** *Whatever:* An appealing, sound-alike twist on the more common **Tamara.**

Tamra (Hebrew: palm tree). Also, **Tamrah.** Familiar, **Tammy.**

Tana (Slavic: variation of **Tanya,** "fairy queen"). Also, **Tanna.**

Tandy (English: team). Also, **Tandee, Tandey, Tandi, Tandie.** *Whatever:* You say kindergartens are filling up with **Taylors** and **Shelbys**? **Tandy** to the rescue. It's preppie, unisex, and looks great in evening wear—or dress-casual-Friday khakis. A pick to click.

Tanis (Lithuanian: immortal). Also, **Taniss, Tanys, Tanyss.**

Tanya (Russian: variation of **Tatiana,** "fairy queen"). Also, **Tania.** *Whatever:* Baby names rise and fall with pop-culture figures. **Tonya**

Harding's ice-rink misadventures during the 1994 Winter Olympics sucker-punched this usually reliable selection.

Tara (Irish: hill). Also, **Tarra.** *Plus:* Finally, a comely Irish lass that's not being reproduced in mass quantities. *Minus:* There's a reason **Tara** isn't burning up the popularity charts. Been there, done that. **Tara** was a 1970s attempt to raid the Emerald Isle for baby names.

Taran (Irish: variation of **Tara,** "hill"). Also, **Taren, Tarran, Tarren, Tarryn, Taryn.** *Whatever:* **Tara** for today.

Taro (English: tropical vegetable). Also, **Tarro.**

Tasha (Russian: variation of **Natasha,** "born on Christmas Day"). Also, **Tashe.**

Tashawna (American: variation of **Shawna,** "God is gracious"). Also, **Taseana, Tashauna, Tashona, Teseana, Teshauna, Teshawna, Teshona.**

Tashka (Russian: variation of **Natasha,** "born on Christmas Day"). Also, **Tashca, Tashcka.**

Tasma (Hebrew: twin). Also, **Tasmah.**

Tasmin (Hebrew: twin). Also, **Tasminn, Tasmyn, Tasmynn.** *Whatever:* An über little princess entry—rhymes with **Jasmine,** no less. Very, very today.

Tasmind (Hebrew: variation of **Tasmin,** "twin"). Also, **Tasmynd.**

Tate (English: cheerful). Also, **Tait, Tayte.** *Whatever:* Another **Tandy,** although arguably not as perky-cute as that classic.

Tatiana (Russian: fairy queen). Also, **Tatianna, Tatyana, Tatyanna.**

Tatum (English: cheerful). Also, **Tatem, Tatym.** *Plus:* Twenty-five years past **Tatum** O'Neal's trailblazing Gen X–era Oscar win, this name is now safely past its trendy phase. *Minus:* Unfortunately, it hasn't really transitioned into its compelling, relevant phase.

Taura (Latin: from Taurus, the bull). *Whatever:* Perfect for astrology buffs.

Tawny (French: tanned, the color of light brown). Also, **Taunee, Tauni, Tawnee, Tawney, Tawni, Tawnie.**

Tayanita (Native American: a beaver). Also, **Tayaneeta, Tayanyta.** *Whatever:* A fine pretty girl candidate. Especially if you take into account that you're the only one who needs to know what the thing *really* means.

Taylor (English: a tailor). Also, **Tayler.** *Plus:* A quintessential power name pulling down monster numbers on the popularity charts. *Minus:*

Be suspicious of names that owe their monster numbers to the daytime soaps. In 1990, *The Bold and the Beautiful* introduced a character called Dr. **Taylor** Hayes. The name started climbing the charts shortly thereafter. Coinky-dink? A telltale sign of trendy suspenders.

Tazmin (Hebrew: variation of **Tasmin,** "twin"). Also, **Tazminn, Tazmyn, Tazmynn.**

Tazmind (Hebrew: variation of **Tazmin,** "twin"). Also, **Tazmynd.**

Tehara (Egyptian: blooming). Also, **Tihara, Tyhara.** *Whatever:* A less literal alternative to its rugged sound-alike cousins **Sahara** and **Sierra.**

Tela (Latin: web). Also, **Tella.**

Telma (Greek: determination).

Tempest (English: stormy). Also, **Tempesst, Tempestt.**

Teodora (English: ruler of the people; Slavic: variation of **Theodora,** "gift from God"). Also, **Teodorra.**

Teresa (Greek: to reap; English: the hunter). Also, **Tereesa.** Familiar, **Terry.** *Plus:* Dependable, doable—and, hey, it's got vowel action! *Minus:* Tired.

Terra (Italian: baked earth). Also, **Tera.**

Terry (English: ruler of the people; Greek/English: variation of **Teresa, Theresa**). Also, **Teri, Terree, Terrey, Terri, Terrie, Tery.**

Tess (Greek/English: variation of **Teresa, Theresa**). Also, **Tes.** *Whatever:* Understated sophistication. It's a style that worked in Thomas Hardy's nineteenth-century novel *Tess of the d'Urbervilles;* it's a style that works today. A pocket T.

Tessa (Greek: fourth). Also, **Tesa.** *Whatever:* An uncommon pretty girl for spelunkers.

Tessella (Latin: small, square stone). Also, **Tesela, Tesella, Tessela.**

Tessie (English: variation of **Teresa, Theresa**). Also, **Tesi, Tessee, Tessey, Tessi, Tessy.**

Thalia (Greek: blooming). Also, **Thalya.**

Thayer (English: army of the people). Also, **Thayor.**

Thea (Greek: divine). Also, **Theea, Thia, Thya.** *Whatever:* A contemporarly little princess sound with a timeless feel. That's a pocket T.

Theda (Greek: divine). Also, **Theeda, Thida, Thyda.**

Thelma (Greek: determination). *Plus:* Your daughter is **Thelma.** Hear her roar. *Minus:* Your daughter is **Thelma.** Hear people ask, "Where's **Louise**?"

Theodora (English: ruler of the people; Greek: variation of **Theodore,** "gift from God"). Also, **Theodorra.**

Theora (Hebrew: God's voice). Also, **Theorah, Theorra, Theorrah.**

Thera (Greek: wild). Also, **Therra.**

Theresa (Greek: to reap; English: the hunter). Also, **Thereesa, Therisa, Therysa.** Familiar, **Terry.**

Therna (Norwegian: a bird).

Thora (Norse: from Thor, god of thunder). Also, **Thorra.** *Whatever:* A pick to click. It's amazing what one little letter—especially a vowel—can do. Without the *a,* it's **Thor,** a virtually unusable boy name. With the *a,* it's **Thora,** a Viking that can pass itself off as an old-fashioned, *Little House on the Prairie* **Sarah** type.

Tia (Spanish: aunt; Greek: princess). Also, **Teea, Tya.**

Tiffany (Greek: from Theophania, epiphany). Also, **Tifani, Tifany, Tifeni, Tifeny, Tiffanee, Tiffaney, Tiffani, Tiffanie, Tiffenee, Tiffeney, Tiffeni, Tiffeny.** *Plus:* Give credit where credit's due. Defying conventional wisdom, this name is demonstrating more staying power than singer **Tiffany**'s own recording career. *Minus:* It's still a *Dynasty* name with a strong chance of one day looking as outrageous as reruns of the old Joan Collins TV series. A pair of trendy suspenders.

Tilly (Latin: shade tree). Also, **Tili, Tillee, Tilley, Tilli, Tillie.**

Tina (Greek: variation of **Christina,** "follower of Christ"). Also, **Teena, Tyna.** *Plus:* Pretty 'n' nice **Tina** makes you nostalgic for old middle school chums. *Minus:* That kind of nostalgia ought to tell you something: You're lonesome for the name because you don't hear it anymore. Why? Because it's *not* happening.

Tira (Hebrew: camp). Also, **Tirah.**

Tita (Latin: safe). Also, **Teeta, Tyta.**

Toby (English: God is good). Also, **Tobee, Tobey, Tobi, Tobie.** *Plus:* A cuddly bear for girls . . . *Minus:* . . . that's slightly on the 1970s side.

Toni (Greek: variation of **Antoinette, Antonetta**) Also, **Tonee, Toney, Tonie, Tony.**

Tonya (Russian: variation of **Tatiana,** "fairy queen"). Also, **Tonia.**

Topaz (English: precious stone).

Tory (English: victorious; Latin: variation of **Victoria,** "conqueror"). Also, **Toree, Torey, Tori, Torie.** *Plus:* A spunky, of-the-moment cuddly bear. *Minus:* A constant reminder of **Tori** Spelling.

Tova (Hebrew: God is good). Also, **Tovah.**

Trace (English: to sketch; variation of **Tracy,** "balcony"). Also, **Traice, Trayce.**

Tracy (English: balcony). Also, **Tracee, Tracey, Traci, Tracie.** Familiar, **Trace.** *Plus:* A state-of-the-art pretty girl . . . *Minus:* . . . in the 1960s.

Trella (French: trellis). Also, **Trela.**

Tressa (Greek: variation of **Teresa, Theresa**). Also, **Tresa.** *Plus:* Makes a delightful alternative to **Tess.** *Minus:* Sounds disturbingly like an ode to big hair.

Treva (Celtic: judicious).

Tricia (Latin: variation of **Patricia,** "noble"). Also, **Tricya, Trycia, Trycya.** Familiar, **Trish.** *Whatever:* What the "in" crowd is wearing . . . if you hop a ride on a time capsule to 1982. It's still doable, it's just not going to feel as fancy in our Brave New **Ashley** World.

Trilby (English: soft hat). Also, **Trilbee, Trilbey, Trilbi, Trilbie.** *Whatever:* Could easily be mistaken, or mispronounced, as "tribble." A *Plus* or *Minus* depending on your affection for *Star Trek.*

Trish (English: variation of **Tricia, Trisha**). Also, **Trysh.**

Trisha (Latin: variation of **Patricia,** "noble"). Also, **Trysha.** Familiar, **Trish.**

Trista (Celtic/French: variation of **Tristan, Tristina, Tristine**). Also, **Trysta.**

Tristan (Celtic: din; French: sad). Also, **Tristen, Tristyn, Trystan, Trysten, Trystyn.** Familiar, **Trista.**

Tristina (Celtic: din; French: sad). Also, **Tristeena, Tristyna.** Familiar, **Trista.** *Whatever:* The new **Tina.**

Tristine (Celtic: din; French: sad). Also, **Tristeene, Tristyne.** Familiar, **Trista.**

Trixy (French: variation of **Beatrice,** "blessing"). Also, **Trixee, Trixey, Trixi, Trixie.** *Whatever:* **Trixie** was the spunky navigator/girlfriend in the 1960s 'toon *Speed Racer.*

Tru (English: true; German: variation of **Gertrude,** "spear, strength"). Also, **True.**

Trudy (German: variation of **Gertrude,** "spear, strength"). Also, **Trudee, Trudey, Trudi, Trudie.** *Whatever:* From hopeless, outmoded **Gertrude** this comes: a sprightly entry that's every bit the contemporary of recently recovered throwbacks such as **Sadie** and **Sophie.**

Tucker (English: cloth cleaner). Also, **Tukker.**

Tuesday (English: third day of the week). Also, **Tuesdae.**

Turney (Irish: lord). Also, **Turnee, Turni, Turnie, Turny.** *Whatever:* Schoolyard taunt alert: rhymes with "gurney."

Twaina (English: two). Also, **Twayna.**

Tyler (English: tile layer). Also, **Tiler, Tilor, Tylor.** *Whatever:* Can you really steal this favorite from the boys just to fashion it as your own private **Taylor?** Sure. All's fair in baby names.

Tyndall (English: burning light). Also, **Tyndal, Tyndel, Tyndell, Tyndyl, Tyndyll.**

Tyne (English: river). Also, **Tine.**

Tyra (German: strong; English: dress). Also, **Tira.** *Whatever:* Supermodel-approved.

U

CRIB NOTES

Famous Us: Lieutenant **Uhura** (communications officer, *Star Trek*); **Uma** Thurman (actor, *Pulp Fiction*); **Ursula** ('toonland gal-pal, *George of the Jungle*)

Pocket Ts: Take a look at the gang above. Two of the "famous" Us aren't even *real* people. This ought to give you a clue that U isn't exactly a prime baby name breeding ground. On the plus side, this is a great stop for the unique and uncommon.

Trendy suspenders: Uh, no.

Think long, think hard: Unity (Hippie city).; **Urania/Uriana** (Too close to **Uranus**. 'Nuff said.)

Udella   (English: variation of **Udelle,** "valley of yew or evergreen trees). Also, **Udela.**
Udelle   (English: valley of yew or evergreen trees). Also, **Udell.**
Uhura   (Swahili: freedom). Also, **Uhurra.** *Whatever:* Pretty and timeless in its own way—and as Trekker monikers go, a much wiser *Star Trek* choice than, say, **Bones.**
Ukeisha   (American: variation of **Aisah,** "life"). Also, **Ukeesha, Ukeysha, Ukisha, Ukysha.**
Ula   (Irish: jewel of the sea). Also, **Uula.**
Ulanda   (German: variation of **Uland,** "noble country").
Ulani   (Hawaiian: cheerful). Also, **Ulanee, Ulaney, Ulanie, Ulany.**
Ulanna   (African: variation of **Ulan,** "firstborn twin"). Also, **Ulana.**
Ulima   (Arabic: wise). Also, **Uleema, Ulyma.**

Ulrica (German: wolf, ruler). Also, **Ulreeca, Ulreecka, Ulreeka, Ulricka, Ulrika, Ulryca, Ulrycka, Ulryka.**

Ultima (Latin: ultimate). Also, **Ulteema, Ultyma.**

Uma (Hebrew: nation). Also, **Uuma.** *Plus:* Thanks to *Pulp Fiction*'s **Uma** Thurman, this entry is the hippest U on the block. *Minus:* Conjures memories of David Letterman's interminable "**Uma,** Oprah. Oprah, **Uma,**" Oscar-night mantra.

Umar (Arabic: bloom). Also, **Umaar, Umarr.**

Umbra (Latin: shade).

Ume (Japanese: plum). Also, **Umee, Umey, Umi, Umie, Umy.**

Umher (German: around, about). Also, **Umherr.**

Umiko (Japanaese: child). Also, **Umeeco, Umeecko, Umeeko, Umicko, Umico, Umycko, Umyco, Umyko.**

Una (Latin: one). Also, **Uuna.** *Whatever:* This one's the **Uma** Less Traveled.

Unica (Latin: variation of **Unique,** "unique"). Also, **Uneeca, Uneecka, Uneeka, Unicka, Unika, Unyca, Unycka, Unyka.**

Unikwa (American: variation of **Unique,** "unique"). Also, **Uneekwa, Unykwa.**

Uniqua (American: variation of **Unique,** "unique"). Also, **Uneeqa, Uneequa, Uniqa, Unyqa, Unyqua.**

Unique (English: unique). *Plus:* Arguably, the bomb as far as "unique" names are concerned. *Minus:* Yeah, it's a bomb, all right.

Unna (Latin: variation of **Una,** "one"; Teutonic: woman).

Uri (Hebrew: light; Hebrew/Welsh: variation of **Uriah, Urian, Urielle, Urienne**). Also, **Uree, Urey, Uric, Ury.**

Uriah (Hebrew: light). Also, **Uria, Urya, Uryah.** Familiar, **Uri.**

Urian (Welsh: fortunate). Also, **Urien, Uryan, Uryen.** Familiar, **Uri.**

Urie (Scottish: yew trees). Also, **Uree, Urey, Uri, Ury.**

Urielle (Hebrew: variation of **Uriel,** "light"). Also, **Uriell, Uryell, Uryelle.** Familiar, **Uri.** *Whatever:* More common as a boy name, **Urielle** also can offer wiggle room on little princess supreme **Ariel.**

Urienne (Hebrew: variation of **Urien,** "light"). Also, **Urien, Uriene, Urienn, Uryen, Uryene, Uryenn, Uryenne.** Familiar, **Uri.**

Ursa (Latin: bear). *Whatever:* More than a little princess, **Ursa** sounds like a "little goddess." It's pretty, modern, and alluring.

Ursina (Latin: little bear). Also, **Urseena, Ursyna.**

Ursula (Latin: female bear). Also, **Ursulla.** *Whatever:* Lisa Kudrow occasionally plays a character named **Ursula** on TV's *Friends* and *Mad About You*. If **Ursula** doesn't get a boost out of this (not to mention *George of the Jungle*), nothing's going to rescue it from its 1960s sex-kitten reputation.

Ushi (Chinese: ox). Also, **Ushee, Ushey, Ushie, Ushy.**

Usra (Sanskrit: immortal).

Uta (Japanese: lyric, poem). Also, **Uuta.**

Utina (Native American: my country). Also, **Uteena, Utyna.**

Uva (Latin: grape). Also, **Uuva.**

Uzielle (Hebrew: powerful). Also, **Uziell, Uzyell, Uzyelle.**

Uzra (Sanskrit: variation of **Usra,** "immortal").

V

CRIB NOTES

Famous Vs: **Valerie** Bertinelli (good daughter Barbara Cooper, TV's *One Day at a Time*); **Vanessa** L. Williams (singer/actor, *Soul Food*); **Vanity** (former Prince cohort); **Vanna** White (professional pointer, TV's *Wheel of Fortune*); **Venus** Williams (tennis player); **Veronica** Lodge (gal-pal, "Archie" comics); **Victoria** Principal (actor, TV's *Dallas*); **Vivica** A. Fox (actor, *Independence Day*); **Vonda** Shepard (*Ally McBeal* songstress)

Pocket Ts: **Vanessa, Vivian**

Trendy suspenders: None

Think long, think hard: **Valene** (Joan Van Ark played ditsy drama queen **Valene** on TV's *Knots Landing* for fourteen long years. Today, the entry looks about as sophisticated as a leopard-skin couch.); **Vanna** (Game shows are for entertainment purposes only.); **Vanity** (Uh, no.); **Velma** (True, **Velma** was the smart one from *Scooby-Doo, Where Are You?* Unfortunately, she was outshined by a scraggly bum and a dog with whiskers. Not exactly a shining moment in the history of the name.); **Velvet** (It's a *fabric,* people.)

Vail (English/Scottish: valley). Also, **Vaile, Vale, Vayle.** *Whatever:* Isn't **Vail** a ski resort town in Colorado? Yeah, and since when is that going to discourage a nation of **Dakota**-heads? This is just as much a "real" name as anything else. Go for it.

Val (Latin: variation of **Valencia, Valentina, Valentine, Valeria, Valerie**).

Valencia (Latin: strength). Also, **Valencya, Valincia, Valincya, Valyncia, Valyncya.** Familiar, **Val.** *Plus:* To the majority of residents in the United States, this is an exotic map name in the tradition of **Cheyenne.** *Minus:* To Californians, this is about as exotic as **Burbank.**

Valentina (Latin: variation of **Valentine,** "strong"). Also, **Valenteena, Valentyna, Valinteena, Valintina, Valyntina.** Familiar, **Tina, Val.**

Valentine (Latin: strong). Also, **Valentyne, Valintine, Valintyne, Valyntine.** Familiar, **Val.** *Whatever:* A name that doesn't hide its heart, but that's OK. It works for girls.

Valeria (Latin: variation of **Valerie,** "strong"). Also, **Valerya.** Familiar, **Val.**

Valerie (Latin: strong). Also, **Valeree, Valerey, Valeri, Valery, Valiri, Valyri.** Familiar, **Val.** *Plus:* A *nice* name. It reminds you of **Valerie** Bertinelli, who seems like a nice person and who once starred in a nice sitcom of your youth called *One Day at a Time* (1975–84). *Minus:* "Nice" is getting trampled by the regal little princesses and the take-no-prisoners power names.

Vaneisha (American: unknown origin). Also, **Vaneesha, Vaneysha, Veneysha.**

Vanessa (Greek: butterfly). Also, **Vanesa, Vanisa, Vanissa, Vanysa, Vanyssa.** *Whatever:* This is an assured, stylish name that's always dressed to kill. A pocket T.

Vanita (Sanskrit: hoped for). Also, **Vaneeta, Vanyta.**

Vanora (Celtic: white wave). Also, **Vanorra.**

Vara (Greek: stranger). Also, **Varra.**

Vega (Arabic: star; Spanish: meadow). Also, **Vaega, Vaga, Vayga, Veyga.** *Plus:* Not just for cheap Chevys anymore. This nifty, offbeat entry swings. **Vega** sounds like a kicky diet soda, circa the 1960s. *Minus:* Two words: Viva Las.

Venetia (Latin: blessed). Also, **Veneetia, Veneetya, Venetya, Venitia, Venitya, Venytia, Venytya.** *Plus:* Mysterious and romantic . . . *Minus:* . . . unless, of course, it happens to remind you of dusty venetian blinds.

Venice (latin: blessed). Also, **Venyce.** *Whatever:* The Eurostyle map name.

Ventura (Latin: venture). Also, **Ventera, Venterra, Venturra.**

Venus (Latin: goddess of love). Also, **Venuss.** *Whatever:* Until recently this entry would have been destined for the *Think long, think hard* department. But now it's got a champion, teen tennis star **Venus** Williams. And you know how these things work—**Venus** suddenly sounds more than OK.

Ver (Latin: spring). Also, **Verr.**

Verda (Latin: young).

Verde (Latin: fresh). Also, **Verdae, Verday.**

Verena (German: guardian). Also, **Vereena, Verina, Veryna.**

Verona (Latin: truthful). Also, **Veronna.**

Veronica (Latin: true image). Also, **Veronicka, Veronika, Veronyca, Veronycka, Veronyka.** Familiar, **Ronnie.** *Whatever:* Like **Victoria** but without the underwear baggage.

Veronique   (French: variation of **Veronica,** "true image"). Also, **Veroniqe, Veronyq, Veronyqe.**

Verra (Sanskrit: faith). Also, **Vera.**

Vesta (Latin: goddess of fire).

Vicky (Latin: variation of **Victoria, Viktoria**). Also, **Vickee, Vickey, Vicki, Vickie, Vikki, Vikky.**

Victoria   (Latin: conqueror). Also, **Victorya.** Familiar, **Tori, Vicky.** *Plus:* Popular and historic—a queenly little princess. *Minus:* Could get plowed under like so many **Kimberly**s if, and when, the little princesses get overthrown.

Vida (Hebrew: life). Also, **Veeda, Vyda.** *Plus:* A kicky, contemporary compact—the Geo Metro of baby names. *Minus:* Geo Metro? **Vida** ain't that modern. It's strictly a horse-and-buggy mode of transportation.

Viktoria (Slavic: variation of **Victoria,** "conqueror"). Also, **Viktorya.** Familiar, **Vicky.**

Villa (Latin: farm). Also, **Vila, Vyla, Vylla.**

Vina (Italian/Spanish: wine; Sanskrit: a stringed instrument). Also, **Veena, Vyna.**

Vinessa (American: variation of **Vanessa,** "butterfly"). Also, **Vinesa, Vinisa, Vinissa, Vinysa, Vinyssa.**

Viola (Latin: violet). Also, **Vyola.** *Plus:* **Viola** is a name that's pretty and would-be contemporary (yea, vowel action!) . . . *Minus:* . . . But it's ultimately for orchestra lovers only.

Violet (Latin: the color of deep purple-blue). Also, **Violett, Vyolet, Vyolett.**

Violetta (Italian: variation of **Violet,** "the color of deep purple-blue"). Also, **Violeta, Vyoleta, Vyoletta.**

Virginia (Latin: maiden). Also, **Virginya, Virginia, Virgynya.** Familiar, **Ginny.** *Plus:* If **Victoria,** why not **Virginia?** Why not indeed? It's dignified. It's stately. It's queenly. *Minus:* The only **Virginia**s you've ever known lived in old black-and-white TV Westerns.

Vita (Latin: life). Also, **Veeta, Vyta.**

Vitoria (Spanish: variation of **Victoria,** "conqueror"). Also, **Vitorea, Vitorya.**

Vittoria (Italian: variation of **Victoria,** "conqueror"). Also, **Vittorea, Vittorya.**

Viv (Latin: variation of **Vivian,** "alive"). Also, **Vivv, Vyv, Vyvv.** *Plus:* **Viv** is a nickname bursting with vim and vigor. *Minus:* There's only so much vim and vigor you can stomach.

Viva (Latin: long life). Also, **Veeva, Vyva.** *Plus:* Pretty, lively. *Minus:* Paper towel-esque.

Viveca (Latin: alive). Also, **Vivecka, Viveka, Vivica, Vivicka, Vivika.**

Vivia (Latin: lively). Also, **Vivya.**

Vivian (Latin: alive). Also, **Vivien, Vivyan.** Familiar, **Viv.** *Plus:* A pocket T, **Vivian** is a never-in, never-out, graceful classic. *Minus:* You think **Vivian,** you think **Vivian** Vance, you think *I Love Lucy,* you think Ethel. You think you're not enjoying this train of thought.

Viviana (Latin: alive). Also, **Vivianna, Vivyana, Vivyanna.**

Vonda (Slavic: variation of **Vondra,** "loving").

Vondra (Slavic: loving). *Whatever:* Exotic sound-alike for **Sandra/ Sondra.** Very cool.

Vonna (French: variation of **Yvonne,** "young archer"). Also, **Vona.** *Whatever:* Another hipster. Timely, pretty—not at all precious.

Vonni (Scandinavian: variation of **Von,** "hope"). Also, **Vonee, Voney, Voni, Vonie, Vonnee, Vonney, Vonnie, Vonny, Vony.**

CRIB NOTES

Famous Ws: Wendy Wasserstein (playwright, *The Heidi Chronicles*); **Whitney** Houston (singer/actor/diva); **Whoopi** Goldberg (Oscar-winner, *Ghost*); **Winona** Ryder (actor, *Little Women*); **Wynonna** Judd (country singer)

Pocket Ts: None

Trendy suspenders: Whitney, Winona, Wynonna

Think long, think hard: Wanda (Life ain't fair. **Wanda** ain't cool. You can deposit those two truisms in the bank. By the time the investment matures, **Wanda** will still be *out*.); **Whoopi** (**Whoopi**s are made, not born. A-list celeb Ms. Goldberg began life as **Caryn**. She *chose* to become **Whoopi** as an adult.); **Wilhelmina** (Another time, another place. Not here, not now.); **Windy** (A Gen X name of your youth that likely won't be joining us in the twenty-first century. About as hip today as a macramè purse.)

Wadi (African: dry river valley). Also, **Wadee, Wadey, Wadie, Wady.**
Wallis (Scottish: foreigner; English: from Wales). Also, **Walis, Waliss, Walliss, Wallys, Wallyss, Walys, Walyss.** *Whatever:* A girl name? Well, it worked for **Wallis** Simpson, aka, the woman who famously stole the heart of the would-be king of England.
Warner (English/French: guardian). *Whatever:* A fancy-pants power name that meshes with the popular, unisex likes of **Bailey** and **Jordan.**
Wednesday (English: fourth day of the week). *Whatever:* **Wednesday** is the name of the daughter in *The Addams Family* from the comic

strip, the movies, and the 1960s TV show. Make of that factoid what you will.

Wela (English: wealth). Also, **Wella.**

Wendy (English: wanderer). Also, **Wendee, Wendey, Wendi, Wendie.** *Plus:* A peanut-butter-and-jelly sandwich . . . *Minus:* . . . that was much hipper (and less ditsy) when Gen Xers were busy being kids, rather than having them.

Wenona (Native American: variation of **Winona,** "firstborn"). Also, **Wenonah, Wenonna, Wenonnah.**

Whitley (English: white woods). Also, **Witley, Whitlee, Whitleigh, Whitli, Whitlie, Whitly, Wytley.** *Plus:* A very today little princess, **Whitley** is full of splendor and would-be sophistication. Given a trial run on TV's *A Differrent World* (1987–93) via Jasmine Guy's preppie antagonist, **Whitley** Gilbert.

Whitney (English: white island). Also, **Witney, Witny, Whitnee, Whitni, Whitnie, Whitny, Wytney, Wytni.** *Whatever:* This one's a lot like its sound-alike **Whitley** with one key exception: **Whitney**'s got a megapopular champion, singer **Whitney** Houston. The diva's divaness is helping prime the day care centers with tons o' little namesakes. The faster they rise . . . You know the rest. Potential trendy suspenders material.

Willa (German: determined). Also, **Wila, Wyla, Wylla.** *Whatever:* The **Wilhelmina** for today.

Willow (English: the willow tree). Also, **Willoe, Wiloe, Wilow.** *Whatever:* newscaster **Willow** Bay proves this tree-hugger of a name can be done with no apparent side effects.

Wilona (German: determined). Also, **Willona.**

Winifred (German: friend of peace). Also, **Winifredd, Winfred, Winfredd, Winyfred, Winyfredd.** Familiar, **Winnie.** *Whatever:* **Winifred** is arguably no more doable than **Wilhemina,** but it's included here on the off-chance you're leaning toward **Winnie** and want to start the name off with something bigger.

Winnie (Celtic: famine; German: variation of **Winifred,** "friend of peace"). Also, **Winnee, Winney, Winni, Winny.** *Plus:* Winsome, perky, Pooh-esqe. *Minus:* A name that illustrates the danger of naming babies after public figures: On *The Cosby Show,* eldest daughter Sondra gave birth to twins. She named them Nelson and **Winnie,** in honor of the first couple (in spirit) of South Africa. Seemed like a fine idea—at the time. Fast forward about ten years, and Nelson Mandela is the inspiring president of the country. (Cool.) **Winnie** Mandela, his now ex-wife, is trying to salvage her reputation after being placed on trial for murder. (Not so cool.) Just a long way of saying this name ain't all it used to be.

Winola (German: charming friend). Also, **Winolla, Wynola, Wynolla.**

Winona   (Native American: firstborn). Also, **Winonah, Winonna, Winonnah.** *Plus:* A very today name with two very popular champions, A-list celebs **Winona** Ryder and **Wynonna** Judd. *Minus:* It's tricky to use a name so strongly linked with one, even two, persons. Go ask all the **Marilyn**s born in the 1950s. Or the **Winnie**s of the 1980s. Potential trendy suspenders fodder.

Winter (English: the cold season; German: wind, army). Also, **Wynter.**

Wray (German: isolated). Also, **Wraye.**

Wrenna (English: small songbird). Also, **Wrena.**

Wright (French: carpenter). Also, **Wrighte.**

Wyatt   (French: little battler). Also, **Wiat, Wiatt, Wyat.** *Whatever:* Commonly a boy name but doable as daughter material too. It has a contemporary, Western, unisex feel. Plus, it's a safe and sane alternative to **Montana** or even **Wyoming.**

Wynette (Scottish: little meadow). Also, **Winete, Winette, Wynete.** *Whatever:* A tribute to the late First Lady of Country Music, Tammy **Wynette**?

Wynne (Scottish: meadow; English: friend). Also, **Winn, Wyn, Wynn.**

Wynona (Native American: variation of **Winona,** "firstborn"). Also, **Wynonna, Wynonnah.** Trendy suspenders.

Wyoming (Native American: A Great Plains state). Also, **Wioming, Wiomyng, Wyomyng.** *Plus:* This one's a map name of manageable popularity; a worthy peer of **Montana** and **Dakota.** *Minus:* Should we fear turf wars?

Wythe (Scottish: willow tree). Also, **Withe.** *Whatever:* **Blythe,** with a Western flair.

CRIB NOTES

We interrupt Famous Xs, Pocket Ts, Trendy suspenders, and Think long, think hard to bring you this special message:

This is what Americans think of the letter X: It's an eight-point Scrabble tile. A game-breaker. An albatross. The letter that leaves you praying for an open *a* on the board, so you can spell "ax" and be done with it.

In short, we don't know what to do with X. We know it makes car models sound faster, secret formulas more mysterious, and generations cooler. But baby names? There, we're clueless. It's all Greek to us. Appropriate, considering the usual list of baby X names reads like a phone book for ancient Athens. Honestly, **Xylia**? Who names a kid **Xylia**? But because we promised you the entire alphabet, and because it's your right to award a baby name you're not even sure how to pronounce, we present— with the above provisos—the letter X.

Xan (Greek: variation of **Alexandra**, "protector, defender"; Spanish: variation of **Xandra, Xantha, Xanthe, Xanthine, Xanthus, Xanthippe, Xantippe**). Also, **Xann**. *Plus:* Kind of kicky. *Minus:* Kind of Wondertwins-esque.

Xandra (Spanish: variation of **Alexandra**, "protector, defender"). Familiar, **Xan**. *Whatever:* Exotic sound-alike alternative to **Sandra**.

Xantha (Greek: yellow-colored). Familiar, **Xan**.

Xanthe (Greek: yellow-colored). Also, **Xanth**. Familiar, **Xan**.

Xanthine (Greek: yellow-colored). Also, **Xantheen, Xantheene, Xanthyne**. Familiar, **Xan**.

Xanthippe (Greek: variation of **Xantippe**, "yellow horse"). Also, **Xanthipp, Xanthypp, Xanthyppe**. Familiar, **Xan**.

Xanthus (Greek: yellow-colored). Also, **Xanthuss**. Familiar, **Xan**.

Xantippe (Greek: yellow horse). Also, **Xantyppe.** Familiar, **Xan.**

Xat (Native American: totem pole). Also, **Xatt.**

Xata (Native American: variation of **Xat,** "totem pole"). Also, **Xatta.**

Xaviera (Arabic: bright). Also, **Xavierra, Xavyera, Xavyerra.**

Xebeca (English: variation of **Xebec,** "ship"). Also, **Xebecca, Xe-becha, Xebecka, Xebeka, Xebekka.**

Xena (Greek: stranger). Also, **Xeena, Xina, Xyna.** *Whatever:* How to trump the little princesses? Christen your own little warrior princess (chakra not included). Can the outrageous popularity of the grrl-power, sword-and-sorcery TV series *Xena: Warrior Princess* translate into an actual baby name trend? Never underestimate a nation that's still naming its kids after *Dynasty* reruns. This is one to watch.

Xenia (Greek: hospitable). Also, **Xenya.**

Xenona (Greek: variation of **Xenon,** "a gas"). Also, **Xenonah, Xenonna, Xenonnah.**

Xeres (Spanish: older).

Xerxas (Greek: variation of **Xerxes,** "lion king"). Also, **Xerxis, Xerxys.**

Xerxes (Greek: lion king). Also, **Xerxis, Xerxys.**

Xhosas (African: South African tribe). Also, **Xhoses, Xhosys.**

Xiang (Chinese: fragrant). Also, **Xiange.**

Ximena (Spanish: variation of **Ximenes,** "obedient"). Also, **Ximeena, Xymeena, Xymena.**

Xin (Chinese: beautiful). Also, **Xinn, Xyn, Xynn.**

Xosas (African: variation of **Xhosas,** "South African tribe"). Also, **Xoses, Xosys.**

Xuan (Vietnamese: spring). Also, **Xuann.**

Xyla (Greek: wood). Also, **Xila.**

Xylia (Greek: forest). Also, **Xilea, Xilia, Xilya, Xylea, Xylya.**

Y

CRIB NOTES

Famous Ys: **Yasmine** Bleeth (ex-*Baywatch* thespian); **Yoko** Ono (John Lennon's widow); **Yvonne** DeCarlo (TV's Lily Munster, *The Munsters*)

Pocket Ts: Interesting choices but nothing that can be safely put in the bank

Trendy suspenders: **Yasmine**

Think long, think hard: **Yentl** (For die-hard Streisand fans only.); **Yoko** (In theory, a lovely name of Japanese origin meaning "goodness" and "nature." In practice, a Madonna—owned by **Yoko** Ono.)

Yael (Hebrew: ascending). Also, **Yaele, Yayl, Yayle.**
Yaeshona (Americanvariation of **Shawna,** "God is gracious"). Also, **Yaeseana, Yaeshauna, Yaeshawna, Yayseana, Yayshauna, Yayshawna, Yayshona.**
Yaffa (Hebrew: beauty). Also, **Yafa, Yafah, Yaffah, Yapha.**
Yale (English: nook). Also, **Yaile, Yayle.** *Plus:* A classy classic. (**Yale** University's been around since 1701). *Minus:* Harvard University's been around since 1636. You gonna name your daughter **Harvard**?
Yamilla (English: variation of **Yamille,** "noisy"). Also, **Yamila, Yamyla, Yamylla.**
Yamille (English: noisy). Also, **Yamill, Yamyl, Yamyle, Yamylle.**
Yana (Slavic: God is gracious). Also, **Yanna.**
Yancy (French: from England). Also, **Yancee, Yancey, Yanci, Yancie.**
Yanessa (American: variation of **Vanessa,** "butterfly"). Also, **Yanesa, Yanisa, Yanissa, Yanysa, Yanyssa.**

Yanisha (American: variation of **Aisha**, "life"). Also, **Yaneesha, Yanysha.**

Yardley (English: enclosed meadow). Also, **Yardlee, Yardleigh, Yardli, Yardlie, Yardly.**

Yashona (American: variation of **Shawna**, "God is gracious"). Also, **Yaseana, Yashauna, Yashawna, Yeseana, Yeshauna, Yeshawna, Yeshona.**

Yasmin (Persian: variation of **Jasmine**, "flower"). Also, **Yasminn, Yasmyn, Yasmynn.**

Yasmina (Persian: variation of **Jasmine**, "flower"). Also, **Yasmeena, Yasmyna.**

Yasmine (Persian: variation of **Jasmine**, "flower"). Also, **Yasmeen, Yasmeene, Yasmyne.** *Whatever:* This little princess variation is as close as the Ys get to a pair of trendy suspenders.

Yazmin (Persian: variation of **Yasmin**, "flower"). Also, **Yazminn, Yazmyn, Yazmynn.**

Yazmina (Persian: variation of **Yasmina**, "flower"). Also, **Yazmeena, Yazmyna.**

Yazmine (Persian: variation of **Yasmine**, "flower"). Also, **Yazmeen, Yazmeene, Yazmyne.**

Yeardley (English: variation of **Yardley**, "enclosed meadow"). Also, **Yeardlee, Yeardleigh, Yeardli, Yeardlie, Yeardly.** *Whatever:* **Yeardley** Smith is the voice of *The Simpsons*' Lisa Simpson.

Yetta (German: singer). Also, **Yeta.** *Plus:* Old-fashioned, traditional. *Minus:* It only works if your *real* first name is either "Aunt" or "Grandma."

Yoanna (Hebrew: variation of **Joanna**, "combination of **Jo** and **Ann**"). Also, **Yoana, Yoanah, Yoannah.**

Yoella (Hebrew: variation of **Joella**, "God is Lord"). Also, **Yoela, Yoelah, Yoellah.**

Yoelle (Hebrew: variation of **Joelle**, "God is Lord"). Also, **Yoele.**

Yohanna (Hebrew/German: variation of **Johann**, "God is gracious"). Also, **Yohana, Yohanah, Yohannah.**

Yolanda (Greek: violet). Also, **Yolande.** Familiar, **Yoli.** *Whatever:* Evokes exotica, circa the 1940s. A nice fit in the talk-show 1990s—a worthy peer of **Oprah, Leeza,** and its sound-alike **Rolanda**.

Yoli (Greek: variation of **Yolanda**, "violet"). Also, **Yolee, Yoley, Yolie, Yoly.**

Yon (Korean: blossom). Also, **Yonn.**

Yona (Hebrew: dove). Also, **Yonah, Yonna, Yonnah.**

Yonina (Hebrew: little dove). Also, **Yonyna.**

Yonit (Hebrew: dove). Also, **Yonitt, Yonyt, Yonytt.**

Yordaine (Hebrew: variation of **Jordan,** "down-flowing river"). Also, **Yordane, Yordayne.**

Yordan (Hebrew: variation of **Jordan,** "down-flowing river"). Also, **Yorden, Yordyn.** Familiar, **Yori.**

Yordana (Hebrew: variation of **Jordan,** "down-flowing river"). Also, **Yordanah, Yordanna, Yordannah.**

Yori (Japanese: truthful; Hebrew: variation of **Yordan,** "down-flowing river"). Also, **Yoree, Yorey, Yorie, Yory.**

Yoshe (Japanese: beauty). Also, **Yoshee, Yoshey, Yoshi, Yoshie, Yoshy.**

Yovona (Slavic: variation of **John,** "God is gracious"). Also, **Yovaana, Yovanna, Yovhana, Yovhanna, Yoviana, Yovianna.**

Ysabel (Spanish: variation of **Isabel,** "God's oath"). Also, **Ysabell, Ysabelle, Ysebel, Ysebell, Ysebelle, Ysybel, Ysybell, Ysybelle.**

Ysabella (Italian: variation of **Isabella,** "God's oath"). Also, **Ysabela, Ysebela, Ysebella, Ysybela, Ysybella.**

Yvette (English: little ivy vine). Also, **Yvett.** *Plus:* Pretty and posh, **Yvette** is the **Alexis** Less Traveled. *Minus:* Makes you think of French maids. And French maid uniforms, or lack thereof.

Yves (French: evergreen).

Yvonne (Hebrew/French: young archer). Also, **Yvon, Yvone, Yvonn.** *Whatever:* **Yvonne** Craig played Batgirl on TV's *Batman* from 1967–68. **Yvonne** DeCarlo played Lily Munster on *The Munsters* from 1964–65. That was sort of the peak of the **Ivonne/Evonne/Yvonne** craze in America.

Yule (English: Christmas).

Yzabel (Spanish: variation of **Isabel,** "God's oath"). Also, **Yzabell, Yzabelle, Yzebel, Yzebell, Yzebelle, Yzybel, Yzybell, Yzybelle.**

Yzabella (Italian: variation of **Isabella,** "God's oath"). Also, **Yzabela, Yzebela, Yzebella, Yzybela, Yzybella.**

Z

CRIB NOTES

Famous Zs: **Zelda** Fitzgerald (author/F. Scott's wife); *Frannie and Zooey* (J. D. Salinger novella); **Zsa Zsa** Gabor (famous person)

Pocket Ts: Zoe

Trendy suspenders: No pick

Think long, think hard: Zsa Zsa (The perfect name for **Zsa Zsa** Gabor—so colorful, so eye-catching. But unless your daughter intends to carve out a life as an international celebrity famed for being, well, famous, then you may want to go with something a tad less La-La Land.)

Zabrina (Latin: variation of **Sabrina**, "princess"). Also, **Zabreena, Zabryna.**

Zada (Arabic: prosperous). Also, **Zadda.**

Zaida (Arabic: hunter). Also, **Zayda.**

Zaire (African: the nation). Also, **Zairre.**

Zale (Greek: wave). Also, **Zaile, Zayle.**

Zamilla (Arabic: variation of **Jamilla**, "beautiful"). Also, **Zamila, Zamyla, Zamylla.**

Zamir (Hebrew: songbird). Also, **Zameer, Zamyr.**

Zan (Chinese: praise). Also, **Zann.** *Plus:* **Jan** for a new millennium. *Minus:* A *Superfriends* Wondertwin for eternity.

Zandra (Greek: variation of **Sandra**, "protector, defender").

Zane (Hebrew: grace of God). Also, **Zaine, Zayne.** *Whatever:* Handsome on a boy (as in Western author **Zane** Grey); equally handsome and smart-looking on a girl.

Zanna (Hebrew: grace of God). Also, **Zana, Zanah, Zannah.** *Plus:* Modern, unique, pretty. *Minus:* The name around the corner from **Vanna.**

Zara (Persian: lucky; Arabic: sunrise). Also, **Zarra.** *Whatever:* Sound-alike for **Sarah.**

Zarena (Latin: variation of **Zerena,** "calm, serene"). Also, **Zareena, Zarina, Zaryna.**

Zashawna (American: variation of **Shawna,** "God is gracious"). Also, **Zaseana, Zashauna, Zashona, Zeseana, Zeshauna, Zeshawna, Zeshona.**

Zea (Latin: grain). Also, **Zia, Zya.**

Zeandrea (American: variation of **Andrea,** "brave"). Also, **Zeandraea, Zeandraya, Zeandria, Zeandrya.**

Zel (Turkish: bell). Also, **Zell, Zelle.**

Zelda (German: gray warrior). *Plus:* You think **Zelda** was the real writing talent in the F. Scott Fitzgerald (*The Great Gatsby*) household. *Minus:* You think **Zelda** Fitzgerald was a loon who drove F. Scott to drink.

Zelma (Irish: variation of **Selma,** "fair").

Zena (Greek: variation of **Xena,** "stranger"). Also, **Zeena, Zina, Zyna.** *Plus:* A scenario: You really want to name your little warrior princess **Xena.** You don't want the neighbors to know that you watch the TV series. You try to sneak one by them by opting for **Zena.** *Minus:* The only one you're fooling is yourself.

Zenda (Persian: commentary). *Plus:* If *Dynasty* was still in production, **Zenda** would be **Alexis'** mysterious cousin. *Minus:* Two words: Prisoner of.

Zenia (Greek: gift). Also, **Zenya.**

Zera (Hebrew: dawn; Greek: life). Also, **Zerah, Zerra, Zerrah.**

Zerafina (Hebrew: on fire). Also, **Zerafeena, Zerafyna.**

Zeraphina (Hebrew: on fire). Also, **Zerapheena, Zeraphyna.**

Zerena (Latin: calm, serene). Also, **Zereena, Zerina, Zeryna.**

Zeta (Greek: dwelling). Also, **Zeeta, Zita, Zyta.**

Zia (Hebrew: to tremble). Also, **Zeea, Zya.**

Zilia (Greek: variation of **Cecilia,** "blind, gray-eyed"). Also, **Zillia, Zillya, Zilya.**

Zillah (Hebrew: shadow). Also, **Zila, Zilah, Zilla.**

Zinnia (Latin: lilac). Also, **Zinia, Zinnya, Zinya.** *Whatever:* In some ways this is the most usable flower name among the outmoded likes of **Daisy, Rose,** and, of course, **Flower.**

Ziona (Hebrew: hill). Also, **Zionah, Zyona, Zyonah.**

Zita (Hebrew: woman of authority). Also, **Zeeta, Zeetah, Zyta.** *Plus:* To use appropriate Z terms: **Zita** is zesty and zippy. *Minus:* It sounds like a pasta dish.

Ziz (Hebrerw: blossom). Also, **Zizz, Zyz, Zyzz.**

Zoa (Greek: variation of **Zoe,** "life").

Zoe (Greek: life). Also, **Zoey.** *Whatever:* Love this name. So modern, so classic, so adaptable. It's spunky. It's perky. No, wait—it's elegant. It's cultured. . . . And this is no fly-by-nighter, either. **Zoe** has been around since the third century. Happily, a pocket T.

Zofia (Slavic: variation of **Sophia,** "wisdom"). Also, **Zofya.**

Zola (Italian: earth).

Zona (Latin: a belt).

Zooey (Greek: variation of **Zoe,** "life").

Zora (Arabic: dawn). Also, **Zorra.**

Zore (Slavic: for a princess). Also, **Zorae, Zoray.**

Zorna (Teutonic: passion).

Zosa (Hebrew: holy). Also, **Zosah.**

Zowie (Greek: variation of **Zoe,** "life"). Also, **Zowee, Zowey, Zowi, Zowy.**

Zuma (Arabic: angel).

Zuriel (Hebrew: God is my rock). Also, **Zuriell, Zurielle, Zuryel, Zuryell, Zuryelle.** *Whatever:* A unique spin on sound-alike **Ariel.**

Other People's Names

Hollywood Babes

What Gen Xer Celebs Are Naming Their Offspring

Gillian Anderson (actor, *The X-Files*) (born 1968):
   Piper, daughter.
Pamela Anderson (ex-*Baywatch* thespian) (born 1967):
   Brandon, son; **Dylan,** son.
Tami Anderson (roommate, *Real World*/Los Angeles) (born 1970)
and Kenny Anderson (NBA star) (born 1970):
   Lyric, daughter.
Nicolas Cage (actor) (born 1964):
   Weston, son.
Kurt Cobain (rocker, Nirvana) (born 1967, died 1994)
and Courtney Love (rocker, Hole/actress) (born 1965):
   Frances Bean, daughter.
Sean "Puff Daddy" Combs (rapper/producer) (born 1970);
   Christopher, son; **Justin,** son.
Harry Connick Jr. (singer/actor) (born 1967):
   Georgia, daughter; **Sara Kate,** daughter.
Jennifer Flavin (model/Mrs. Sylvester Stallone) (born 1968):
   Sophia Rose, daughter; **Sistine Rose,** daughter.
Tracey Gold (actor, *Growing Pains*) (born 1969):
   Sage, son.

Cuba Gooding Jr. (Oscar-winner, *Jerry Maguire*) (born 1968):
Spencer, son; **Mason,** son.
Ken Griffey Jr. (baseball player) (born 1969):
Trey Kenneth, son; **Taryn Kennedy,** daughter.
Teri Hatcher (actor, *Lois and Clark*) (born 1963):
Emerson Rose, daughter.
Whitney Houston (singer/actor) (born 1963) and Bobby Brown (singer) (born 1969):
Bobbi Kristina, daughter.
Nicole Kidman (actor/Mrs. Tom Cruise) (born 1967):
Conor Antony, son; **Isabella Jane,** daughter.
Lisa Kudrow (actor, *Friends*) (born 1963):
Julian, son.
Ricki Lake (talk-show host) (born 1968):
Milo, son.
Elle Macpherson (model) (born 1964)
Arpad Flynn Alexander, son.
Gena Lee Nolin (ex-*Baywatch* thespian) (born 1971):
Spencer, son.
Sinead O'Connor (singer) (born 1967):
Jake, son.
Lisa Rinna (actor) (born 1965):
Delilah Belle, daughter.
Darius Rucker (rocker, Hootie and the Blowfish) (born 1966):
Carolyn, daughter.
Holly Robinson (actor) (born 1964) and Rodney Peete (football player) (born 1966):
Rodney Jackson, son; **Ryan Elizabeth,** daughter (twins).
Rick Schroder (actor, *NYPD Blue*) (born 1970):
Holden Richard, son; **Luke William,** son; **Cambrie,** daughter.
Elisabeth Shue (actor, *Leaving Las Vegas*) (born 1963):
Miles, son.
Will Smith (actor) (born 1968):
Willard Smith III (Trey), son.
Will Smith (actor) (born 1968) and Jada Pinkett (actor) (born 1971):
Jaden Christopher Syre, son.
Nikki Taylor (model) (born 1975):
Hunter and **Jake,** twin sons.

Uma Thurman (actress) (born 1970) and Ethan Hawke (born 1970):
  Maya Ray, daughter.
Tiffany (former teeny-bopper singer) (born 1971):
  Elijah, son.
Vanessa L. Williams (singer/actor) (born 1963):
  Melanie, daughter; **Jillian,** daughter; **Devin,** son.
Robin Wright (actor, *The Princess Bride*/Mrs. Sean Penn) (born 1966):
  Hopper, son; **Dylan,** son.

The Information Superpotty:
Baby Name Websites

Parent Soup's **Baby Name Finder** (http://www.parentsoup.com): Here's
a fantabulous, full-service site with everything from general parenting
stuff (chats, discussion groups, resources, etc.) to the most authoritative
baby name on-line search engine around. For origins and meanings, go
to "Find What's in a Name." For popularity rankings, click on "Popularity Finder." "Finder Potpourri" is the perfect stop for the spelunker, with
tips on "unique" entries like **Congo** and **Copper.**

BabyCenter (http://www.babycenter.com): Like Parent Soup, Baby-
Center is an everything-including-the-kitchen-sink site. Its baby name
section is especially loaded. There's the usual good stuff (chat rooms,
popularity lists, etc.) plus there's the unusual good stuff, like this handy
tip: Don't give your kid a name that ends in the same letter as the first
letter of his last name. Why? Makes for difficult pronunciation. Or so
says BabyCenter.

Baby Names! (http://www.babynames.com): This is a handy guide to
more than 4,500 names established by two sisters who have been col-
lecting monikers for wee ones for more than five years. Fun categories
include: "Soap Names" and "Baby Pic of the Month," for when your
head hurts from figuring out how to spell **Zachary** funny, and you just
want to look at a cute ol' baby for a while.

The *New* Baby Name Index (http//www.electricalsocket.com/Baby
Names/): Established in 1996, this site is dedicated to giving users not

just the baby name facts (spelling, origin, meaning), but the baby name "feel." What *does* a **Mabel** look like, after all? The site links most of its database names to real people (sometimes accompanied with real pictures) to help answer that mystery. Also, in case you can't wait to see your carefully chosen baby name on the birth certificate, try out the online one provided by the Baby Name Index—a good way to gauge how the thing will play in the real world.

The Utah Baby Namer (http://www.geocities.com/Heartland/3450/): A site specializing in baby names for Utah Mormons (or, presumably, anyone who wants to sound like one). A great stop for spelunkers—revel in the unique, from A (**Adelvade** for a girl) to Z (**Zurl** for a boy).

Baby Names (Indian) (http://www.rajiv.org/iu/babyn.html): Just like the name says, this cyberspace hang lists names from India—almost 3,000 of them, from **Aanaud** to **Zev**. (P.S. This isn't the place to search for origins and meanings. There are none included here.)

Internet Baby Namer (http://www.webabc.com/baby.html): Let the cyber fates help you select a name. At the prompt, tell the program what you're looking for—a boy name or a girl name. The Internet Baby Namer will think it over for a second and then, like your mother, offer its two cents. Its advice can run from the sensible (**Matthew** for a boy) to the dubious (**Bertha** for a girl).

The Dream Is Over: Just Say No to Hippie Names

"[My mother] and my father liked the name because of what it said about them, not about what it would mean for me," an assistant magazine editor by the name of **Summer** Flint lamented in a 1997 essay for *Swing* magazine.

In the article, Flint wrote of coming to terms with her crunchy granola moniker—finally, at age twenty-five. We can only imagine what a long road from the Summer of Love to acceptance that must have been.

Lesson learned: Peace and love are worthy ideals, not names. If you

get the urge to give your baby any of the following names, force yourself to listen to a little "Freedom Rock" until the feeling passes.

Hippie Names

Donovan	Rainbow
Flower	River
Freedom	Serenity
Leaf	Star
Love	Sunshine
Moon	Vegan
Peace	

Alison. Billy. and Jake:
Baby Names from *Melrose Place*
(and Other TV Soaps)

Looking to raise a little drama queen named **Amanda**? How about a
handsome yet ultimately dim-bulb hunk called **Billy**? Well, all right,
maybe these aren't exactly the aspirations you had in mind. But there's
no denying, *Melrose Place* isn't just for laughing at Heather Locklear's
idea of a hemline anymore. The twentysomething-friendly prime-time
soap is prime source material for baby names. Really. One main reason:
lots of characters, lots of corresponding proper nouns—pick and choose
your favorites.

Below are suggested names, culled from the annals of *Melrose Place,*
and for good measure, a handful of other daytime and prime-time dra-
mas. The key here is to look for names that capture the bold, maybe even
exotic feel of the soap you love, without getting too Harlequin romance,
à la **Cord** or **Bolt.** Good rule of thumb: No matter what soap writers say,
inanimate objects, particularly those relating to toolboxes, are not acceptable substitutes for people names.

Possibles

Alison (*Melrose Place*)	Eleni (*As the World Turns*)
Amanda (*MP*)	Brandon (*Beverly Hills, 90210*)
Jake(*MP*)	Andrea (*90210*)
Jo (*MP*)	Dylan (*90210*)
Matt (*MP*)	Bobby (*Dallas*)
Jane (*MP*)	Austin (*Days of Our Lives*)
Peter(*MP*)	Frankie (*Sisters*) (as girl's name)
Grant (*Another World*)	Neil (*The Young and the Restless*)

Borderline

Billy (Infuse a couple of I.Q. points in this name, and go with William.)
Michael (*MP*) (Overused, and used on *MP* by a sociopath—not a good combo.)
Kimberly (*MP*) (The mother of all sociopathic characters.)
Sydney (*MP*) (Wouldn't want to be a **Sydney** girl in the fourth grade when the little boy classmates discover old *MP* reruns.)
Erica (*All My Children*)
Tad (*All My Children*)
Pamela (*Dallas*)
Justus (*General Hospital*)
Bo (*One Life to Live*)
Dru (*Young and the Restless*) (Short for the even more chancy, Drucilla.)

Impossibles

Chas (*MP*)
Brenda (*90210*) (Too much bad karma.)
Fallon (*Dynasty*) (*Très* 1980s. Just about everything from this series reeks of stale Reagan administration aires, including **Blake, Krystle, Alexis, Dex,** and **Sable.** And although **Sammy Jo** doesn't fit this definition, she should be considered off-limits too.)
Thorne (*The Bold and the Beautiful*)
Sue Ellen (*Dallas*)

Patch (*Days of our Lives*)
Cricket (*The Young and the Restless*)

The Yearbook Method:
Find Inspiration from Forgotten Schoolmates

OK, since you've (likely) bought this book, now it can safely be revealed: There's already a perfectly good baby name book sitting beneath a fine coat of grimy dust in the back of your closet. We speak, of course, of your yearbook. Junior high, middle high, high school, college, doesn't matter. Any old one will do. So, go on, dig it up. With yearbook in hand, follow these four easy steps:

1. Skip the "Have a bitchen summer!" inscriptions, the oh-so poignant candid photo spreads offset with snatches of lyrics from "The Way We Were," and thumb straight to the class mugshots.
2. Look for familiar faces. Remember that girl Amy who was sorta nice? Fine, put that one (**Amy**) in the possible pile. Remember that girl **Kristen** who kinda bugged you and refused to acknowledge your existence after elementary school? Of course, you do. You bear a grudge, you have a long memory, mark **Kristen** a reject. (As perfectly fine a name as **Kristen** is, if you grew up hating one, you're not going to want to pass down that demon seed to your kid.)
3. Repeat this who-I-liked/who-I-hated game until you have a solid list of ten possibles—ten for boys, ten for girls.
4. Scan your list for anachronisms, edit appropriately. Remember, if you're using one of your old yearbooks, you burgeoning geezer you, you're spelunking for material from a bunch of kids who got tagged with their **Dena**s, **Joey**s, and **Greg**s in the 1960s and early 1970s. This, of course, is not to say you can't name your newborn **Gary,** this is just to say: **Gary** used to sound cool, but then so did Wang Chung.

Here's a list of possible boys and girls names I came up with utilizing my own 1983 sophomore-year yearbook. These are names that have legs— and were used by people who weren't unduly cruel to me in my youth. A potent combo:

Girls

Ann	Grace
Amy	Maureen
Candice	Sophia
Caroline	Justine
Donya	

Boys

Carter	Jeffrey
Christopher	John
Eric	Paul
Jan	Reuben

The All-New Rat Pack:
Lounge Scene—Inspired Baby Names

You worship cocktail lounges, lava lamps, houndstooth fedoras, slip-on Hush Puppies. You'd just as soon wing it to a Steve and Eydie concert as check out what's new in MTV's "Buzz Bin." You are retro—New Frontier–style. Sure, some of the attitude is affected irony, but some of it, maybe even most of it, is genuine affection. Sinatra *is* cool. Tiki music *does* float your boat. Orange shag carpet *is* an acceptable interior design choice.

But here's the really cool thing: Sinatra's Rat Pack isn't just for boozy late-night performances at the Sands Hotel anymore. The Pack is a fine source for names that project (in the eye of the lounger, anyway) just a hint of swagger, just a touch of tuxedo-clad class, and barrels of show-biz moxie.

One note of caution: The Rat Pack's girl tag-alongs, frankly, aren't the best baby names for the 1990s—what with **Angie, Shirley,** and **Ruta** having seen their best days decades ago. Instead, may we suggest some very fine, classy-sounding monikers from their jazz-era counterparts.

Possible Girls

Julie (as in Miss Julie London)
Keely (as in Smith)
Eartha (as in Kitt)
Ella (as in Fitzgerald)
Dinah (as in Washington)
Etta (as in James)

Possible Boys

Frank (as in Sinatra)
Sammy (as in Davis Jr.)
Dean (as in Martin)
Peter (as in Lawford)
Joey (as in Bishop)

These lists cover the Pack fraternity. Here are some other swingin' names of swingers:

Bobby (as in Darin)
Henry (as in Mancini)
Martin (as in Denny)
Nelson (as in Riddle)
Mel (as in Tormé)

Flannel Blanket:
Grunge Scene—Inspired Baby Names

At first glance, this doesn't seem a good idea at all: What? You're supposed to name your kid after some greasy-haired, flannel-wearing mopey head? Well, yeah. Maybe.

Aside from occasional excesses in the angst department, grunge was about being (excuse the term) "real." Low-key. Stripped down. Laid-bare. Fancy-schmancy hair-band posers need not apply

Accordingly and/or coincidentally, the purveyors of the scene had names to match the no-frills attitude. (Particularly the boys.) Taut, sturdy, durable, if a tad *Leave It to Beaver*-ish—this is the stuff that grunge names are made of. And when you think of it that way, they're not bad choices at all. A splendid name-a-palooza awaits you below:

Possible Girls

Courtney Love (Hole)
D'arcy (Smashing Pumpkins)
Juliana Hatfield
Kelley Deal (the Breeders)
Kim Gordon (Sonic Youth)
Kristin Hersh (Throwing Muses)
Linda Perry (4 Non Blondes)
Shirley Manson (Garbage)
Tanya Donelly (Belly)

Possible Boys

Billy Corgan (Smashing Pumpkins)
Butch Vig (Nirvana producer/Garbage)
Chris Cornell (Soundgarden)
Daniel Johns (Silverchair)
Dave Grohl (Nirvana)
Eddie Vedder (Pearl Jam)
James Iha (Smashing Pumpkins)
Jeff Ament (Pearl Jam)
Kim Thayil (Soundgarden)
Kurt Cobain (Nirvana)
Perry Farrell (Jane's Addiction)
Scott Weiland (Stone Temple Pilots)
Stone Gossard (Pearl Jam)

(Note: Yeah, yeah. Some of the above bands and/or artists are arguably not-quite grunge. Just trying to even out the temperament of your choices.)

New Jack Babies:
Hip-Hop/Rap-Inspired Baby Names

Looking for variety? You found it.

The hip-hop/rap scene is loaded with the stuff. This is where the classically mundane (i.e., **Bobby, Lisa**) rub figurative shoulders with the left-of-center marvelous (i.e., **Shawntea, O'Shea**).

Below you'll find workable baby names inspired by leading artists of the field. The key word here is "workable." Not a **Sir Mix-A-Lot** or **Snoop Doggy Dogg** in the bunch. Fact is, nobody names a kid Snoop. Not even Mrs. Snoop, *er,* Brodeus. (Snoop's given name is Calvin Brodeus.) Lesson learned: Don't go getting too creative on your newborn. If he or she wants to be known as Boo-Berry, let the kid make the call.)

Possible Girls

Cheryl "Salt" James (Salt 'N Pepa)
Foxy Brown
Lisa "Left Eye" Lopes (TLC)
Lauryn Hill
Mary J. Blige
Neneh Cherry
Queen **Latifah**
Sandra "Pepa" Denton (Salt 'N Pepa)
Shawntae Harris (Da Brat)

Possible Boys

Ali Shaheed Muhammad (A Tribe Called Quest)
Andre Young (Dr. Dre)
Bobby Brown
Chuck D (Public Enemy)
Oshea Jackson (Ice Cube)
Sean Combs (Puff Daddy)
Treach (Naughty by Nature)

Tupac Shakur
Warren G
Wyclef Jean (the Fugees)

Very Brady Names:
Large TV-Family Baby Names

If you're planning a large family, which today roughly means (what?) one child and a house plant, the name game business gets even trickier to negotiate. The chief concern: Should you attempt to build a theme—something along the lines of (a) Alliteration 'Til You Drop (**Cathy, Carlton, Cody, Connor**); (b) All Rhyme, All the Time (**Bill, Will, Jill, Phil**); or (c) Tribute City (**Franklin, John, George, Lyndon,** for our nation's presidents . . . **Chris, Martina, Monica, Bjorn,** for our globe's tennis players)?

The rhyming method is the least desirable of these choices. Remember, your goal here is to raise good little citizens, not a circus act. (Unless, of course, you are currently employed in the circus industry, in which case, please, go right ahead—rhyme away.)

The key in naming multiple offspring is to give children something unique, something that lets them exert individuality, even in a crowded group portrait. Usually, this happens by default. We tend to get more creative, more adventurous with our name choices as we age. Take Tom Hanks, for instance: The actor's first two children (by wife number one) were named **Colin** and **Elizabeth.** By the time he got to his third and fourth (by wife number two), he was dragging out **Truman** and **Chester.**

For inspiration, and for example, let us now turn to the last great purveyors of big broods: TV families (minimum four kids, oldest to youngest).

The Bradys of *The Brady Bunch:*
   Greg, Marcia, Peter, Jan, Bobby, Cindy, Cousin **Oliver.**
The Bradfords of *Eight Is Enough:*
   David, Mary, Joannie, Susan, Nancy, Tommy (Tom Jr.), Elizabeth, Nicholas.
The Partridges of *The Partridge Family*:
   Keith, Laurie, Danny, Christopher, Tracy.

The Ingalls of *Little House on the Prairie:*
   Mary, Laura, Carrie, Grace, Albert.
The Salingers of *Party of Five:*
   Charlie, Bailey, Julia, Claudia, Owen.
The Huxtables of *The Cosby Show:*
   Sondra, Denise, Theo, Vanessa, Rudy.
The Waltons of *The Waltons:*
   John-Boy (John Jr.), Jason, Mary Ellen, Ben, Erin, Jim-Bob, Elizabeth.
The Seavers of *Growing Pains:*
   Mike, Carol, Ben, Chrissy.

Baby Brats:
What the Brat Pack Is Naming Its Offspring

Emilio. Demi. Rob.
   Along with the likes of **Anthony, Andrew,** and **Ally,** these were the essential movie stars of the Generation X era, circa 1982–87. They worked together, hung together, and endured together that loathsome tab . . . "the Brat Pack."
   Funny thing is, even as we measured ourselves against them, they weren't *one* with us. Most were tail-end baby boomers. Getting a head start on this adulthood business, the Brat Packers (or at least a couple of them) began populating the earth in their likeness in the mid-1980s.
   And so, because we still haven't gotten over *St. Elmo's Fire,* and because we still *care* about Rob Lowe, we present a peek into the nurseries of our screen icons:

Founding Members

Ally Sheedy (born 1962)
Key credits: *St. Elmo's Fire* (1985); *The Breakfast Club* (1985)
Offspring: **Rebecca** (daughter)

Emilio Estevez (born 1962)
Key credits: *St. Elmo's Fire* (1985); *The Breakfast Club* (1985)
Offspring, **Taylor Levi** (daughter); **Paloma Salley** (daughter)

Rob Lowe (born 1964)
Key credits: *The Outsiders, Class* (1983); *St. Elmo's Fire* (1985).
Offspring, **Edward Matthew** (son); **John Owen** (son).

Demi Moore (born 1962)
Key credits: *St. Elmo's Fire* (1985)
Offspring: **Rumer Glenn** (daughter); **Scout Larue** (daughter); **Tallulah Belle** (daughter).

Auxiliary Members

Robert Downey Jr. (born 1965)
Key credit: *Less Than Zero* (1987)
Offspring: **Indio** (son)

Michael J. Fox (born 1961)
Key credit: *Bright Lights, Big City* (1988)
Offspring, **Sam,** (son); **Aquinna Kathleen** and **Schulyer Frances** (twin daughters)

Timothy Hutton (born 1960)
Key credit: *Taps* (1981)
Offspring: **Emmanuel Noah** (son)

Sean Penn (born 1961)
Key credits: *Fast Times at Ridgemont High* (1982); *Bad Boys* (1983)
Offspring: **Dylan Francis** (daughter); **Hopper Jack** (son)

James Spader (born 1960)
Key credits: *Pretty in Pink* (1986); *Less Than Zero* (1987)
Offspring: **Sebastian** (son); **Elijah** (son)

Lea Thompson (born 1961)
Key credit: *Some Kind of Wonderful* (1987)
Offspring: **Madeline** (daughter); **Zoey** (daughter)

Name-a-Rama:
How to Create Baby Names at Home—
in Your Spare Time

"Unique. Unique. Unique." That's your mantra. Big deal. Everybody talks about finding unique baby names, but how many are brave enough to *actually* forge new wilderness. And we're not talking about adding an *e* to the end of **Mark** and calling yourself a visionary. We're talking about the surest way to get a certifiably unique baby name—making up the blinkin' thing yourself.

Scary, invigorating, frightening, freeing—this is what it's like to stare down the likes of **Brandon** and **Brianna,** and say, "No, thanks, we think we'll try something different." If you don't mind the extra sweat or extra work, you *can* dream up a moniker that is the worthy peer of the current trendsetters. Here's how:

Keep it close: Don't mean to damper your enthusiasm from the get-go, but there are certain realities that must be heeded even if you're winging it. Namely, your brand-spanking-new name should sound like something approximating names used by humans of the latter twentieth century. In short, **Xwkdeedio-124** ain't gonna fly. Really. You can't afford the therapy bills. While you may want something ultraunique, all your kid is going to want is something that doesn't get him pounded at lunch.

So, instead of reinventing the wheel, start with a popular name you sort of like—say, **Emily**—and go from there. Your mission, should you wish to accept it, is to create a name that feels and sounds like a peer of the standard model.

Classic combos: OK, you've got your goal—**Emily**-esque. Now what? One suggested method, the old "Little Bit Me, Little Bit You" gambit.

How it works: Mom's first name is, say, **Pamela.** Dad's first name is **Richard.** Take a couple letters from Mom, take a couple letters from Dad. Put them together *Electric Company*–style ("Ch." "Air." . . . "Chair."), and see if you've got any magic. The **Pamela-Richard** combo, for example, can yield doable entries like: **Riela, Rila,** or **Lari**. (Not exactly **Emily** doppelgängers, but not that far off either.)

Obviously, you can substitute middle names for first names, mix and match surnames with given names, whatever. Just as long as you don't settle for **Richpam.**

Sounds right: The other suggested baby-naming method is "Sounds Right." There are certain sounds, certain letter combos, that are—for inexplicable reasons—very happening in a particular era. You got a name starting with "Dar"—from **Daria** to **Darian** to **Darrius**—and chances are, you got a hip name. Same goes for "Juh" and "Kee."

So, to get to your unique **Emily,** mess around with the "Sounds Right" combos and watch stuff like this emerge: **Darmaly, Keeyem.**

This method also works when you want to dress up any existing, one syllable common name: **Shawn** becomes **Keshawn, John** becomes **Darjon, Ron** becomes **Jaron.**

Be prepared for resistance: The second-hardest part of making up your own baby name is holding your ground once you inform family, friends, and officials of your intentions.

In 1967, my parents, feeling as if they'd taken care of familial obligations and religious nods with their first two children, decided they could afford to get creative with their next child, me. My father takes credit for concocting **Joal**—"Jo" from **John,** "Al" from **Alice,** a combination dreamed up on a family shopping trip to Thrifty's drug store in Burbank, California.

Everyone—from my mother to siblings number one (Charlie) and two (Judy)—agreed **Joal** sounded like a fine choice.

Then they broke the news to the head nurse at the maternity ward. She said, "**Joal**?!? Are you sure you want that? That's kind of weird for a girl's name, isn't it?" my mother remembers.

The nurse, in fact, withheld issuing a birth certificate to give my parents some cool-down time, presumably hoping they would see the error of their ways and retag me **Jennifer** like every other baby on the floor.

But my parents held their ground and kept the "weird" name—to the eternal displeasure of the official who would have me be **Darcy,** no doubt.

Addendum: My mother wasn't kidding when she says the nurse didn't like **Joal.** My parents recently got around to requesting my official birth certificate from the hospital. The document was blank where a first name should have been. **Joal** was never entered.

And so for eternity, or until we pay some stupid paperwork fee, I am now, simply, Baby Ryan.

The moral of this story: Make sure your maternity ward nurse has a good sense of humor. The identity of your child may depend on it.

Totally:
1980s Retro Names

Ronald Reagan. *The A-Team.* New Wave. *Glasnost.* Yuppies. *Dallas.* The *Challenger* explosion. Jim and Tammy Faye. AIDS. MTV. "Thriller." Geraldo Rivera in Al Capone's vault.

That was the decade that was—a key one in Gen X history: the one where we came of age (if not of reason).

Relive those thrilling days of painter pants and Pac-Man with a baby name that evokes the times:

Newsmakers

Ronald Reagan
Mikhail Gorbachev
Margaret Thatcher
George Bush
Gary Hart
Walter Mondale
Geraldine Ferraro
Princess **Diana**
Christa McAuliffe
Samantha Smith

Music

Michael Jackson
Madonna
Cyndi Lauper
Tina Turner

Simon Le Bon (Duran Duran)
Billy Idol
Steve Perry (Journey)
Bono (U2)
Michael Stipe (R.E.M.)
Morrissey (the Smiths)

Movies/TV

Alex P. Keaton (*Family Ties)*
J. R. Ewing (Dallas)
Molly Ringwald
Eddie Murphy
John Rambo (*Rambo)*
Arnold Schwarzenegger
Corey Feldman/**Corey** Haim
Michelle Pfeiffer
Brooke Shields
Martha Quinn (original MTV veejay)

Only in the '80s

Bret Easton Ellis (*Less Than Zero*)
Jay McInerney (*Bright Lights, Big City*)
Tama Janowitz (*Slaves of New York*)
Malcolm Forbes
Ivan Boesky

State-of-the-Art Baby Names

Michael, Jason, Brian (boys); **Jennifer, Jessica, Heather** (girls).

Bell-Bottoms:
1970s Retro Names

Richard Nixon. *The Brady Bunch.* Disco. Vietnam (still). Moonies. *Saturday Night Live.* Kent State. Steve Austin and Jaime Sommers. Swine flu. Pong. The *Grease* soundtrack. Singles bars.

This was the mood ring of a decade in which Gen Xers cut their collective teeth. Relive those trippie days of designer jeans and *H. R. Pufnstuf* with a baby name that evokes the times:

Newsmakers

Richard Nixon
Leonid Brezhnev
Jimmy Carter
Gerald Ford
Spiro T. Agnew
John Mitchell
Martha Mitchell
Henry Kissinger
Golda Meir

Music

Bruce Springsteen
Sid Vicious (Sex Pistols)
Glenn Frey (the Eagles)
Victor Willis (Village people)
Olivia Newton-John
Karen Carpenter (the Carpenters)
Toni Tenille (the Captain and Tennille)
Helen Reddy
James Taylor
David Cassidy

Movies/TV

John Travolta
Tony Manero (*Staurday Night Fever*)
Clint Eastwood
Burt Reynolds
Farrah Fawcett
Diane Keaton
Arthur Fonzarelli (*Happy Days*)
Chevy Chase
Goldie Hawn
Archie Bunker (*All in the Family*)

Only in the '70s

Bob Woodward (*All the President's Men*)
Carl Bernstein (*All the President's Men*)
Hunter S. Thompson (*Fear and Loathing in Las Vegas*)
Gloria Steinem
Vidal Sassoon

State-of-the-Art Baby Names

Michael, David, Scott (boys); **Jennifer, Kimberly, Kelly** (girls).

Tie-Dyed:
1960s Retro Names

John F. Kennedy. *Gilligan's Island.* The British invasion. Vietnam. Hippies. *Speed Racer.* Assassinations. Liz Taylor and Richard Burton. Cuban missile crisis. *Sgt. Pepper's Lonely Hearts Club Band.* Moon walk.

   This was the dawning of the Gen X era. Relive those hippie-dippie days of Woodstock (the concert) and Woodstock (the bird) with a baby name that evokes the times:

Newsmakers

John F. Kennedy
Robert F. Kennedy
Martin Luther King Jr.
Malcolm X
Jacqueline Onassis
Lyndon B. Johnson
Robert S. McNamara
Walter Cronkite
Abbie Hoffman
Eldridge Cleaver

Music

John Lennon (the Beatles)
Paul McCartney (the Beatles)
George Harrison (the Beatles)
Ringo Starr (the Beatles)
Mick Jagger (the Rolling Stones)
Janis Joplin
Jimi Hendrix
Nancy Sinatra
Paul Simon and **Art** Garfunkel

Movies/TV

Dustin Hoffman
Benjamin Braddock (*The Graduate*)
Paul Newman
Steve McQueen
Natalie Wood
Faye Dunaway
Barbra Streisand
Dick and **Tom** Smothers
Jack Webb
Captain **Tony** Nelson (*I Dream of Jeannie*)

Only in the '60s

Truman Capote (*In Cold Blood*)
Philip Roth (*Portnoy's Complaint*)
Hugh Hefner (*Playboy*)
Twiggy
Joe Namath

State-of-the-Art Baby Names

David, Steven, Gary (boys); **Karen, Amy, Linda** (girls).

Happy Days:
1950s Retro Names

"I Like Ike." *I Love Lucy.* Elvis' hips. The Korean war. Beatniks. *Leave It to Beaver.* Communist witch-hunts. Grace Kelly and Prince Ranier. Polio. Frisbee. "Come Fly with Me." Civil disobedience.

What Gen Xers know about the 1950s we learned from books, old TV clips, and *Happy Days.* Far from feeling distant, however, the era is as instantly retrievable as the nearest VCR or Internet connection.

Newsmakers

Dwight D. Eisenhower
Nikita Khrushchev
Harry S. Truman
Fidel Castro
General **Douglas** MacArthur
Thurgood Marshall
Joe McCarthy
Princess **Grace**
Pope **John** XXIII

Music

Elvis Presley
Little **Richard**
Buddy Holly
Carl Perkins
Chuck Berry
Bobby Darin
Perry Como
Pat Boone
Patsy Cline
Julie London

Movies/TV

Doris Day
Rock Hudson
Jack Lemmon
James Dean
Lucille Ball
Desi Arnaz
Charlton Heston
Elizabeth Taylor
Jerry Lewis and **Dean** Martin
Marilyn Monroe

Only in the '50s

Dr. **Benjamin** Spock
John Updike (*Rabbit, Run*)
Allen Ginsberg ("Howl")
Charles Van Doren
Mickey Mantle

State-of-the-Art Baby Names

Dennis, Roger, Craig (boys); **Mary, Barbara, Susan** (girls).

Victory Garden:
1940s Retro Names

FDR. WWII. Nylon stockings. D-day. Bobby-soxers. *It's a Wonderful Life*. Hiroshima. Bogie and Bacall. Big bands. "You're in the Army Now." War rations.

What Gen Xers know about the 1940s we learned from books, news reels, and *Hogan's Heroes*.

Newsmakers

Franklin D. Roosevelt
Eleanor Roosevelt
Winston Churchill
General **Dwight** D. Eisenhower
General **George** S. Patton
General **Omar** Bradley
Queen **Elizabeth**
Ernie Pyle
Thomas Dewey

Music

Frank Sinatra
Bing Crosby
Tommy Dorsey
Benny Goodman
Duke Ellington
Ella Fitzgerald
Judy Garland

Jo Stafford
Billy Eckstine

Movies/TV

Clark Gable
Bette Davis
Humphrey Bogart
Lauren Bacall
Gary Cooper
Katharine Hepburn
Spencer Tracy
Ingrid Bergman
Errol Flynn
Carole Lombard

Only in the '40s

Edward R. Murrow
Louella Parsons
Hedda Hopper
Walter Winchell
Joe DiMaggio

State-of-the-Art Baby Names

James, Donald, Ronald (boys); **Mary, Betty, Shirley** (girls)

Oh, Shaun!:
Names for Future Teen Idols

Your *Bop* and *Tiger Beat* subscriptions were *not* in vain. Rather, teen idols provide us with valuable insight into breaks in the baby name game.
   Consider: **Alan, Wayne, Merrill, Jay,** and **Donny**. Which one do you

think became the breakout star? **Donny,** of course. While the other four were Osmond Brothers in good standing, they lacked the essential tools (read: name) to stand out.

Is the secret to an appealing, cute-as-a-button boy name really as simple as tacking on an *ie* or *y*? Yes and no.

In the 1960s and 1970s, that was about all you had to do. Little creativity was required in the era of the peanut-butter-and-jelly sandwich. As the baby name game grew more complex in the 1980s, so too did the monikers worn by our youngest male stylesetters. (Would **Jonathan** Taylor Thomas cut it today as plain old **Johnny** Thomas? Doubtful.)

Next time you're wondering which way the wind is blowing for boy names, check out the following chronology of the teen idols of the Gen X era. It's a near peerless guide to the evolution of the boy name. So goes our nation's teen idols, so go we. (And you thought **Joey** Lawrence was just a flyweight.)

Teen Idols

Mid-1960s to mid-1970s
Frankie Avalon
Bobby Sherman
Dino, Desi, and **Billy** (Dean Martin Jr., Desi Arnaz Jr., Billy Hinsche)
Jack Wild
Johnny Whitaker
David Cassidy
Donny Osmond
Jimmy Osmond
Barry Williams
Tony DeFranco
The Bay City Rollers: **Alan, Derek, Eric, Leslie, Woody**

Mid-1970s to mid-1980s
Shaun Cassidy
Leif Garrett
Andy Gibb
Rick Springfield
Simon Le Bon

Mid-1980s to Today
Kirk Cameron
New Edition: **Bobby, Johnny, Ralph, Michael, Ricky, Ronnie**
New Kids on the Block: **Danny, Donnie, Joe, Jonathan, Jordan**
The Two Coreys: **Corey** Feldman, **Corey** Haim
Joey Lawrence
Jonathan Taylor Thomas
Elijah Wood
Devon Sawa
Hanson: **Isaac, Taylor, Zac**
The Backstreet Boys: **Alexander James (A. J.), Brian, Kevin, Nick**
Leonardo DiCaprio
The Spice Girls: **Emma, Melanie (B. & C.), Victoria**
Ex–Spice Girl: **Geri**
Brandy Norwood

Picks for the Future
Brandon
Jacob
Justin
Tyler

Millennium Kids:
New Names for a New Century?

Futuristic movies are often bleak affairs. Sterile environs. White-on-white interior design. Unitards all around.

And then there's the matter of names—or lack of them. Science fiction likes to tell the grim tale of a world so dehumanized that names are eschewed with numbers and serial codes. **Cody,** say hello to your new classmate: THX 1138.

Well, the future is here and the question is: Do baby names really stand a chance of becoming obsolete?

No, says Bellevue University psychology professor Cleveland Evans, a longtime student and chronicler of the history and trends of American given names.

"People are never going to use their social security numbers as their name," Evans says. "I'm sure there may be some numbers that become names—I wouldn't be surprised if I started hearing of **Seven of Nines** (after the *Star Trek: Voyager* TV character). But once you do that, it's not a number—it becomes a name."

As far as Evans is concerned, the *real* baby name revolution is already underway—and it has nothing to do with IBM datacards.

"Everybody wants to look for something different. Nobody wants to name a child after somebody anymore," the Nebraska-based educator says. "Names have become an arena for individualism."

Part of this drive, according to Evans, stems from a fragmentation of our lives, our culture, our media. The TV nation, for instance, is no longer made up of sixty million sets tuned to *The Ed Sullivan Show* on Sunday night. It's made up of one hundred million sets sampling one hundred channels, thousands of videocassettes, and countless video games. We simply don't take in the same experiences, don't share the same influences anymore. This diversity of culture is slowly leading us away from the usual **Michael, Jennifer, Emily** lockstep, Evans argues.

That said, Evans feels certain that some names are here to stay for the twenty-first century and beyond. "I think it'll be difficult to imagine a **Michael,** or **John,** or **Elizabeth,** or **Katherine** sounding too odd," Evans says. "At least everybody has to keep learning about people with those names in school."

Hmm. Think this means somebody named **Brianna** better make the history books—pronto. Otherwise, it may be a long century for certain little princesses.

Bert and Ernie:
Kids' TV—Inspired Names

Sad but true: *Sesame Street* didn't just teach us how to spell, it introduced us to our first set of friends—as did other staples of our morning TV show diet. First impressions die hard. Some of us may still be harboring a soft spot for **Grover.** Some may even be considering naming (*gasp!*) a human being in honor of the dear blue Muppet. In such a case, some of us may want to peruse the lists below, refresh our memories, recharge our batteries, and get a grip. If you're going to pay tribute to the

Saturday morning TV of your youth, such things must be handled with delicacy. And a minimum of **Grovers.**

Sesame Street Possibles

Bert
Bob
Ernie
Maria
Oscar

Sesame Street Impossibles

Grover
Kermit
Big Bird
Mr. Hooper
Elmo

Sid and Marty Krofft Possibles

Jimmy (*H. R. Pufnstuf*)
Will (*Land of the Lost*)
Holly (*Land of the Lost*)
Marshall (*Land of the Lost*)
Mark (*Lidsville*)

Sid and Marty Krofft Impossibles

Witchiepoo (*H. R. Pufnstuf*)
Sleestack (*Land of the Lost*)
Sigmund (*Sigmund and the Sea Monsters*)
Whoo Doo (*Lidsville*)

The Archie Comedy Hour Possibles

Archie
Sabrina
Reggie
Betty
Veronica

The Archie Comedy Hour Impossibles

Jughead
Moose
Groovy Goolies

Speed Racer Possibles

Trixie
Spridle

Speed Racer Impossibles

Speed
Chim-Chim

The Breakfast Club:
Names Inspired by John Hughes' Movies

If you are a fan of peanut-butter-and-jelly sandwiches, believe them to be essential to the well-balanced baby name, and think it's somehow "wrong" that they are under siege by the fancy-pants likes of **Conner, Spencer, Brooke,** and **Taylor,** then it may interest you to know that your distress is all John Hughes's fault.

Through seven key Gen X–era films from 1984–88, the prolific writer/director, intentionally or not, championed the cause of the little princesses, power names, lil' cowpokes and cuddly bears that dominated the baby name world in the coming decade—not so coincidentally, around the same time Gen Xers began procreating.

Regular old **Richard** or **Katie** weren't good enough for a John Hughes script. No, those stalwarts were considered the stuff of another, older generation. Hughes's on-screen teen protagonists, and antagonists, needed cooler, classier, preppier stuff. We watched, we memorized lines, and we—apparently—agreed.

A sampling of our baby name education, as administered from the pen of John Hughes:

Sixteen Candles (1984)

Samantha (Molly Ringwald)
Jake (Michael Schoeffling)
Bryce (John Cusack)

The Breakfast Club (1985)

Andrew (Emilio Estevez)
Brian (Anthony Michael Hall)
John **Bender** (Judd Nelson)
Claire (Molly Ringwald)
Allison (Ally Sheedy)

Weird Science (1985)

Gary (Anthony Michael Hall)
Wyatt (Ilan Mitchell-Smith)
Ian (Robert Downey Jr.)

Pretty in Pink (1986)

Andie (Molly Ringwald)
Blane (Andrew McCarthy)
Duckie (John Cryer)
Steff (James Spader)
Jena (Alexa Kenin)

Ferris Bueller's Day Off (1986)

Ferris (Matthew Broderick)
Cameron (Alan Ruck)
Sloane (Mia Sara)

Some Kind of Wonderful (1987)

Keith (Eric Stoltz)
Watts (Mary Stuart Masterson)
Amanda (Lea Thompson)
Hardy (Craig Sheffer)
Duncan (Elias Koteas)
Shayne (Molly Hagan)

She's Having a Baby (1988)

Jefferson "Jake" (Kevin Bacon)
Kristy (Elizabeth McGovern)
Davis (Alec Baldwin)

Mirror Names:
The Consequences of Creating Mr. John Johns

Scenario: You love the name **Daniel**. It's classic. It's handsome. It was the name of your beloved grandfather. One problem: The baby's last name is going to be Daniels. . . . **Daniel** Daniels? Can you do that? . . . Legally, yes.

Should you do that? A thornier question. Maybe we should let **Ryan** Ryan answer: "I wouldn't put my kid through what I went through. It was complete brutality from Day One."

Ryan Ryan—full name, **Ryan** O Ryan—is my younger brother. He was born in 1970, when our parents, apparently bored with doling out peanut-butter-and-jelly sandwiches to the first two kids (**Charlie** and **Judy**) dabbled with baby-name experimentation.

It was well-meaning Mother Ryan's idea to opt for **Ryan** Ryan.

Her side of the story: "Well, first, there was **Ryan** O'Neal who was popular at the time. And then I was thinking about how [your father] always said the English took the *O* off *O'Ryan,* and I said, 'Let's put it back and make him **Ryan** O Ryan.'

"And he was actually delivered by Dr. **Morgan** P. Morgan!"

Ah, the fun, the merriment, the laughs—they were only beginning, right? Let's return for a moment to the person who actually had to wear the name.

"Every day was like fear going into school," Ryan says. "It especially got bad when the teacher started laughing when she announced it. . . . She thought at first it was a typo."

Then there was the comedian who sat behind him in junior high: " 'So, what are you going to name your kid—Ryan Ryan Ryan? And then your second kid is going to be named Ryan Ryan Ryan Ryan?' . . . He used to go on a half hour with this."

Meanwhile, back at Mom's: "No, I never thought of anybody being teased. . . . I really liked [the name]." (Parents say the darndest things.)

Anyway, to end this cautionary tale on an upbeat note, let it be noted that **Ryan** O Ryan did not grow up to be a social outcast, but rather a skilled kitchen designer. And get this: He *likes* his name—now. "The name works because it's unique. . . . When you hear the name you can't forget it."

All's well that ends well, but even **Ryan** O Ryan doesn't plan to tempt fate by passing down the moniker to any potential offspring. "Why make your kid suffer?"

Place Holders:
The Thing About Middle Names

If middle names didn't exist, Gen Xers would have to invent them—increasingly that's where we're doing the family obligation thing.

Instead of naming the boy **Ronald** in honor of his uncle, you tag him **Hunter** (the name you *really* think is cool) and let **Ronald** (the name you feel a strong emotional tie to but just don't click with) find a nice home, safely tucked between the given name and surname. Perfect.

Here are some things to keep in mind when selecting middle name(s):

Finding the middle ground: As in the above example, middle names can make for great peacekeepers. They can be used to help appease the extended family (maybe there's a middle name for the mother's father *and* stepfather), the immediate family (like the mother who's pressuring you to name the girl **Mildred** after her mother), and even the mother herself (assuming the child is going to adopt the last name of her/his father, how about passing down the mother's maiden name as a sneaky middle name?).

One word of caution: Don't go tacking on multiple middle names in an ill-conceived attempt to make *everybody* happy. There is only so much you can do, there is only so much your child's name can do—at some point you're going to have to tell Cousin **Walter** that there's no room at the inn. If pressure from familial types continue, as nicely as you can, try suggesting: *Go have your own kid.*

Rhythm: Just as rhythm is important to the first name/last name combo, it's important to the whole first name/middle name/last name shebang. Maybe **Ty** Hutchins sounds great. But **Ty Guy** Hutchins sounds ridiculous.

You can also use the middle name to help lighten and balance the impact of a syllable-heavy first and last name, à la **Alexander Ben** Raefelson.

The monogram issue: You know how in certain states you can't request personlized auto license plates that spell "suggestive" or "offensive" phrases like "BRA" or "ASS"? The same safeguards should be in place at maternity wards. You try innocently naming your kid **Samuel Harold** Taylor, and some official points out that "SHT" wouldn't be the choicest of monograms to stitch on sweaters and bath towels.

Relax: Middle names are middle names. If your kid really grows up hating it, there's something called an initial.

The Carbon Copy Question: To Junior or Not to Junior?

There doesn't seem to be a lot of room for Juniors in the Gen Xer lifestyle. This is, after all, an age group of baby name spelunkers, of prospective parents consumed by one thought: "Oh, please, don't let anybody else know I found the name **Asha**!"

That said, the Junior question is probably going to come up at least once during your time with child, so you may as well get your story straight. Here are some pros and cons to consider:

Five Reasons **NOT** *to Junior*

1. The concept strikes you as archaic.
2. You don't like your name.
3. You don't like your partner's name.
4. You're planning on becoming internationally renown in your profession and always kind of felt bad for **Frank** Sinatra Jr.
5. Oh, there's this little issue you have—something about how babies have a really tough time being born and all, and the least they deserve is a warm crib *and their own name.*

Five Reasons to *Junior*

1. You want to start your own family tradition.
2. You happen to like your name very much, thank you.
3. You think your partner's is pretty cool.
4. You think it was really cute how Lucille Ball and Desi Arnaz had a little **Lucie** for Mom and a little **Desi** for Dad.
5. You have a really tough time with deadlines and don't think you'll be able to think of anything original by the due date.

eXpert voices
Summer
(born 1971)
Meridian, Idaho

Children: ***Morgan, Dominic*** (twin sons).

In her own words: "I wanted names that would be unusual—but not as unusual as my name. I've always liked my name, but I got a lot of teasing about it and *still* get a lot of really stupid jokes. I've heard of a few other **Morgan**s and **Dominic**s (some of them girls), but it's nothing like the number of **Mike**'s or **Joe**'s or **Chris**es. . . . I also did not want 'twinny' names that rhymed or started with the same letter or sounded a lot alike."

Runner-up Names: ***Marjorie*** (girl).

Reject-pile names: "Anything that was on a top ten, top twenty, top fifty baby name list was out!"

Did you select baby names differently than your parents? "I think I was a little more concerned with what my boys will have to put up with [as far as teasing] than my parents were when they named my brother and me.

I was also more determined to be prepared. When my brother was born in 1969, they had one boy name [**Forrest**] and one girl name [**Summer**] picked out. When I was born in 1971, they still hadn't found another boy name yet, so it's a good thing I [turned out] a girl!"

eXpert voices
Suzy
(born 1969)
Buzzards Bay, Massachusetts

Children: **Kendyl Ellery** (daughter).

In her own words: "We looked on maps, on food labels, on movie credits, phone books—anywhere to find an unusual name that would [work] for either gender and would prevent our kid from being teased in school. We wanted him/her to (hopefully) be the only one in his/her class with that name. . . . We wanted something original but not far-out.

"Still, we hadn't decided completely until we arrived at the hospital. There [we saw] triplets who . . . were still in the nursery. Their last name was **Kendall**. Bingo!"

Runner-up names: **Carson** (boy); **Carstyn** (girl).

Reject-pile names: "Anything cutesy (**Lindsey**). Anything trendy (**Hanna**). Anything that could be shortened (**Samantha**). Anything conservative (**Jennifer**). Anything common (**Megan**)."

Did you select baby names differently than your parents: "My parents named me for relatives. . . . I don't think they had the freedom to name their children truly unusual names as we do nowadays. Although **Suzy** caused quite a stir because it was not **Susan** or **Suzanne**."

eXpert voices
Patricia
(born 1972)
Canada

Children: **Bronson Nicholas** (son).

In her own words: "For a boy we wanted a name that was strong but unique at the same time, and something that could not be shortened or turned into a joke. For a girl we wanted something strong and unique but still feminine.

"We were considering a 'junior' name for a son but felt that this would be too egocentric for us. We chose the second name in honor of my father-in-law. We were considering **Nicholas** or **Nicole** as a first name, but my husband felt it would be awkward for him to be calling anyone but his father '**Nick.**' [Plus,] two cousins on his side of the family had already named their sons **Nicholas**."

Runner-up names: **Dylan** ("and all the other names from popular TV characters"): **Walter, Agnes** ("too old-fashioned"); **Cheyenne, Dakota, Austin** ("names that were after states and Indians and the like").

How did your experience with your own name influence your choice? "We felt our names were OK, but both of us hated the names and jokes that came with them. For me it was '**Patty**' that I hated. Especially the '**Fatty Patty**' two-by-four rhyme from school. I was not fat, but it bothered me."

Did you select baby names differently than your parents?: "My parents had been convinced that I would be a boy and only had a boy name chosen. I ended up being named after my mother's best friend at the last minute. We made sure that we had two names chosen, and agreed-upon, before [our son] was born."

eXpert voices
Denise
(born 1963)
Aliquippa, Pennsylvania

Children: **Kathryn Denise** (daughter); **Luke Daniel** (son).

In her own words: "We wanted [our daughter] to have a name with lots of possible variations—**Katy** (which is what we usually call her), **Kathy, Kate, Kay, K.D.,** et cetera. We chose the spelling we did because I had a great-aunt who used that spelling, but also because we wanted a less-than-common spelling.

"[For our son] we wanted a Bible name, yet not the usual **Matthew, David,** or **Jonathan.**"

Runner-up names: **Alexandria** (girl); **Samuel** (boy). ("We didn't settle on **Luke** until we saw him. He was born just after midnight on July 5, so we seriously considered **Samuel,** as in Uncle Sam! Then we saw him and he looked like **Luke,** not **Sam.** Although he *was* red, white, and blue when he was born!)

Reject-pile names: **Taylor, Jordan, Spencer.** ("Anything that was too trendy. . . . We didn't want our kids' names to date them. . . . And we didn't want them to be one of four kids with the same name in their classes at school.")

How did your experience with your own name influence your choices?: "I spent a few of my junior high years wanting to change my name. In fact, I spelled it **D-e-n-i-c-e** for a while, just to differentiate myself from the other **Denise**s. I also went by the nickname, **Dini,** most of my college years, and still go by that with certain friends. **Denise** is OK, but *too common*. I wanted my daughter to have options, to be able to pick the nickname that fits her at each stage of her life."

eXpert voices
Janet
(born 1965)
Long Island, New York

Children: **Jonathan Rhys** (son); **Sydney Lauren** (daughter).

In her own words: "It was hard coming up with a name. You don't want a name that you have a bad past association with—and that's hard. The older you get, the more morons you know."

Runner-up names: **Rhys, Daniel.** ("**Jonathan** was supposed to be **Daniel.** But then in the delivery room, I just said, '**Jonathan.**' And that was it.")

Reject-pile names: **Caitlin, Briana.** ("I just think it's going to be funny in forty years when you have all these Grandma **Brianas**.")

Did you select baby names differently than your parents?: "My brother was named for my father. My sister was named for my mother. I got **Janet Marie** because it rhymed with my last name. . . . I wouldn't pass on my own name."

Appendix 1

Pocket Ts:
The Compendium

Boys

Aaron
Adam
Andrew
Anthony
Ben
Benjamin
Cameron
Christian
Christopher
Daniel
David
Derrick
Edward
Elijah
Eric
Erik
Ethan
Frank
Fred
Gabe
Gabriel
George
Hal
Hank

Henry
Ian
Isaac
Isaiah
Jack
Jacob
James
John
Jonathan
Joseph
Joshua
Lincoln
Lewis/Louis
Luke
Mark
Martin
Matthew
Michael
Nathan
Nathaniel
Neal
Neil
Nick
Noah
Oliver
Oscar

Owen
Patrick
Peter
Reed
Reid
Richard
Robert
Sam
Samuel
Saul
Seth
Stephen
Steven
Terence
Thomas
Timothy
Vaughan
Victor
Vincent
William
Wyatt
Yale
Zachary
Zeke

Girls

Abigail
Amelia
Anne
Audrey
Becca
Belle
Bridget
Caroline
Catherine
Clare
Diana
Diane
Ellen
Elizabeth
Emily
Emma

Eva
Faith
Grace
Hillary
Hope
Isabel
Jane
Jessica
Julia
Kate
Katherine
Kathleen
Lily
Lucy
Maria
Marie
Martha
Meg

Natalie
Nina
Nora
Olivia
Paige
Quinn
Rebecca
Rose
Ruth
Sarah
Simone
Sonya
Sophia
Tess
Thea
Vanessa
Vivian
Zoe

Appendix 2

Trendy Suspenders: The Compendium

Boys

Alexander
Austin
Brandon
Coby
Cody
Cory
Dakota
Dillon/Dylan
Fletcher
Frasier
Frazier
Garth
Harley
Hunter
Jesse
Jordan
Justin
Kobe
Kyle
Logan
Max
Nevada
Parker
Shane
Spencer
Walker

Girls

Alexandra
Alexis
Amanda
Ashley
Brianna
Brittany
Brooke
Caitlin
Carissa
Cassidy
Dakota
Desiree
Dylan
Erica
Felicia
Geneva
Gwyneth
Harley
Hayley
Heather
Jacinda
Janita
Jasmine
Jordan
Kaitlyn
Kayla
Madison
Megan
Moesha
Montana
Morgan
Nevada
Paloma
Rachel
Samantha
Savannah
Shelby
Sierra
Taylor
Tiffany
Whitney
Winona/Wynonna
Yasmine

Appendix 3

Picks to Click:
The Compendium

Boys

Ari
Beck
Bern
Brody
Carter
Clint
Clive
Conlan
Darius
Ellis
Ezekial
Finn
Gib
Gordon
Harper
Hutch
Innis
Jude
Keagan
Killian
Lane
Lionel
Malcolm
Marshall
Miles
Mitch
Nolan
Palmer
Porter
Pryor
Quince
Ram
Rhodes
Riordan
Robin
Roman
Sandy
Sawyer
Shepherd
Sy
Theo
Titus
Tobias
Trey
Vance
Ware
Weaver
Wheat
Whit
Wright
Yul
Zane

Girls

Carson
Chloe
Connor
Dalia
Dara
Daria
Flannery
Glenys
Greer
Hollis
Keilly
Maeve
Moira
Nola
Palmer
Peri
Remy
Ren
Tandy
Thora

Appendix 4

Comers:
The Compendium

Boys

Bailey
Connor
Dalton
Donovan
Fox
Gil
Harry
Jeremiah
Jonas
Keenan
Leo
Levi
Liam
Monte
Nathaniel
Parker
Quentin
Stocker
Tighe

Girls

Alice
Ava
Cali
Cameron
Kelsey
Larkin
Leann
Lilith
Liv
Mackenzie
Mariah
Martha
Maya
Mira
Poe
Sabrina
Schylar
Shania
Skylar

Sources

Armenians' Names
  Martha Atikian
  (Atikian & Atikian, 1973)

British Family Names: Their Origins and Meanings
  Rev. Henry Barber
  (Gale Research Co., 1903; reprinted 1968)

The Book of African Names
  Molefi Kete Asante
  (Africa World Press, 1991)

Concise Heritage Dictionary
  (Houghton Mifflin, 1976)

Dictionary of American Family Names
  Elsdon C. Smith
  (Harper & Bros., 1956)

Dictionary of Given Names
  Flora Haines Loughead
  (Arthur C. Clark Co., 1933)

A Dictionary of Jewish Names and Their History
  Benzion C.Kaganoff
  (Schocken Books, 1977)

The Everything Baby Names Book
Lisa Shaw
(Adams Media Corp, 1997)

Hispanic First Names
Compiled by Richard D. Woods
(Greenwood Press, 1984)

Internet Movie Database
(www.imdb.com)

Leonard Maltin's 1997 Movie & Home Video Guide
Leonard Maltin, editor
(Signet, 1996)

The Merriam-Webster Thesaurus
(Pocket Books, 1978)

Mike's Page of Baby Names
(www.charm.net/~shack/name/babynm.html)

The New Jewish Baby Book
Anita Diamant
(Jewish Lights Publishing, 1993)

The Origin and Signification of Scottish Surnames
Clifford Stanley Sims
(Avenel Books, 1959)

Oxford Dictionary of English Christian Names
Compiled by E. G. Whithycombe
(Oxford University Press, 1947)

Parent Soup Baby Finder
(www.parentsoup.com)

Random House Dictionary
(Ballantine Books, 1996)

The Very Best Baby Name Book
Brush Lansky
(Meadowbrook Press, 1995)

Webster's Encyclopedic Unabridged Dictionary of the English Language
(Portland House, 1989)

What Is Your Name?
Sophy Moody
(Gale Research Co., 1863; reprinted 1976)

Maze
Reign